Too Valuable
To Lose

GLOBALIZATION OF MISSION SERIES

Too Valuable TO LOSE

Exploring the Causes and Cures of Missionary Attrition

Edited by William D. Taylor

William Carey Library

Pasadena, California

Editor: William D. Taylor
Technical Editor: Susan Peterson
Cover Design: Jeff Northway

World Evangelical Fellowship
International Headquarters
141 Middle Road
#05-05 GSM Building
Singapore 188976
Telephone: 65 339 7900
Fax: 65 338 3756
E-mail: WEF-Int@xc.org

World Evangelical Fellowship
North American Office
P.O. Box WEF
Wheaton, IL 60189-8004, USA
Telephone: 630 668 0440
Fax: 630 668 0498
E-mail: WEF-NA@xc.org
     or 76043.1576@compuserve.com

Published by:
William Carey Library
P.O. Box 40129
Pasadena, CA 91114
Telephone: 626 798 0819

ISBN 0-87808-277-8

Printed in the United States of America

*To the global, cross-cultural mission force
and their children,*

*past, present, future,
disciples of the Triune sending God,
from every nation to every nation,*

*who serve in order that
the beloved Lamb who was slain
might receive the reward of His sufferings.*

5115

Contents

PASTORAL CARE OF THE MISSIONARY

Effect of attrition factors in relation to the pastoral care of the
missionary, working in light of the four foundational papers and
specific discussion.

Preface

David Tai-Woong Lee

Does God really care about His servants? Throughout the Scripture there are unmistakable evidences of the fact that "He cares for us." The crux of the matter is: Do we care for our people who are serving the Lord out there in the world of cross-cultural ministry?

Reducing Missionary Attrition Project (ReMAP), launched by the World Evangelical Fellowship Missions Commission, is one of the clearest and most vivid evidences that, like our God, we do care about all of our members who are serving the Lord, from both the old and the new sending countries. There is, at the very least, a unanimous agreement in terms of our motivation, proven by the response of the international mission communities. Close to 115 persons from 35 nations gathered at All Nations Christian College in Easneye, UK, to work on the task of reducing undesirable attrition of our missionaries. The workshop came as a culmination of the 14-nation study on attrition issues for the previous two years.

One of the sobering facts that surfaced during the workshop was the tremendous lack of resources to help the field missionary both to survive and to thrive in ministry. This is particularly true for the new sending countries.

In view of this situation, needless to say, both the workshop itself and this book, utilizing the findings of the 14-nation study done by the task force (carried further by the selected authors from both old and new sending countries), will be of rare value.

This book, then, presents perspectives of mission executives, pastors, missionaries, and counselors hammering out some of the ambiguities in the area of member care on the one hand, and on the other, attempting to formulate better ways to care for our field colleagues.

Countless hours were poured into ReMAP's stages: identification of the issues, the research process, data evaluation and interpretation, and then the workshop itself, as well as at the follow-up stage. There is no doubt that a book of this caliber will be at the forefront in the area of member care for years to come.

WEF Missions Commission staff, task force members, and international participants who worked diligently to produce a sensible plan for member care deserve full recognition for their task. A word of deep appreciation is also extended to the authors representing both old and new sending countries, and lastly to the WEF Missions Commission Executive Director/editor for his prophetic ministry.

Let God receive all the glory and honor.

David Tai-Woong Lee is the current chairman of the WEF Missions Commission. Together with his wife, Hunbok, and two sons, Samuel and Benjamin, he resides in Seoul, Korea. He is the founder of Global Missionary Fellowship, Inc., and is the current chairman of their Board of Directors. He is also the director of the Global Missionary Training Center in Seoul.

Prologue

William D. Taylor

Brief, personal stories of seven people launch us into this book. Harold and Marion, a young couple finishing pre-missions theological study, were just recently in my home. They asked point blank, "Bill, in light of your attrition study, what else should we do prior to leaving for Russia that will help to keep us out of your next attrition research as casualties?" What a challenging question! But I was grateful that this gifted couple, committed to long-term cross-cultural service, were probing. And I believe God gave me something to say to them.

Magdalena spent three years in a tough Muslim context and has returned to her home country riddled with intestinal parasites and other sickness. She longs to return to her task, but the reality of her broken health has prohibited it, at least for now. As we talked during the months of her recovery, some disturbing questions came to my mind. Would her health situation have been different had she received more careful field shepherding, thus allowing her to continue her ministry to this restricted access people group after home leave? Do we do right in placing single women in such contexts? What can Magdalena

do now, back in her home country, about her passionate commitment to missions?

Marcos and Mary just sent me an e-mail from another tough part of the world. They are working on their second difficult language and have made a very long-term commitment to see the church planted amongst this unreached population. I know them well, and my prognostication regarding them is that, barring some radical change, they are en route to a life investment of ministry. I do not see them vulnerable to attrition. For one, they entered cross-cultural ministry after a strong base of years of university student ministry where results were not easy. Second, they have a solid foundation of intercessors in their home country. Third, they are part of a healthy team of three families, all of whom know and trust each other well. Fourth, they are members of a solid mission society with evident pastoral commitments.

Ian and Susanna served with a well-known denominational agency in Asia for some years. For various reasons, they left the field as well as their church. Now, they apparently have little spiritual drive, much less an interest in missions. I met them in a social setting, and when they found out I was working on these attrition issues, their attention rose keenly, saying, "Well, if you want to know how we feel about attrition, we have some things to say!" But I wonder whether we are ready to listen to them!

These stories, and thousands of others, form the flesh-and-blood foundation of this publication. The causes and solutions of undesirable attrition are complex; personal, family, and institutional cultures are difficult to change; the spiritual warfare is nothing to laugh about; and the long-term cross-cultural ministry is frankly tough. But ultimately we are talking about people, real-life individuals—children, youth, and adults. And that's what drives our study.

THOUGHTS ON THIS BOOK AND THE RESEARCH VENTURE, REMAP

Welcome to this historic and unique book. It is historic because it records and addresses issues related to the attrition of long-term missionaries, both in broad sweeps and in specific applications. The book is unique because it presents these issues from a truly global perspective—from the point of view of the "old sending countries" as well as the "new sending countries."

ReMAP

This book is the result of the World Evangelical Fellowship (WEF) Missions Commission venture called ReMAP (Reducing Missionary Attrition Project), our multifaceted and long-term study on this important issue. The aim of ReMAP was not to arrive at a "body count" nor a "blame calling" of mission-

ary "dropouts." Rather, our desire was threefold:

+ To identify the core causes of undesirable long-term (career) missionary attrition and to determine the extent and nature of the problem.
+ To explore solutions to the problem.
+ To deliver products and services to mission agencies and churches worldwide that will help reduce undesirable attrition.

Our long-term focus was and is pastoral and is directed to the global mission force in the areas of selecting and screening, preparing and training, sending and supporting, strategizing and shepherding, and encouraging missionaries during their lifelong pilgrimage to find God's purpose for them, regardless of geography or specific ministry.

ReMAP was designed to produce several kinds of outcomes: **research outcomes** (for example, new data on international and national rates of attrition); **process outcomes** (for example, the effect that completing the survey would have on the nearly 600 mission leaders, for as they worked through the survey it would stimulate them to reflect on attrition related to their own sending agency or church); and **product outcomes** (for example, the international workshop held in 1996, as well as this book).

This publication emerges from three primary sources. The first was the process of our international research, carried out during 1994–1996, with primary contribution by Jonathan Lewis, then Rudy Girón, Peter Brierley, and others who have written for this book. The second source was our international workshop on attrition held at All

Nations Christian College, UK, in April 1996. This conference brought together a rich mixture of generations, genders, pastors, trainers, and executives in the 110 key participants from around the world (41% from the new sending countries and 59% from the old sending countries). The writers of this book comprised our third source of information. Only three papers were presented in the attrition workshop, and they were then modified for publication. This entire book has been written by participants at the 1996 workshop. This is truly a global perspective, a multidisciplinary approach, and an international team of writers, who are from or currently working in 12 nations.

The ReMAP Research

ReMAP used the WEF Missions Commission's extensive global network to collect data from 14 of the most prominent missionary sending nations. The ReMAP researchers utilized the data, first of all, to identify and define the actual and perceived causes of missionary attrition among Western and non-Western missionary movements, both in specific national contexts and in global terms. Second, the data were analyzed to try to identify the specific factors and combinations of factors which may contribute most to increasing or reducing missionary attrition. Through creative dialogue with the missions community, the ReMAP task force then sought to identify solutions that will enhance the ability of sending churches and mission agencies to send and retain effective cross-cultural servants. The result of this concerted international effort is in your hands.

We are not finished with this process. The research must continue. Tools must be developed, information disseminated, and training undertaken that will address the underlying issues of why valuable workers are lost to the missions effort. This volume is but an initial platform, an opening gambit, a threshold to address issues which go well beyond attrition and must ultimately result in the increased effectiveness and greater health of the global missions movement.

We pray that this volume becomes a serious invitation to self-analysis and reflection by the diverse leadership of the great missionary enterprise. Above all, we desire the book to serve our current field missionary force, as well as the future generation that will move into the battleground on behalf of the Triune supernatural God and the glorious message of His Story.

THE STRUCTURE OF THE BOOK

We invite you to take another look at the table of contents to preview the structure of the book. As mentioned above, only three of the chapters were first given as papers at the UK workshop, and they were modified in preparation for this publication. All the others were written expressly for this book.

Part 1 presents the foundational papers from a diversity of perspectives. Following a sweeping overview by Bill Taylor, Paul McKaughan insightfully attempts to define the real problem of attrition. A broad-scope perspective on attrition comes from Rudy Girón's pastoral heart. Then comes a provocative generational study by Kath Donovan and Ruth Myors.

Part 2 moves into the research project itself. Jonathan Lewis defines the project's original design, followed by the fundamental statistical analysis by Peter Brierley of the UK. The data are subsequently reexamined by Detlef Blöcher and Jonathan Lewis, with some clear implications for the missions movement.

Part 3 shifts into national attrition studies, and again the viewpoint is distinct. Korean Steve Moon has done an excellent job of analyzing attrition over a three-year span—in essence a study of first-term Korean attrition. Brazil-based Ted Limpic takes a comprehensive brush that for the first time gives Brazilian leaders grounds for encouragement as well as challenge. Stanley Davies surveys the British context, while Seth Anyomi does the same for Ghana. Finally, North American Phil Elkins evaluates attrition issues from the dual perspective of sending churches and mission agencies in the USA and Canada.

Part 4 changes the focus, and 11 authors writing from eight nations study five major categories that affect missionary attrition: the selection process with a particular focus on the role of the sending church; formal and non-formal pre-field training; mission agency screening and orientation; on-field training and supervision; and the pastoral care of the missionary. We present a key chapter addressing specific items related to missionary kids. We also include a multinational interview of pastors. The section concludes with a global directory of field-based pastoral care providers. The unique component in this section is that each category is addressed from the point of view of both

the old sending countries and the new sending ones.

In **Part 5**, Bill Taylor summarizes some of the challenges directed specifically to the primary "stakeholders" of the missionary movement. This section also suggests avenues for further attrition research.

Part 6 includes a copy of the survey instrument, a suggested Tracking Guide to use in monitoring attrition, and a general index.

SPECIFIC DEFINITIONS USED IN THE BOOK

We faced a number of problems in our study. One was the fact that the term "attrition" did not have easy equivalents in other languages, thus requiring our colleagues to adapt their own descriptive terms to fit their own reality—a challenge in any language!

Portuguese speakers used terms meaning both "abandon" and "wearing out"; those from the Spanish world used the equivalents of "deserting" or "premature abandonment of field service"; one Swede used a term that gives the compound idea of "retiring, withdrawing, leaving"; our colleague from Ethiopia talked about "losing interest and finally dropping out"; one Dutch speaker simply said, "Attrition is difficult to translate"; a Filipino said, "This has to be explained in a series of sentences or phrases in Tagalog. But it is not hard to do."

Using English as our international research language, we found it necessary to define the key terms which are used throughout this book. Here are some of them:

Attrition is the most general term to work with and refers simply to the departure from field service by missionaries, regardless of cause. Our concerns were primarily related to the study of the attrition of long-term (career) missionaries, with a particular focus on the "premature or avoidable return from field service." Leaders of short-term missions must grapple with their own manifestations of the problem.

Attrition rate refers to a percentage which expresses the number of departures of field missionaries within a specific time framework, compared to the overall number of field missionaries for a given organization or movement.

Unpreventable attrition is understood as acceptable or understandable attrition, such as retirement, completion of a contract, medical leave, or a "legitimate call" to another ministry.

Preventable attrition points to a more delicate issue—attrition that could have been avoided by better initial screening or selection in the first place, or by more appropriate equipping or training, or by more effective shepherding during missionary service. Paul McKaughan (chapter 2) has called this type of attrition "problem attrition." He says that it occurs "when missionaries, because of mismanagement, unrealistic expectations, systemic abuse, personal failure, or other personal reasons, leave the field before the mission or church feels that they should. In so doing, missionaries may reflect negatively on themselves, but of greater concern is the negative impact on the specific mission structure and the cause of world missions."

PAR refers to "preventable attrition rate."

UAR refers to "unpreventable attrition rate."

Old sending countries (OSC). Our research project included 14 nations. For the sake of category comparisons, OSC referred to the six nations with a longer history of modern missions: Australia, Canada, Denmark, Germany, the United Kingdom, and the United States.

New sending countries (NSC) refers to the eight nations in our study with a younger history of modern missions: Ghana and Nigeria in Africa; Costa Rica and Brazil in Latin America; and India, South Korea, the Philippines, and Singapore in Asia.

FINALLY

We have written this book with special people in mind—the "stakeholders"—those men and women who have a particular investment in the issues related to attrition. Stakeholders include missionaries (previous, current, and future); missions mobilizers (who motivate the church towards missions); church leaders (pastors, missions pastors, and committees); those involved in missionary training (whether in undergraduate or graduate programs, agencies, training programs, or centers, formal or non-formal); missionary sending agencies (whether churches or societies); national receiving churches (where they exist); and member care providers (pastors and medical and health professionals).

We invite all of our readers to plunge into this publication, grow your own understanding of these critical themes, and reflect on your own situation as an individual or one involved in leadership. Then do all you can within your own sphere of influence to address these matters in a corrective manner.

William D. Taylor, Director of the WEF Missions Commission since 1986, was born in Costa Rica of missionary parents. He lived in Latin America for 30 years, 17 as a career missionary on the faculty of Seminario Teológico Centroamericano in Guatemala. Married to Yvonne, a native Texan, he has three children (all Generation Xers) who were all born in Guatemala. Taylor has edited **Internationalizing Missionary Training** (1991) and **Kingdom Partnerships for Synergy in Missions** (1994) and has co-authored **Crisis and Hope in Latin America** with Emilio Antonio Núñez (1996). His passion is to finish well and to pack heaven with worshipers!

Part 1

The Foundational Papers

Introduction:
Examining the Iceberg
Called Attrition

William D. Taylor

Most of us know something about icebergs, those floating ice masses that have broken off from glaciers, with their largest portion under water and dangerously hidden from view. Attrition reminds us of icebergs, for we tend to see only the visible evidence—missionaries who, for whatever reason, have permanently left cross-cultural service. But over the course of these last three years, our WEF Missions Commission leadership team has been reminded again and again of the hidden dimensions of attrition—the "real" reasons that missionaries leave, or the invisible culture of the mission society/agency that clearly affects attrition positively or negatively. So keep these factors in mind as you read not only this chapter, but also the others in this book. You might discover some new dimensions of this iceberg yourself, both visible and invisible!

THE HUMAN STORIES
AND DIMENSION OF ATTRITION

I never want to forget Betty, whom I met shortly before our 1996 UK work-shop on attrition. She was a sweet, gracious, gifted disciple of Christ who was preparing for ministry. Her young adult face reflected a two-volume set of emotions. She would smile in our conversations, but her eyes never smiled. They were etched with permanent pain. As her story poured out, her just anger, hurt, and tears roiled through me. Both of her parents were graduates from a premier missionary training school. They were accepted by a major mission agency and, supported by friends and churches, they went to the mission field. But once there, reality emerged, and Betty's father revealed himself as a quiet, cruel, violent abuser of his wife. Betty and her younger brother saw it all. But the "family secret" was never unveiled. The family returned home and resigned from the mission. The parents divorced, and the family fragmented. Betty's mother slipped away from faith, and in mid-life she married a non-Christian who, ironically, truly loved her in a way that her "Christian" husband never had. The father today is a bitter man; the brother is isolated from the family and is angry with all, including God. When Betty heard about our attrition study, she asked me, "Do you think your study will help discern what happened to my family so as to prevent other similar cases?"

The fact is that this attrition research has been anything but exciting, thrilling, and filled with joy for me. There are too many personal stories, now shared very freely when people (including the "attrits") discover what we are doing in this investigation. We never wanted simply to do "body counts" nor to major on "failures"—whether provoked by the individual, the family, church, school, or agency. We wanted to go beyond the numbers into human lives and church/mission "cultures," to discern just why we are losing so many good people from long-term cross-cultural ministry. We also wanted to discover what keeps people on the field. We desired to profile those mission agencies which are doing a good job in preventing attrition. This complex task requires them to face their own history of attrition and to provide proper pastoral and member care, detecting those who are vulnerable to attrition and stimulating necessary change within the mission culture and structure.

I have been greatly encouraged by personal stories of both young and veteran missionaries who have hung in there over the years, regardless of difficult circumstances. Recently, a most gifted single woman serving in Central Asia spent the better part of a day in our home. We had prayed her to the Muslim world years ago, and now she was back on her first home leave. Hers was a multilayered story of tensions with co-workers, personal grief, a broken heart

when a romantic relationship dissolved, difficulties with language learning and cultural adjustment, ministry as a single woman in a Muslim culture, and even changing mission agency while on the field. To our astonishment, this woman desires to return! What is it that keeps such a person on the field, while others with less difficult situations withdraw from cross-cultural service?

Attrition is a multifaceted creature providing touches of dark humor, personal reality checks, and painful stories, as well as forcing churches, training schools, and mission societies into serious self-evaluation. A colleague from the South Pacific passed on a touch of dark humor on this subject. He told me that of the first five missionaries to the Cook Islands, two left the field (attrition), one went native (assimilation), and two were eaten (nutrition)! I was told that the Solomon Islanders ate one missionary but had a hard time with the shoes. They kept cooking them but never got them tender enough to eat!

Not too long ago, I spoke at a major North American conference of mission leaders. I posed three "personal reality check" questions and was jolted by the responses. First, I asked how many of those present had been field missionaries at one time but had left the field for any variety of reasons. Most of the audience raised their hands. Second, I asked how many of them, upon leaving the field, had been classified under the category of "undesirable attrition," either by their agency or perhaps by their colleagues or home churches. Again, most said yes. Third, I asked how many of those who had left the field had participated in a final interview with either mission or church leadership. Most indicated that they had not had such an interview. The generalized conclusions were not very encouraging.

I also well remember the case study of a young missionary family in Latin America. The husband was a missionary kid who had returned to his beloved region with a young wife and a baby daughter. He had dreamed since the age of eight that he would be a missionary, and having made that decision, he allowed it to shape his life. Finally, after three years of Bible school, a university degree, four years of seminary, and a term of staff ministry with InterVarsity, they were off to the field, to his "home." Little did the young man know what he would encounter when his expectations faced reality, or that his dreams would be torpedoed due to a conflictive mission leader. Towards the end of the first term, this aspiring missionary was absolutely worn down and was on the verge of throwing in the towel and returning to his "passport culture" (certainly not his "home country").

During the worst of that darkness, one evening the doorbell rang. To his astonishment, the struggling young missionary found outside the gate a greatly respected veteran mission leader, who at that time lived in the USA. "What are you doing here in Guatemala? We had no idea you were coming here." He simply stated, "I have come." So into the house he came. He sat down and asked simply, "How are you doing?" The young husband and father broke, and with his wife alongside, he told his painful story in tears. The veteran listened. He discerned the deeper cries. He spoke healing, and gradually new perspectives of hope came into focus. Humanly speaking,

God used this man to "save" that young family from being an early case of crushed attrition. That man was not only the mission president; he was a beloved visionary shepherd. He was also my father, for I was that young man.

Attrition issues are extremely important to me now, for I have witnessed both the visible and the invisible dimensions of the iceberg.

BACKDROP ITEMS

The WEF Missions Commission venture called ReMAP (Reducing Missionary Attrition Project) emerged into a major international concern as we listened and dialogued with our colleagues around the world. For years we had emphasized the need of proper pre-field training, but we concluded early on that training was but one of three major components of an interrelated, functional missions infrastructure. The three components were:

1. Pre-candidate component—the mobilization of the church and the selection of the missionary, including screening, sending, and supporting.

2. Training component—effective equipping of the cross-cultural force.

3. Field component—supporting, strategizing, shepherding, and supervising the global missionary force.

From the perspective of our WEF team, the international missionary enterprise seemed to have done a relatively good job in the first area, general mobilization. They had researched and "adopted" the unreached people groups and had sent out cross-cultural workers, both short-term and long-term. Relative to the second component, the training vision was growing worldwide, and this gave us encouragement. **But** was the global movement scoring as high in the strategic dimensions related to the pastoral care of field missionaries? Were we keeping our new and younger mission force in long-term, effective, cross-cultural service? Were we sending people to the field who should *not* have been sent? Our primary concern began to focus not on longevity of service, but rather on effectiveness in long-term ministry. What truly was the international attrition rate for long-term (a better word than "career") missionaries, and why were these workers leaving? We were greatly encouraged by the requests from the newer sending countries for help in addressing their own unique attrition issues.

We launched ReMAP in 1994 to address specific issues related to long-term (not short-term) missionaries and undesirable attrition from active field service. While attrition applies to all categories of missionaries who return earlier than expected, we felt that the strategic nature of this project must focus on the long-term personnel. While we praise God for the growth and impact of short-termers, we also feel that most of the underreached and unreached peoples will see vital churches planted primarily by those willing to invest a sufficient number of years to learn the language well, understand the heritage and culture of the people, love the people deeply, and thus build credibility for telling the transformational Story of the Triune God.

Our overall goal of the study was to reduce undesirable attrition in the long-term missionary body and thus increase the effectiveness of the global mission task force. The study led to a five- to seven-year process which is now revealed in this publication. However, we are not finished with the research, and we are challenged as we discern what paths to take in the coming years of this investigation.

EXPLORING THE ICEBERG: PERSONAL OBSERVATIONS ON ATTRITION

1. Attrition in the Secular World

Attrition is a genuine, high-dollar problem in the secular world of military, diplomacy, and business. It is not just a missions concern. I have spoken with people familiar with these diverse vocations and employment categories. Note these insights from the business world:

"Approximately 30% of managers from the US return home early from an overseas assignment" (Shames, 1995). This striking statement is followed by a discussion of why attrition occurs. Shames observes that personal and family stress are the primary factors. What is the financial cost to business? For a single, middle-level professional, the figure is close to $150,000, but for a senior professional with a family, the number is $350,000 or more. But there are different price tags also. The article goes on, "The human costs defy calculation. Emotional havoc, broken families, derailed careers, and illness are the price of neglecting personal well-being on the global circuit."

In June 1996, the *Personal Journal* offered a brief but sober report entitled, "Expatriate Assignments May Not Be Fulfilling Their Objectives." Some of the questions:

1. Has your organization experienced early repatriation of expatriates?

No 27%   Yes 73%

2. Has your organization experienced the early return of expatriate families without the employee?

No 55%   Yes 45%

3. Has your organization experienced the failure of the expatriate to meet the business objectives of the expatriate assignment?

No 18%   Yes 82%

4. Do you suspect that many business problems occur in the international location because of cultural problems that may never come to the attention of senior management?

No 9%   Yes 91%

5. Does someone in your office have regular contact with the expatriate to monitor how the assignment is progressing?

No 36%   Yes 64%

2. Change in Language Needed

We must change our language on attrition, reduce the use of pejorative terms related to the subject, and begin to see strong positives in attrition. Some of the negative terms are "dropout," "failure," "they quit," "quitters," "body count," and "blame calling." Many times these words underscore a judgment placed on the wrong people. Perhaps the missionaries were pushed out by negative field leaders or colleagues who were threatened by new and gifted leaders. Or they may have burned out due to inadequate pastoral care or unrealistic expectations from themselves, their churches and supporters, the sending body or agency, the field ministry, or even the national church. Perhaps the focus of judgment should be directed to the mission leadership, the administrative structures, or the agency culture.

But there is another side to this coin, which sees "attrition" as the best thing that could happen to a missionary, even "the will of God in Christ" for the person. Perhaps church and mission leaders should restructure their attitudes and actions in the direction of finding the right place of ministry for this particular person. Perhaps God in His sovereignty will allow a person to serve in a cross-cultural context to work on character, skills, or some other testing. Then it is time to move into another ministry, perhaps back in the home culture.

Some other leaders have suggested that attrition is God's plan to encourage the nationalization of certain ministries that need to be fully transferred to national church structures. Some of these organizations would not reject a missionary whom they could get "for free," but is this the best thing for both mission and national church?

3. Divergent Attitudes

Mission and church leaders revealed divergent attitudes towards attrition issues and this study. Some North Americans were very frank, saying things like, "Don't bother me with another study which we don't need!" Or, "This is a waste of money," or, "Our church really doesn't have a problem with attrition." Others said, "If we only had a real hard-data research [i.e., what are the numbers?], then we might be able to complete the job of world evangelization." From others, we encountered passive resistance. "Well... I guess if you have to do it, but really...." Or the "blood and guts" people: "This is war, so expect attrition. Stuff happens! Get tough."

From some, the attitude was denial, "circling the wagons" to protect their history, traditions, and structures. The latter reaction comes from too many agencies and primarily older leaders. Many do not value their missionaries honestly and do not acknowledge that they and their families are hurting or that something is seriously wrong with the mission policy or leadership. This becomes a major constituency issue for agencies, and again it reveals denial and fear.

We were encouraged by many: "We really need this study!" This comment came from primarily outside the USA, certainly from every leader we spoke with from the Two-Thirds World, but also from some younger mission leaders in the West. One missions pastor of a large American church told me, "I have just had to deal with some of the most messy attrition cases in my life. Please tell people that we in the sending churches must pay more attention to the selection of missionaries, as well as to their field-based pastoral care." And significantly, some of the "attrits" supported the study and had a lot to say about it, offering their candid opinions. I often wondered why they were so interested, and then the answer became obvious. They are the ones who have personally experienced the pain!

4. Agency Tracking Studies

Some agencies have done an admirable job of tracking and addressing their attrition factors. We have been greatly encouraged by agencies such as the Christian and Missionary Alliance, whose studies spanning decades are models of careful tracking. The Foreign Mission Board of the Southern Baptist Convention is another example, as is the Assembly of God. Peter Brierley carried out a study for OMF which was revelatory in many senses. Some other agencies, such as OC International and WEC, have done their own studies.

What agencies have done with the results of their studies has varied. Some have truly grappled with the implications and have introduced changes. One non-denominational society's attrition study revealed a serious absence of field-based pastoral care. They acknowledged the deficiency and appointed someone to meet the need. But was that sufficient to stem their major losses? Many agencies say they track attrition, but they have never seriously analyzed their results. Frankly, too many simply deny that attrition is a problem for them. One mission executive told me, "Our missionaries don't need pastoral care." At the other end of the spectrum, thankfully, more and more agencies are desirous of help in tracking their attrition and in addressing their particular issues.

Several studies have clarified that while attrition hits first termers especially hard, it is *not* a phenomenon limited to the first term. One mission found that serious attrition was taking place at the level of their emerging, experienced leaders.

5. Newer Sending Nations

Following are some vignettes with attrition implications from the newer sending nations, which have a younger force with few retirees.

Singapore: "A minimum bond of S$75,000 has to be paid to the government if the parents choose to continue with overseas schooling for boys after they reach the age of 12."

India: "On an average, each missionary working in the Malto region has had malaria more than 15 times. There are missionaries who have been affected by malaria 25 to 30 times. But they stay." India has its martyrs also, and this category emerged in the results of the ReMAP statistics.

Philippines: The prime reasons for attrition were lack of home support, lack of call, outside marriage, inadequate commitment, and health problems.

Brazil: Based on unconfirmed reports, they feared attrition was 15% per year, but their ReMAP study showed 7% annual undesirable attrition. The five primary causes of undesirable attrition are inadequate training, lack of financial support, lack of commitment, personal factors such as self-esteem and stress, and problems with colleagues. The major attrition causes focused on character problems and not skill limitations, which will have a great impact on Brazilian training programs.

Korea: In 1992, only 23% of the agencies reported attrition, but by 1994 the figure had jumped to 44% of the agencies. The attrition rate is much higher for single women missionaries, primarily due to parental pressure toward marriage. For the year 1994, the first-term attrition was 2.75%. The main perceived causes for attrition were problems with peers, weak home support, health problems, children, change of job, and outside marriage.

6. Deeper Issues

Attrition is only the tip of the iceberg. We have to evaluate the entire process of selection, training, sending, supervision, and pastoral care of missionaries, as well as agency structure and culture. These dynamics have emerged over and over again, both at the April 1996 workshop and in this book. Kath Donovan and Ruth Myors (see chapter 4) addressed this area directly and at length in their presentation at the ReMAP workshop. Each church and mission agency has a particular "culture" or "system" which it preserves as part of its history. But too many churches and agencies deny the reality of missionary pain and attrition. Perhaps too many agencies are led by visionaries (or functionaries), who do not have the required pastoral gifting to be sensitive to hurting people.

Donovan and Myors also focused on understanding the issues of "spirituality," "call," and "staying power." Of particular value was their chart which gave a perspective on the three Australian generations. Many workshop participants were especially attracted to their observation that, "The older generation is driven by the parable of the plow, and the younger generation is driven by the parable of the talents."

Paul McKaughan's profound, insightful chapter (chapter 2) addresses this theme directly, with specific application to both the new and old sending countries.

7. Reasons for Attrition

We identified four categories of reasons as to why people leave the mission field. Peter Brierley was the initial person to identify the first three elsewhere, and I have added one.

1. The reasons the agency and church leaders believe they have heard and understood.

2. The recorded reasons in the files.

3. The reasons departing missionaries hold in private or may share with closest friends.

4. The real reasons—are they knowable?

Many questions emerge from these four categories. One of the challenges in dealing with a missionary family unit returning "early" is to attempt to discern the real reasons in ways that are truly helpful for them, their families, supporting churches, and mission societies.

8. Faces of Attrition

We saw four faces of attrition emerge:

Acceptable Attrition

We can understand "acceptable" attrition that comes from normal retirement, issues related to children (although some of these are a cover for unresolved parental conflicts), a legitimate change of job, or health problems. Significantly, in North America, with an older mission force, these are the top four reasons for missionary attrition. There are others we can accept as well.

Preventable Attrition

There are attrition causes that we feel are preventable, such as lack of home support (not just financial), problems with peers, personal concerns, lack of call (dealt with prior to departure to the field), inadequate pre-field equipping/training, poor cultural adaptation, and a cluster of others that came up in our research. It was these causes that we felt could be dealt with prior to field service, as well as during field service. Equally significant is the fact that the younger mission force faces its own set of four primary causes of attrition, all of which could be categorized as prevent-

able: lack of home support, lack of call, inadequate commitment, and disagreement with the agency.

Desirable but Unrealized Attrition

This is the attrition that should have taken place but didn't. No formal study that I know of can document this fact, but some missionaries stay who should leave, and they compound the tragedy, in that their staying makes some of the better people leave. So not all attrition is bad. It can be a healthy thing to reduce the number of missionaries who should not be allowed to stay on the field. But doing this requires courageous, proactive leadership from the agency or responsible church. It also points out a major structural flaw that is faced particularly in the so-called "faith missions," but I suspect it exists across the board. To stay alive and apparently relevant, mission agencies depend on missionary units—and their finances. So when individuals come with an apparent call to missions and with tangible financial support, and they somehow fit into the mission agency, they tend to get in. And some will never leave nor be removed! It takes great courage for leadership to act responsibly here, and ultimately they do missionaries a high good by getting them "home" and off the field. Such action certainly benefits local churches and other missionaries.

Attrition Among the Vulnerable

Finally, there's a group we would call "those vulnerable to attrition." This was a category that emerged in the OMF study on attrition done by Peter Brierley, which focused on the younger-to-middle segment of their mission force. Understanding this phenomenon led

OMF to take corrective measures. What are the factors in a particular mission society or in a subteam of that agency, perhaps different from one national context to another, that cause this segment of the missionary force to be vulnerable to attrition? Mission leaders are wise to address this issue right away.

9. Churches and Agencies

Churches and agencies have their particular concerns with attrition issues. Not only across North America, but also in countries around the world, churches are brewing with their own global missions ferment. Some are profoundly dissatisfied with the way schools have "mis-trained" people and agencies have misused human and financial resources. "We can do it better and cheaper ourselves!" Some churches are selecting, training, and sending their own church-planting ministry teams, even into the tough, unreached parts of the world. But have they truly counted the cost of providing the imperative field-based support system to enable their teams to live and serve effectively and for longer terms? I tend to doubt it. Few churches have analyzed their own missionary attrition history or the realities they will face if they don't change their way of doing things.

Other churches that have carried a major portion of a missionary's financial support must invest more concern with attrition matters. One American missions pastor called me shortly before I began writing this chapter to say, "Your attrition study is absolutely crucial to our church. I have just gone through a gruesome experience with two families, and the tragedy is that we could have prevented a lot of the pain." Another

church "lost" three missionary families within one month: one due to genuine sickness of a child, one due to sinful behavior of a parent, and the third from a combination of reasons.

What about the agencies themselves? Some USA and international agencies are grappling with attrition issues in a serious way. But unfortunately, many mission agencies have *not* faced their own attrition history. This is the case in both old and new sending nations. Why so? Uneasiness? A sense that it isn't necessary? Lack of knowing how to do it?

Significantly, the attrition workshop caused many agency leaders to work on their own attrition factors. M. Patrick Joshua of the Friends Missionary Prayer Band of India wrote me: "Our Research and Development Department took the initial notes I brought from the missionary attrition conference seriously and applied some of the principles to our system. There is enormous effect in the observance of intensive pastoral care, having a different outlook in dealing with younger generations of missionaries, etc. There is much reduction in our attrition rate."

We noticed during the ReMAP workshop that the further a missions leader is from field/pastoral realities, the greater the tendency to minimize the attrition issues. It was the men and women close to the nitty-gritty of people's lives who sensed the critical nature of the topic at hand.

10. "Eschatology" of Attrition

Using "eschatology" in this sense, I refer to attrition factors that might affect the future generation of missionaries, particularly those yet in high school and college, as well as recent graduates. Can we attempt to predict what will happen to these young people within current or newly created mission structures?

Again, Kath Donovan and Ruth Myors have stimulated many of us to evaluate the future profile of both mission force and mission society. Prior to the workshop, one Western participant wrote heatedly that the grid prepared by Donovan and Myors was another imposition upon the Two-Thirds World of something from the West. My response was twofold: We had asked the speakers to address the issue from their experience and national perspective, but I suspected that every country had some kind of generational factor to consider in terms of both church and mission movement. Fortunately, I was right on both counts! One Filipino leader said that when he first read of the generational element, he felt it had no application to his nation, but when he shared those ideas with some younger colleagues, they helped him see their own home-grown generational problem. Worldwide, a similar phenomenon is taking place that will require great creativity on the part of older Christian leaders.

When I evaluate the younger generation in North America—let's call them "Generation X" (with "X" representing the unlimited algebraic possibilities, not a generic blandness!)—I wonder how many of these young people will fit into current mission structures, particularly the agencies with the weight of history and tradition. These particular Christian subculture structures come in all stripes, styles, and shades of doctrines, policies, unspoken rules, and unique particularities/peculiarities. After I

spoke on attrition at the 1996 EFMA/IFMA conference in Florida, a 31-year-old mission leader from a well-known agency asked me point blank: "Do you really think Generation X is going to fit into these agencies?"

I gave him this fourfold response: First, yes, some of them will fit in, because Generation X is so diverse. There are always some who have grown up in a subculture that matches that of the agency. They may be missionary kids who find that world "normal" and will return to the mission field. Some may be unable to fit in elsewhere or unable to fit into their "passport culture." They may be graduates of Bible schools and seminaries who fit that world. Second, there is hope that some older agencies will make substantive, even structural changes to make room for these gifted and godly young adults. Third, other Generation Xers will find their global community in the context of vibrant local churches where pastoral, mission, and business entrepreneurs merge their visions and create new sending/supporting structures. Finally, yet other creative Generation Xers will start their own unique organizations, which will reflect their values, commitments, and passions. This is already happening across the USA. But the fact is that many Generation Xers will struggle with frustration as they work out their global commitment.

Frankly, I am profoundly distressed by the attitude of older "boomer" missionaries and leaders, who have harshly judged the Xers and have shown such little compassion, grace, and mercy to a broken generation. Why are boomers reacting so negatively, when so many Xers are their own children? Michael

Schwartz, creative and committed Generation X editor of *Vox: The Voice of a Generation* (a magazine written by and for Xers), recently told me that his generation has found a more compassionate hearing from the older generation than from boomers. And for that reason, the Xers respect the elders much more. Generation X is a generation that is closer to the socio-moral-spiritual condition of first century Christians than we can imagine. However, as they acknowledge and deal with their brokenness in the power of the Spirit, they will become also a generation of glorious promise both for the church and for the global cause of Christ!

11. Revisiting Attrition Studies

Attrition evaluation by mission agencies is not a new item, as most of us already know. I discovered in my files a copy of an unpublished four-page report by Dr. J. Herbert Kane entitled, "An Analysis of Missionary Casualties." It reported a study done by the Missionary Research Library of New York, covering the decade 1953–1962. During that period, 1,409 "casualties" were reported by 36 boards, both large and small, both denominational and faith missions. The study had two categories, "avoidable withdrawals" and "anticipated withdrawals," covering career missionaries with 20 or more years of service.

Statistics are tricky under just about all circumstances, and their reliability is justifiably questioned. We have faced this problem in ReMAP, and we cautiously offer our numbers within their context and reality. Already some have exaggerated the figures to build their own cases. One old sending country (OSC) agency wrote shortly after our

1996 workshop: "47% of missionaries leave the field during the first five years. 71% of them do so for preventable reasons. Effective training, or the lack of it, plays a critical role." The fact is that for the OSC countries, inappropriate training ranked 20th in the study. However, for the new sending countries (NSC), it came in 11th place.

Perhaps a better way to state the case for training is to address the top five causes of OSC "preventable" attrition and realize that these causes have to do primarily with issues of character and relationships. Then we can ask the question: In what ways do our formal and non-formal training equip missionaries in these two crucial dimensions? Formal theological institutions that say they train missionaries often address primarily knowledge components, not character nor even skills needed to survive and thrive in cross-cultural missions. What must be done to change the way we do missionary training? Do our church, mission, and educational leaders have the courage to forge a new path?

Let's take a look at one of the prime findings of the ReMAP research: In terms of the global missions force, it is estimated that 1 career missionary in 20 (5.1% of the mission force) leaves the mission field to return home *every year*. Of those who leave, 71% leave for *preventable* reasons. What might these numbers mean? If we estimate the current long-term, international, cross-cultural missionary force at 150,000 strong—a very conservative number—an annual loss of 5.1% would be 7,650 missionaries leaving the field each year. Over a four-year term, this figure jumps to 30,600. This is the total loss figure for all reasons. The preventable percentage is 71% of 30,600, or 21,726.

Just the financial implications are dramatic and rather calculable. But the human implications are staggering and incalculable. Can we simply continue to do business as always? Absolutely not!

FINAL REFLECTIONS ON ATTRITION FROM A PERSONAL EXPERIENCE

In March of 1996, my wife and I stood on the windy, frigid shores of the distant, northwestern Scottish island of Iona, a crucial pilgrimage site for students of Celtic history and Christianity. We felt history washing over us as we relived the powerful testimony of those unique men and women of faith who so shaped their world and beyond. In the year 563 A.D., St. Columba (Columcille), both pilgrim and missionary, journeyed across the Irish Sea to establish his base on this tiny island. The island became the platform for the Celtic evangelization of what we know as Scotland. Christian Celts from Ireland would eventually send their missionaries as far away as the Ukraine.

Of particular interest to my own study of attrition is the Celtic missionary vision, which they called *peregrinatio* (pilgrimage, or wanderlust to explore the unknown), under one of their symbols for the Holy Spirit, the wild goose. Over the years, the Celts developed a fascinating, tricolored martyrdom: *red* martyrdom symbolized persecution, bloodshed, or giving one's life for Christ; *green* martyrdom spoke of self-denial and severe penitential acts that would lead to personal holiness; and *white* martyrdom spoke of the pain of leaving

family, clan, and tribe to spread the cause of Christ, perhaps never returning home again.

As I think of these diverse attrition issues which come out of ReMAP and our own modern Christian missions *peregrinatio*, I sense that those Celtic men and women of missionary faith might be able to understand some of our problems. They would have much to say to us today about the relevance of their tricolored martyrdom. Perhaps we can adapt their wisdom and vision to our time and reality.

This is a glorious day to be alive, serving the supernatural, Triune God in global missions. And while we must not avoid the price to be paid, nevertheless we can do a much better stewardship job with our missionary force.

REFERENCES

Expatriate assignments may not be fulfilling their objectives. *Personal Journal* (1996, June).

Shames, G. W. (1995, February). United Airlines *Hemispheres*.

William D. Taylor, *Director of the WEF Missions Commission since 1986, was born in Costa Rica of missionary parents. He lived in Latin America for 30 years, 17 as a career missionary on the faculty of Seminario Teológico Centroamericano in Guatemala. Married to Yvonne, a native Texan, he has three children (all Generation Xers) who were all born in Guatemala. Taylor has edited* **Internationalizing Missionary Training** *(1991) and* **Kingdom Partnerships for Synergy in Missions** *(1994) and has co-authored* **Crisis and Hope in Latin America** *with Emilio Antonio Núñez (1996). His passion is to finish well and to pack heaven with worshipers!*

Missionary Attrition: Defining the Problem

Paul McKaughan

Not long ago I was in a meeting of mission leaders, discussing one of the hot topics of missions today, missionary attrition. It was one of those "Aha!" experiences when we discovered that in one way or another, we had all "attrited." None of us was in the place where we had started out in ministry. We were not doing what we thought the Lord had first called us to when we responded to the challenge of world evangelization. Most of us had planned and trained to be career field missionaries, and here we were in academic missiology, in missions administration, or in other staff roles with mission agencies. Were we failures? We were all surely attrition statistics.

For most of us, there would have been a point at which those who knew us well would have said that, yes, we were at least disappointments. Most of our sending missions at one point had lamented the fact that personal frustration, shifts in ministry interests, family responsibilities, or other factors caused us to "take our hand from the plow"—to "look back" and leave the field for other "lesser" ministries. Sometimes more than leaving the field, we had left the mission with which we had served, and at times those leavings were not as graceful as they might have been. The whole experience had left an abundance of psychological and spiritual bumps and bruises for the Holy Spirit and the body of Christ to heal.

WHAT IS A PROBLEM ANYWAY?

Some years ago I came across a very helpful management textbook entitled *Rational Manager* (Kepner & Tregoe, 1976). The point of this book was that too often we jump to conclusions in declaring what the problem is. Then we precipitously leap in to resolve the ill-defined problem. We alter a symptom but do not resolve the real problem. By acting this way, we often create even more complications, while the real problem remains festering and unresolved. As a missions community, we may be doing this with the issue of attrition. Kepner and Tregoe affirm that we start to solve a problem when we define it properly. They define a problem as a deviation from a norm or expectation that we can choose to do something about.

I must admit that I have many more questions on the topic of attrition than I have answers. My questioning starts with, what is the missionary norm today? Is the normal term of service for a missionary what it was when I began my career 35 years ago? Do we carry with us a mental picture or norm for missionary service that was created 100 years ago, when it took several months to physically get to the field and people often got sick or died in a matter of a few years or even months, and if they survived they labored long years without even returning to the country of origin? Or have issues such as the ease of travel, a society of multiple careers, and a church which frequently replaces its pastors all changed what should be considered normal for missionaries today?

I present the following reflections from the perspective of decades of experience in cross-cultural ministry, from years as a field missionary as well as the CEO of a mission agency, and now from the vantage point of a North American evaluating his own understanding of the global task before us.

NORMAL?

To define normal, one must always question, as compared to what? It is important to note the standard against which we are considering a normal term of missionary service. Normal, for my children, is not spending a life with one company or even in one career. The normal way that my son, an engineer, gets increased responsibility and the raises which go with it is to change from company to company, from project to project. Normal for another son, who is in ministry here in the States, is to move from place to place in order to acquire

the reservoir of experiences and skills necessary to qualify him for leadership in his chosen field of service. The expectations by which we measure missionary normalcy are important, if we are to evaluate missionary attrition accurately.

Many in the missions system continue to hang onto and propagate a model of normalcy which is considered not only abnormal but irrelevant to many in the church and in the broader society. The model is normal only in our little missions world, yet it is the standard against which we measure a missionary career. This is not to say that some people do not stay a long time in a single company or career field. It is not to say that we do not need men and women on the mission field who are experts and, more importantly, who have established an empathetic understanding of a specific culture and long-term trust relationships with people in that culture. The issue is that the standard we are using simply may not be the relevant norm against which we can measure all missionary attrition.

PROBLEM DESCRIPTIONS

Deviation From the Norm

In problem solving, one of the first things we are taught to do is to describe the deviation from whatever norm we are considering. Let me try to describe three fairly typical cases.

Case 1

A highly trained and competent missionary, who has gone through a rather rigorous screening process and has spent many months raising his support, finally gets to his field of service. But sometime before he completes his first term (three years), having given the majority of that time to language acquisition and learning the culture, he comes to the conclusion that missionary life is not what the Lord intended for him. Therefore, he just picks up and comes back home.

Case 2

A missionary family complete two or three terms on the field and are reaching the point of maximum knowledge and influence with the national church leaders. They are coming home permanently because their children are starting high school or college, because they need to take care of an elderly parent, or because the husband has discovered that he has a contribution to make in some other area. They leave behind a void, because the field already has a shortage of mature, effective missionary leadership.

Case 3

A missionary has a sense of growing unrest and anxiety. She has needs which she feels are not being met on the field or within the mission. She feels drawn to grow in a direction not provided for by her missionary career. At times, she has grown tired of a somewhat paternal or even oppressive mission administration—an administration which insists that when she is home, she must spend the majority of her time raising support or engaging in other activities which she finds incompatible with her gifting or calling.

In all of these cases, there seems to be articulated by the missionaries a sense of God's leading in their lives. They feel they are following the Master. They are not in conscious rebellion, but rather they are seeking to be obedient.

Isn't that the sense of calling that has drawn them to missions in the first place? This quest for a statement of the problem has been long and involved, but the bottom line is that missionaries leave the field before the mission or church thinks they should.

What, Where, When?

A second problem-solving exercise we embark on is determining what the problem is or what the problem is not. Then, where does the problem occur? After that, when did it first occur? Only then can we look for possible causes and, it is hoped, some solutions.

Case 1

There are significant issues of credibility in Case 1, the person who returns during or at the end of the first term. The case is normally seen as a stewardship issue, because the missionary took a long time to raise support in the church and expended a lot of resources acquiring not only a theological education, but also missiological understanding and specialized skills in language learning and cultural exegesis. The missionary leaves the field without fulfilling expectations commensurate to the funds and effort invested in him.

Case 2

Case 2 is seen as a strategic loss to the field and missions community, even though there may be a battery of reasonable and rational personal conclusions which, in a sense, force veteran workers to take this drastic step.

Case 3

In Case 3, the perceptions of the missionary and the sending agency are in conflict and cannot be easily reconciled. There is also a mismatch of expectations. The missionary sees her situation as God's leading through many different circumstances, while the agency tends to perceive the same set of circumstances as a failure on the part of the missionary.

Let's go on to see where the problem of attrition may occur and when it was first observed. I emphasize again that in these three cases the problem is *not* one of conscious rebellion against God or a lessening of commitment to follow Him. The problem isn't even giving up on an obedient response to disciple the nations. Rather, it is a sense that the place or context for the fulfillment of the call has changed.

Where is the problem which we have labeled as attrition occurring? Attrition seems to be happening all over the world, and it seems to be happening in all types of mission agencies. I would say it is not even geographically or ministerially confined. The same phenomenon is described in the pastorate here in North America, as ministers seek fulfillment in other areas of their lives.

Lastly, **when** was the problem first observed in the life of the church? I would say that it was first described in the Scriptures. It was chronicled in the book of Acts in the experience of John Mark (Acts 13:5, 13). At the very least, a change of missionary team was necessary for John Mark (Acts 15:36-40), but over a period of time, even the people with whom he had split, headed by the Apostle Paul, came to realize that this "dropout" had later become valuable (2 Tim. 4:11).

The problem of attrition has been with us from the beginning of the mis-

sions movement. However, today time has been telescoped, and the context has changed. Where once missionaries died or became totally debilitated by health problems, the reasons for attrition today tend to be much more psychological and centered in the felt needs of missionaries and their families.

How serious is the problem? I don't know if anyone knows the answer to that question. In some agencies and countries, the fallout from attrition is severe and threatens the missionary movement. In other places, attrition is just another item seen as a negative that is associated with the missionary movement, which is itself falling from public favor. Attrition is aligned with other stewardship issues, which observers feel are pricing Western missionaries out of effective ministry.

ATTEMPT AT A PROBLEM STATEMENT

Let me try to state our problem which has been called attrition: **Problem attrition occurs when missionaries, because of mismanagement, unrealistic expectations, systemic abuse, personal failure, or other personal reasons, leave the field before the mission or church feels that they should.** In so doing, missionaries may reflect negatively on themselves, but of greater concern is the negative impact on the specific mission structure and the cause of world missions.

POSSIBLE CAUSES OF ATTRITION

What are some of the possible causes of this phenomenon of missionary attrition or dropout? We hear that people are much softer, that they are unable to "take it," that there is spiritual immaturity in the lives of today's missionaries, that missionaries are not prepared for the work that they encounter. These are all plausible hypotheses. However, to put the phenomenon in historical perspective, it seems that each generation judging its junior successor has these same built-in prejudices. Often this generational reflection is compounded by our sense that those of us who are older have achieved a level of commitment and have paid the price to a degree unapproached by the younger generation. There are, however, other possible reasons to consider besides the apparent increased immaturity and self-serving of today's younger missionaries.

There is the possibility that the decreased distance between the ministry at home and the ministry overseas makes it much easier to go back and forth. Geographic distance is no longer a significant barrier between nations or peoples. It takes much longer to drive across the USA, Canada, Brazil, or India in an automobile (a feat unheard of 100 years ago) than it does to fly to the farthest place on planet Earth. In a day we can be almost anywhere. Also, we find that church members today do not see a hierarchy of need based on geographical distance. To many people, geographic distance is almost meaningless today.

The missionary ministry is not as different or as far away as it was in times past. In comparison to the mission field, all of our major Western cities seem just as needy, if not more so. The Western church is familiar with sanitized, far-away places seen on the TV's Travel Channel, Learning Channel, or CNN. Because all these places seem so close, returning from the field does not seem as big a deal as it was when one had to get on a ship and sail for six months to get home. Correspondingly, the field is not nearly as exotic, mysterious, or compelling as it used to be.

There may be yet another cause of attrition, as well. The day in which people would apprentice themselves for years to learn a trade has ended. People today graduate from college and seminary with a sense of immediate competency. Young people today have expectations of several major career moves. Therefore, they don't consider extensive time garnering experience to be necessary for advancements. They look at acquiring new and different experiences as a broadening process which adds to their resume and skill set. Why should it be any different if one is going into missions? Is it not technical competency that we are primarily looking and advertising for? Don't classroom-acquired technical competencies prepare one for immediate effectiveness when reaching the field?

Unfortunately, the projections of those who create missionary advertising may clash with the expectations of those who respond to such promotions, even before new missionaries arrive on the field. Also, the mission agency may have a very unrealistic and antiquated view of the length of time which is really necessary to become effective on the field. When we in missions have clear performance expectations, the norms are not always relevant.

OTHER ATTRITION-RELATED CHALLENGES

The more I study the issue, the more I ask myself, what kind of problem is attrition, or is it really a problem at all? Would the kingdom of God really have been advanced farther if there had been less attrition? We will probably never be able to answer that question conclusively, but one thing seems certain: Attrition is *not* a problem if people leave a particular place of ministry because they find themselves ineffective or miscast, especially if, subsequent to that decision, they move into a context of productive kingdom ministry. Most of the time, such moves are a part of the normal learning and maturation process—a process that teaches us who we are and for which work God has gifted us.

The impact of a decision to leave the mission field may be problematic for the mission and the church community. Its fallout must be dealt with. Following are several attrition-related problems.

The Problem of Discredit

The fallout from attrition is a problem if leaving service early brings discredit to the kingdom or to its King, Jesus. Those who fail because of a moral lapse due to lack of self-control leading to uncontrolled anger, factious behavior, illicit sex, or some other sin cause grave consequences. However, in the majority of cases, the returning missionaries have not lost their faith, nor are they leaving because they have experienced public disgrace as a result of their moral lapse.

The Problem of Sickness

Many missionaries become sick, a fact of biology. Although sickness often constitutes a more socially acceptable reason to leave the field, it can also reflect the body's response to high levels of protracted stress. Attrition is a problem if it is caused by stress-induced sickness, if it causes lasting and debilitating personal trauma, or if it is a public symbol of individual defeat.

The Problem of Systemic Abuse

We must admit that there are people who, because of a mismatch in giftedness, calling, or spiritual resources, have terminated a period of time under the care of a mission board, feeling great bitterness toward a mission which they believe has misused them. Too often it has. This is a problem. But often, rather than evaluate and admit our organizational guilt or ineptness, we mission leaders abdicate our responsibility and too easily write off the individual as somehow not having measured up—another casualty of missionary attrition. Individuals become the problem, not the management or system which has misused them. When this situation happens frequently, the system should be judged as abusive or sick, not the individuals.

The Problem of Margin

Attrition can be a problem for an organization when people whose skills and abilities are needed leave before they should. The departure of competent workers often creates hardship and overwork for those left behind. When personnel resources are withdrawn, there are often jobs left undone, sometimes bringing discredit to the organization because of its failure to complete tasks promised to the supporting constituency or national church. On the other hand, in missions is there ever a "right" time to leave? Is the problem attrition, or could it be that we overcommit our organization and staff, leaving no margin or slack for the emergency which always surfaces? One management guru said that a contingency which happens more than twice is not a contingency and should be planned for. This usually is not done in missions; we leave no margin.

The Problem of Stewardship

The loss of personnel creates a problem if it demonstrates a wasteful use of very scarce and precious personal or financial resources. Attrition is a problem if it raises the question before the greater body of Christ of organizational credibility because the ministry is unable to make people really effective over the long haul. However, the management system may be the real problem, and attrition itself is but a symptom.

The Problem of Staying

There is an even larger challenge than attrition. Too often, people fail to recognize the mismatch of job and talent. Instead, they accommodate themselves in the all-enveloping comfort of suboptimum performance when they should "attrit." These are missionaries who adjust performance expectations downward and validate ineffectiveness. This type of behavior is one of the major ministry challenges we face, both in the church at home as well as around the world. On the mission field, it is a huge problem when this accommodation to survival and to minimal standards of ministry performance becomes normative for new missionaries or for the national leaders who look to missionaries for leadership and example. Here are some thoughts which may stimulate your thinking on this topic:

REINVENTING THE MISSION SYSTEM

One of the biggest issues that we face in attrition is systemic. We have a system in which we put all of the training and investment in the individual up front. It causes us great anxiety when we "lose" the investment of hundreds of thousands of dollars in the acquisition of theological, cultural, and linguistic understanding, along with time spent in raising funds. Perhaps the matter is not so much a problem of the individual as it is a problem with the system, which front-loads all this development before really gaining the experiential understanding as to the giftedness and/or the ability of a person to be effective in a particular cultural setting.

On the other side, the missionary has not seen the specific work first-hand, so that a proper judgment can be made as to its suitability to the missionary's calling, gifts, and style of ministry. Though tests can determine many things, the ultimate reality as to the giftedness and effectiveness of a person in a particular situation is a function of on-site and in-depth experience. Management theorists allude to this fact when they say that in staffing, the best predictor of the future is the past. Would we not deal with our attrition problem if we were to institute a series of experiences in short and mid-length terms (whether in the home church or in cross-cultural contexts), which would give us and the

ls involved a clear under-
s to their giftedness and abili-
would then evaluate people by
their past performance and not just
dwell on the extremely difficult task of
predicting their future promise.

A wise man once said that the number one determinant in staffing is personality and not skills. He went on to
say that skills can be acquired, while
personality is basically a given. If this is
the case, then probably we could determine the personality traits in action
through early and repeated short-term
experiences. These experiences would
lead naturally to the skill acquisition
phase, as people move through the cycle
of lifetime involvement with the Great
Commission.

Every short-term ministry that I
know has become a long-term ministry
within a given missions organization.
Every short-term ministry has also produced individuals for other mission organizations, as people discovered their
gifts and abilities and found that there
were other venues in which they could
be more effective. Rather than bemoan-
ing the rates of attrition, should we not
redo the system, so that the whole Great
Commission community would nurture
its effective people and thereby create a
much more flexible career path for those
who will follow Christ for a lifetime,
some of which will be spent in cross-
cultural ministry in other countries?
With computer technology, we can now
monitor a large number of people over
time, keeping track of their performance, training, and giftedness. Why not
form a consortium of missions for training and tracking short-term personnel,
so that we could as a Great Commission
community benefit from the discovery

and maturation process of these people
who are so highly committed to Christ?

If indeed geography is meaningless
in a multicultural world, should we not
have an integration of the mission
world, focusing on peoples and working
with those peoples wherever they might
be found? In a more flexible approach to
missions, should we not be open to
missionaries spending time, because of
family responsibilities, working in their
home country with the various people
groups with which they have become
familiar? It is the tribes or peoples of
planet Earth which must be discipled,
not merely some distant geopolitical entity.

If such a system were developed, we
as mission agencies would also have to
create more realistic measures of ac-
complishment. We would have to begin
to determine what is normal and what
is to be expected in terms of performance and expectation. I once brashly
told a mission executive that I was far
more concerned about the ineffective
people who stay on the field than I was
about those missionaries who become
statistics of attrition. That assertion was
somewhat of an overstatement, but it is
true that I am very concerned about the
ineffective missionary who creates his
or her own comfortable environment
and does not seem to be drawn to the
urgency of the endeavor. Many times
the person who drops out is looking for
and even taking risks to discover effectiveness, spiritual significance, and fulfillment in ministry. The person who
stays and becomes a veteran of years,
but who is not effective, undermines the
expectations of each subsequent generation of missionaries. That person is
a real problem.

Once again, a management guru hit the nail on the head when he said that it was a leader's or manager's responsibility to make average people effective. The buck stops with the leader who cannot evaluate because there are no standards or because the standards are irrelevant. Leaders are responsible when the system is causing a problem, because they can change the system. When the ineffective veteran becomes the model against which attainment is measured, that is very poor management, leadership, and spiritual stewardship.

We need a missions system which allows people to move in and out easily, without trauma, but also without inordinate cost. We need to develop a system that moves out the marginal and ineffective workers or that brings them back home, where they can possibly find points of contribution. If we are going to take these steps, I think we also need to create a new vocabulary.

REINVENTING OUR TERMINOLOGY

The designation "missionary" carries with it a lot of baggage, such as the baggage of training, the baggage of qualification, the baggage of expertise, and at times even the baggage of elitism. We need to create a terminology which allows people to learn and grow and contribute without being seen necessarily as experts. We need to develop a designation which allows people to be servants in New York or New Delhi, without being seen as different from their national brothers and sisters who also love the Lord and who are desperately burdened to see lost people come to Christ. We need to develop a language which does not make people who take their summer vacations and sabbaticals to work in another part of the world seem like second-class citizens who are less than career missionary professionals. The phrase "short term" sounds as if a ministry is begun and ended in a transitory beat of the clock. What people want and need is to be able to live out a lifetime of commitment to Christ and the discipling of the nations, utilizing new, different, and creative life patterns which are available to us today as never before.

We need to develop vocabulary which does not create a dichotomy between church planting and church nurture, between pioneering and the work necessary to prepare a church in one part of the world to pioneer in another. Our categories of language tend to make for primary and secondary ministries, when this distinction is not necessarily true in practice. A contribution that makes the whole body function more like Christ in today's world is just as important as is the function of assisting the birth of a new congregation.

In today's world, there are many new modes of ministry for people wishing to express their faith and God's call on their lives to disciple the nations. Technology, the ease of transportation, and more flexible career paths have given us many different avenues for missionary service. We dare not lock ourselves into one mode from the past and beat our chests lamenting that the past pattern is not being reproduced today. We need to be creative, utilizing the gifts that God has given us now, in this day, for the fulfilling of the Great Commission.

SO, IS ATTRITION REALLY A PROBLEM?

Is attrition a problem? Well, it could be, but I think that the issues of stewardship, management, and a system that needs to develop new patterns and free itself from the tyranny of past expectations are far more serious. Failure to grasp the new opportunities from the hand of a sovereign Lord and failure to recognize developments which can be employed to extend Christ's kingdom are much greater problems than attrition as we know it in our missionary community.

REFERENCE

Kepner, C. H., & Tregoe, B. B. (1976). *Rational manager: A systematic approach to problem solving and decision making* (2nd ed.). Princeton, NJ: Kepner-Tregoe.

Paul McKaughan and his wife, Joanne, spent 13 years as missionaries in Brazil, where their three children were born. Then he served as Coordinator and CEO of Mission to the World, of the Presbyterian Church in America. In the late 1980s, he was also Associate International Director for the Lausanne Committee on World Evangelization and was Congress Coordinator for Lausanne II in Manila. Since 1990, McKaughan has been President and CEO of the Evangelical Fellowship of Mission Agencies (EFMA), composed of both denominational and para-ecclesiastical mission boards. He serves as a WEF Missions Commission Associate.

3

An Integrated Model
Of Missions

Rodolfo "Rudy" Girón

The issue of attrition has a direct relation to the way a missionary is selected, prepared, and sent. In this chapter, we would like to set forth a foundational statement that **avoidable attrition will be minimized to the extent that we properly choose, train, send, pastor, and supervise our missionaries**. We will discuss a model in which we propose that unless we are more integrative in the way we send missionaries, we will see an increase in the attrition rate among our workers.

It is instructive to begin by quoting an article by Robert T. Coote (1995, p. 6), in which he stated:

In a world where hundreds of millions have yet to hear the name of Christ and additional millions have not heard the gospel presented effectively in their cultural context, there is no substitute for the career missionary. Making this assumption, one can take only limited satisfaction in reports of uncounted thousands of short-termers engaged in missions, of local churches and schools undertaking cross-cultural "exposure" forays, and of various forms of high-tech media lending support to the proclamation of the gospel. These and other posi-

tive factors cannot balance a real decline in long-term commitments by men and women who are prepared to take a profoundly incarnational approach to communicate the gospel of Jesus Christ to people of other cultures.

This quotation reflects the state of the missionary movement in the USA and Canada today, but it is not far from the reality of what is happening in much of the remaining Western world and increasingly in the Two-Thirds World.

Career missionary commitment cannot be achieved through simple recruitment in conferences, seminars, or training centers. Rather, it results from a solid foundation laid in the family and in the local church. It takes a process to produce a career missionary. It takes time.

Career missionary commitment presupposes staying on the field, overcoming attrition, and living in such a way that the field becomes home, and home becomes the field.

Our tendency when we look at the subject of sending missionaries is to look either to the missionary agency or to the local church. Both are vital parts of the missionary sending process, but they are not the only parts. We need to see the sending of missionaries as an integrated process in which the church, the mission agency, training centers, and other entities take part.

Historically there has been a tension between the church and the missionary agency in the recruiting and sending of missionaries. Some missiologists have even clearly defined both entities as having distinctive characteristics that make each one suited for what it does best. The church is called a *modality*, defined as a fraternity structured in such a way that there are no limitations of gender or age. The mission agency is called a *sodality*, a fraternity determined because the members have to make a second decision regarding membership. In a sodality the matters of gender, age, and marital status are considered.

The concepts of modality and sodality have been much a part of the Western missionary movement. We find some influence of these ideas in other areas of the world, but for the most part we have a different paradigm being developed in the Two-Thirds World

churches. In the New Testament, there does not seem to be a distinction between the church and the missionary agency, although some may argue that both entities operated throughout the Apostle Paul's missionary career.

In this chapter, we would like to propose another way of looking at the missionary sending enterprise. The model presented here is an integrated missionary model that unites four distinct elements: selection, training, sending, and the pastoral care and supervision of the missionary. Implementation of this model should result in more career missionaries who are committed to staying on the field where God has called them, thus decreasing attrition in the missionary force. Figure 3-1 illustrates this model.

We will not see a successful missionary work unless we integrate the four elements represented in the illustration. In the Western world, for instance, it has normally been thought that the best way to train pastors and leaders is to send them to a Bible institute or seminary before they begin their ministries. Such an approach has been exported to

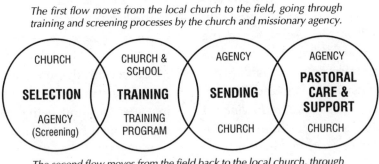

The first flow moves from the local church to the field, going through training and screening processes by the church and missionary agency.

The second flow moves from the field back to the local church, through the process of reentry and cultural adaptation, passages which are nurtured by the agency and the church.

Figure 3-1. An Integrated Model of Missions

the nations where Western missionary work has been conducted. However, in countries which are experiencing amazing church growth, not only among Pentecostal churches, but also among many other new churches in the Two-Thirds World, the reality is that pastors and leaders are first identified, authenticated, and recognized by the local church. After these individuals become pastors or leaders, they are then sent to a Bible institute or seminary for training.

Just as church leaders are not produced by a Bible institute or seminary, so missionaries are not produced by a mission agency or training center. Rather, they are produced first by local churches, which train and disciple them, recognize their call, and test them as individuals and as future leaders and missionaries. Then the churches send the prospective missionaries to a training center, which gets them ready to go to the mission field and then passes them on to a mission agency. The mission agency screens the candidates and equips them for specific tasks. Once on the field, missionaries must receive proper supervision of their work and must be shepherded by their local church pastor or mission leader, as well as by the pastoral supervisor of the mission agency. When missionaries return home for furlough or partnership development, both the agency and the church must be involved, to ensure that the experience is satisfying for the missionaries and their children alike.

The above description sounds idealistic; however, this kind of integration is needed if we are to see a successful career missionary movement.

Let us look at each of the components in our model.

SELECTION

Selection includes all of the elements that make it possible for a missionary call by God to be recognized by the missionary, by the Christian community, and by the missionary agency. In some instances, the local church will do the selection of the missionary by itself. In these cases, the missionary is discipled by the church and then is sent to the mission field without going through the screening of an experienced agency. For many candidates, there is no problem with this approach, but in the long run, the lack of screening by an agency will compromise the process of good selection and may diminish the effectiveness of the missionary on the field.

Typically, the missionary agency will do the screening of the missionary. Some people call this process selection, but we prefer to call it screening, since selection includes much more than a mere analysis done through psychological tests and other tools. Many agencies will approve a candidate for missionary service, regardless of what the church thinks about the individual. Based on their screening tools, agencies will send a missionary to the field without proper discipleship experience, which can only be obtained in the church. The result is high attrition due to immature Christian character. Problems arise between the missionary and others on the team, or in the relationship with the national leaders or agency leaders.

Unquestionably, the best entity to authenticate the missionary call of a given person is the church. **No matter how professional an agency may be,**

it will never take the place of the screening of the local church. In Acts 13, we see a biblical model in the experience of the church at Antioch. The Apostle Paul was well-known to the Antioch church. When God through His Holy Spirit called Paul and Barnabas, the church validated the call through prayer and fasting. This is a beautiful model of how the church confirms the call of a missionary.

Below we discuss in more detail the elements involved in the selection of a missionary.

Discipleship
Of the Missionary

The model that Jesus established when He took 12 men from a wide variety of backgrounds and made them into disciples is without doubt the best example for us when we think of missionary work. There is no single method of training that can take the place of a discipleship process in laying the foundation for successful missionary work.

Normally the discipleship process will be conducted mostly by the local church. The agency will just take what the church has done and will finalize the process by giving the missionary the necessary tools to adapt his or her ministry to the specific culture served by the agency. But two weeks or even three months of orientation will not produce a true Christian disciple. That is something that comes from a longer period of instruction, during which the pastors, leaders, and members of the local church disciple the missionary candidate.

In looking at the life of Paul, we see the process of discipleship in action when Paul went to Jerusalem as a young believer (Acts 9:26-30). Because of the threats against his life, Paul was sent first to Caesarea and then to Tarsus, his place of origin. This may well be the period during which Paul endured most of the hardships described in 2 Corinthians 11 (Bruce, 1977, p. 127). He also witnessed great spiritual growth among his fellow Jews. These years constituted a discipleship period, during which Paul was under the spiritual care of the synagogue in Tarsus.

Identification
And Authentication
Of the Missionary Call

This element is crucial, since many candidates may claim to have a call from God to become a missionary. Others may decide to go to the mission field simply because there is no ministry or occupation for them at home.

When a person expresses interest in becoming a missionary, the church or agency needs to be sure that the call or motivation is genuine *before* the individual goes to the field. There is a great risk of loss if it is discovered, after a missionary is on the field, that the person lacks a true missionary call. Such a realization not only affects the life of the missionary, but also affects the lives of those working with the person. **The local church plays an important role in authenticating the call of a given person before the individual goes through a process of screening at an agency and eventually heads for the mission field.** Both the local church and the agency need to have clear procedures for identifying and validating God's call of the prospective missionary.

As we noted above, the church at Antioch recognized and authenticated the call of Paul and Barnabas to the Gentile mission. This authentication was needful throughout Paul and Barnabas' whole career as missionaries, since the Antioch church was their base of operation and source of support.

Coming Alongside The Missionary

Once a church has recognized the call of a person for missionary work, it is then necessary to come alongside the individual in order to prepare the missionary for the next step in his or her career. This expression of support is important, not only to guide the missionary regarding the best option for ministry, but also to identify the field to which God is calling the person and to select a mission agency.

The appropriate agency for this partnership may be chosen when a channel of communication is established between the missionary committee or leadership of the local church and the existing agencies that offer the best options for the prospective missionary's future field of service.

In summary, selection is not just screening a prospective missionary. Rather, it is a natural process of recognition and validation of a person who has a genuine call from God to missions. At the same time, it is the natural way of rejecting those whose call is not authentic. Much harm to the missions enterprise will be avoided if we pay attention to these aspects of selection.

TRAINING

Figure 3-2 on the next page represents the development of a missionary throughout life, using as a model the basic features of the facade of a Greek temple.

In any building, the foundation is the key to the support of the whole structure. Usually the foundation is hidden from view, but that doesn't alter its importance. The endurance of the whole building depends on the quality of the foundation. Paul emphasizes the importance of a spiritual foundation in 1 Corinthians 3:11, where he affirms, "For no one can lay any foundation other than the one already laid, which is Jesus Christ."

Above the foundation, the columns with their bases and capitals form the second part of a temple facade. The columns are responsible for raising the building up from ground level and supporting the roof. In our model, when a person comes to faith and then engages in the process of growth and development in a local church and at a biblical or theological training center, in a sense that individual is raised up from the ground level to the level of being a missionary candidate.

Finally, the most visible part of a Greek temple facade is the triangular area near the top, known as the tympanum, where elaborate decorative figures are usually found. In our illustration, this level is the most visible phase in the life of a missionary candidate. At this level, the local church sends the missionary to a training center, where the person's performance is evaluated. It is assumed that the training will accomplish all that is necessary to prepare the missionary for the field; however, the individual's performance will also be closely related to his or her past development in life and in the church.

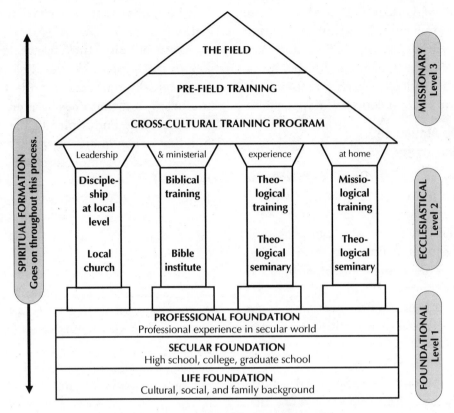

**Figure 3-2. Lifelong Process of Missionary Formation:
The Building of Training**

Although a model can never fully represent the realities of life, it does help to illustrate what we are trying to say. Our model of missionary development has a foundational level as the support structure in the missionary's life and being. Level 2 is where the missionary's call is confirmed and where the missionary is raised up from being a new believer to being ready to go to a training school. Level 3 is what we see of the missionary on the field.

We refer here to the growth and development of the missionary as a means of becoming properly equipped to fulfill God's call. The process includes more than mere instruction in a missionary orientation program. Rather, it is a lifelong process in which God prepares the candidate to become a missionary. Family upbringing, social environment, educational development, and professional experiences all play a part in the process. The local church, through a program of discipleship, brings the candidate to the point of being ready to go to a Bible institute or seminary. At such an institute, the candidate is equipped to present the gospel effectively in his or her own culture. Upon completion of this educational program, the individual is ready to receive cross-cultural training in the home culture. Finally, the person goes to a pre-field training program conducted in the host culture, where he or she is polished to fit the demands of the specific mission field.

Once again, this scenario sounds too idealistic to be real; nevertheless, we must seriously consider the overall process of development of the missionary as a person and as a Christian if we want to see positive results in the missionary endeavor.

Spiritual Formation

Before examining each level of development in detail, let us note that a prominent feature in this model is the spiritual formation of the missionary. We have represented this formation by means of an oval to the left of the temple facade. Spiritual formation is something that goes on at every level of training. If somebody is born in a Christian home, that person's spiritual development will begin from childhood. In many cases, this is a great advantage, and many good missionaries have developed in this way. In other cases, people can be born again at a time in their lives when they are already professional in some way. In these cases, the church plays the role of nurturing the spiritual life of each person. Even if a person's earlier life has developed outside the will of God, God can still use that life for His glory. This is part of God's mysterious way. He can use fishermen as fishers of men and tent builders as builders of holy temples.

Spiritual formation is essential throughout the overall development of a missionary. It does not end when the missionary arrives on the mission field either. On the contrary, a new level of spiritual development begins at this point. The real test of a missionary is whether the person is able to cope with the new spiritual realities and demands of missionary life.

Spiritual formation must be present at every step along the path of a missionary. We must avoid the tendency to reduce missionary training to a mere academic exercise. To be truly effective, any training program must have at its core a very strong spiritual element.

With this introduction, let us look at each of the components of Figure 3-2 to understand better this developmental process in the life of a missionary.

Foundational Level 1

Apart from what the church or any biblical or theological institution can do to mold a person's character, there lies a foundational level of life. This level consists of three layers: a life foundation, a secular foundation, and a professional foundation. The foundational level as a whole has to do with the way an individual is reared. No one can escape the influence of his or her cultural, social, and family background. As we examine each element of the foundational level, we will find clues to what a person may be able to do in life. God will use and mold what He finds in a person when that individual comes to Him.

Life Foundation

It is relatively easy to understand this level of development, but not many churches or agencies consider the life foundation in placing missionaries. God took life development into account when He chose Paul instead of Peter to be the missionary to the Gentiles. He used Peter, of course, as the Apostle to the Jews. God places each person in the proper setting for effective ministry.

In looking at Paul's life, we can understand how God molded Paul and choose him even before he was born. Paul was a descendant of a Pharisee family. He was born outside the Palestine area in a Greek/Roman city, into a Hellenistic cultural background. He had the advantage of being from a well-to-do family and was privileged to be born a Roman citizen. He was trained as a Hebrew, both at home and at school. As a youth, Paul was sent to Jerusalem to study under Rabbi Gamaliel, who held to a strict Pharisaic school of thought. Yet Paul was still able to understand and appreciate the Hellenistic world.

We may say that through Paul's life situation, God prepared him to minister to the Gentiles. Paul did not have the ethnocentric orientation of Peter, who experienced many difficulties throughout his ministry in relating to Gentiles. God gave Peter the charge of working with his fellow Jews, while Paul was sent to the Gentiles.

One wonders how many times missionaries have been sent out without anyone's giving serious consideration to the characteristics of their life foundation. To all of us who are part of the emerging Two-Thirds World missionary movement, this point is significant. In sending out a missionary, it is not enough just to have financial resources to support workers, as some countries in Asia may have. It is necessary to consider the missionary's background in life and God's call. It is not enough to have the enthusiasm of the Latin people to send missionaries to Spain or to other European countries. We need to select workers based on their life foundation. In this way, we may avoid a great deal of frustration and attrition in the missionary force.

Secular Foundation

The secular foundation of a missionary may include all of the person's educational background, from elementary school through college or graduate school. It may also include vocational training. In a world that expects more and more expatriate workers to possess professional qualifications, missionaries will be better suited for work on the field if they pursue such training.

The growth of the bi-occupational missionary force is one evidence of the importance of professional training for the missionary enterprise today. We need to encourage more non-professional missionaries to consider getting such training to enhance their missionary career.

Secular training, then, is an asset to missionary work. With more and more secular professionals entering the missionary work force, we are seeing increased opportunities for reaching countries having restricted access. The next century will undoubtedly witness even larger numbers of secular professionals joining the ranks of missionaries. For all such workers, spiritual development through discipleship will be the key to balancing a professional ministry with a spiritual ministry on the field.

Professional Foundation

We refer here not to the schooling or academic side of professional development, but to the period during which a person emerges from college or graduate school and becomes established as a professional. This is the time to become acquainted with the world of business and commerce, apart from the academic world. Missionaries who receive this kind of practical training become more aware of the realities of life. They begin to understand the big difference between the academic world and the real world.

Having professional experience in the secular world is especially important for missionaries who desire to serve in countries where vocational missionary work is restricted. We need to encourage more entrepreneurs to consider this approach to missionary work. Many Latin missionaries are using such an approach and are gaining entrance into the restricted countries of the Muslim world through the secular business world. This element of professional experience must be considered when choosing the field where the missionary will work.

Ecclesiastical Level 2

When we come to this level of training, we understand that the more ecclesiastical training a missionary has, the better the missionary task will be done. Let us look at each component.

Discipleship
At the Local Church Level

Once again, we emphasize the importance of discipleship at the local church level. Over the years of missionary work, it has been proven that a missionary who has such training within the church will much better be able to meet the demands of the field. We cannot overstate the value of church experience when we consider the kind of missionary needed for initiating a church planting movement among unreached people groups of the world.

Discipleship training in a local church is considered informal training or informal education. Pastors and

church leaders should be aware of the benefits of such training. A missionary will reproduce (in a contextualized manner, it is hoped) what he or she has received from the local church.

Biblical Training

Biblical training has to do with formal and non-formal education. It may be done through education by extension or in the residential mode. Either way, biblical training will prepare the missionary to give a solid presentation of the gospel to those who have not yet heard the message of salvation. **The local church can often supply the biblical training that a missionary requires**, if the minister or ministers of the church have sufficient biblical training themselves.

As simple as this approach may be, many prospective missionaries, especially those in the Two-Thirds World, may discount the value of this kind of training. The cost and the time demands of biblical training will cause some missionary candidates to pass over this needed stage. We cannot specify how much training is necessary. We emphasize, though, that going to the mission field without biblical training will greatly diminish the impact a missionary can make.

Theological
Or Missiological Training

In the Western world and increasingly in some non-Western countries, entry-level theological or missiological training is a prerequisite to being accepted as a missionary. This level may include a B.A. degree or, even better, a master's degree. The degree can be in the area of theology or missiology. In some areas, a doctoral degree is required.

Bypassing this level of development results in sending missionaries who lack a solid biblical and theological foundation. In areas where the preaching of the gospel is restricted, a high level of theological education may be critical. Apologetics is at the heart of the proclamation of the gospel. Missionaries going to the unreached areas of the world should spend time in advance acquiring the theological and missiological foundation they will need.

The preceding statement notwithstanding, we must be careful not to place too much emphasis on theological and missiological education at the expense of well-rounded development throughout the earlier stages of life. Some agencies, for instance, may focus more on theological and missiological training than on the earlier stages of missionary development. This mistake results from the influences of a developed society, in which diversification and specialized knowledge are required for a person to be accepted in a given role in society. In addition, the religious educational industry sells its products (degrees) to the church and makes the church believe that without such education a person will never do well on the mission field.

While we agree completely with the great advantage of having a theological or missiological degree, we disagree with the idea that a missionary will do a better job on the field just by having such a degree. Those of us from countries that have been recipients of missionary outreach can testify to the error of such a presupposition.

The best missionary is not always the most educated one. The best missionary is the person who is blessed with a solid biblical and theological foundation, who knows what the church is and how it functions, and who relates effectively and respects people in the host culture where he or she serves.

Leadership And Ministerial Experience

The best missionaries are those who have proven in their home culture that they can minister in a relevant way to other people. Experience provides the kind of informal education that molds more of the good habits and skills that missionaries need. Christians who take seriously their role as disciples of Jesus may at this stage enjoy many ministerial opportunities, including short-term missionary experiences.

Missionary Level 3

At this stage of missionary development, specific cross-cultural training is required. Many agencies and institutions, especially in the Western world, neglect this step and send out missionaries with only a short, entry-level course to acquaint their candidates with the culture served by the agency.

Our contention is that a missionary at this stage is not yet ready to go to the field. It is first necessary for the person to participate in a training program in which various cross-cultural phenomena are explained. The training may be done in one or two stages, depending on the quality of the programs offered by the training centers at the disposal of the missionary. Ideally, we suggest two stages at this level.

Cross-Cultural Training Program

We refer here to programs that students may receive in their own cultural setting. Several such programs have been developed, especially in the non-Western world. The prospective missionary may go to a school or center to receive specialized training in areas such as cross-cultural communication, linguistics, missiology, history of missions, and related subjects. Some candidates may have already taken similar courses if they have achieved a general missiological degree. The difference between this course and earlier ones is that the students and their families experience communal life at the center while taking the course. They learn how to cope with different styles of living, especially in relation to their peers at the center.

How valuable it is to know—*before* expending thousands of dollars getting to the mission field—that one is not easily able to adapt to changes or to live in community, which many times will be required on the mission field.

We need to encourage the development of more training programs such as the ones offered by All Nations Christian College in the UK, the Global Missionary Training Center in Seoul, Korea, and the Centro de Capacitacion Misionera Transcultural in Córdoba, Argentina. Programs such as these make a big difference in the way missionaries are being sent.

Pre-Field Training Program

Besides having a training program at home, ideally the missionary will attend a field training program as well. Such a program should be close to the host culture where the missionary will work.

It may be a language school or a short-term program (three to six months). Programs such as the Outreach Training Institute of the Indian Evangelical Mission in Bangalore, India, are of great value. Another pre-field training program is offered by the Asia Cross-Cultural Training Institute in Singapore. For many missionaries from America and Africa, attending this program will be a rewarding experience before proceeding to the final field of service.

The Field

Finally, the missionary is ready to go to the field. At this point, many will be saying, "It will take a lifetime to arrive on the field!" Yes, it does take a lifetime to go to the field for long-term career missionary commitment. Think of an airplane. Most of us have taken short trips by air. Usually a small airplane is used in such cases. These small aircraft need only a short runway and require only 18 to 20 seconds to take off. But when we are going on an overseas trip, we usually will take a Boeing 747. An airplane that large needs a much longer runway, and it will take 35 to 38 seconds to take off.

In a world of "instants," where things are accomplished at the touch of a finger, we need to remind ourselves that career missionaries are not produced in six months or even in two years. It takes time. We believe that we need to reach the world for Jesus Christ before the turn of the century. But it is difficult to see how we are going to accomplish this goal, if we consider the fact that in order to reach the remaining 10,000 unreached people groups, we need to have career missionaries who are committed to spend their lives on the mission field. We must calculate the investment that will be needed to send those missionaries to the unreached and to keep them there.

Going to the field is itself a training experience. It is worth mentioning that a missionary going to the field who is willing to learn is more likely to be successful. David de la Rosa, a Puerto Rican missionary in Spain, after five years of successful missionary service, stated that the key to his success among the Spanish churches was that he was willing to die to himself. He said that he was willing to die to his knowledge and to know nothing. That attitude made him teachable, and the Spanish brethren were happy to teach him how to do missionary work in their country. We want to see more people like this brother. Regardless of a missionary's refined level of education, he or she must be willing to be taught by the host culture or the host church. The best training ground for a missionary is the mission field.

SENDING

The West has so much experience in sending missionaries that a Two-Thirds World leader may not be the most suitable person to talk about this area. However, some significant aspects of the sending component should be noted.

The work done by many mission agencies is so valuable that we need to pray that God will enable these agencies to keep doing what they are doing. Agency services include conducting research regarding the various mission fields, recruiting new missionaries, orienting missionaries to the particular culture served by the agency, channel-ing funds to missionaries, providing missionaries with base support, sending out prayer letters, and communicating with donors. Agencies also furnish missionaries with medical and life insurance best suited to their needs. In case of emergencies due to accidents, political crises, or hostilities directed against missionaries, agencies are able to deal with these special situations and help resolve them.

Churches may well take care of some of the details that agencies handle, but their expertise lies in other areas. Overall, churches need missionary agencies to assume responsibility for many of the details of sending out missionaries and keeping them on the field.

In spite of the recognized need that churches and mission agencies have for each other, when it comes to sending missionaries, there is a well-known and documented tension (already mentioned) between the church and the agency. Sending a missionary out without the proper logistical support is as dangerous as sending one out without the necessary discipleship period in the local church or the proper training by specialized schools and programs. A well-developed system of support must exist in order for missionaries to be successful in their service on the mission field.

There is a growing trend among churches of the Western world to bypass the mission agency when sending out missionaries. Many churches have made the decision to send out their missionaries without the help of a missionary agency. Usually a missionary committee is appointed in the local church to take care of the logistics of sending missionaries. The reasons given for such actions are numerous, but one of the most commonly mentioned is: "Agencies take too much money in order to do their work. We will have more profit for our missionary dollar if we do the work ourselves. God will be pleased that we are taking good care of His money."

This argument sounds plausible, but it is wrong. God has established the church as a body in which many members perform different functions and ministries. The church is not the best entity to do all of the logistics required in order to send out a missionary. The result of bypassing the agency is that what seems to be a less expensive option actually becomes much more expensive. The inexperienced personnel used in a local church require more resources than those from an agency. In Latin America a popular proverb says, "Cheap things always become expensive." That proverb may be applicable to a church that attempts to assume the role of a mission agency.

We recognize that many agencies are spending too much money on promotion, administration, and overhead, but the solution may not necessarily be to do things by ourselves. The solution may be for agencies to reengineer their operation in order to better invest the money given by donors, so that the funds will support missionaries on the field and not executives in hotels. Such restructuring will encourage churches to give to missions and to support the missionary agencies which are best equipped to do the job.

When we look at the churches of the developing countries of the Two-Thirds World, the situation takes on another dimension. Most churches in the Two-

Thirds World simply do not have enough money to pay an agency to do the work of sending out missionaries, so they decide that since they have only enough for the support of the missionary on the field, they will do the sending work by themselves. The thought is always that God will be pleased because of the wise use churches are making of the few resources He is giving to do missions. Also, in many countries there are not enough sending structures to channel the many people who are ready to go to the field, so churches and denominations are doing the work by themselves.

Our suggestion is that experienced agencies of the Western world may help by opening up opportunities for missionaries from the non-Western world to go through their sending channels. An even better solution would be for Western agencies to help develop sending structures in countries where they are needed.

A second reason which churches give for bypassing the agency is that the churches want to have contact and direct communication with their missionary. This argument merits consideration, since the local church gains a sense of ownership and mutual belonging with the missionary when the church sends out the missionary apart from an agency. The bottom line is that whether we send our missionaries through a denominational board of missions or through an independent agency, local churches need to have a sense of participation in the sending of their missionaries.

Where possible, we suggest that agencies be started in response to churches expressing a desire for help in the placing and sending of their missionaries. In sending countries where tension exists between church and agency, the only viable solution may be to reengineer the process of sending missionaries by creating new partnerships between existing agencies and the new sending groups.

PASTORAL CARE AND SUPERVISION

This phase of the missionary enterprise has been neglected more than any other area in missions. Frank Allen (1986, p. 121), in writing about why missionaries leave the field, stated, "Probably one of the keenest disappointments that new missionaries face is that everyday life on the field is a far cry from what was told them." Allen concluded that the primary causes of attrition are unfulfilled expectations, moral problems, and family difficulties. In the same study, Allen presented interviews with missions executives from four major sending agencies: The Evangelical Alliance Mission, Christian and Missionary Alliance, Conservative Baptist Foreign Missions Society, and World Gospel Mission. All of these leaders cited personal and family problems as the major reasons missionaries leave the mission field.

Pastoral care and supervision are at the heart of successful missionary work. While missionaries are on the field, they frequently experience personal needs. They may also have concerns relating to children, parents, or family life, or they may be faced with stresses such as illness or the death of a spouse. All of these problems come under the heading of pastoral needs.

Other problems may include dissatisfaction with the mission or the assigned task, differences with the leadership, disagreement with the policies of the mission, and problems of adjustment to a new culture and language. These problems all require supervision.

Pastoral care is one thing, and supervision is another. The work done by a field leader or supervisor typically focuses on administrative and operative matters rather than on pastoral care. A visit by a supervisor to the field usually is spent checking on how things have been done. Very seldom does a supervisor take time to inquire about the welfare of the missionary family or the problems a missionary couple may face in educating their children. Supervision is necessary, of course, to ensure the successful completion of the job assigned to each missionary, but in the long run, pastoral work is even more important than supervision.

Pastoral work requires field leaders who are people oriented and not just goal oriented. In a society in which goals and programs take precedence over people, we need to be careful not to be trapped by the models of the world in doing our work. We need to pray that Jesus' attitude toward Peter when he failed Jesus (John 21) will capture our hearts as we pastor missionaries on the field. What a challenge to follow the example set by Jesus when Peter and his companions went back to their nets. They felt discouraged, but Jesus sought them out and restored them to His kingdom.

Much more could be said about pastoral care. Let us close by mentioning just one more point. A local church through its leadership can make a tremendous contribution to the pastoral dimension of missionary support. By encouraging the members of a church to keep in contact with their missionaries, a pastor is contributing to the moral support of the missionary.

Pastoral support is also needed when missionaries return home. Missionaries coming back to the home culture may be as shocked as they were when they first went to the mission field. A story told by Neal Pirolo (1991, pp. 11-13) illustrates the problem of reentry:

"Beth! Wake up! Please, Beth! Wake up!" Beth's roommate held the empty Valium bottle in her hand and knew Beth wouldn't wake up. But instinct said get help. The people in the next apartment helped her carry Beth to the car. A mile that seemed half way around the world brought them to the hospital. They pumped Beth's stomach. She stirred and opened her eyes.

Months later Beth could talk about it:

"I had a normal life before this.... I had just returned from a six-month missionary venture in the Orient.... I just wanted somebody to acknowledge that I was back home!

"One Sunday morning after church, I gathered the strength to again go to my pastor and say, 'I am at the end of my rope! I think I'm losing it! I need your help!' With his arm around me, he said, 'Beth, I am busy. I am so tied up this week. But if you must, call my office to set an appointment for a week from Wednesday. Beth, if you would just get into the Word more....'

"Through the dazed fog of an existence I had been living in, all of a sudden it became crystal clear: 'Pastor, I am not worth your time!' I had made other desperate calls to various counselors. One guy tried to date me. A psychiatrist had given my condition a fancy label. But

now it was clear: 'I am not worth anybody's time.'

"I decided to take the rest of the bottle of Valium."

Sad as it is, this story reveals the dilemma a missionary may face when coming back home from the mission field. How many missionaries face similar conditions on the field without anybody helping them?

How many churches argue that they want more participation in the process of sending a missionary, but when they have the chance to do something significant for that person, they are simply too busy to take care of these critical needs? May God help us to realize how important it is to pastor the missionaries we send and how important it is to help them when reentering their home culture again.

CONCLUSIONS

The issue of attrition in the missionary enterprise may be analyzed in different ways. Our proposal has postulated that we will see a decrease in the avoidable cases of attrition if we take into consideration the overarching integration of missionary work. The church, the agency, and the training center must enter into dialogue to see how they can best integrate their resources. Missionaries who go to the field must have a solid foundation, be well-trained, and be well-supported, so that they can be effective and efficient in their work.

Fulfilling the Great Commission of Jesus Christ requires more than we may realize. The Great Commission is a holistic mandate which is to be carried out by the church of Jesus Christ. Every element of the missionary endeavor is as important as the others. Selection, training, sending, supervision, pastoral care, and reentry are all facets of the same reality. Let us look at this reality not with a compartmentalized mentality, but with an integrated one.

The unity of the body of Christ is the premise to which we cling in striving to fulfill this ideal. The world will be reached more easily if we just combine all of our resources. Cooperation and partnership will be necessary. Western, non-Western, Two-Thirds World, First World, North, and South—all must contribute to the goal of establishing the kingdom of God on this earth.

In conclusion, here are some questions for reflection:

1. How can we achieve an integrated model of missions, given the great diversity of approaches and ministries available to do missions?

2. How can we improve our selection procedures, integrating the church and the agency into the process?

3. How achievable is the model that has been presented?

4. Can the church and the agency work hand in hand in order to place and send missionaries?

5. What are the most critical elements the church and the agency are overlooking when it comes to shepherding the missionary family?

6. How does this model speak to your reality? Is it relevant? Why or why not?

REFERENCES

Allen, F. (1986). Why do they leave? Reflections on attrition. *Evangelical Missions Quarterly*, **22**, 118-122.

Bruce, F. F. (1977). *Paul: Apostle of the heart set free*. Grand Rapids, MI: Eerdmans.

Coote, R. T. (1995). Good news, bad news: North American Protestant overseas personnel statistics in twenty-five-year perspective. *International Bulletin of Missionary Research*, **19**, 6-8, 10-13.

Pirolo, N. (1991). *Serving as senders*. San Diego, CA: Emmaus Road, Intl.

Rodolfo "Rudy" Girón was born in Guatemala in 1952 and was graduated as an architect from the San Carlos University of Guatemala. God called him to full-time ministry in 1980. He has been an evangelist, pastor, and educator in his denomination, the Church of God, Cleveland. Since 1990, he has been President of COMIBAM International, has worked as the Coordinator for the ReMAP project, and is a member of the Executive Committee of the WEF Missions Commission. In 1997, he and his family moved to Moscow, Russia, where he is serving as the President of the Eurasia School of Ministries, a denominational undergraduate seminary. He is married to Alma and has four children: Rudy (21), Marta (20), Carolina (18), and Karla (17).

4

Reflections on Attrition In Career Missionaries: A Generational Perspective Into the Future

Kath Donovan and Ruth Myors

Note: This paper was written from a Western perspective and reflects observations of Western countries and their missionary personnel. Since we were unaware of anything having been written in this area from non-Western countries, we were very interested to hear the comments of delegates from those countries at the consultation. Among those who spoke at the plenary session of the WEF conference, there was agreement that similar trends were being seen in their own countries. These delegates were from Asia, South America, and Africa. We were therefore encouraged to believe that what we were saying could have global relevance.

In 1983, Myron Loss (1983, p. 1) wrote, "Numerous workers with excellent potential drop out of cross-cultural ministry." Our experience as people who work closely with returned missionaries is that this phenomenon is still happening to-day—despite the best efforts of many mission societies to address the problem. Many missionaries return brokenhearted and crushed in spirit. This is not only a serious loss to mission but a personal tragedy to those concerned. Why is it happening? What can be done?

One clue is that missionary attrition is a fairly recent phenomenon. In 1966, in the mission with which one of us worked, the only reasons for attrition were death and reaching the mandatory retirement age. To-day, the attrition picture in that mission is as Loss described. Some have left because their work was completed, many for the sake of children's education, and others for a wide variety of other reasons. Deane (1994) has excellently reviewed the factors perceived to contribute to attrition in these days. He lists 16 avoidable factors including work, personal and family problems, difficulties having to do with location, and relationships. The interesting thing is that a good many of these factors were just as real in 1966— but people didn't leave. So what lies behind this change?

We have approached the subject by reflecting on the question, "What does the current loss from cross-cultural ministry of people with excellent potential say to us?" We believe that it is saying that to-day's missionaries are so different from those of 30 years ago that they no longer fit traditional missionary models. In other words, we are putting new wine into old wine skins or, at best, into patched up old wine skins. This practice is disempowering missionaries and mission societies alike.

Of to-day's missionaries, Elder (1991, p. 51) says, "The differences in generations are so significant ... that I can't see the younger generations being incorporated with just a few minor adjustments.... Fundamental changes are required in the missions industry if we are to attract, harness, and release their contribution." Elder (1991, p. 55) goes on to ask the question, "Can the majority of agencies to-day make sufficient adjustments soon enough to capture the potential of the boomers and busters?" We believe that they can and that some have already made some of the necessary modifications. However, the radical changes required, although difficult and daunting, need to be happening now.

This paper is written first to highlight the implications for mission of the cultural gap between generations and then to suggest a practical mission response to enable the younger missionaries to carry on the task of mission without losing heart.

IMPLICATIONS FOR MISSION OF THE CULTURAL GAP BETWEEN GENERATIONS

Tom Sine (1991) suggests that the church needs to wake up to the reality of the "generational revolution." So do traditional mission societies. The historic events and societal changes of the last 70 years have brought with them significant changes in the attitudes, values, and behaviour of people. So significant have these changes been that clear generational groupings can be identified—groupings which are so different from one another that they really constitute cultural gaps.

Sine (1991) distinguishes three such major groupings—the boosters (born between 1927 and 1945), the baby boomers (born between 1946 and 1964), and the busters (born between 1965 and 1983). To-day's missionaries come mainly from the last two groups. For ease of discussion, we will group them together as post-boosters.

Overview of Generational Characteristics

1. Boosters: Missionaries Of the Traditional School

The boosters were brought up in a world which had experienced the Great Depression and World War II. In both events, people endured great hardship and won through.

Boosters were hardworking, single-minded, persevering, committed, stable, frugal, and willing to turn their hands to whatever needed doing for the sake of the goal. Those in leadership were strong, authoritarian, and respected because of their position. The boosters were strong in institutional loyalty, whether the institution were leadership, marriage, the organisation employing them, their country, or their church.

As missionaries, boosters provided the model of missionary service still followed by traditional missionary societies to-day. They went out in response to a clear, firmly held sense of call to a particular country with a particular mission society for life, sight unseen. They were prepared to go anywhere and do anything. No sacrifice was too great for the sake of the gospel, and however great the hardship, resignation was unthinkable. These dedicated servants lived very simply and frugally and applied themselves to whatever the situation demanded of them with great diligence.

Independent, rugged individualists, boosters brought about marvellous advances of the gospel in previously unreached areas. They planted churches, translated the Bible, ran schools, performed medical work, conducted literacy programmes, trained pastors, and endured physical and social deprivation without complaint and by relying only on the Lord, in many remote places of the world. They were paternalistic and authoritarian in leadership and were respected and followed by young national Christians (Donovan, 1992). Their approach is encapsulated in the caveat, "No-one who puts his hand to the plough and looks back is fit for service in the kingdom of God" (Luke 9:62).

Many boosters are still in leadership on mission councils and boards, where they provide stability and tenacity. They often perceive the approach of to-day's young people as signifying lack of "commitment" and "obedience."

2. Post-Boosters: The New Breed of Missionaries

BABY BOOMERS

The baby boomers were born into material prosperity as a result of the hard work of their fathers. Their corporate memory is of Vietnam, the war which they neither owned nor approved and which in the end was not won. They were also made aware of the horrors rather than the glory of war—through hearing about the Holocaust and Hiroshima and the devastating consequences of blindly following leaders.

Baby boomers became the protesting, questioning, pragmatic, yet idealistic generation. They hold themselves responsible for their own lives and choices and respect the right of others to do the same. Thus they are tolerant of abortion, homosexual life style, and de facto relationships. In their life time they have experienced and/or benefitted from huge technological changes and have become part of those changes. They are usually well educated, specialists, agents of change, and pursuers of excellence. They are intolerant of waste, inefficiency, and incompetent leadership. Their loyalty is to people rather than institutions. Work *and* family are very important to them. Both marriage partners work, and as a result, their quality of life and family nurture have declined. There has been significant increase in marriage breakdown. The boomers have low institutional loyalty, high expectations, high tolerance for diversity, a desire to be seen and treated as professionals, impatience with hierarchical structures, and a need for informal, participative, grass-roots leadership style. They are impatient with what is perceived to be outmoded and are constantly seeking meaning in life (Anderson, 1990).

The baby boomers bring to mission specialised knowledge, skill, vision, energy, and willingness for hard work. They place great importance on using their God-given skills and training to the maximum to His glory. Fulfilment in their work is very important to them, as is continuing professional development. If these things are not available or do not seem likely to happen, boomers will become frustrated and discouraged and may leave the mission. They will challenge mission direction if they think it necessary and will find perceived incompetence in missionary leadership very difficult to handle. Some of the most deeply discouraged, frustrated, and angry first-termers come from this group (Donovan, 1992).

The boomers also attach great importance to family responsibilities and often insist on home schooling for their children. They return to their home country to get the best education they can for their children. Being low on institutional loyalty, they see commitment to an organisation as much less important than commitment to ministry. Boomers characteristically, therefore, want to try missionary service before becoming committed to it. Thus they are comfortable with short-term service with the option of a longer term if things work out. Short-term experience programmes are also the best way of recruiting these workers. If boomer missionaries are to be retained, mission societies need to give attention to careful placement, professional development, good job fit, roles for wives appropriate to their gifts, participative leadership, and provision of a platform for personal

and professional development. Missions also need to provide emotional support and pastoral care for boomers.

BUSTERS

The busters have been called by Sine (1991, p. 157) "the harbingers of our very uncertain future." The most indulged materially and the least nurtured of all generations, the busters were born into a world under threat from nuclear weapons and a diminishing ozone layer. This has created in them what Grenz (1996) calls "a gnawing pessimism" and an awareness of the fragility of life upon this planet. The positive side of this way of thinking is concern with environmental issues, but the negative side is a sense of hopelessness and futurelessness.

A significant number of busters have never been employed. Many are products of fragmented families and often have been victims of sexual abuse and other forms of violence. Many become street kids and turn to prostitution and drugs to blot out their low self-esteem. They feel alienated, forgotten, abandoned, and cheated by the boomers. All these factors have contributed to a deep disillusionment with life. Busters look to one another for support and tend to form closely knit groups among their peers. They are intensely loyal to the group or community of which they are a part. Because of their own vulnerability, they are very sensitive to people and look for deep, lasting relationships. They were brought up with change and are comfortable with it.

In strong reaction to the modern mind-set of previous generations which enshrined rationalism, busters want to be "whole" people—to cultivate all dimensions of life, to explore the mysterious (Grenz, 1996). This way of thinking, together with their need to find meaning in life, has generated a deep interest in spiritual things. Like the boomers, busters are pragmatic and tolerant of diversity. They have a deep longing for spiritual growth, while appreciating the guidance and nurture of people perceived to be real. Busters are honest and open, acknowledging their need for discipline, nurture, and guidance (Barna, 1994).

Out of this generation come missionary applicants from broken homes, who often have a great deal of pain in their lives to work through. They may be particularly vulnerable to emotional problems on the field. Because of their group orientation, busters work best in teams and can not be expected to cope with isolated places without adequate support from their peers. On the other hand, they are sensitive and accepting, making excellent team members. Their self-esteem is easily eroded, and so they are particularly vulnerable during their first term and in times of crisis.

As members of the disillusioned generation, busters are also very vulnerable to disillusionment. They may be perceived by fellow missionaries as self-centred, being unwilling to be overloaded in their work and being very sensitive to any perception of rejection. Busters want to live balanced lives—enjoying life as well as working. They feel in great need of pastoral care and of continuing help and guidance in their spiritual development. Because of their strong community-orientation, they work very well among relationship-oriented people and understand very well the concept of being embedded in one's own community (Grenz, 1996).

Because of their strong tolerance of diversity, they work very well with people from other ethnic groups. They also work very well with and under national church leaders. They are honest and open and willing to face up to even painful issues. However, their tendency to tell it exactly as it is may be quite threatening to booster leaders.

In that so many busters have come from broken homes, are struggling with past pain, may have been sexually abused, and are struggling to get their lives together, they need very careful screening and often counselling before departure. They also need continuing pastoral care and encouragement on the field and need to be part of supportive teams.

Points of Difficulty Between Missionary Generations

As Dave Daugherty (cited in Elder, 1991, p. 54) of OMF put it, "Boomer and buster characteristics collide head on with the agencies." Following are some of the points of collision:

1. Call, Commitment, And Length of Service

For boosters, the call is the chief motivation for going overseas and for remaining there, come what may. Boomers and busters don't talk about a call so much as about thinking it right to go. Often they arrive at this conclusion by asking questions of a number of mission societies, getting job descriptions, and then applying to the society for whatever job seems to fit their gifts, training, and other requirements best.

Whereas boosters understand commitment to mean long-term service with a particular organisation in a particular place, boomers understand it to mean making the very best use of gifts and talents wherever this can best be done (i.e., their commitment is to ministry rather than to a specific organisation or place). While being open to extended service if things are going well, boomers are also open to the idea of moving to a position perceived as potentially more fruitful in another place. Thus they may set up excellent programmes and then move on. Sometimes this means that what they have done is likely to fall in a heap. Busters will only commit themselves in short bursts, because they don't know what the future holds and because they doubt their own ability to persevere.

2. Attitude to the Mission Society

This is closely related to the first point. Because of their calling to a mission society long term, boosters will usually be very loyal to their mission. Wilcox (1995, p. 102) comments, "During my 12 years of missionary service, I have been struck by the importance veteran missionaries place on their sense of linkage to the missionary organisation. The phrase 'our mission family' is an often-heard term which carries great feelings of valued linkage." In his study of factors influencing decision to continue by teachers of missionaries' children, Wilcox (1995) found that *affective commitment* (i.e., the strength of an employee's willingness to exert considerable effort on behalf of the organisation and acceptance of the goals and values of the organisation) was significantly related to the decision to continue, and that this was in turn related to older age. Such institutional loyalty, as we have seen, is low in both boomers

and busters because of their perception of ministry.

3. Leadership Issues

Boosters work well under authoritarian leaders, treating them with respect and obedience. Boomers see themselves as professionals and expect to be treated as such, including being consulted in their areas of expertise. Thus they look for participatory consensus leadership and competence in the leader. Elder (1991, p. 54) gives an example of a boomer who, after resigning from a traditional mission, said that the work at hand seemed of higher value to leaders than the development of the people doing it. He felt "crushed in their order-giving style of leadership."

Another boomer missionary said to us, "The leadership held sacrifice and performance high, and we felt robbed of our individuality and decision making powers."

Busters challenge decision makers to explain exactly what is required and why (Barna, 1994). Their attitude can cause leaders to feel irritated and insecure because they may feel their competence is being questioned. If busters are satisfied with the response to their challenge and are convinced that they will be supported in what they are being asked to do, they will co-operate. This difference in attitude across generations was encapsulated for us at an orientation course, at which we asked each of the generational groups present to respond to a leader's request that they should JUMP. The boosters' response was, "How high?" The boomers asked, "Why? If you can convince us that it is necessary, we'll jump." The busters said, "If you jump with us, we'll do it."

4. Approach to Conflict Situations

Gish's (1983) study of the leading stressors of missionaries found "the need to confront" at the top of the list. Boosters tend to sweep things under mats or approach conflicts indirectly. Often the result is escalation or suppression of the conflict—both having a negative effect on relationships. Boomers prefer to bring things into the open and work towards reconciliation, this being the most efficient way of managing a team. Their tolerance of other viewpoints makes conflict resolution much easier for them than for the typical booster. Busters come straight to the point, tell it as it is, and look for resolution for the sake of the team.

5. Need for Support And Pastoral Care

Boosters are independent self-starters and maintainers of their own spiritual lives. When offered pastoral care, they tend to respond that they have the Lord. If offered debriefing, they murmur something about not wanting to see "a shrink." Boomers find good team relationships very helpful to effective ministry and are willing to try psychological assessment to see whether it works. Busters come straight to the reality that without a good team, mentoring, and pastoral care, they will not cope. When asked why they chose a certain mission, many busters say, "Because it seemed the most caring." One of the greatest fears of busters, according to Engel and Jones (cited in Elder, 1991), is of isolation in mission, of not being with a team.

6. Role Issues

Boosters were willing to take on whatever job was asked of them, even if they were not trained for it and even if it meant sacrificing personal goals. They were innovative and very good at making do with things.

Boomers, on the other hand, given their commitment to excellence in ministry, expect accurate job descriptions and are likely to become extremely angry with the mission if the job descriptions don't prove true. They also bring with them the sense of entitlement characteristic of their generation (Sine, 1991): "We gave up a good job and a beautiful home and put our future and the future of our children on the line to come here. We are entitled to expect from the mission reasonable housing at the very least." Further, boomers' ministry expectations are high. Since the realities of the average overseas situation almost invariably fall short of their expectations, boomers are very vulnerable to disillusionment.

In her interesting comparison between combat-related stress and missionary stress, Miersma (1993) suggests that one of the first casualties of both groups is loss of ideals, leading to disillusionment, and that this is a leading psychological risk factor for these individuals.

7. Role of Women

Booster women tended to be comfortable supporting their husbands and fitting into whatever role was available where they were posted. In many missions, they were not eligible for council membership and certainly not for leadership over male missionaries. Boomer women, on the other hand, have very often had professional training, and many expect to have a recognised role commensurate with their training. "I need to have my own role and ministry in my own right," they claim. There is now considerable scope for single women to develop professionally and to exercise a ministry according to their gifts and training, even in Muslim countries. However, for married women, finding an appropriate ministry is often much more difficult. Thus some cases of attrition occur because of wives' dissatisfaction with their ministries.

8. Devotional Life

The average booster missionary was quite disciplined about the daily quiet time ("no Bible, no breakfast"). In contrast, missionaries of the new breed find it difficult to discipline themselves to a

regular time. The busters in particular cry out for help in disciplining themselves and maintaining their devotional lives. Spiritual mentors and times of retreat are therefore especially needed for them.

9. Relationship To the Local Community

Booster missionaries came with a strong sense of knowing what people needed and a commitment to ensure that they received it. Thus they operated in a paternalistic way. Boomers come as specialists to meet needs expressed by the churches. They are willing and ready to teach what they have in a relationship of brother to brother and, in

A GENERATIONAL PERSPECTIVE ON MISSIONS ISSUES			
Issue	**Boosters (Over 50)**	**Boomers (Ages 30–50)**	**Busters (Under 30)**
Call	Mystical	Best job fit	"Best" mission: often most caring
Focus of commitment	Particular people or country with particular mission organisation	Ministry in which and wherever gifts are best used	Particular project
Length of commitment	Life	Short term and review	Short term
Attitude to mission agency	High loyalty	Low loyalty	Low loyalty
Leadership	Authoritarian; respect status	Participatory, consensus; respect competence	Participatory team; respect genuineness and openness
Approach to conflict	Indirect or denial	Clarify and work towards reconciliation	Direct, open, and honest
Attitude to support and pastoral care	Independent	Expect opportunity for both; willing to try and see	Perceive both as essential to well-being
Role issues	Generalists; prepared to do anything; make do	Specialists; pursue excellence; agents of change	Function best in teams, each with focused ministry
Wives' roles	Supporting husband	Contribution in own right	Prefer husband-wife team; egalitarian marriage
Devotional life	No Bible, no breakfast	Wherever it can be fitted in	Find discipline hard but long for spiritual things
Relationship to local community	Paternalistic	Fraternalistic	Work well under church

Figure 4-1

turn, to learn from what others have to impart to them. Like most host communities, busters are strongly relationship-oriented and also work well under the direction of national church leaders. Both boomers and busters are used to working with people of other cultures and feel no sense of superiority to them.

10. Attitude to Resignation

A booster missionary once commented, "As far as I can see, the greatest sin a missionary can commit is to resign" (Donovan, 1991). A boomer missionary, on the other hand, asked, "What's the problem? What's so bad about resigning?" If more effective ministry beckons elsewhere, a boomer feels it's appropriate to resign. The average boomer is said to change careers two to three times during his or her working life.

The differences discussed above are summarised in Figure 4-1.

Predicted Causes of Attrition In Post-Booster Missionaries

We recognise that, as one missionary put it, "A respectable reason such as children's education or health is given as the primary reason when there are other reasons for a person's return from the field." This is not to suggest that the given reason is not real, but it does underline the fact that unexpressed reasons are often very powerful.

Based on the differences between generations noted above, we made the following theoretical predictions of underlying factors which might contribute to attrition of post-booster missionaries:

+ **Job issues**, such as unsatisfactory placement, lack of opportunity for professional development, inaccurate job description, lack of oppor-

tunity to use gifts and training, and unsatisfactory role for wife.

+ **Leadership issues**, such as lack of consultation in areas of expertise, perceived lack of competence of leaders, and lack of participation in decision making.
+ **Support issues**, such as lack of pastoral care, lack of encouragement, lack of mentoring, lack of emotional support, lack of spiritual guidance, and lack of input.
+ **Family issues**, including children's education needs, security of family, housing, lack of recreation, lack of time for family relationships, and risk of illness.
+ **Relationship issues**, particularly inadequacies in communication and conflict resolution, perceived lack of genuineness and honesty, and insufficient emphasis on team building.

Reasons for Early Return From the Mission Field

We asked a group of 61 baby boomer missionaries to identify the main contributing factors in their decision to return prematurely from overseas missionary service. Most reported several contributory factors. By far the most commonly given were **family issues** (children's education and needs of elderly parents), **job issues** (including role deprivation, lack of professional development, unsatisfactory role for wife, overwork to the point of burnout), and **attitude of leadership to missionaries** (authoritarian, non-caring, treating them like pawns, and not consulting them in areas of their expertise or in decisions affecting their families).

When asked whether anything might have inclined them to change their minds about leaving, 15% responded in the negative. Of the 85% who said that certain changes could have influenced them to stay, 32% mentioned job issues (different role, chance for professional development, and suitable role for wife), 25% mentioned support issues (72% of these identified emotional support from leaders, and 27% listed support from other missionaries), 20% mentioned leadership/management issues, and 14% mentioned children's education. This was a very preliminary survey for the purpose of collecting items for a questionnaire and is not suitable for any kind of statistical analysis. However, it does lend support to the suggestion that the fundamental differences between generations are likely to be significant contributing factors to decisions by baby boomer missionaries not to continue.

We suggest that, given the emotional vulnerability of baby busters and their need to work in teams, the issue of support is likely to be an even more important contributory factor to their attrition rate.

Apart from family issues, usually outside the control of the mission, the main factors mentioned as influencing the decision not to continue seem to be closely related to generational differences in viewpoint. In the next section we will consider changes designed to address these problems.

A PROACTIVE MISSION RESPONSE TO MISSIONARY ATTRITION

If poor fit between generations is a contributor to attrition of missionaries, what changes could mission societies make to address this problem?

We suggest that there needs to be a paradigm shift in thinking about generational differences. From this base, creative change could be brought about to make best use of our post-booster missionary resources and so reduce attrition.

A Paradigm Shift in Thinking About Generational Differences

There needs to be understanding by both boosters and post-boosters that, as Elder (1991, p. 54) puts it, "Much of the dissonance between generations is due to a cultural difference in which biblical aims and principles are carried out differently." To the degree that attitudes are not biblical, they should not be accepted. However, basic assumptions on both sides which hinder needed change (encapsulated in the complaint, "Why can't they be like us?") need to be addressed. For booster leaders, steps toward resolution might include understanding why they're "not like us," seeing post-booster missionaries as the right people for this day, and moving from generational collision to synergy.

1. Understanding Why They're "Not Like Us": Movement From Modernity to Postmodernity

One of the most significant changes in the second half of this century has been the movement from modernity to postmodernity (Grenz, 1996). Boosters belong to the era of modernity, busters to postmodernity, and boomers somewhere in between.

In essence, **modernity** elevates the human intellect, human reason, and individualism and sees the universe as mechanistic (operating according to predictable laws). A basic assumption is that knowledge is certain, objective, and good. The path to human fulfilment is presumed to lie in unlocking the secrets of the universe, mastering nature for human benefit, and so creating a better world. Twentieth century modernity sees advances in technology through scientific discovery as the means to this end. Christians brought up in a world with a modern mind-set tend to be people of action, task-oriented, persevering, hardworking, optimistic, and committed to obedience and sacrifice for the sake of the gospel.

Postmodernism came into being as a response to modernism. It questions the ideals, principles, and values of modernity. According to Grenz (1996), postmodernism has been the most significant philosophy shaping society since the mid-1980s. Following are key elements of postmodern consciousness:

1. There is deep **pessimism** over the reality that the world is clearly not getting better, despite remarkable technological achievements. The rational application of knowledge does *not* appear to be solving the world's problems.

2. An awareness of the **fragility of life** on this planet necessitates urgent action to survive through co-operation with nature, rather than mastery of it.

3. **Reason is dethroned** as the sole arbiter of human destiny, leading to an appreciation of the non-rational dimensions of truth and a desire to cultivate affective and intuitive as well as cognitive dimensions of life. This explains the new interest in spiritual and social aspects of life characteristic of the buster. **Busters are experiential rather than cognitive, relationship-oriented rather than task-oriented.** Thus, relat-

ing to God and spending time with Him take priority over doing things for Him. Busters are contemplative, reflective, and meditative. Therefore they appreciate times of retreat and spiritual direction or mentoring rather than undiluted Bible teaching.

4. Recognition of the failure of the modern cult of the individual has given rise to an awareness of the **importance of community**. There is a perception of truth as being rooted in the community of which each person is a part. Truth is understood to be whatever is needed for the well-being of each community. Since there is a multiplicity of different groups and communities in the world, postmodernists are tolerant of and even celebrate diversity—whether cultural or religious. Associated with this community-orientation is movement away from centralised and hierarchical authority to networking and participatory decision making.

5. **Egalitarianism** is a striking feature of the buster generation. This is symbolised in a fascinating way in many Western churches, where the trend is away from pews in rows with the minister six feet above, to chairs in circles with everyone equally valued and invited to participate. The philosophy also shows itself in the buster refusal to use titles, robes, and degrees and in their use of Christian names only. Along with these attitudes is a lack of respect for experience and authority.

6. There is a **global consciousness** (resulting from the global village), which erodes national loyalty. Along with this global consciousness is a celebration of cultural diversity. We belong to a "multiverse" rather than a universe (Grenz, 1996).

7. Group orientation and acceptance of diversity have led to a **centrelessness**. There are no common standards to which people can appeal and no acknowledged common source of authority.

Given these values, it is not surprising that Christian busters, having been brought up in postmodernity, are prepared to face painful realities, are deeply concerned about the environment, are experiential in their faith, are community-oriented, are low in institutional loyalty, and are celebrators of diversity. Although they are neither centreless nor hopeless, they remain vulnerable in these areas, easily losing confidence and becoming discouraged.

2. Seeing Post-Boosters as the Right Missionaries for To-day

There needs to be an acceptance by mission societies that, far from being problems, the younger generation of missionaries are God's men and women for carrying on the task of mission in this day. AEF's Canadian Director, Scott Forbes, suggests that the explanation for crisis in mission to-day lies not with the new generation of missionaries, as some have suggested, but with the mission societies (Forbes, n.d.).

Just as booster missionaries were ideal for the job in their day, so the boomers and busters have many strengths particularly geared for to-day's needs. For example, they bring specialist skills appropriate to current needs; they are able to work comfortably beside and under national churches; they are comfortable with contributing their expertise and then moving on to other places of service; they are relationship-oriented, like the host cultures; they are geared to training, mentoring, and discipling while maintaining an attitude of learner; they are realistic enough not to feel indispensable and so are not inclined to outstay their welcome (Forbes, n.d.).

Special strengths of boomers:
+ Concerned with excellence in ministry.
+ Well-trained, agents of change, visionaries.
+ Focused on personal and professional development and on good management of resources.
+ Team builders.

Special strengths of busters:
+ Community-oriented.
+ Concerned with the whole person.
+ Accepting of people as and who they are.
+ Acting from the heart, from inner resources.

If the boomers and busters are the missionaries God has given us for this next stage of missionary work, they need to be welcomed and helped in every way to carry on the task of mission in a way appropriate to the modern world.

3. Moving From Collision to Synergy

In Figure 4-1 (page 48), collision points across generations were noted. Changes in thinking, as above, could open the way instead to a synergistic outcome.

Synergy refers to the extra mysterious dimension which develops beyond the sum of individual contributions when two or more people work together in harmony. We are aware of this effect when we hear a magnificently performed symphony or oratorio. Synergy is something which should characterise our teamwork as Christians. Romans 15:5-7 gives the key. The needed ingredients of endurance and encouragement are God-given so that, as we all follow Christ Jesus, we can work together in such harmony that we together glorify God. This is the spirit that we're looking for in the proposed changes. We don't want to discard anything that is relevant and valuable from the old, nor do we want to incorporate anything that is unbiblical or of no value from the new. We want to blend the strengths of both in a new model to the glory of God. The greater the diversity, the greater the potential for synergy.

Some positive strengths of the boosters which need to be passed on to the younger generations:

+ Experience.
+ Knowledge of culture and language.
+ Spiritual discipline and methods of spiritual growth.
+ A capacity to keep the goal of missionary work firmly in focus.
+ Continuity with the great traditions of the past.
+ Perseverance against odds—enduring hardship as good soldiers of Christ.
+ Helping the younger missionaries to be constantly looking at how to link their real strengths and capacities into the ongoing purposes of God and the extension of His kingdom.

These assets, working together with the strengths of the post-boosters mentioned in the last section, have great potential for synergy. At the same time, things which could hinder synergy need to be faced and dealt with.

Aspects of the traditional approach which need to be allowed to pass into history:

+ Authoritarian leadership.

+ Tendency to overextend and therefore overstretch missionary staff.
+ Expectation that missionaries will look after themselves and not need pastoral care.
+ Sweeping conflicts under mats.

Characteristics of boomers/busters in special need of tempering with the wisdom of booster leaders:

+ The sense of entitlement. Boomers in particular have a strong sense of entitlement. They feel that the government, the education system, and the health system "owe" them something (Sine, 1991). Some come to overseas situations with the idea that the mission owes them things, such as a certain standard of housing. This can cause a great deal of stress on the team financially and relationally. Boomers need to be challenged with the idea that *they* owe their home church and their supporters something. For example, there needs to be some degree of commitment to a reasonable length of service to justify the financial outlay of supporters. There also needs to be teaching and modelling of "our right to give up our rights," to quote Oswald Sanders.
+ The temptation of professional development for selfish reasons. It is difficult for members of the generation whose watchword is, "I have a duty to myself," to be clear about motives. We call this *goal confusion* and suggest that professional development needs to be addressed in the light of the goals of the organisation, as well as in light of the missionary's personal goals. There needs to be balance between profes-

sional development and giving out from what has been gained.

+ Lack of respect for experience and authority. This is the downside of the capacity to think independently, to dream dreams, and to be agents of change. These gifts can be greatly enriched as the wisdom of elders is genuinely appreciated.

+ Outspokenness. This is the downside of openness and honesty. The buster tendency to tell it exactly as it is can be hurtful and counterproductive to team relationships.

Suggested Changes To Facilitate the Ministry Of Post-Booster Missionaries

In Figure 4-2, special strengths and special needs of post-boosters are summarised. Each special strength points to change which could facilitate its expression. For example, the commitment of boomers to minister wherever their skills and training can be used best points to the need for a good match between the person and the job and to the need for professional and career development. For the buster, community-orientation prompts working in teams and use of participatory, consensus leadership.

Further links of this sort will be explored in the important areas which follow (see also Figure 4-3).

1. Recruitment

ACCURATE INFORMATION

The specialist mentality and efficiency of boomers shows itself in a desire for honest and accurate information as a basis for making informed choices. One of the complaints of some boomers is that they were "recruited under false pretences." They felt that the information they were given by the recruiter did not match with the reality of what they found. "The home countries project a worn-out image of mission which doesn't match reality," said one missionary who is now in field leadership. This points to the need for frequent updates from overseas so that recruiters can be current with their information.

SOME SPECIAL STRENGTHS AND NEEDS OF POST-BOOSTER MISSIONARIES		
	Strengths	**Needs**
Boomers	Specialist skills; good training; pursuit of excellence	Good job match; good management; professional development
	Visionary, change agents	Participatory leadership
	Wives bring specialist skills	Appropriate role
	Family-oriented	Educational choices for children
Busters	Community-oriented	Work in teams
	Genuine, accepting, sensitive	Pastoral care
	Holistic	Balanced programme
	Deep interest in spiritual things	Time for reflection and retreat
	Egalitarian	Participatory, consensus leadership
	Acquainted with pain	Pastoral care

Figure 4-2

SUGGESTED CHANGES TO RESPOND TO POST-BOOSTER CHARACTERISTICS		
	Characteristics	**Suggested Changes**
Recruitment	Want accurate information Want several options Want to try out before commitment Group orientation; fear isolation	Regular updates from field List suitable jobs Short-term experience Recruit teams
Screening	High unemployment High tolerance of diversity Traumatised backgrounds "Call" not mentioned	Careful professional screening, including psychological assessment Understand use of terms and different focus
Orientation and Training	Need to learn from own experience	Use experiential learning Newcomer orientation on field
Field Leadership	Work best with participative, consensus-style leadership Work best with good management Intolerant of "incompetence"	Suitable training for leaders Identify and train for leadership early
Support Issues	Emotionally vulnerable (busters) Need to work in teams Holistic (busters) Spiritual discipline difficult	Regular debriefing/pastoral care programme, especially in first-term crises Recruit teams Avoid overwork; encourage balance Regular guided retreats
Job Issues	Want to use gifts in best way Wives want roles	Career development programme Short-term contracts Look for husband-wife team positions

Figure 4-3

SHORT-TERM EXPERIENCES

The need that post-boosters have to experience things before making a commitment can be met by short-term experience programmes. Mission societies that use such programmes are finding them a very fruitful means of recruitment. According to Barnes (1992), 22% of all baby boomers have visited a Christian organisation on site overseas and, of these, almost 75% are interested in short-term service. Barnes emphasises, however, that if short-term experience programmes are to be successful in recruitment, they must be done well, i.e., by careful selection and preparation of participants, good organisation of the programme, and working in partnership with the national church and long-term missionaries.

We should note, however, the importance of tempering the impressions gained through short-term experience with an accurate overall picture of the realities of missionary life. Otherwise missionary newcomers recruited through short-term programmes may arrive on the field expecting all missionary work to be done at the level they experienced. This unrealistic outlook may contribute to early disillusionment and attrition.

TEAMS

The group-orientation of busters and fear of working in isolation point to the desirability of recruiting teams for train-

ing and working together. This also
leads to synergy and mutual care.

SHORT-TERM SERVICE

The pragmatism of post-boosters
and the lack of buster confidence in
their staying power make short-term
service an attractive option. In fact, as
Barnes (1992, p. 376) has observed,
"The number of short-term personnel
serving at least two months continues
to be the fastest growing segment of the
missions force." In light of this trend,
traditional societies need to move away
from the conviction that the only missionaries worth their salt are those who
offer for long-term service. Short-term
models need to be embraced as normal
and valid. The tension is that, to be
effective, missionaries need to learn the
language and culture well and then,
from that base, develop a ministry. Few
would argue with this ideal. However,
we are dealing with a group of people
who think it normal to change careers
two or three times during their working
life. On the other hand, they are also
committed to the pursuit of excellence.
They are creative thinkers. They dream
dreams. Well thought out and planned
contracts may be one way to accommodate baby boomers. [1]

If those doing short terms are challenged, fulfilled, and developed professionally and personally during their
period overseas, they may well renew
their commitment for a further term.

2. Application Issues
SCREENING

Because of the traumatic backgrounds and emotional fragility of busters and the high tolerance for diversity
of both boomers and busters in a generation in which "anything goes," there
is a need for very careful screening.

The conservation of missionaries begins with selecting the right people and
identifying those who are not suited to
cross-cultural ministry before they are
too far down the assessment track. More
pain is caused by accepting the wrong
people than by not accepting those who
might have made it.

In these days of high unemployment,
motivation must be carefully examined.
In addition, questions need to be asked
about experience of the occult, sexual
abuse as a child, substance abuse, and
extra-marital sex. Many applicants have
come from broken homes and have experienced a great deal of pain in their
lives. Given their emotional vulnerability, they need thorough and careful professional assessment and perhaps
counselling prior to departure. We see
psychological assessment as an important tool for helping missionaries understand themselves and their partners
and recognise areas in which they may
struggle in a cross-cultural situation.
Psychological assessment is also valuable in predicting the ability of applicants to cope under cross-cultural
pressure.[2]

---

1. See pages 64–66, "Job Issues," for further detail.

2. For further details about assessment methods, see Appendix A to this chapter, pages
68–70.

CALL VS. DECISIONS

The failure of post-boosters to think in terms of a call probably reflects different terminology and a greater capacity to look reality in the face than was the case with some members of the traditional school. We suggest that if booster calls were compared with boomer decisions that "this is the way to go," there may be little difference between them. In any case, the situation should prompt mission societies to decide whether the post-boosters' terminology can be understood and accepted as biblical.

One boomer missionary wrote that he saw the idea of a call as being responsible for many problems. Among these are lack of careful screening of missionaries; separation of missionaries from their home churches due to a sense of individualistic call as opposed to the church as primary sender; and missionaries struggling on with inappropriate methods and outstaying their welcome.

3. Working With the Candidate To Identify Overseas Location

The job description came in with the baby boomer missionary. In the days of the booster missionary, accepting postings without consultation was part of the job. Nowadays it is not acceptable. Post-booster missionaries are simply not prepared to go overseas without full information about their placement and ultimate ministry. Many mission societies have already responded to this requirement by providing quite detailed job descriptions. The boomer candidates with whom we have contact often mention good job descriptions as being an important reason for choosing a certain mission.

The importance of accurate information being given prior to departure needs to be emphasised again. The applicant will have sifted through a number of job positions before choosing this one. We know of two families—with different mission organisations—who recently went overseas with the expectation that they would be going into a certain position, only to find that the job did not exist or had been given to someone else. One person was then told by the field leadership to do a job for which he was not trained, and the other was told to look for another ministry. The first family is already back in Australia, and the other is likely to return soon. This is a clear waste of missionary resources.

At the same time, it is very important that post-boosters be challenged to count the cost and to give some degree of commitment to their home support network. The situation is often complicated by unrealistic expectations, to which baby boomers are especially prone.

4. Orientation and Training

ADDRESSING HIGH EXPECTATIONS AND EXPERIENTIAL LEARNING STYLE

Missionary organisations which expect candidates to live at the mission headquarters for weeks or even months have a very good opportunity to observe daily functioning and reactions of prospective missionaries. The headquarters facilities are also good venues for learning about the mission's ethos and for becoming familiar by necessity with its operating methods and policies. It will be interesting to determine whether the length of the orientation course relates to the tendency to remain overseas. Another interesting question is whether the method of teaching before departure relates to the ability to retain what is taught.

Attendees at missionary orientation courses often seem unable to hear much of what is taught in lectures. Comments such as, "It's mostly common sense," or, "They all seem to be repeating themselves," are very common. However, on the first leave there is often the cry, "We should have been told such and such" about something that had been stressed repeatedly, confirming the suspicion that people who are excitedly preparing for work overseas cannot hear about missionary stress, the cost of adjustment, etc. Friedman (1985) describes a similar phenomenon with trainee clergy. "Clergy have an experience in their own professional lives ... inability to hear before experiencing the real world of commitment ... when advice is given. Clergy in the field constantly lament that what they learn in the workshops after ordination should have been taught when they were still in school. It was."

For busters, more emphasis is needed on experiential learning, generic orientation, and training in teams and groups, rather than any kind of formal lecturing. Generic orientation courses being conducted by Missions Interlink in Australia, using experiential and competency-based learning, are proving very popular among missionary candidates. It can be predicted that competency-based training would especially meet the needs of boomers, and experiential training would meet the needs of busters.

FIELD ORIENTATION

Given the difficulties that candidates have in hearing what they are taught prior to departure, it might be better to give the most attention to orientation after new missionaries arrive overseas, when they are actually experiencing the things being taught. Support, monitoring, and mentoring also need to be given priority during the first year overseas, when people are most vulnerable and at risk of attrition (Deane, 1994). In addition to the initial entry-orientation during language school, there should be regular times when a senior missionary sits down with the newcomer. The purpose should be to ask and answer questions, teach, and assess coping. Regular evaluation, feedback on performance, and review of goals with encouragement should be part of the process. At least one session with a senior four times during the first year and at least twice each subsequent year of the first term on the field is highly desirable.

Another priority has to be adequate time for language learning. In some missions, where there has been a strong language-learning policy for 30 years, there are still some newcomers serving in specialised roles, such as accountancy, who do not receive adequate language study time. Yet experience shows that they would have had a much higher quality of life and work satisfaction if they had had special, protected time for language study. Work satisfaction and ministry are enhanced through a knowledge of the local language.

SPIRITUAL DISCIPLINES

Busters' longing for spiritual growth, their orientation towards experience, and their difficulty over discipline need to be addressed. We see it as highly desirable that post-booster missionaries be given an opportunity prior to their departure for the development of spiritual disciplines. Periods of guided retreat are likely to be particularly helpful. These should also be continued regularly in the overseas situation, along with periods of Bible teaching.

5. Field Leadership Issues

Movement away from authoritarian, non-consultative, task-oriented leadership is probably the single most important needed change.

Dissatisfaction with leadership was one of the contributors to attrition most often mentioned by participants in our survey. Some of the stated reasons for dissatisfaction were the leaders' lack of human resource management skills, not giving staff opportunity to be heard, and treating new workers "like pawns." Some complained of feeling dehumanised or undervalued. Many mentioned not being consulted in areas which directly concerned them and/or their families.

Changes in leadership style and an understanding of leadership responsibilities are needed. Then those with leadership potential need to be identified early and given appropriate training.

LEADERSHIP STYLE

Baby boomers are most comfortable with friendly leadership using personal rather than positional power. They prefer leaders who lead by example, inspiring and equipping. They want those who can work as facilitators and coaches and who motivate by keeping a sense of involvement and partnership. The more grass-roots the processes, decisions,

and work, the more comfortable the boomers are (Elder, 1991). They want to be on a Christian-name, equal-terms basis from day one. They expect to be treated as professionals and value straight talk and truthfulness, with participation encouraged. They like layers of management to be kept at a minimum and leaders to be sensitive to individual needs (Anderson, 1990). Busters work best in teams with participative, consensus-style decision making and shared leadership.

LEADERSHIP RESPONSIBILITIES

Leaders of the new generation of missionaries have a responsibility to lead in a way which is growth-inducing both for individuals and for the organisation. "Young missionaries," says Finzel (1992), "should go with a group that will look after them, lead them with integrity and excellence, and keep their best interests at heart. It is a question of stewardship—missionaries stewarding their gifts and agencies stewarding their people."

Finzel points out that Christian organisations can be quite stressful working environments. While it is true that they are communities of God's people working in the power of the Holy Spirit, they are also human institutions with often much to learn about how humans work together. What is needed is the dynamic of the Spirit's influence *and* good management.

Finzel lists nine organisational elements that are needed by to-day's leaders:

+ Consistent personal devotional life.
+ Commitment to facilitating the ministry of every missionary.
+ Commitment to vision, goals, and strategies.

✦ Consistency and flexibility.

✦ Use of clear job descriptions, organisational charts, and delegation of authority and responsibility.

✦ Good communication with staff.

✦ Good financial stewardship.

✦ Commitment to providing care in crises.

✦ Commitment to quality and excellence.

SYSTEMS APPROACH

Because it is group-oriented, a systems approach to training is particularly suited to busters, and because it is team-oriented, it is well-suited to boomers. Instead of seeing a mission as a collection of individuals working side by side, the systems approach looks at the interrelationships between people. A healthy mission is one in which people work together with healthy patterns of cohesion, boundaries, adaptability, regulation, and communication (White, 1992). Thus, a difficulty faced by an individual missionary is seen within the context of the dynamics of the whole group. It generates questions like, "What in our system has contributed to this crisis?" and, "How should our way of operating be changed as a result of this experience—or modified to prevent a recurrence?" The loss of a missionary by attrition is then seen as a failure in the system, rather than being the sole responsibility of the person who leaves.

For example, a young mother was seen as a problem missionary and was believed to be on the field as a result of poor assessment procedures. However, the reality was that she had been coping well until there had been a violent robbery shortly after her first child had gone to boarding school. There had been no debriefing following this incident,

nor had anyone empathised with her in her grief over the separation from her child. The team dynamics had clearly been inadequate, and change needed to be made at that level.

Some other concepts used in the family systems approach also have relevance to missionary team dynamics:

Differentiation. In selection of leaders, missions will do well to look for people who are well differentiated. Poorly differentiated people look at life through the grid of their emotions, spending energy seeking approval and demanding validation. On the other hand, people with good differentiation are capable of clear thinking and decision making, are able to look at criticism and others' opinions objectively, and can problem solve and see coping options clearly. This is not remoteness or radical independence, but a capacity to distinguish between thought and feeling (Bowen, 1978).

Triangulation seems to be fairly common in missions. Since confrontation is very stressful to missionaries (Gish, 1983), a less anxiety-provoking way of dealing with a problem is to create a triangle and focus on a third person or thing. An inexperienced or unskilled leader who chooses to do this will impoverish the team. For example, a leader who was concerned about the low level of language acquisition in a team decided to deal with it by constantly drawing the team's attention to the performance of one member who was a keen linguist and was doing well. This did nothing to correct the problem and made it very difficult for the person being praised. The right approach would have been to discuss the problem with the team and work out a mutually acceptable strategy. Sometimes two missionaries and a project may form a triangle, as both look at the problem through the grid of blocked goals instead of discussing options and individual ideas.

Scapegoating. This is the situation in which one person in an upset family or team is identified as the problem. We have frequently been aware of this in stressful missionary situations, and it is a sure route to attrition.

It is of particular importance for the leadership team to have within it people who are pastoral carers. Such leaders will take an interest in all missionaries and will allow them time to express what they are feeling. They will also consult missionaries about any proposed changes affecting their work.

MANAGEMENT INSIGHTS FROM THE SECULAR WORLD

In the secular scene these days, it is well recognised that care for and development of staff facilitates the achievement of organisational goals (Shedlosky, 1992). Mission societies have not always paid enough attention to this relationship. However, in that boomers are particularly asking for professional development and busters for pastoral care, it is a very appropriate time to learn from secular experience. Instruments which are well cared for and used in the right way perform better and have a longer effective life than those which are not. This principle is very relevant to attrition.

Shedlosky (1992) points out that organisations consist of four systems, each of which needs to be in a healthy condition. First is the *structural system*, which includes the interrelation between individuals, departments, and management, as well as lines of authority, responsibility, and accountability. Blurring in these areas can be very stressful. Second is the *human resource system*, which encompasses the care and development of personnel. Third is the *political system*, which covers power and the allocation of resources. Fourth, there is the *symbolic system*, or the organisational ethos and culture.

The structural system needs to be clear; the human resource system, well-developed; the political system, fair; and the symbolic system, such as to inspire loyalty. In addition, all four need to be in appropriate balance.

It is interesting to consider what can be learned from the widely used concept of **total quality management**. The aim of this management system is excellence, and the system uses four basic principles in achieving this: customer-defined quality, continuous improvement, involvement of every member, and teamwork.

In mission, customer-defined quality might mean discovering and focusing on felt needs and on what is really relevant in a target culture. It will include aiming for the highest possible level of language and culture acquisition for every missionary, spending much time in building relationships, and not spreading missionaries too thinly.[3]

---

3. Further details of total quality management may be found in Appendix B to this chapter, pages 70–72.

LEADERSHIP IDENTIFICATION
AND TRAINING

Post-booster missionaries do not respect the status of a leader and so do not easily tolerate perceived incompetence in leaders. One of the most serious deficiencies in the traditional missionary model has been in identifying and equipping leaders. Many missionaries have been put in field leadership positions because no one else could be found for the job. Often these people have been taken from fruitful ministries and are left to sink or swim as leaders without any prior training or experience. It is therefore not surprising that the whole experience at times proves painful and diminishing for leader and led alike.

We can learn from secular organisations that potential leaders can be identified early and trained appropriately for the job. As one returned missionary commented, "Secular organisations would be bankrupt if they managed their organisations the way missions very often manage theirs!"

Training in systems theory and in appropriate management skills would be a useful beginning. Every leader needs to have a commitment to team building and facilitating member care. Leaders also need to be aware of the synergistic potential of team harmony (see Rom. 15:5-6).

6. Support Issues

The positive benefit of social support for people in situations of high stress has been well established (Elliott & Eisdorfer, 1982). Such support may be *tangible* (e.g., practical help in crisis), *informational* (keeping people informed in an open and honest way), and *emo-*tional (having someone to listen and with whom problems can be discussed). **Post-booster missionaries are in special need of support, firstly, because of the situations in which many work and, secondly, because of their emotional vulnerability.**

WORK SITUATIONS

The movement from colonial rule to independence in many countries has meant that expatriates in general and missionaries in particular are often held in much lower regard than they used to be. Therefore, there is higher risk of rejection for the missionary to-day. To this, busters in particular will be very sensitive.

Many missionaries have also been subjected to violence or threat of violence or have witnessed terrible cruelty, poverty, and famine. All these experiences increase their need to feel part of supportive teams. It is also important that contingency plans be in place to deal with such occurrences.

The fact that missionaries in some places are working under national church leaders points to the welcome fact that national churches have become independent. However, the arrangement may cause problems for some of the missionaries concerned. Among these are the overuse of skills to the point of burnout and the lack of culturally appropriate pastoral care. Both circumstances signal a need for increased emotional and tangible support from mission leadership.

Threat of exposure to serious illness, especially affecting children, is another valid source of distress. A few missionaries have become infected with HIV through contaminated medical equipment and blood transfusions. Chronic malaria has caused some to return home permanently. Contingency plans, e.g., for HIV/AIDS, provide helpful tangible support.

People working in countries where there are significant cultural constraints to ministry, e.g., wives in Muslim countries, are also very vulnerable and so need special care.

EMOTIONAL VULNERABILITY

Busters in particular are very vulnerable, since many have had a great deal of pain in their backgrounds. Since missionary life is very stressful due to the pressures which are an inevitable part of it (see, for example, Donovan, 1984; Donovan, 1992; Dye, 1974; and Wilcox, 1995), busters need continuing care, including the support of a team. They find isolation very hard to handle, and our recommendation is that they should not be in situations where they are away from the support of friends.

There should be contingency plans in place for care in times of special vulnerability, including the first term, moving to another ministry, and crises of all kinds. We have pointed out else-. where that analysis of missionary stressors suggests that many stressors are connected with loss of the basic human needs for belonging (feeling loved, accepted, and cared for) and for role (feeling that what they are doing is making a difference), along with the loss of a sense of predictability and control with regard to the environment (Donovan, 1992). It therefore follows that people who are dissatisfied with their work are in special need of care. The importance of satisfaction with role is also underlined. Since role is of special importance to boomers, their vulnerability and need of care when their job is not right can be

readily understood. "I probably would have made it," said one who was struggling over work issues, "if someone had taken time to listen to me and to explain their reasons for asking me to move." The perception of not being valued as team members can be devastating to missionaries and can act as a powerful incentive to leave the field. Thus leadership commitment to relationship building by all means is likely to do much to prevent attrition.

WHOLE PERSON

Serious commitment by mission leadership to caring for the whole person is vital to the care of post-boosters. Even if things work out less than perfectly, people who know that they are cared for, that they are regarded as adults, and that they are trusted in their ministry will cope far better than others. We have outlined elsewhere a programme of pastoral care of missionaries throughout their careers, involving the local church, the mission society, and the missionary team (Donovan, 1992).

Priority should be given to listening and regular debriefing. Missionaries can learn to do this for one another.

In her comparison of missionaries with Vietnam veterans, Miersma (1993) notes that both groups lacked opportunity for debriefing, discussion, and decompression—either overseas or at home. Leading areas of need for debriefing were failure to see progress in their work, feeling that their work was not done well or well enough (because of constant interruptions, limited availability of materials and labour, and undependability of bureaucratic systems in host countries), and a perception of having wasted their time or their life.

Regular debriefing or defusing as part of member care and adequate time away from the job for rest, recreation, and reflection are mandatory for the new generation of missionaries. Times for spiritual retreat are also vital.

Debriefing after any traumatic incident is mandatory and should be built into team practice. Debriefing not only helps the person tell his or her story with the encouragement of another's full attention, but also facilitates the clarifying, acknowledging, and expression of negative emotions. This is a very important step in the healing process (Mitchell & Bray, 1990). The leader should then follow up the debriefing by making contact with the missionary at regular intervals to check progress. Leaders need to be aware of early symptoms of critical incident stress and should have a plan in place for dealing with that contingency (Carr, 1994).

There is also need for leaders and team members to have basic knowledge and skills in grief counselling, since so much of what missionaries experience even in moving between cultures is grief over loss (Donovan, 1992).

It is interesting to note that the World Health Organization in 1976 identified four social situations which increase vulnerability by erosion of normal support: uprooting, being devalued as humans, psychosocial effects of innovations, and psychosocial constraints on programmes and activities (Elliott & Eisdorfer, 1982).

DISILLUSIONMENT

Boomers and busters are both particularly vulnerable to disillusionment—the former because of inappropriately high expectations and the latter because of their emotional vulnerability

and proneness to disillusionment. Some workers can be helped by what Sell (1991) calls "de-illusionment." This approach deals with the distance between one's dream and one's achievement of it. This really consists of modifying and personalising (contextualising) dreams so that they better fit present realities. Perhaps it is only the time span which needs modifying, but often there will be constraints in another culture which will never permit the fulfilment of dreams in their present form. Sell (1991, p. 159) says that de-illusionment "can result in a beautiful increase in self-knowledge and refreshing self-acceptance. It represents a mature look at one's abilities, energies, and future decades." In the cross-cultural situation, de-illusionment can also be a powerful stimulus to personal growth, out of which flows more effective ministry. It may be that this concept can be introduced and practised predeparture and then continued through mentoring, regular evaluation, and encouragement by leadership overseas.

The other side of the emotional vulnerability of the busters is their sensitivity to others' feelings and their capacity for deep relationships. Thus they can make very good team members.

7. Job Issues
JOB SATISFACTION

The parable of the talents is of special significance to boomers. They see their training and skills as God-given for their particular ministry. Therefore, it is especially stressful to them if they are in work which is not suitable or which underutilises them. Asked reasons for attrition in his team, David Camburn

(1986, p. 128) quoted a field chairman as saying, "The structure can jump up and strangle creativity." Camburn goes on to suggest that the emphasis should be on efficiency and fulfilment rather than on restrictions and confinements. Of course, many of the restrictions and confinements are beyond the control of field leadership. However, some are not, and these will be minimised if the leader is committed to identifying the potential of every team member and facilitating its development as far as possible. This applies to women as well as men, single as well as married. Wilcox (1995) points out that overseas educators "seem to remain as long as they sense that the organization is moving along with them, facilitating their ministry." This is another way of saying that if the missionary has confidence in the leadership, he or she is more likely to put up with a less than ideal situation. Closely related to this is the need mentioned earlier of ensuring that the mission gives the missionary a clear and accurate job description prior to departure. In these days of e-mail, it should be possible to keep candidates up to date with any changes likely to affect their jobs. Such efficiency and thoughtfulness do much to build confidence and trust.

We suspect that the seeds of attrition may be sown in the early days in the new culture or even predeparture. As one young buster candidate said in my hearing to a certain home administrator, "It's time that you people got your act together!" Obviously, this young man didn't know that there was a time to remain silent. However, at the same time he was voicing a cry of his generation about the proper use of resources. It is a cry to which we must respond if

we are to avoid losing some of these dedicated servants of the Lord.

Wilcox (1995) also demonstrated in his study that continuing overseas was strongly correlated with job satisfaction. Part of this satisfaction, as expressed by the missionaries who talk to us, relates to the opportunity for professional development. Such development needs to be obviously linked both to the present job and to the long-term goals of the organisation. Younger boomers may actually seek refuge in further study if things are getting too hard, so one of the tasks of the leader is to ensure that study for professional development is done at the right time and for the right reasons.

If people are well matched with jobs, the effect is generally wonderfully enriching. However, it is important, as Wilcox (1995) suggests, to analyse the characteristics of the job to see whether the job is reasonable or just survivable. This brings us to one of the most effective underminers of missionary relationships, health, and ministry—**overwork**. This state usually also provides a very confusing model to the local people, who know the value of letting time pass gently by and savouring it and who give the highest priority to relationships. Overwork is like a blight on missionary work everywhere. Taken to its all-too-frequent conclusion, it causes burnout and attrition.

There is urgent need for missions to find ways of protecting their staff from overcommitment. The malady affects mission organisations at every level. Younger missionaries easily become caught up in it. Then they feel trapped. As one young boomer put it, "It's not true that it's better to burn out than to rust out. Both are dishonouring to God."

The situation will continue until someone is brave enough and farsighted enough to say that the only solution is to be sufficiently focused in our ministry to ensure that our capacity to minister is not impaired. This may mean saying no to an exciting new opportunity until there are enough appropriately qualified staff to handle it. The ministries of too many young missionaries have come to grief on the rock of some missionary leader's extravagant ideas of expansion. No missionary in these days should be sent anywhere overseas without adequate support from more senior experienced personnel.

Two Initiatives
To Meet Post-Booster Needs

1. Career Development Programmes

Post-booster missionaries come from backgrounds in which career development programmes are normal components of job descriptions. Since professional development is very important to boomers, mission societies who take time to have career development programmes seem more likely to retain boomer staff.

Peter Shedlosky (1992) describes YWAM's approach to missionary career development. YWAM is concerned with developing the maximum potential of the individual in line with the overall goals of the organisation. This means giving attention to the goals of both the individual and the organisation, with a view to progressive improvement in the match between them. The concept is that a career development plan is developed at the beginning of a missionary's career in consultation with an appropri-

ate leader. The plan is then reviewed and adjusted at regular intervals. Training programmes are always considered in light of the goals of the organisation and of the individual before they are undertaken.

As part of their Los Angeles career development programme, the staff at YWAM-LA run career development workshops. They consider personality, interests, work cluster abilities, and work values, and they test each individual in all these areas. At the end of the time, the participant works out his or her own career development programme. Other components of the programme are personal counselling in problem areas, offering placement listings to assist in a job-career profile match, and utilising promotability forecasting. The last is really a way of identifying those likely to go on to advanced ministry. Provision is also made for in-service training and a leave of absence for other appropriate training. Suggested benefits for mission societies of this kind of programme are more fulfilled and therefore more effective missionaries, increased staff motivation, and improvement in the mission's reputation.

2. Short-Term Projects

Short-term projects seem a good way of linking into the boomers' search for excellence, their needs for professional development and participative leadership, their pragmatism, and their reluctance to make a long-term commitment. The way the projects are set up has the busters' need for holism in mind also. In the following example, a contract to set up a health centre programme is outlined.

EXAMPLE OF A SHORT-TERM, TIME-LIMITED PROJECT

This project has a time limit of eight years and review.

Goal: To set up a health centre in Woopwoopland in response to an expressed felt need of a local community.

Person sought: Team leader with medical qualifications and administrative skills.

Recruitment steps:

1. Make known a detailed description of the proposed project, including country profile, disease profile, and profile of the local community.

2. Give a mission profile and describe how this project fits into the mission's overall purposes.

3. Describe the qualifications and experience needed for this project (use expert advice).

4. Describe the supporting team proposed.

Screening: Interviewing panel to include an expert in the field.

After acceptance:

1. Visit to the field. Gather information, become involved in initial planning, and assess needs (professional and personal) and constraints. Begin problem solving. Begin to develop relationships with key people, e.g., government officials, other missionaries in a similar field, etc. Work on what needs to be done predeparture, e.g., management training, home contacts, recruitment of the rest of the team, and professional and personal development.

2. Predeparture preparation. Network with experts in home country. Set up professional development methods, e.g., via computer. Complete orientation and acquire needed skills. Network with future missionary team.

After arrival overseas: It is suggested that a flow chart be devised having four strands. These would occupy different amounts of time at each stage (see Figure 4-4).

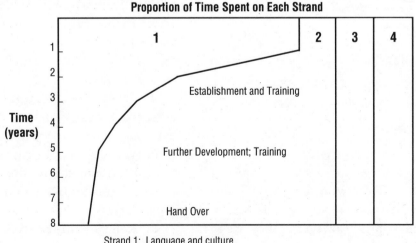

Strand 1: Language and culture
Strand 2: Project development
Strand 3: Professional development
Strand 4: Personal development including team building

Figure 4-4. Short-Term Contract Development Strands

1. Language and culture acquisition. It is predicted that if this area is seen as vital to the success of the project, it will be acquired more rapidly than otherwise. It is also suggested that the method of acquisition which best suits the individual be used.

2. Project establishment and development. In the first stage, when language and culture acquisition have first priority, project planning meetings, visits to the site, preliminary relationship building, and networking with government officials could be taking place. In the next stage, more time would be given to establishing the health programme and beginning training. As time went on, most time would be given to the project.

3. Professional development. This would be set in place immediately and continue throughout the project, matching the aims of the project and meeting the needs of the missionary.

4. Pastoral care, team building, and personal development. In the first stage, most time would be given to pastoral care, but all would receive attention throughout the project.

High-quality, appropriate care would be the aim of the project. In its final stage, handing over to someone else would be an important component.

CONCLUSION

In the present generation of missionaries, we have an excellent group of young people who are very well equipped to take the task of mission on to its next stage. However, if they are to do the job and do it as well as the boosters did their part, they need a great deal of support.

In particular, they need mission organisations that are prepared to change to accommodate them. They need leaders who will trust them with the job and provide the right kind of leadership to facilitate and inspire them. They need the right kind of organisational management and personal/professional development to facilitate personal well-being and high-standard ministry. They need the right kind of support to keep them on the field when their courage threatens to fail.

The direction of needed change is clear. Some mission agencies have already made changes, but a great deal of hard work is still needed to arrive at the fundamental change of which Elder spoke in 1991. To conclude, we come back to Elder's question, "Can the majority of agencies to-day make sufficient adjustments soon enough to capture the potential of the boomers and busters?"

APPENDIX A:
IMPORTANT CONSIDERATIONS FOR CANDIDATE ASSESSMENT

1. Past history. What can be learned from this person's past history that will provide evidence of characteristic ways of coping?

2. Stress management. How is the person currently coping with stress? If there is stress overload in the home country, it does not augur well for successful adjustment to the stresses of cross-cultural adjustment and missionary life.

3. Relationships. How does the person relate to others? Is there evidence of resolving conflicts? Is there an attitude of being willing to ask forgiveness? A tendency to always blame others when things go wrong has to be an orange light. Does the person have sufficient interpersonal skills for successful team interaction? Would there be enough confidence to confront a difficult or disappointing situation rather than just skirting around it? What evidence is there of long-term relationships being successfully maintained?

4. Self-expression. During the interview, is the person open and cooperative or defensive and unwilling to talk? Is there adequate ability in self-expression? If the person is excessively shy, it would be good to recommend some training in communication skills.

5. Family of origin. What helpful information can be gained from the history of the family of origin and the candidate's place in that family? Poor family-of-origin communication is an important factor to consider. Broken relationships should be discussed. Leaving home is much easier if everything possible has been done to deal with hurts of the past. The more a person can resolve family-of-origin issues, the more ability there is to cope with change and to be a functional team member.

6. Motivation. What can be discovered about the person's motivation in applying for missionary service? This is currently more difficult where unemployment is a problem and there has not been satisfactory employment at home. The possibility that there is a rebound reaction due to a broken relationship or a job disappointment should also be carefully examined.

7. Time management. How does the candidate handle time? What has he or she ever organised from scratch? This question is especially important for peo-

ple going into unstructured jobs such as church planting.

8. Marriage relationship. For married candidates, careful attention should be paid to the marriage relationship. Under God, the marriage should be the number one coping resource. Any tension in the marriage, either emotional or physical, should be dealt with prior to departure.

9. Children. If there are children accompanying missionary parents, careful attention should be given to the needs of the children. Psychological problems or learning difficulties should be discussed and the implications considered. What is the attitude of teenage children to being uprooted? There is also a need to discuss the attitude of older teenagers who are being left at home. Maladjustment in any of these situations will add to the stress that the parents are already enduring through cross-cultural adjustment.

10. Sensitive issues. Because of the make-up of our present society, it is important to talk frankly on certain issues. Sensitive questions need to be asked concerning experience of the occult, child sexual abuse, and attitudes toward homosexuality and extra-marital sex. If there has been immorality of any kind, then there should have been a period of restoration (four years has been suggested by one writer). Some responses to questions in these areas will indicate a need for counselling prior to departure.

11. Psychological testing. Psychological testing is an essential tool in the assessment process for ruling out any emotional disorders. The test profiles should also provide information on current emotional functioning, personality type, areas of strengths and weaknesses, abilities such as IQ and language aptitude, and tendencies to be impulsive or obsessive. A high score on hostility may point to an unresolved grief that should be dealt with before departure. The profile may indicate high depressive scores or high anxiety or tension. Because the tests are self-reported, the test profiles should be congruent with the interview data and the references. Whatever the battery of tests chosen, there should be one projective test included. The psychologist should have had some experience with what is involved in missionary work and should have a good working knowledge of the tests being used.

12. References. The results of psychological assessment and the interview data need to be combined with references from people who know the candidate well, including a reference from a recent employer and from the Bible college personnel. However, it needs to be pointed out that research has shown that there is no significant correlation between positive references and success. Referees tend to cast around for positive things to say. There is, however, significant correlation between negative references and failure. A phone call follow-up of a reference is often a good idea, as referees are often hesitant to put negative comments in writing.

13. Short termers. Many societies which use psychological assessment for career missionaries deem that such assessment is not necessary for short termers. However, experience has shown that visits as short as three weeks have been problematic if an unsuitable or emotionally unstable person is allowed to go. Some experiences have

been highly traumatic, not only for the person who has had to be despatched home, but also for the team on the field.

In spite of all the care and prayerful consideration, there will still be times when someone who seemed suitable will not make it. A wonderful asset in candidate assessment would be a crystal ball! Although we learn from experience, the fact is we cannot predict the set of variables awaiting the prospective missionary or how a person will react in some situations. Some who have not made a successful adjustment would have done so, had they not been hit by a series of losses with inadequate support. Others, about whom there had been some question, have blossomed and grown as people, because of good support and effective field orientation or other factors not always humanly explicable.

APPENDIX B:
TOTAL QUALITY
MANAGEMENT (TQM)

It is fascinating to read of the effect on the Japanese manufacturing industry since World War II of the implementation of total quality management. TQM was the brain child of Edward Deming and Joe Juran in the U.S. They theorised that as the quality of a product improved, so would productivity. When the Japanese took hold of the TQM concept and ran with it, the effect on both quality and productivity was dramatic.

The relevance of this theory to post-booster attrition is that the aim is excellence. The key principles in TQM's achievement are as follows:

1. Customer-defined quality. In the mission scene, this might involve spending far more time discovering what is really relevant to the cultures in which missions work. It will also mean the highest quality achievable in language and culture acquisition, in relationship-building, and in specific ministries. In many situations, this may mean becoming much more focused in ministry—resisting the temptation to spread ourselves too thin.

2. Continuous improvement. All team members are held responsible not only for the quality of their work, but for continuously improving it. This taps into the baby boomers' need for professional development.

3. Involvement of every member. The Japanese speak of "creative involvement of everyone." They recognised very early that their strength lay in using the creativity and intelligence of every single person in the organisation. They also recognised that people need training and support to make their best contribution. To accomplish their goals, the Japanese:

+ Make every effort to match skills to jobs.
+ Provide a great deal of training to upgrade skills and so increase capacity and interest.
+ Make every effort to educate everyone to understand how their part in the operation fits into the total process.
+ Invite people to contribute improvement ideas on a continuous basis.
+ Invite everyone to anticipate problems before they happen and to deal with them then.

4. Teamwork. Part of the leader's role is to maintain consistency of purpose and to keep reminding members of that purpose and how they fit into it. There is also commitment to fostering an attitude of trust in the organisation so that people feel free to expose problems.

Role of Team Leaders

It is acknowledged that 85% of problems are with the system and not with the workers. Deming suggests a number of points. Those of particular relevance to mission are:

+ Create consistency of purpose (see above).
+ Encourage commitment by every member to that purpose.
+ Identify problems early and work with those concerned in order to deal with them.
+ Institute modern methods of training for everyone. (Computer technology now makes this possible for even the most isolated missionary.)
+ Break down barriers to the team outcome, e.g., misunderstandings between generations or missionary cultures, competition between departments.
+ Remove barriers between the individual and his or her capacity to do a good job.
+ Invite maximum participation and suggestions by team members.
+ Maintain respect for everyone at every level.
+ Learn and apply appropriate skills and techniques.
+ Ensure that overall purposes of the organisation are understood.
+ Ensure that improvements are relevant to the organisation's goals.
+ Give credit for results achieved.
+ Recognise that the creativity and knowledge of the work force are major assets. Seek improvement with the help of the workers.

✦ Recognise that most problems can be attributed to the system. Constantly try to improve the system.

✦ Engender trust and build relationships.

Application to Missions

It seems to us that transferring these principles to our operation might not only reduce post-booster attrition, but also result in better use of the resources we have.

One of the maxims of TQM is that "best efforts directed at the wrong tasks destroy pride in performance, cause waste and error, and mean unnecessary cost." Our impression is that some missionaries feel that their best efforts are being directed at the wrong tasks—or at so many tasks that effectiveness is being lost.

For additional information, see Stace (1994), Standards Australia (1992), and University of Newcastle (1994).

REFERENCES

Anderson, L. (1990). *Dying for change*. Minneapolis, MN: Bethany House.

Barna, G. (1994). *Baby busters: The disillusioned generation*. Chicago, IL: Northfield.

Barnes, S. (1992). The changing face of the missionary force. *Evangelical Missions Quarterly*, **28**, 376-381.

Bowen, M. (1978). *Family therapy in clinical practice*. New York, NY: Jason Aronson.

Camburn, D. (1986). Why do they leave? Reflections on attrition: The Conservative Baptist Foreign Mission Society. *Evangelical Missions Quarterly*, **22**, 127-128.

Carr, K. L. (1994). Trauma and post-traumatic stress disorder among missionaries: How to recognize, prevent, and treat it. *Evangelical Missions Quarterly*, **30**, 246-255.

Deane, H. (1994). *Staying missionary*. Auckland, NZ: Impetus.

Donovan, K. (1984). *The concept of stress and its effects on the quality of missionary life*. Unpublished manuscript.

Donovan, K. (1991). Beauty for ashes: Redeeming premature field departure. *Evangelical Missions Quarterly*, **27**, 18-22.

Donovan, K. (1992). *The pastoral care of missionaries*. Leonard Buck lecture. Bible College of Victoria, Lilydale, Victoria, Australia.

Dye, T. W. (1974). Stress-producing factors in cultural adjustment. *Missiology*, **2**, 61-77.

Elder, A. (1991). Boomers, busters, and the challenge of the unreached peoples. *International Journal of Frontier Missions*, **8**, 51-55.

Elliott, G. R., & Eisdorfer, C. (Eds.). (1982). *Stress and human health: Analysis and implications of research: a study*. New York, NY: Springer.

Finzel, H. (1992). Nine essentials for organizational development. In K. O'Donnell (Ed.), *Missionary care: Counting the cost for world evangelization* (pp. 219-234). Pasadena, CA: William Carey Library.

Forbes, S. (n.d.). Crisis? What crisis? *Action Africa*.

Friedman, E. H. (1985). *Generation to generation: Family process in church and synagogue*. New York, NY: Guilford Press.

Gish, D. (1983). Sources of missionary stress. Journal of Psychology and Theology, **11**, 236-242.

Grenz, S. J. (1996). A primer on postmodernism. Grand Rapids, MI: Eerdmans.

Loss, M. (1983). *Culture shock*. Dallas, TX: Word.

Miersma, P. (1993). Understanding missionary stress from the perspective of a combat-related stress theory. *Journal of Psychology and Theology*, **21**, 93-101.

Mitchell, J. T., & Bray, G. P. (1990). *Emergency services stress: Guidelines for preserving the health and careers of emergency services personnel*. Englewood Cliffs, NJ: Prentice-Hall.

Sell, C. M. (1991). Transitions through adult life (2nd ed.). Grand Rapids, MI: Zondervan.

Shedlosky, P. (1992). Career development and the mission agency. In K. O'Donnell (Ed.), Missionary care: Counting the cost for world evangelization (pp. 247-259). Pasadena, CA: William Carey Library.

Sine, T. (1991). *Wild hope*. Dallas, TX: Word.

Stace, R. (1994, July 26-29). TQM and the role of internal audit. *Australian Accountant*.

Standards Australia (1992). *Stepping stones: A practical criteria-based approach to total quality management.* Standards Association of Australia.

University of Newcastle (1994). *Total quality management*. Staff seminar.

White, F. (1992). The dynamics of healthy missions. In K. O'Donnell (Ed.), *Missionary care: Counting the cost for world evangelization* (pp. 235-246). Pasadena, CA: William Carey Library.

Wilcox, D. K. (1995). Who perseveres? A discriminant analysis of missionary school personnel by intention to extend service. *Journal of Psychology and Theology*, **23**, 101-114.

Kath Donovan was a medical missionary in Papua New Guinea for 17 years. Since returning to Australia in 1983, she has been involved in missionary health care, including research into issues relating to the quality of missionary life and ministry—particularly stress and coping, selection procedures, singleness, pastoral care, and adjustment issues. Donovan is the author of **Growing Through Stress** (Aquila Press) and **Pastoral Care of Missionaries** (BCV). In partnership with Ruth Myors, Donovan runs the Christian Synergy Centre, providing care for missionaries through seminars, counseling, and debriefing.

Ruth Myors was a missionary for 23 years with the Somali people in Somalia (13 years), Ethiopia (4 years), and Kenya (5-1/2 years). She worked as a nurse and also as a radio script writer. Myors returned to Australia and trained as a psychologist, specializing in missionary candidate assessment, counseling, and debriefing. With Kath Donovan, she is co-director of the Christian Synergy Centre.

Part 2

The Research
Analysis

5

Designing the ReMAP
Research Project

Jonathan Lewis

Participants in the 1993 National Missions Congress in Caxambu, Brazil, were shocked at the report given by a respected Brazilian missionary that 75% of that nation's cross-cultural missionaries quit their posts during their initial five-year term of service or don't return after the first furlough. Could this 15% per annum attrition figure possibly be true? None of the participants at the congress could confirm or refute the figure. There were simply no reliable data available.

The need of emerging missions nations for information regarding their rate of attrition was one of the important reasons that the WEF Missions Commission (WEF/MC) decided to undertake a global study on attrition. This project was soon called ReMAP (Reducing Missionary Attrition Project). Originally, the "newer" sending countries with the greatest numbers of missionaries were to be surveyed. These included Brazil, Nigeria, Korea, the Philippines, and India. A representative from Spanish Latin America, Costa Rica, was soon added to the list, as were Ghana and Singapore.

With the project conceived, it became apparent that some of the Western nations also wanted to participate in the study. While attrition studies have been made in many of the "older" sending countries, there is no clear picture of the overall attrition of these historical sending bases as a whole. A comparison between "older" and "newer" sending countries could also provide information never before acquired, which could give insight into the aging of mission agencies. The UK and Australia seemed eager to join, and eventually Germany and Denmark also participated. After a couple of false starts, the USA and Canada also took part.

As the project began to shape up, WEF/MC staff struggled with what we really wanted to achieve. We knew it was important to get some numbers from the newer sending countries that would help them understand where they stood on the attrition rumors. Beyond the numbers, we wanted strategic mission leadership to take a "reality check" and to better understand the cost and nature of all kinds of attrition—understandable, unavoidable, preventable. Perhaps of most interest was the possibility of exploring the roots of missionary attrition and seeing some creative solutions applied to this costly problem.

Our discussions led us to the conviction that the ultimate success of the project must be measured not in the statistical information we managed to produce or the new information garnered. Rather, our success would be marked by the overall reduction of missionary attrition, particularly among the mission agencies and sending churches that participated in the study. Furthermore, we understood that the process itself of gathering and compiling the data would be extremely important in achieving some of these ends.

The initial challenge would be to create a generalized awareness of the significant issues in attrition (an unpleasant subject for many missions executives) and sensitively to seek leaders' "buy in" for the project. This step was particularly necessary in the problem-solving aspects of the project, with subsequent creation and application of forthcoming solutions. In tangible terms, the greatest value of the project would be in its process outcomes, not in the statistical products, which seemed its most obvious objective. Too many Western mission leaders simply wanted numbers ("body counts"), but we were seeking to provide the catalyst for a long-term process.

So how were we to go about tackling a 14-nation, four-language, comprehensive study on missionary attrition in which we hoped to involve hundreds of missions executives and influence a global movement? And how were we to do it with two already "full" full-time WEF/MC staff and a non-existent budget? It was obvious from the start

that the project would have to "fly" on faith, if at all.

On a practical level, a coordinator for the project was the first and most urgent need. Happily, MC Executive Committee member, Rudy Girón, who was serving as President of COMIBAM, was in a transition period and accepted the responsibility to administrate the project on a half-time basis. His primary efforts centered first on coordinating the volunteer task force we would muster from the 14 nations under consideration and, second, on managing the process towards the attrition workshop in April 1996.

From a research point of view, we had an enormous challenge. Sampling, the foundation of any research effort, was going to be a problem. A mail survey, which is the only affordable alternative in most cases, would simply not work in some of the Two-Thirds World countries. At best, it would produce a "self-selecting" sample which could skew the overall results. As for validity and reliability issues, comparison studies between cultures are always open to question. Rigorous translation procedures and the hands-on supervision which would have been ideal to help control discrepancies would have required 10 times the budget we hoped to raise for the study. In the end, such measures still might not produce much more satisfactory data for statistical analysis than what we would get otherwise.

Had we been focused primarily on the numbers, we might have faltered on these points. We weren't, and we didn't. We focused on the process and trusted that God was as interested in this study as we were. We also knew that the country coordinators Girón had selected were highly committed to the project and would do their best to gather reliable data from the most complete sample possible. In several countries, coordinators resorted to interviewing a large sample of their mission agencies one by one in order to obtain adequate data. In Ghana, every single agency participated in the survey because they were individually interviewed. A similar situation took place in the Philippines.

The results rewarded our confidence. Even though the effort made to secure this information was enormous and was done on a "faith budget," a large enough sample was obtained in most cases to give us fair confidence in the generalizability of the findings to the mission scene in general. It bears mentioning that while our Two-Thirds World colleagues were making a huge effort to complete this study in a timely manner, the North American endeavor was beleaguered by delays, which severely affected our time-frame-work for the data analysis.

GIVING THE STUDY DIRECTION

The instrument as originally conceived was constructed with our process objectives in mind. Whenever an attempt is made to determine why a missionary leaves the field in an untimely manner, there are at least two major perspectives—that of the missionary and that of the missionary's supervisor. The reasons given by the two parties for the missionary's leaving the field don't always coincide, and they may also vary from the "recorded" reason at mission headquarters. Although some agencies, notably the Southern Baptist Conven-

tion, have gone to great lengths to determine the "true" reason their missionaries leave the field, we realized from the outset that we would not be able to do this in our study. Even to attempt this would have required extensive interviews with the 4,400 missionaries eventually identified who left their mission during the three-year period studied. We would also have had to interview missionary supervisors from the 453 missions that returned questionnaires. While interviews would have been conceivable at the level of a single mission (and we want to encourage this very thing), such an undertaking would have been nearly impossible for us even to attempt with our global study.

The WEF/MC serves the mission agencies and their national and continental affiliations around the globe. To meet our process objectives, it was important to involve the decision makers in these organizations which comprise our primary constituency. Since we could not interview departing missionaries, we took an approach which was not only achievable, but would involve the very people who could most likely take measures to reduce unnecessary attrition. We targeted missions administrators.

Do missions administrators really understand why their missionaries leave the field? What are their perceptions of the causes of missionary attrition? If through the survey process we could get missions administrators thinking seriously about attrition issues, we would achieve a first important step towards our objective of creating a general awareness of the problem and its causes throughout our missions constituency.

CAUSES OF ATTRITION

In order to survey missions administrators about their perceptions of missionary attrition, we would have to design an instrument with a valid and relatively complete list of the causes of attrition. The generation of such a list in itself would be a valuable contribution to research on this subject, if done in a broad and consensus-building manner which could span across the nations.

An "expert panel" was convened from the participating countries in February of 1995, to discuss at length the possible causes of attrition and to organize these causes into a manageable list. The panel included the majority of the Re-MAP country coordinators, as well as the WEF/MC staff. Three intensive days were spent at the Foreign Missions Club in London defining the causes of attrition. Eventually a list of 26 individual reasons classified into seven general categories emerged. An eighth "other" category was also added to the questionnaire. This list became the first item on the survey form.[1] It was used to ascertain the seven top reasons which missions administrators *perceived* to be the major causes of missionary attrition in their mission. It was also used to rank these reasons in importance.

OTHER FEATURES
OF THE SURVEY DESIGN

The second item on the survey attempted to determine the overall numbers of missionaries that were leaving the mission. While we were not after a "body count," it was important to understand the dimensions of the losses. Comparing this number with the size of the missions involved, we later determined that about 5% of all missionaries leave their missions each year for all reasons. This was an important baseline figure. This survey question also became the basis for calculating the preventable attrition rate by relative agency size and for determining factors which most contributed to reduced attrition (see chapters 6 and 7).

Question 3 was a control question to see whether the missions administrators' perceptions of the causes of attrition aligned with the recorded reasons. When taken as a whole, perceptions did coincide with recorded reasons when comparing the general rating of the eight categories in question 1, with the minor exception that the overall first and second reasons were inverted by a relatively small margin. This agreement was an important finding, because it suggests that missions administrators do indeed have a feel for why their missionaries are leaving the field.

MISSION DEMOGRAPHICS

Questions 4–7 of the survey were designed to obtain information which might help in understanding the relationship between rate of attrition and the demographic profiles of missions. Essentially, we wanted to try to get answers to the following questions:

1. Do missions from the "older sending nations" have higher or lower attrition rates than missions from the "newer sending nations"?

---

1. The complete survey instrument is reproduced on pages 363–370.

2. Do larger and/or older missions have higher or lower attrition rates than smaller and/or younger missions?

3. Do frontier or pioneer missions involved in church planting have more or less attrition than those missions which are involved primarily in relief and church-related support roles?

4. Do missions involved in same-culture ministries lose missionaries at the same rate as those involved in cross-cultural ventures?

With the answers to these questions, a profile of missions that are most at risk and/or least at risk of attrition might be determined.

MISSIONS PROCEDURES

During the course of its work, the WEF/MC has identified four critical procedural arenas in which inadequate attention can result in missionary attrition down the road. The first is the critical selection process, with a primary focus on the crucial role of the local church. The second is the pre-field equipping stage, where the candidate may undergo formal and non-formal training to become a missionary. The third is the mission's own pre-field orientation, which may be supplemented by an initial on-field briefing. The fourth arena involves the ongoing, on-field support, supervision, and pastoral care of the missionary.

Beyond the demographic profile of the mission, it was our intent to begin to understand what procedures common to missions agencies might affect the preventable attrition rate. We attempted to identify the kinds of procedures and the amounts of each item that missions required or provided. The

following questions related to these issues:

1. How do on-field and support measures affect attrition?

2. How important are screening procedures and training requirements?

3. Does the amount of time and money we spend on missionary care really make a difference? If so, how much of each is needed?

In other words, we wanted to identify those procedural areas over which missions administrators (and other decision makers) have some control and through which they might produce a lowering of the preventable attrition rate by applying information we could provide.

Question 12 of the survey again aimed at a gut-level perception of what missions administrators believe are the most important elements in missionary endurance. It was important to end the survey process with reflection on what missions administrators intuitively know needs to be reinforced, supported, or screened. We believed that even as the administrators performed this exercise, a learning moment could occur. And significantly, this did happen!

THE DATA ANALYSIS

In order to expedite the processing of the data, Peter Brierley of Christian Research was contracted to do the initial data analysis. The full, 120-page initial report of his findings is available through the WEF/MC offices. While adequate time for the survey work was designated, late returns from North America delayed the process, and the report was not available to the WEF/MC staff much before our major working consultation entitled "Causes and

Cures of Missionary Attrition" in April 1996. Unfortunately, the data could not be subjected to as complete an analysis as we had hoped before this important consultation at All Nations Christian College in England. Nevertheless, further analysis was completed subsequent to this event, which is shared by Detlef Blöcher and myself in chapter 7 of this book.

During the 1996 consultation, Peter Brierley's initial report was presented in a plenary session, and participants were able to interact with the report as well as with the papers which were offered during the other plenary sessions. In addition, the larger group was divided into smaller groups which focused on the selection, training, orientation, field supervision, and pastoral care of the missionary. Another group dedicated itself to attrition as it relates to missionary kids and their unique needs. Each team discussed pertinent issues and provided a basic outline to be developed into sections of this book.

The consultation was extremely beneficial in achieving many of our objectives. Some 115 church and mission leaders gathered from over 30 nations to gain better understanding of the issues and to reflect together on how to stanch the flow of unnecessary attrition. A heightened awareness of the broader dimensions of the problem was achieved, as participants began to understand attrition as symptomatic of deeper structural and programmatic aspects of mission agency work. A profound sense of concern gripped all of us as we considered not only those who leave, with the attendant pain and frustration, but many who "hang on" in spite of it all.

While the statistical information may need to be revalidated by further study, countries such as Brazil learned that their attrition rate was high, but not nearly what had been announced at that conference in Caxambu. The yearly attrition rate of 7% (which translates to 28% for a four-year term) for Brazil now not only offers missions leaders a clear figure, but also provides a deeper understanding of the causes and possible cures of attrition. Our Brazilian colleagues are aiming to bring this figure down in the coming years. The Brazilians, along with the Ghanaians, the Koreans, the Filipinos, the Costa Ricans, and our other Two-Thirds World colleagues, experienced the satisfaction of successfully undertaking this kind of investigation as they gathered valuable information which could aid their missions movements.

The WEF/MC's new calling is to help turn this important information regarding the causes and cures of missionary attrition into helpful tools for our missions colleagues around the world. This will mean, among other things, translation of this book into other languages and implementation of transferable training through workshops, to help churches and agencies work together towards lowering attrition figures.

One important emphasis of the training workshops will be how to keep records on attrition which will generate the kind of in-house information for the sending body (whether a local church or mission agency) that will help them control and reduce losses. Such information is essential if we are to be able to carry out the more valuable longitudinal studies over time.

Another focus of the training will be helping the sending bodies to understand the systems that are involved in developing and supporting missionaries. There are critical points where additional input is needed to achieve greatest overall effectiveness and efficiency, which will equate to reduced preventable attrition. We pray for God's grace in meeting these great challenges in the coming years. As always, we are counting on the enthusiasm, commitment, and support of the WEF/MC's global volunteer network in carrying out these programs to the glory of our Savior.

Jonathan Lewis was born in Argentina of missionary parents. He and his wife have been cross-cultural missionaries in Honduras, Peru, and Argentina. He has served as a church missions pastor in the USA. He authored the three-volume *World Mission* (1987, 1993) and edited *Working Your Way to the Nations* (1996). Currently, he is on staff with the Missions Commission of the World Evangelical Fellowship as a missionary training consultant and director of publications. He is married to Dawn, and together they have four children.

6

Missionary Attrition: The ReMAP Research Report

Peter W. Brierley

We have a problem! A growing number of missionaries are coming home for preventable reasons. How this concern became focused into a major research project is described in detail elsewhere in this volume. In 1994, the Missions Commission of the World Evangelical Fellowship (WEF) decided to sponsor a fact-finding exercise to ascertain how far the reports of early return might be true and what the perceived causes of this attrition were. The overall objectives of the Reducing Missionary Attrition Project (ReMAP) are to help mission agencies analyse why they are losing missionaries and to help them reduce attrition and increase their effectiveness.

In February 1995, Dr. William Taylor, Missions Commission Director of WEF, and Rudy Girón of COMIBAM, Task Force Chairman of the International Missionary Research Project, asked the UK Christian Research Association[1] to analyse the data collected by the WEF Missions Commission.[2] An expert task force from participating countries designed a questionnaire based on a listing of 26 major reasons for departure, which were broken down into eight major groups.[3] The survey was undertaken through national missions commissions in a sample of countries. Altogether, 14 countries participated in the study—six from the "old sending countries" (OSC) of Australia, Canada,

---

1. Information about the work and other activities of Christian Research may be obtained from Dr. Peter Brierley, Christian Research, Vision Building, 4 Footscray Road, Eltham, London, England SE9 2TZ; phone, 44 181 294 1989; fax, 44 181 294 0014; e-mail, <100616.1657@compuserve.com>.

2. The statistics presented in this chapter may differ from those given in other chapters. There are three reasons for the variations: (1) The calculations in this chapter were based on the first examination of the data. (2) Detlef Blöcher and Jonathan Lewis (chapter 7) had additional data from which to work. They examined the data from a different perspective, asking different questions. (3) Some of the statistics in the national case studies reflect new surveys and different ways of reading the numbers.

3. For details, see the survey instrument, which is reproduced on pages 363–370.

Denmark, Germany, UK, and USA, and eight from the "new sending countries" (NSC) of Brazil, Costa Rica, Ghana, India, (South) Korea, Nigeria, the Philippines, and Singapore. All continents were therefore included.

THE PROBLEM IS SERIOUS

Christian Research analysed the data and concluded that, measured over the years 1992–1994, the average number of workers who leave is 3.4 per society per year, or 5.1% of each society's mission force. That is to say, 1 missionary in 20 is being lost from missionary service each year. This average percentage is calculated across all sizes of society. It does vary by country, as described later.

The 5.1% figure needs to be confirmed by other studies, if possible. There have not been many studies quantifying attrition, but the figures in this survey are broadly comparable to those in previous studies. The human cost in personal development, the frequent need for counseling, the expense of training and travel and support, the impact on the churches, the gaps that are left in ministry, and the turmoil for mission leaders all point to this topic as being one of major significance.

OTHER CONSIDERATIONS

There are a number of other factors which are relevant to the overall across-the-board figure of 5.1%.

First, some attrition cannot be prevented. The survey found that overall 29% of the attrition that societies had experienced during 1992–1994 was for reasons that could not be helped, such as normal retirement, a political crisis, death of a spouse, marriage outside the

mission, or a change of job. Thus, to consider just preventable attrition, a multiplication factor of 0.71 should be used. This would reduce the 5.1% to 3.6% for preventable reasons.

Second, some missionaries who leave one mission subsequently return with another agency, and this factor must also be considered. Each mission agency is able to report the numbers it loses for whatever reason. It cannot say how many of these workers remain on or return to the mission field working with another agency. One large international missionary society (see Back & Johnson, 1988, p. 28) sent a questionnaire to all of its 345 recruits over a seven-year period. It found that while 13% had left the mission, 2% had not left missionary service. Other research which might replicate this figure is not known. If relevant to other societies, then to consider missionaries totally lost, we must use a multiplication factor of 0.85 of the attrition rate (the other 15%, 2/13, return to the field). Thus the 5.1% becomes 4.3% for attrition from the field, and the 3.6% becomes 3.1% for preventable attrition from the field.

Third, the number of missionaries serving in their first term was not asked, but a 1986 UK study showed that the average number of recruits per year from 1980 to 1986 across 25 different societies averaged 9.1% of their mission force (Brierley, 1986). Suppose that the average first term for all societies is three years and that the UK proportion of recruits in the 1980s is valid both in the 1990s and across all missionary sending countries. That would suggest that 27.3% (= 3 x 9.1%) of the mission force are serving in their first term—a sizable proportion if attrition hits them harder, as a study by the World Gospel Mission (WGM) suggests (Bushong, 1986).

The WGM study found that half of WGM attrition occurred by the end of the first term. While some reasons for leaving, such as failure to learn the new language or adapt to the culture, could occur more in the first term than in later terms, the reverse is true of other factors. Health problems are more likely to surface later than earlier, as is the need to return to look after elderly parents or because of the children's education. Marriage conflicts and problems with other missionaries or with local church leaders are all likely to emerge after the first term of service. The results of the ReMAP study show that it is these latter reasons which dominate.

SOME BACKGROUND INFORMATION

According to the *World Churches Handbook* (Brierley, 1997), there were 0.92 billion Christians in 1960 throughout the world (including many nominal Christians). This figure had increased to 1.61 billion by 1995 and, if present trends continue, will reach 1.90 billion by the year 2010. This is a current growth rate of around 60,000 people a day. Perhaps a third of these are children, and perhaps a fifth are in the great nation of China alone. The rate of expansion between 1960 and 1995 has varied across the world. In North America the church has gained new members at the rate of +1.4% per year over these 35 years; in Oceania, +1.1%; and in Europe, +0.1%. Against these figures are the growth rates in Latin America of +2.2%; in Africa, +3.8%; and in Asia,

+4.1%. It is quite clear that the non-Western church is growing much faster than the Western, and the lands south of the equator more quickly than those north.

From his work in *Operation World*, Patrick Johnstone (1986) estimated the growth of evangelical Christians between 1960 and 1985 to be from just under 60 million in 1960 to 85 million in 1985 for those living in North America and Europe. The figures for the Third World went from 25 million to over 160 million in the same time period—a massive expansion. At the same time, Johnstone (1986, p. 35) estimated that in 1978 the total number of cross-cultural missionaries worldwide was 63,000, of which 90% were Westerners. By 1985 the total number had increased to 81,000, of which 87% were from Western countries. In 1990, Johnstone (1993, p. 643) estimated that there were 88,000, of which 79% were from the West.

This increase in the number of non-Western missionaries is in accordance with the figures produced by Larry Pate (1989, p. 52), who includes near-cultural missionaries in his figures, so the overall numbers are different. Pate estimates 75,000 missionaries in 1980, of which 80% were Western; 121,000 in 1988 with 68% Western; 137,000 in 1990 with 64% Western; 197,000 in 1995 with 55% Western; and 296,000 in the year 2000 with 45% Western. That Pate's percentages of Western missionaries decrease so much faster than Johnstone's reflects the huge increase Pate sees in the number of near-cultural missionaries. Whether the West will drop behind so greatly in view of George

Verwer's 1996 call for 200,000 more missionaries remains to be seen.[4] Pate (1989, p. 45) likewise gives a steep increase in the number of Two-Thirds World mission agencies, from 750 in 1980 to 1,100 in 1988. He forecasted that these would increase to 1,200 by 1990, to 1,500 by 1995, and to 2,000 by the year 2000.

The ReMAP study seems to indicate that the NSC are placing greater emphasis on pioneer work and church planting than are the missions from the OSC. The ministry in which missionaries were most likely to be serving varied

TOP MINISTRY IN OLD AND NEW SENDING COUNTRIES		
	Country	**Top Ministry**
Old Sending Countries	Australia	National church (20%)
	Canada	Pioneer work (18%) Support services (18%)
	Denmark	Relief (25%)
	Germany	Relief (30%)
	UK	Pioneer work (21%)
	USA	Church planting (21%)
New Sending Countries	Brazil	Pioneer work (24%)
	Costa Rica	Church planting (25%)
	Ghana	Church planting (24%)
	India	Pioneer work (29%)
	Korea	Pioneer work (23%)
	Nigeria	Pioneer work (36%)
	Philippines	Pioneer work (23%)
	Singapore	Pioneer work (28%)

Figure 6-2

across the different countries (see Figures 6-1 and 6-2).

METHODOLOGY

The in-country survey work was conducted by nationally representative missions associations. For example, in the UK, the surveys were conducted by the Evangelical Missionary Alliance; in Denmark, by the Danish Missions Council; in Brazil, by the Cross-Cultural Missions Association of Brazil. These organisations were each sent a master copy of the final version of the questionnaire by Christian Research in May 1995. Where necessary, the questionnaire was translated locally. The missions associations then sent copies of the questionnaire to the agencies on their list. In some countries, interviews were conducted in order to ensure the

TYPES OF MINISTRY IN WHICH MISSIONARIES ARE INVOLVED			
Ministry	**Overall %**	**OSC %**	**NSC %**
Pioneer work	21	19	24
Church planting	20	18	21
National church	17	19	15
Relief	16	16	16
Local church	13	14	12
Support services	13	14	12
Total (=100%)	446	242	204

Pioneer work: Involved in pioneer mission work among unreached, unchurched people groups where there is little or no evangelical presence.

Church planting: Involved in evangelism and church planting in areas where the evangelical church has an established presence.

National church: Helping the national church through administrative, pastoral, teaching, theological training, and other support work.

Relief: Involved in relief and development or institutional work such as famine relief, hospital work, etc.

Local church: Helping the local church through administrative, pastoral, teaching, theological training, and other support work.

Support services: Providing a support service for evangelism and church planting, such as Bible translation, aviation, literature, radio, etc.

Figure 6-1

---

4. On January 17, 1996, George Verwer, International Director of Operation Mobilisation, launched a passionate appeal for (mainly Western) churches to send another 200,000 missionaries in cross-cultural evangelism in the next five years.

NUMBER OF REMAP SURVEY FORMS RETURNED				
Country	Total Received	Total Usable	# From Agencies	# From Churches
Australia	44	44	44	0
Brazil	22	22	22	0
Canada	37	35	33	2
Costa Rica	7	6	6	0
Denmark	10	10	10	0
Germany	22	20	20	0
Ghana	52	52	40	12
India	21	20	20	0
Korea	64	54	54	0
Nigeria	14	13	12	1
Philippines	18	18	18	0
Singapore	7	7	6	1
UK	39	37	37	0
USA	194	190	126	64
Total	551	528	448	80

Figure 6-3

representative nature of the sample. A total of 551 forms were returned (see Figure 6-3). Of these, 37% were from the NSC.

One response in seven, or 14%, was from those who categorised themselves as being a church, not a mission agency. These churches totaled 80 in all—66 in the OSC (64 in the USA) and 14 in the NSC (12 in Ghana). Where global figures are given, they have been analysed en masse and weighted by the number of replies from each country. If one assumes that the proportion of agencies which responded would be roughly the same in each country, then this method is valid.

OVERALL NUMBERS ON ATTRITION

Agencies were asked for the actual number of missionaries lost over the preceding three years—1992, 1993, and 1994. Surprisingly, in terms of the per-centage of the average mission agency, the OSC have more missionaries come home than the NSC—1 in every 18 (5.6%) compared with 1 in every 24 (4.1%), but a greater percentage come home from the OSC for unpreventable causes. With this adjustment, overall preventable annual attrition runs at 4.0% and 3.4%, respectively, for the OSC and NSC.

The reasons that missionaries leave vary according to the source of the information! First, there are the reasons mission agency leaders will give when requested—their perceptions. The bulk of this study focused on these perceptions. Second, there are the recorded reasons which may be found in the official documents held by the society, which this study also gathered. Third, there are the reasons which the missionary who leaves may give, which would have been impossible to address in a study such as this. In this survey, both the perceived and the recorded reasons were

RECORDED / PERCEIVED REASONS THAT MISSIONARIES RETURNED HOME			
Reason	Overall %	OSC %	NSC %
Unpreventable	29 / 24	36 / 29	13 / 16
Personal	23 / 25	20 / 21	28 / 32
Marriage/Family	13 / 13	15 / 17	11 / 9
Society	11 / 12	9 / 10	15 / 15
Work-related	10 / 10	9 / 8	13 / 12
Team	6 / 9	4 / 8	9 / 10
Cultural	2 / 5	2 / 5	2 / 5
Other	6 / 2	5 / 2	9 / 1
Total (=100%)	4,131	2,893	1,238

Figure 6-4

requested. These are compared in Figure 6-4.

The ReMAP survey showed that the perception by leaders of why their missionaries left was not always accurate—or perhaps it was deemed better not to record in writing (for fear of being sued?) the "real" reason, and a "safe" reason was substituted instead. If this sounds like harsh judgment, it is not meant to be so, and it is written in all Christian charity, conscious that many leaders know the pain felt when people leave a mission to which they have devoted years of their lives, and the leaders do not wish to add to that pain by writing something that some might feel is somehow unfair. This issue was almost entirely seen in the two main causes of leaving—unpreventable and personal. Leaders were more likely to write down an unpreventable reason than they believed was actually the case (29% to 24%). By the same token, they were more reluctant to write down a personal reason than they thought was actually the case (23% to 25%). These variations are not huge, but they are significant.

The NSC were less likely to record unpreventable or personal reasons, but they recorded "other" reasons much more than they believed actually happened (9% to 1%). In the OSC, two other factors also appeared. Mission leaders recorded marriage or family reasons for departure slightly less than they felt was actually the case (15% against 17%), and they recorded problems with the team much less than they believed was the reason (4% against 8%).

The "actual" reasons were measured over the years 1992–1994, and the "believed" reasons would have been based on the leaders' experience, mostly over a much longer period. It is always possible that the years 1992–1994 were special in a mission's losses, but this is most unlikely to be a valid explanation of the observed differences in all but a handful of cases. The variations therefore are almost certain to be real, and they probably express a type of pastoral concern by the agency leaders. This is both good news and bad news—good for the heart of concern it represents, but bad in that it could mean that some missionaries are not brought face to face with issues relevant to them, which, if worked through, would strengthen them for their future ministry.

MOST IMPORTANT REASONS

Societies were asked to identify the seven most important reasons they believed missionaries had left their agency in the previous five years. They were then asked to indicate which was the most important, the second most important, on up to the seventh most important reason. It should be noted that these reasons related to missionaries leaving the agency, rather than returning home per se, as some who returned home might have been offered another job in their home country with the same agency. These individuals would not qualify for inclusion. Likewise, it should be noted that the study was primarily concerned with long-term missionaries, not short-term, although some of the reasons why short-termers might come back prematurely could be the same. In order to be able to examine the detail of the results more easily, the various stages of importance in leaving have been amalgamated into a single score. This was done by giving each order of importance a value or weight rather than taking a simple average, since that would give equal weight to all categories of importance.

The weight used was 7 points for the item of most importance, 6 points for the item of second importance, 5 points for the third most important item, etc., down to 1 point for the seventh. Thus an overall table may be drawn up, the results of which are given in Figure 6-5. The numbers in the "Total" row give the sum of the number of reasons in each group multiplied by the appropriate weight for that order of importance.

Half of the curtailments to missionary service come from either unpreventable reasons or personal reasons. This is so for both the OSC and NSC, with unpreventable reasons being slightly more important in the OSC, but personal reasons being twice as likely in the NSC.

Marriage/family and society reasons account for a further quarter of reasons that missionaries come home, with marriage/family being more important for the OSC and society reasons for the NSC.

Work-related, team, cultural, and other reasons account for the remaining quarter of reasons, with work-related and team reasons being rather more important in the NSC than in the OSC.

Figure 6-6 lists all of the various reasons for leaving missionary service as a weighted percentage of the total number of times each was ticked in the overall order. After the double vertical line, the ranked order of these reasons is shown, ignoring "other" reasons for this purpose.

It is patently obvious that the reasons for leaving vary enormously between the two groups of countries. Of the overall top five reasons—normal retirement, children, change of job, health problems, and lack of home support— four appear in the list for the OSC, but only one is in the top for the NSC, and it is the first in order for them! This one (lack of home support) is the fifth one for the OSC. The orders of the lists are so different that it is actually misleading to look at the overall figures and talk about the "top five" reasons. They simply aren't the top five in reality, when the country of origin is taken into consideration.

Figures 6-7 and 6-8 give the country detail, but arranged in the rank order given above for the OSC and NSC, respectively. The variations in order for individual countries can be readily seen, but they are far less dramatic. In Figure 6-7, even amongst the OSC the main cause of returning home varies. It is normal retirement for the North American societies and the UK. For those on Continental Europe the main cause of returning home is personal concerns in Germany, and children and marrying outside the mission in Denmark. In Australia it is changing jobs. However, the top four reasons listed

OVERALL WEIGHTED REASONS FOR LEAVING THE AGENCY			
Reason	Overall %	OSC %	NSC %
Unpreventable	24	29	16
Personal	25	21	32
Marriage/Family	13	17	9
Society	12	10	15
Work-related	10	8	12
Team	9	8	10
Cultural	5	5	5
Other	2	2	1
Total (=100%)	13,302	8,270	5,032

Figure 6-5

	Overall %	OSC %	NSC %	Rank Order All	OSC	NSC
TOTAL WEIGHTED REASONS FOR LEAVING MISSIONARY SERVICE						
Reason						
Normal retirement	9.4	13.2	3.2	1	1	14
Child(ren)	8.1	10.1	4.8	2	2	8
Change of job	7.4	8.9	4.9	3	3	7
Health problems	7.2	8.4	5.1	4	4	6
Lack of home support	6.2	5.0	8.1	5	7	1
Problems with peers	5.9	6.0	5.7	6	5	5
Personal concerns	4.9	5.2	4.5	7	6	9=
Disagreement with agency	4.7	3.9	6.1	8	8	4
Inadequate commitment	4.4	2.7	7.3	9	14	3
Lack of call	4.1	1.8	8.0	10	19	2
Outside marriage	3.6	3.4	4.0	11	11	12=
Immature spiritual life	3.3	2.5	4.5	12=	15	9=
Marriage/family conflict	3.3	3.6	2.8	12=	10	16=
Poor cultural adaptation	3.1	3.2	3.0	14	12	15
Problems with local leaders	2.9	2.2	4.0	15=	16=	12=
Elderly parents	2.9	3.8	1.3	15=	9	24
Inappropriate training	2.7	1.6	4.5	17	20	9=
Lack of job satisfaction	2.6	2.9	2.2	18	13	20=
Political crisis	2.4	2.2	2.8	19	16=	16=
Inadequate supervision	2.1	2.0	2.3	20	18	19
Death in service	1.6	1.3	2.2	21=	21	20=
Dismissal by agency	1.6	1.0	2.5	21=	23=	18
Immoral lifestyle	1.4	0.9	2.2	23	25	20=
Language problems	1.3	1.2	1.5	24	22	23
Theological reasons	1.0	1.0	1.1	25	23=	25
Other	1.9	2.0	1.4			
Total weighted (=100%)	13,302	8,270	5,032			

Figure 6-6

Reason	OSC %	Australia %	Denmark %	Germany %	UK %	Canada %	USA %
WEIGHTED REASONS FOR LEAVING MISSIONARY SERVICE ITEMISED BY OLD SENDING COUNTRIES							
Normal retirement	13.2	11.5	11.1	5.1	14.1	18.6	13.7
Child(ren)	10.1	11.4	17.5	8.6	13.7	11.0	8.8
Change of job	8.9	11.8	10.6	9.7	11.3	5.4	8.0
Health problems	8.4	10.1	15.3	9.8	10.0	8.1	7.4
Problems w/ peers	6.0	4.1	0.8	5.7	3.9	4.2	7.3
Personal concerns	5.2	5.8	5.1	16.0	4.5	2.4	4.5
Lack of home support	5.0	2.8	0.0	0.0	3.7	8.7	6.1
Disagreement w/ agency	3.9	3.1	1.7	2.2	2.3	1.0	4.9
Elderly parents	3.8	4.2	0.0	6.6	4.7	5.9	3.3
Marriage/family conflict	3.6	3.7	0.0	2.1	2.1	0.0	4.5
Outside marriage	3.4	3.5	17.4	7.6	5.0	4.7	1.9
Poor cultural adaptation	3.2	3.0	2.5	3.3	2.0	1.9	3.6
Lack of job satisfaction	2.9	1.9	1.3	5.0	4.4	3.4	2.7
Inadequate commitment	2.7	3.8	0.0	2.2	1.8	4.2	2.7
Immature spiritual life	2.5	2.2	0.0	1.3	2.4	3.5	2.7
Political crisis	2.2	0.0	9.2	3.3	3.2	1.6	2.1
Problems w/ local leaders	2.2	3.2	4.6	0.4	3.3	2.6	1.8
Inadequate supervision	2.0	1.2	0.0	0.1	0.7	1.0	2.8
Lack of call	1.8	1.4	0.0	1.6	0.6	3.3	2.1
Inappropriate training	1.6	3.0	0.0	0.1	0.5	1.5	1.7
Death in service	1.3	2.0	0.0	1.4	1.8	1.3	1.1
Language problems	1.2	0.7	1.2	1.2	0.6	0.6	1.5
Theological reasons	1.0	0.4	0.0	1.7	0.0	1.9	1.2
Dismissal by agency	1.0	0.7	1.3	1.2	0.1	0.2	1.3
Immoral lifestyle	0.9	0.7	0.0	0.6	0.4	0.4	1.2
Other	2.0	3.8	0.4	3.2	2.9	2.6	1.1
Total weighted (=100%)	8,270	1,059	241	464	941	473	5,092

Figure 6-7

WEIGHTED REASONS FOR LEAVING MISSIONARY SERVICE
ITEMISED BY NEW SENDING COUNTRIES

Reason	NSC %	Brazil %	Costa Rica %	Ghana %	Nigeria %	India %	Korea %	Philippines %	Singapore %
Lack of home support	8.1	7.9	12.7	8.0	7.6	6.3	8.4	13.9	2.6
Lack of call	8.0	5.0	0.0	12.7	15.3	3.7	6.1	7.5	0.0
Inadequate commitment	7.3	7.8	5.6	9.5	9.7	10.9	3.4	6.3	3.3
Disagreement w/ agency	6.1	6.2	4.5	6.2	7.4	9.5	4.3	4.1	17.3
Problems w/ peers	5.7	7.4	12.8	2.3	0.0	6.8	8.8	5.7	7.9
Health problems	5.1	2.8	8.0	2.5	6.0	4.1	7.4	6.0	3.3
Change of job	4.9	2.6	3.9	4.1	1.9	1.6	6.3	5.8	22.3
Child(ren)	4.8	2.9	2.7	3.7	3.0	5.3	7.4	3.4	7.5
Personal concerns	4.5	7.5	0.0	4.0	4.2	4.1	3.2	3.9	4.4
Immature spiritual life	4.5	4.4	0.0	5.1	7.9	8.9	5.8	4.5	0.0
Inappropriate training	4.5	8.4	5.5	6.8	3.2	0.4	3.5	0.6	2.4
Outside marriage	4.0	6.5	0.0	0.3	3.2	1.4	6.3	6.8	3.9
Problems w/ local leaders	4.0	0.9	7.5	6.9	3.6	0.4	2.8	5.5	2.4
Normal retirement	3.2	1.7	0.0	4.1	3.4	3.7	3.2	5.5	0.0
Poor cultural adaptation	3.0	3.0	3.9	2.8	2.2	3.7	3.2	1.2	0.0
Marriage/family conflict	2.8	1.9	8.1	0.9	2.0	2.5	3.9	4.4	3.3
Political crisis	2.8	0.3	10.3	3.6	4.1	0.0	4.1	0.8	0.0
Dismissal by agency	2.5	5.4	3.9	2.1	6.5	4.8	1.2	0.3	0.0
Inadequate supervision	2.3	1.7	4.6	1.7	0.6	3.8	3.4	0.5	3.2
Lack of job satisfaction	2.2	3.2	0.0	3.3	1.7	1.2	0.4	2.9	4.7
Immoral lifestyle	2.2	3.8	5.1	2.5	3.2	2.4	0.5	1.8	0.0
Death in service	2.2	0.3	0.0	1.6	0.9	7.5	2.7	2.3	0.0
Language problems	1.5	2.4	0.0	2.3	0.6	0.8	2.3	0.3	0.0
Elderly parents	1.3	1.7	0.9	0.4	0.3	2.7	0.8	4.0	7.5
Theological reasons	1.1	0.3	0.0	2.1	1.5	2.2	0.3	1.6	0.0
Other	1.4	4.0	0.0	0.5	0.0	1.3	0.3	0.4	4.0
Total weighted (=100%)	5,032	577	128	1,456	359	552	1,358	476	126

Figure 6-8

above are high on the list for all the countries given.

The fifth reason, problems with one's fellow missionaries, is high on the list because of its high placing in agencies in the USA. It is much lower down for the other countries, including Canada. Note the relatively high percentage of people leaving because of outside marriage in Germany, the problems of political crises for Danish organisations, and the difficulties of lack of home support and elderly parents in Canadian agencies. Lack of home support is third for the Canadians and sixth for the Americans, but it doesn't feature at all for the Continental European societies! Elderly parents are the sixth on the list for Australian, German, and British organisations.

In the NSC in Figure 6-8, lack of home support tops the list of only one country, the Philippines, though it is second for Brazil, Costa Rica, and Korea. It is third for Ghana, fourth for Nigeria, sixth for India, and 13th for Singapore. Problems with missionary peers tops the list for Costa Rican and Korean missionaries and is third for Singaporeans. A lack of call is the major reason for coming home in the African countries of Ghana and Nigeria, and it is the second most important factor for Filipino agencies.

Inadequate commitment is the major problem for Indian missions. It is the second most important difficulty for Ghanaian and Nigerian societies, is third in rank for those in Brazil, and is fourth in the Philippines. Disagreements with the sending organisation are the second most likely reason for coming home for those from India or Singapore, the fifth for Nigeria, and the sixth for Ghana. These problems are not only quite different from those affecting OSC missions, but they require different types of solutions. Some are related more to spiritual and structural issues than to age, family, or health issues, which afflict the OSC. Other problems, such as relationships, are of equal importance to all countries—problems with peers is fifth on both lists.

RESEARCH DESIGN AND DATA ANALYSIS

The following comments relate to the design and data analysis of the ReMAP research project.

First, language is always a problem in international surveys. A word that means one thing to one nationality may mean something different to another, even when both are using the same language, English, to communicate. Thus, while the ReMAP survey was about mission attrition, we have had to assume that each country has understood the meaning of that word in the same way and that each person who completed a form in each country thought likewise. Since great care was taken to explain and discuss every concept at the beginning of the study, when all the researchers gathered together, we trust this problem has been minimised, although it will not have been completely eliminated.

Second, the questionnaire deliberately asked for both "hard" (quantitative) and "soft" (qualitative) data. The hard data came from records and from counts made of different cases. The soft data are people's opinions. There is no reason not to collect both types of data. Qualitative data are useful, as they generally give a greater understanding of the material. This was so in this study.

Third, it is true that not every mission sending agency in each country answered the questionnaire. No survey gets 100% response! The total number of mission agencies was known in five of the 14 countries, and in these between a quarter and a half replied. But the number of agencies in a country which are *sending* agencies is less than the total, and we do not have the number of sending agencies in any country. If we had, the response rate would have been higher. It might be argued that our figures are not representative, because an unknown number of similar agencies in each country did not reply. This is a normal problem with any sample survey. The normal method of procedure is to assume that those who did not reply are similar to those who did reply. The ReMAP survey followed this procedure.

Fourth, it is recognised that some causes of attrition are more relevant to those who have served for many years, while others are more likely to occur in short-term missionaries. This study did not distinguish these categories as such, not because we felt that such variations were not valid, but because we felt that it was important that the main causes of attrition be ascertained first, thus enabling any subsequent study to build on these results, rather than undertaking a long and expensive study in the first place. The ReMAP research should be seen as a starter study, not a definitive answer to the causes of attrition.

Fifth, only relatively simple analyses have been made of the data, so that the results can be understood in the many countries where English is not the first language. More complicated analyses, such as those involving analysis of variance, correlations, or cluster analysis, could have been undertaken, but they were not, since the number of control (or dependent) variables was small.

Sixth, we have assumed that attrition is a problem. It probably is, but it might also be regarded as a transitional phase through which all sending agencies pass. The main reasons for departure may lead to changes by mission leaders, which means that older agencies will tend to have different reasons from younger agencies. How far the types of attrition are simply a transitional phase is not discussed.

Finally, it should be noted that "attrition" and "quitting" are not necessarily the same. Measuring one is not a measurement of the other. And we are called to serve God wherever He puts us, even if we return home.

FINAL THOUGHTS ON WHY MISSIONARIES COME HOME "EARLY"

In this study, the top four preventable reasons for missionary attrition were those designated personal, marriage/family, society, and work-related. These same reasons are cited in numerous other studies. So, what do we do about these results?

There is no shortage of suggestions! Phil Parshall (1975) gives a powerful plea to rethink missionary priorities, both on the field and during home assignment. David Cummings (1987), a past president of Wycliffe Bible Translators, asks for mission boards to help young missionaries grow out of their ingrained, individualistic home culture by investing "the time and energy to model, teach, and disciple these keen young people." Glenn Herr (1987) wants local churches to arrange an accountability programme for their missionaries. Harold Fife (1970) emphasizes the importance of pastoral care, and Robert Eagle (1984) advises on how to handle stress. Dr. Marjory Foyle (1987), in her classic *Honourably Wounded*, focuses on how Christian workers should handle stress, especially in cross-cultural situations; the book ought to be required reading for every missionary.

There are perhaps the following types of issues:

1. Management issues. These matters should be handled before someone leaves for the field. What should a missionary do if his or her parent(s) become(s) ill? What will happen with respect to the education of the children? For the NSC, the questions to be asked relate to what happens if there is a breakdown in support or a problem with the directions given by the agency's leaders. How will poor health be handled? Some of these questions mean more information, more strategic planning, and more answering of "what if" type questions. The size of a society might be important here.

2. Spiritual/pastoral issues. These issues ultimately require someone to be available to the missionary for counsel. This person may be someone on the field in a supervisory position, a friend, or a leader from the home church, but a person to whom the individual missionary can relate. In that relationship, problems such as uncertainty regarding the call and ambivalence regarding commitment can be dealt with. The counselor can pray with the missionary for support, understanding, and wis-

dom in a different culture. The pastoral counselor should probably be a person who has the authority to allow failure whilst urging renewed dedication. The main reasons for preventing loss are all under this heading.

3. Leadership issues. These concerns relate to vision, balance, and overview—seeing things in proportion, being able to discern the key elements in a situation, knowing how much of resources to allocate (time or money), and being able to relate the people in the parts to the process as a whole. Where is the organisation going? What does the society want to become? Such questions not only enable people to get excited, but also help them see their part in the overall scheme of things. Having a blueprint in mind also means missionaries can be brought back to the plan when life gets very tough.

DIRECTIONS FOR FUTURE RESEARCH ON ATTRITION

As we evaluate the long-term process of ReMAP, bringing us to the conclusion of this stage of the research, the following avenues of further research are suggested.

1. Replication. It would be worth considering the possibility of replicating this study in five years' time, ideally with the same societies and countries. While it may be difficult to survey the very same agencies, the attempt would be valuable. It would also give us opportunity to measure one of our goals in ReMAP, which was to significantly reduce the attrition rates in those agencies which participated in the 1995–1996 study.

2. Extension to other countries. Another potentially valuable option is to extend this same study to other countries which did not participate in the first study. This would enable us to strengthen our current analysis based on lessons learned in this foundational project.

3. Qualitative research. Changing the thrust of the research would enable us to explore some categories of "qualitative research," which would focus less on broader numbers and statistics and more on personal case studies. For example, we could analyse the differences among the three types of reasons that missionaries leave the field: the so-called "real" reasons, the "recorded" reason in the personnel file in a mission's headquarters, and the mission leader's "believed" reason as to why that missionary resigned. The present study identified some differences between the "recorded" and the "believed" reasons, and at least one other study has seen differences between "real" and "recorded" reasons. These differences lead us to believe that there are many such discrepancies among the three categories. Identifying what they are and how great these variances are would be of great value to both missionaries and leaders.

4. Reasons for dominance. Yet another alternative would be to elaborate on why certain causes of attrition dominate, especially in the personal and marriage/family areas. Are the factors behind these reasons largely circumstantial, or do they arise from mission policies?

5. Expectations. One cause of loss is lack of job satisfaction, especially in the UK. What are the expectations that missionaries have? Could a study look at a cohort of missionaries over a longer period of time? For example: (a) before they leave for field service; (b) after two years on the field; (c) at the end of their first home leave; (d) halfway through their second term; (e) at the end of the second term. How far were expectations met? How far did vision change? How far did the reality of the actual task change expectations?

6. Assessment. Should research be undertaken in the way that potential missionaries are assessed? To what degree is their spirituality observed, and can this personal aspect even be evaluated by another person? In this light, we remember the significant percentage of NSC agencies that stated a lack of call as the reason for early departure from the field.

7. Variation. Finally, does attrition vary more in some countries than others? If so, why? Do pastoral care and supervision vary over time? Does the attrition rate in a particular country vary over time?

A CONCLUDING WORD

The contemporary word is partnership. We need to look at the promises and pitfalls, as Bill Taylor (1995) says in a recent article. He quotes Phill Butler, Lausanne Senior Associate for Partnerships and President of Interdev, who has given 16 key partnership principles for organisations and societies working together. These principles are true internally as well as externally. Mission is about partnerships—at home, through the agency, on the field. "Effective partnerships," says Butler, "are built on trust, openness, and mutual concern." This isn't just good long-term strategy—it is actually the heart of the gospel.

APPENDIX:
TABLES AND OTHER DATA
RELATED TO THE RESEARCH

THE MOST IMPORTANT REASONS FOR PREVENTING LOSS OF CAREER MISSIONARIES						
	Percent of Mission Agencies Which Ranked the Specified Reason in ...					
	1st Place		2nd Place		3rd Place	
Reason	OSC %	NSC %	OSC %	NSC %	OSC %	NSC %
A clear calling to mission work from God	36	61	31	18	4	5
A very supportive family and/or spouse	42	21	5	2	3	1
Regular contact with friends, church, and prayer partners from home	7	7	4	5	2	2
Good relationships with other missionaries and colleagues	6	2	15	16	11	4
Regular supervision, pastoral care, and other support	3	5	13	14	5	9
Ability to adapt to different cultures and learn languages	2	1	15	17	21	9
Good relationships with supervisors and the missionary society	2	0	4	6	5	5
Regular financial provision from home country	0	2	8	11	8	18
Ability to maintain a healthy spirituality without external support	0	1	3	1	29	36
Ability to cope with stress and heavy workloads	0	0	1	6	10	2
Provision of appropriate and regular training	0	0	1	4	1	9
Other factors	2	0	0	0	1	0
Total (=100%)	212	199	207	199	205	194

Other factors included a clear sense of identity, a healthy self-image, and prayer support. This table shows the importance placed upon the call, the family, relationships with others, supervision, the ability to adapt, and the importance of a healthy spirituality. A simple totalling of the percentages across the page gives the following in terms of order:

A clear call	155%
A supportive family	74%
A healthy spirituality	70%
Cultural adaptation	65%
Good relationships	54%
Pastoral care	49%
Financial provision	47%

None of the other elements total as much as 25%, so these are clearly the top seven reasons for preventing attrition. The split between OSC and NSC is not significant with respect to the call, spirituality, cultural adaptation, good relationships with colleagues, or pastoral care. But it is the OSC which focus very heavily on the need for a supportive family (50% to 24%), and it is the NSC which focus on the need for adequate financial provision (31% to 16%). These emphases agree with the earlier findings.

Figure 6-9

PERCENT OF AGENCIES
SERVING SPECIFIED NUMBER OF CAREER MISSIONARIES

Country	None*	1–10	11–25	26–50	51–100	101–200	201–500	>500	Total # Agen. (=100%)
Australia	5	36	21	12	17	9	0	0	42
Canada	0	36	18	27	14	5	0	0	22
Denmark	0	30	60	10	0	0	0	0	10
Germany	5	24	28	5	24	14	0	0	21
UK	8	21	13	20	13	20	5	0	39
USA	1	22	21	22	11	11	8	4	207
Avg: OSC	2	25	22	20	13	11	5	2	341
Brazil	0	9	32	23	23	4	9	0	22
Costa Rica	0	57	29	14	0	0	0	0	7
Ghana	0	52	21	19	6	0	2	0	52
India	5	15	15	20	15	15	10	5	20
Korea	0	44	24	16	8	2	3	3	63
Nigeria	0	29	43	21	0	7	0	0	14
Philippines	0	33	17	22	17	11	0	0	18
Singapore	0	29	43	28	0	0	0	0	7
Avg: NSC	0	37	25	19	9	4	4	2	203
Avg: World	2	29	23	19	11	9	5	2	544

* The figures in this column reflect agencies which have no career missionaries, only short-term workers.

Figure 6-10

PERCENT OF AGENCIES
SENDING OUT MISSIONARIES FOR SPECIFIED NUMBER OF YEARS

Country	<1	1–2	3–10	11–25	26–50	51–100	>100	Total # Agen. (=100%)
Australia	0	0	12	9	28	28	23	43
Canada	0	0	9	14	38	10	29	21
Denmark	0	0	0	0	10	70	20	10
Germany	0	0	9	29	38	24	0	21
UK	0	0	10	15	23	26	26	39
USA	0	0	7	27	30	28	8	205
Avg: OSC	0	0	8	22	29	28	13	339
Brazil	0	0	27	36	14	18	5	22
Costa Rica	0	0	71	29	0	0	0	7
Ghana	4	10	50	17	13	6	0	52
India	0	0	45	35	20	0	0	20
Korea	0	2	70	23	2	3	0	64
Nigeria	0	7	50	43	0	0	0	14
Philippines	0	6	22	39	33	0	0	18
Singapore	0	0	29	57	14	0	0	7
Avg: NSC	1	4	51	28	11	4	1	204
Avg: World	0	2	24	24	22	19	9	543

Figure 6-11

	PERCENT OF AGENCIES THAT REQUIRE SPECIFIED TYPES OF TRAINING										
Country	Type of Training									Avg	Total # Agen. (=100%)
	A	B	C	D	E	F	G	H	I		
Australia	82	61	32	34	23	39	7	23	2	34	44
Canada	82	77	32	32	18	9	5	18	0	30	22
Denmark	67	67	33	67	22	33	11	11	0	35	9
Germany	62	86	33	52	19	19	10	24	0	34	21
UK	67	54	28	28	26	23	5	21	10	29	39
USA	62	58	28	48	33	14	7	27	8	32	200
Avg: OSC	67	61	29	43	28	19	7	24	7	32	335
Brazil	50	46	59	27	32	41	5	14	14	32	22
Costa Rica	43	71	43	57	43	43	0	0	14	35	7
Ghana	46	87	77	44	48	52	21	10	4	43	52
India	43	33	67	43	33	10	14	14	0	29	21
Korea	60	64	52	40	30	33	10	25	0	35	63
Nigeria	64	29	71	29	50	36	7	0	0	32	14
Philippines	53	53	41	59	59	18	12	24	0	35	17
Singapore	86	57	43	71	43	29	0	43	0	41	7
Avg: NSC	54	61	60	42	40	36	12	17	3	36	203
Avg: World	62	61	41	43	33	25	9	21	5	33	538

A: Cross-cultural orientation
B: Completion of a theological course or other professional training
C: Completion of your organisation's own course in missiological studies
D: Completion of a non-formal missionary training programme
E: A short-term experience of living in a different culture
F: Formal qualification in missiological studies other than a degree
G: Degree course in missiological studies
H: Other skills
I: None required

Figure 6-12

PERCENT OF AGENCIES THAT EVALUATE
CAREER CANDIDATES IN SPECIFIED AREAS

Country	A	B	C	D	E	F	G	H	I	J	K	L	M	N	Avg	Total # Agen. (=100%)
Australia	89	98	93	98	86	77	75	52	64	68	30	18	16	23	63	44
Canada	100	96	96	91	91	77	86	64	73	82	27	18	9	14	66	22
Denmark	60	80	80	100	90	70	50	30	30	50	20	40	20	0	51	10
Germany	86	95	91	91	76	57	67	24	29	5	29	14	19	10	50	21
UK	97	100	90	100	80	82	82	62	62	77	31	5	26	21	65	39
USA	94	93	94	85	77	76	73	63	65	58	44	21	9	13	62	202
Avg: OSC	92	94	93	89	80	76	74	58	62	59	37	19	13	15	62	338
Brazil	82	91	73	59	46	68	55	36	64	32	23	32	18	14	50	22
Costa Rica	86	100	86	86	86	71	57	57	57	29	57	14	14	14	58	7
Ghana	94	96	92	58	79	60	62	79	33	31	35	33	8	8	55	52
India	91	76	86	62	38	48	33	24	19	24	57	5	29	14	43	21
Korea	98	59	62	87	59	56	54	56	75	37	43	38	41	19	56	63
Nigeria	93	79	86	50	64	64	50	50	14	29	36	7	7	0	45	14
Philippines	94	89	194	83	83	67	78	83	56	56	78	6	33	22	66	18
Singapore	86	100	86	100	71	100	86	86	57	71	43	14	29	29	68	7
Avg: NSC	93	80	79	72	64	61	57	59	50	36	43	26	24	14	54	204
Avg: World	93	89	88	83	74	70	68	59	57	50	40	22	17	14	59	542

A: A clear statement of God's calling for mission service
B: Personal character references, such as from the candidate's church
C: Acceptance of missionary society's doctrinal statement
D: Evaluation of health
E: Previous experience of church work
F: Evaluation of a candidate's marriage or singleness
G: Evaluation of communication and relationship skills
H: Evaluation of leadership and pastoral skills
I: Firm promises of financial support
J: Psychological and/or personality testing
K: Previous experience of missionary type work
L: Ordination or equivalent
M: Limits on the age or number of children, or other family restrictions
N: Other conditions

Figure 6-13

REFERENCES

Back, P., & Johnson, A. (1988). *Toughing it out? A study of missionary orientation and attrition for OMF International.* London, UK: MARC Europe.

Brierley, P. W. (1986). *EMA personnel survey 1986.* London, UK: MARC Europe.

Brierley, P. W. (1997). *World churches handbook.* Based on P. Johnstone's *Operation World* database. London, UK: Christian Research and Lausanne Committee for World Evangelization.

Bushong, B. H. (1986). Why do they leave? Reflections on attrition: World Gospel Mission. *Evangelical Missions Quarterly,* **22**, 129.

Cummings, D. (1987). Programmed for failure: Mission candidates at risk. *Evangelical Missions Quarterly,* **23**, 240-246.

Eagle, R. L. (1984). Positive possibilities of mid-life transitions. *Evangelical Missions Quarterly,* **20**(1), 38-45.

Fife, H. W. (1970). The pastoral care of missionaries. *Evangelical Missions Quarterly,* **7**(1), 19-23.

Foyle, M. (1987). *Honourably wounded.* London, UK, and Wheaton, IL: MARC Europe, Evangelical Missionary Alliance, Interserve, and Evangelical Missions Information Service.

Herr, G. (1987). Doing your job: Does your church care? *Evangelical Missions Quarterly,* **23**, 42-45.

Johnstone, P. (1986). *Operation World.* London and Bucks, UK: STL and WEC International.

Johnstone, P. (1993). *Operation World.* Grand Rapids, MI: Zondervan.

Parshall, P. (1975). A "dropout syndrome" you can overcome. *Evangelical Missions Quarterly,* **11**(4), 223-227.

Pate, L. D. (1989). *From every people: A handbook of Two-Thirds World missions with directory/histories/analysis.* Monrovia, CA: MARC.

Taylor, W. D. (1995). Lessons of partnership. *Evangelical Missions Quarterly,* **31**, 406-415.

Peter W. Brierley is a statistician who is Executive Director of Christian Research, a charity which undertakes surveys for churches and Christian organisations and publishes resource books. Previously, he was responsible for MARC Europe, a body dedicated to strengthening Christian leadership, which closed in 1993. He has also worked as a teacher (3 years), for the British Government (Defence, 3 years; Cabinet Office, 8 years), and as Programme Director of the British and Foreign Bible Society (5 years). He lives in south London with his wife Cherry. They have four children aged 24–30.

7

Further Findings In the Research Data

Detlef Blöcher and Jonathan Lewis

Why are there so many casualties in world missions—good people who are lost to the cause? To answer this crucial question, in February 1995, the World Evangelical Fellowship (WEF) Missions Commission launched a study called the Reducing Missionary Attrition Project (ReMAP), involving old sending countries (OSC) such as USA, England, and Australia and new sending countries (NSC) such as Brazil, Nigeria, and India. The data gathered in the 14-country, 453-agency study were then processed and analyzed by Peter Brierley of Christian Research.

Brierley's report (see chapter 6) was shared at the WEF Missions Commission's Consultation on Missionary Attrition in April 1996, at All Nations Christian College, England. These findings provoked further questions, which caused us to look at the data in a differ-

ent manner, as described in Appendix A to this chapter, pages 119–122.[1]

DETERMINING PAR

Missionary attrition includes both expected or unpreventable factors, such as retirement or death, and factors that are preventable and that we can possibly do something about, if we understand the causes and apply ourselves to the cures. We first set out to establish the preventable missionary attrition rate as the most important quantifiable element, against which all other factors would be compared.

In dealing with attrition as a problem, we must subtract unpreventable factors from the equation, since every missionary is an attrition case after 40 years or so, but that is not really our concern here. Also, for statistical analysis, young agencies do not yet have a great loss due to retirement, so includ-

---

1. The statistics presented in this chapter may differ from those given in other chapters. There are three reasons for the variations: (1) Peter Brierley's calculations (chapter 6) were based on the first examination of the data. (2) The analysis in this chapter used additional data and looked at the data from a different perspective, asking different questions. (3) Some of the statistics in the national case studies reflect new surveys and different ways of reading the numbers.

ing this unpreventable attrition element in the total loss leads to a distortion of the overall picture. We have focused, therefore, on the preventable attrition rate, which for the purpose of this study we have denominated PAR to help the reader distinguish it from the general attrition rate for all reasons and from the unpreventable attrition rate, which we have designated UAR.

When we try to calculate the loss per agency, it makes a big difference whether 2 missionaries out of 10 are lost or 2 out of 1,000. Thus the most useful figure is an attrition rate that is expressed in terms of a ratio of loss per number of missionaries on the field, per year. In this study, the number of missionaries on the field is only available in groupings by relative agency size (Q4 of the questionnaire[2]). This is a limiting factor of the analysis.

It would have been more reliable to know exactly how many missionaries each agency has on the field. Since an exact quantification of attrition per agency wasn't the original intent of the ReMAP study, the questionnaire did not collect this precise figure (doing so might have proved too threatening to those submitting the information). Nevertheless, attrition rates could be determined for agencies grouped by size, and this figure was used in both the Brierley report and this one. Although grouping involves some assumptions, care was taken to obtain the most reliable statistical information possible.

In addition to determining PARs, we also wanted to understand which significant relationships existed between PARs and demographic features of mission agencies, such as size, age, origin, and type of field or work. We were also interested in relationships between PAR and procedural factors, such as selection of missionaries, their training, kinds of field support and supervision given to them, and the percentage of time and money dedicated to their pastoral care. Correlational statistics were used to determine how influential each of these variables seems to be in reducing preventable attrition. Information about these areas had been gathered through the original survey instrument and was thus available for analysis.

We have enjoyed reflecting over this information. It is our prayer that the findings we share herein may help to fine tune and, perhaps, reengineer in some cases the work of those dedicated to sending out and maintaining the global missionary force—for the glory of God, the blessing of the church, and the benefit of the unreached who still await salvation in our Lord Jesus Christ.

MISSIONARY CHURCHES VS. MISSION AGENCIES

The study solicited information from missionary sending churches as well as dedicated mission agencies. The range in the number of missionaries sent by these churches was unexpectedly wide: 13 churches had sent out 1–10 missionaries; 16 churches, 11–25 missionaries; 18 churches, 26–50 missionaries; 5 churches, 51–100 missionaries; and 2 churches, 101–200 missionaries. It is clear that many of these churches fit better into the category of a denomina-

---

2. For a listing of the survey questions, refer to the survey instrument, which is reproduced on pages 363–370.

tion rather than single church units. Do these churches do better than agencies in keeping their missionaries on the field?

To answer this question, we compared the subset of 54 churches to the 357 dedicated mission agencies. The total attrition rate for sending churches was lower: 4.91±0.60% per year vs. 5.79±0.10% for mission agencies. Unpreventable attrition was also lower: 1.16±0.35% vs. 1.70±0.10%. The PAR for churches was 3.75±0.60%, compared with 4.10±0.10% for mission agencies.

However, the church sending agencies were smaller than the mission agencies (29.3 missionaries per agency vs. 60.4). They were also younger (61% of the sending churches have been commissioning missionaries for 25 years or less), and they dedicate less means for missionary care (57% of the churches but only 42% of agencies invest 10% or less of their time for missionary care; 59% of churches vs. 44% of agencies dedicate 10% or less of their finances for member care). When statistical adjust-

ments are made for the more rapid growth rate inherent in the younger missions organizations in general (see Appendix B of this chapter, pages 122–123), the PAR of churches about equals that of mission agencies. Because of the close PAR values and because these church missions contributed only 6.3% of the total missionaries included in this study, the decision was made not to segregate the churches from the agencies for this analysis.

DEMOGRAPHIC VARIABLES

Large vs. Small

Having settled the question of whether or not to include churches in the sample to be analyzed, we looked into whether or not the size of the agency influenced the attrition rate. This proved by far to be the most significant demographic factor influencing overall attrition (see Figure 7-1).

It is obvious that both PAR and UAR rates drop tremendously with agency size in new sending countries (NSC) as well as in old sending countries (OSC).

CORRELATION BETWEEN ATTRITION AND SIZE OF MISSION								
Agency Size	Total # Agencies	UAR %	PAR %	Total Loss %	OSC # Agencies	OSC PAR %	NSC # Agencies	NSC PAR %
1–10	121	4.29±0.50	15.70±1.20	20.00±1.60	58	13.22±1.35	63	18.10±1.56
11–25	100	2.60±0.24	7.70±0.44	10.30±0.60	52	7.97±0.66	48	7.38±0.66
26–50	82	1.78±0.16	4.91±0.29	6.69±0.36	47	5.05±0.40	35	4.73±0.44
51–100	49	2.04±0.16	3.91±0.25	5.95±0.34	31	4.46±0.35	18	2.92±0.34
101–200	38	1.93±0.13	4.38±0.25	6.31±0.34	31	4.19±0.28	7	5.02±0.60
201–500	15	1.67±0.24	5.00±0.62	6.67±0.81	8	4.04±0.83	7	5.60±0.87
>500	6	1.78±0.35	3.43±0.65	5.21±0.98	3	3.28±0.76	3	4.22±1.00

UAR % = Annual loss for unpreventable reasons divided by the number of missionaries on the field, expressed as %.
PAR % = Annual loss for preventable reasons divided by the number of missionaries on the field, expressed as %.
Total Loss % = Annual loss of missionaries divided by the number of missionaries on the field, expressed as %.
OSC = Old sending countries (Australia, Canada, Denmark, Germany, UK, USA).
NSC = New sending countries (Brazil, Costa Rica, Ghana, India, South Korea, Nigeria, Philippines, Singapore).

Figure 7-1

GROUPINGS ACCORDING TO SIZE AS DETERMINED BY SIMILARITY IN PARs					
Agency Size	**# Agencies**	**# Missionaries**	**UAR %**	**PAR %**	**Total Loss %**
Size 1: 1–10	121	605	4.29±0.50	15.70±1.20	20.00±1.60
Size 2: 11–25	100	1,600	2.60±0.24	7.70±0.44	10.30±0.60
Size 3: 26–200	169	11,620	1.99±0.08	4.36±0.13	6.35±0.20
Size 4: >200	21	6,061	1.72±0.14	4.01±0.30	5.73±0.43

Missionaries = Estimated total number of missionaries represented by agencies of this size.
UAR % = Annual loss for unpreventable reasons divided by the number of missionaries on the field, expressed as %.
PAR % = Annual loss for preventable reasons divided by the number of missionaries on the field, expressed as %.
Total Loss % = Annual loss of missionaries divided by the number of missionaries on the field, expressed as %.

Figure 7-2

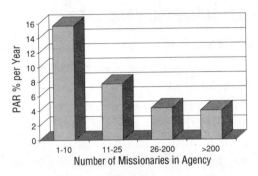

Figure 7-3
PAR as a Function of Agency Size

Although only six agencies fell into the group with >500 missionaries and the statistical accuracy for this group is somewhat limited, we are assuming that the trend is true throughout our range of mission sizes.

We find similar attrition rates for agencies with 26–50, 51–100, and 101–200 missionaries and a similar plateau for 201–500 and >500 missionaries, so that these were grouped for statistical reasons, as shown in Figures 7-2 and 7-3.

Also, since the small agencies represent only some 600 field missionaries (2.5% of our total sample), and since only a few agencies fall into the category >200 missionaries (5.1% of our total sample), we considered the group with 26–200 missionaries to be the most re-liable for statistical analysis (41% of the missions and 48% of the missionaries in our sample).

The discovery of this strong correlation between size and attrition led us to begin speculating on the reasons that this might be true. Does the more developed organizational structure of larger missions create a sense of security for their missionaries? Do they provide better for their members? Is there a "critical mass" of missionaries necessary for survival on the field? Are these missionaries better screened or better trained? We could try to answer only some of these questions with our data set, but our research put us on a productive track.

Young vs. Old

When we first tested the correlation between the age of the agency and preventable attrition, there seemed to be a clear positive relationship, with the exception of the >100 years category, whose attrition rate rose over the 51–100 years category by 1.45%. However, since size is also a function of age in most cases, we ran cross-correlations between these two factors and found that young agencies are in general smaller and thus have a higher PAR, while older agencies are also larger and

PAR AS A FUNCTION OF AGENCY SIZE AND AGE

Agency Size	PAR Total %	PAR % for Agency Age Groups				
		0–10 years	11–25 years	26–50 years	51–100 years	>100 years
1–10	15.70±1.20	16.10±1.80	16.90±2.90	9.80±2.20	15.90±3.80	21.30±7.60
11–25	7.68±0.50	9.04±1.00	7.06±0.80	7.10±1.10	6.08±1.10	9.10±1.80
26–200	4.52±0.13	4.82±0.47	5.52±0.38	3.57±0.23	4.16±0.29	4.79±0.45
>200	2.70±0.20	—	—	2.95±0.40	2.64±0.30	2.18±0.60
Total	4.85±0.11	7.70±0.42	5.36±0.32	3.33±0.20	3.25±0.20	4.70±0.39

Figure 7-4

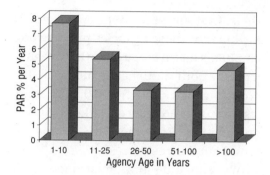

Figure 7-5
PAR as a Function of Agency Age

have a smaller PAR, as reflected in Figures 7-4 and 7-5.

This table also explains why the >100 years agency attrition rate rose as well. These oldest agencies (>100 years) are of significantly smaller average size (66 missionaries) than those of the group 51–100 years (132 missionaries). So size was the determining variable and not age in their higher attrition rate. This finding caused us to ponder why these oldest missions are smaller. Have they failed to grow and maintain their missionaries because they have lost their drive and vision, or are there other factors involved? Are they 19th century denominational missions where there is a pastor position readily available for the returning missionary to drop into? These are questions which await further research.

Old Sending Countries vs. New Sending Countries

For statistical analysis, Peter Brierley's report divided the participating countries into old sending and new sending. Figure 7-6 gives the PARs of the four groups by agency size as it correlates to the OSC and NSC variable.

Both PAR and UAR fall with increasing agency size for both OSC and NSC, as expected. In the NSC, unpreventable attrition is about one-third of what it is

ATTRITION BY SIZE AND BY OSC AND NSC SENDING BASE

	Agency Size	# Agencies	# Missionaries	UAR %	PAR %
Old Sending Countries	1–10	58	290	6.77±0.80	13.20±1.60
	11–25	52	832	3.52±0.35	7.96±0.66
	26–200	109	8,155	2.52±0.20	4.46±0.25
	>200	11	6,829	1.54±0.17	2.50±0.30
New Sending Countries	1–10	63	315	2.01±0.80	18.10±1.80
	11–25	48	768	1.60±0.30	7.37±0.60
	26–200	60	3,465	0.73±0.10	4.65±0.25
	>200	10	3,682	0.60±0.09	3.04±0.30

Figure 7-6

in the OSC. This clearly reflects the youth of the missionary force in the NSC, where retirement has not yet had a significant effect on attrition. In the OSC, the effect of an older mission force is seen in the number of missionary boosters retiring from the force.[3]

The PAR is somewhat higher for NSC agencies. When considered as a whole, and without accounting for statistical skewing, which in the case of some very quickly growing national movements raises the rate considerably (see Appendix B of this chapter, pages 122–123), NSC agency missionaries are somewhat more at risk of preventable attrition (4.37% per year) than those from OSC (3.77% per year).

Same-Culture vs. Cross-Cultural Missionaries

Are cross-cultural workers in a foreign country more prone to attrition? Our correlational analysis showed the opposite to be true. In fact, cross-cultural workers have a (marginally) smaller PAR. In our most statistically reliable group (agencies with 26–200 missionaries, which included 169 agen-

cies with 11,620 missionaries), the PAR was 4.29±0.17% compared to 4.52± 0.13% for same-culture workers.

Pioneer/Church Planting vs. Relief/Support Work

Agencies were asked for their ministry priorities. In Figure 7-7, the preventable attrition rate is given for agencies that stated that a certain ministry was their first or second priority, which means that these agencies put a strong emphasis on this type of work. We again looked at our statistically most reliable group, agencies with 26–200 missionaries, to study the effect of the kind of work on attrition. For other size groups we found similar results.

We conclude that missionaries in pioneer work and cross-cultural ministry do not have a higher PAR (they appear to be hardy people), while those in relief and support ministry do leave more frequently. Is this a factor of short-term vision, are they more easily worn out (overworked), or do they fail to have their expectations met? Another question for further research.

PAR IN KINDS OF MISSIONARY WORK					
Agencies with 26–200 missionaries (169 agencies with 11,620 missionaries)					
Type of Ministry	Agencies Having the Identified Ministry as 1st Priority			Agencies Having the Identified Ministry as 1st or 2nd Priority		
	# Agencies	# Miss.	PAR %	# Agencies	# Miss.	PAR %
Pioneer	50	3,745	4.03±0.23	80	5,810	4.03±0.19
Church planting	49	3,220	4.25±0.27	90	5,565	4.58±0.20
Relief	9	595	7.11±0.98	25	1,890	7.36±0.56
Support	20	1,505	5.66±0.51	37	2,732	4.01±0.30
Total (26–200 miss.)	169	11,620	4.52±0.13			

Figure 7-7

---

3. See chapter 4 for a discussion of the different generations.

PROCEDURAL VARIABLES

There are two ways of looking at the relationship between PAR and procedural variables: (1) Does the kind of procedure affect the PAR (whether the procedure is used or not), and (2) does the number of procedures (overall quantity) affect the PAR? We looked at both areas.

Field Care and Support: What Kind and How Much

Each item on the list for agency support and supervision was analyzed individually to determine which items were the most important. Figure 7-8 summarizes the result for agencies with 26–200 missionaries (a total of 169 agencies, representing 11,620 missionaries).

This analysis shows a clear positive effect only for regular letters or phone calls and a marginal effect for on-the-job training. Surprisingly, the majority of the support items show a negative effect, which means that as single items they are correlated with an increased PAR. The same correlations were found

in all agency size groups. This leads us to the observation that good communication with the missionary may be the single most significant support item in helping lower preventable attrition. It is not likely that the rest of the items in and of themselves actually increase attrition, yet agencies with low attrition rates have invested less into these benefits. This means that support on the field in itself will not keep people in service, unless it has been preceded by careful candidate screening as well as pre-field training and possibly other factors.

On the other hand, the percentage of agencies providing each of these services increases with agency size, with the exception of letters or phone calls, which was constant at a level of about 75% of the agencies irrespective of agency size. Since PAR also drops with agency size, we might conclude that the larger the number of provisions of support and supervision an agency has, the better. But when we isolated this variable and tested it, it actually demon-

KINDS OF SUPPORT AND SUPERVISION AND THEIR EFFECT ON PAR						
Agencies with 26–200 missionaries (169 agencies with 11,620 missionaries)						
Provision	Provided			Not Provided		
	# Agencies	# Miss.	PAR %	# Agencies	# Miss.	PAR %
Field leadership	129	9,380	4.80±0.18	39	2,170	3.42±0.25
Pastoral care	82	5,285	4.62±0.21	85	6,230	4.46±0.20
Job description	95	6,930	5.34±0.22	72	4,585	3.31±0.16
On-the-job training	72	5,425	4.38±0.21	95	6,090	4.68±0.20
Annual leave	120	8,820	4.64±0.18	48	2,730	4.22±0.26
Regular visits on field	100	7,210	5.27±0.22	67	4,305	3.31±0.18
Provision for children	90	7,070	5.02±0.22	77	4,445	3.77±0.16
Team structure	105	7,630	4.82±0.19	63	3,920	4.01±0.17
Letters or phone calls	136	9,030	4.32±0.16	33	2,520	5.34±0.43
Conference	116	8,540	5.01±0.20	52	3,010	3.22±0.19
Total (26–200 miss.)	169	11,620	4.52±0.13			

Figure 7-8

PAR AND THE AMOUNT OF TIME AND MONEY SPENT ON MISSIONARY CARE

| Amount of Time/Money | Time for Care | | | Finances for Care | | |
| | PAR % for Agency Size Groups | | | PAR % for Agency Size Groups | | |
	1–10	11–25	26–200	1–10	11–25	26–200
<1%	20.00±4.66	3.47±1.68	5.36±1.00	11.80±3.20	4.50±1.30	6.70±0.91
1–5%	10.67±1.82	5.02±0.77	7.02±0.59	17.20±2.50	5.40±1.00	5.49±0.38
6–10%	17.97±2.54	9.58±1.39	4.04±0.31	16.50±2.30	8.90±1.00	4.40±0.36
11–20%	19.70±2.78	8.09±1.17	3.68±0.29	16.00±3.00	8.00±1.40	4.35±0.34
21–30%	14.00±3.36	7.50±1.46	3.67±0.35	12.50±3.50	5.20±1.00	4.66±0.63
>30%	17.14±2.62	8.24±1.04	5.07±0.39	17.10±2.40	10.30±1.40	3.28±0.28

Figure 7-9

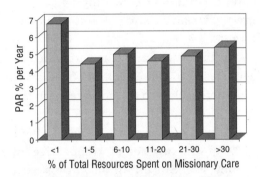

Figure 7-10. PAR of All Missionaries as a Function of the Percentage of Total Resources (Time and Money) Spent on Missionary Care

strated a negative effect. So more may not necessarily be better in the case of support and supervision, and increasing the amount of support and supervision does not appear to be a decisive factor in lowering preventable attrition.

Along the same lines, however, we found a clear positive relationship between lower PAR and the amount of care provided as measured by the percentage of time and money spent, but only up to a certain point (6%). Once this level was reached, the effect was actually negative (see Figures 7-9 and 7-10).

From a statistical point of view, the most reliable result is found in the size group 26–200 missionaries. It appears that the highest efficiency is reached at 6% time and finances for care. A very

high emphasis on care (>30%) seems actually to be detrimental. (In the other size groups, this effect was less pronounced but subject to increased statistical inaccuracy of ±3.) Does this demonstrate too much of a good thing? Does extensive internal communication or hand-holding become a problem in itself?

The average time for care remained constant at 14–16% irrespective of agency size—a figure which is well above the threshold mentioned above (6%). The same result was found for finances invested in personal care (14–15%). Agencies from NSC dedicate a higher percentage of their time and finances to care than those from OSC, but the PAR at similar investment of time and finances (percentage wise) is somewhat higher than from OSC, as shown in Figure 7-11.

Similar results are found in the size groups 1–10 missionaries and >200 missionaries with marginal statistical significance; a reverse trend was found in the size group 11–25 missionaries (NSC do better than OSC). So in general, NSC dedicate a higher percentage of their resources to support and supervision but still end up with a higher PAR.

PAR AS COMPARED TO OSC AND NSC INVESTMENT OF TIME AND MONEY
Agencies with 26–200 missionaries

Investment		OSC			NSC		
		# Agencies	# Miss.	PAR %	# Agencies	# Miss.	PAR %
Time	0–5%	23	1,400	6.23±0.40	6	385	9.69±1.21
	>20%	24	1,820	4.41±0.36	29	1,610	5.21±0.36
Finances	0–5%	36	2,310	5.75±0.34	10	595	6.88±0.68
	>20%	19	1,435	3.74±0.39	25	1,470	3.47±0.40

Figure 7-11

PAR AND PRE-FIELD TRAINING REQUIREMENTS
Agencies with 26–200 missionaries (167 agencies with 11,515 missionaries)

Kind of Requirement	Required			Not Required		
	# Agencies	# Miss.	PAR %	# Agencies	# Miss.	PAR %
Cross-cultural orientation	8	350	3.43±0.60	159	11,165	4.59±0.13
Theological training	74	5,355	3.99±0.20	93	6,160	5.04±0.20
Cross-cultural experience	53	3,465	3.70±0.20	114	8,050	4.92±0.16
Degree in missiology	12	945	3.28±0.50	155	10,570	4.67±0.14
Missiological studies, informal or formal	141	9,765	4.44±0.15	26	1,750	5.18±0.35
Others	38	2,870	4.50±0.30	129	8,645	4.57±0.15
Total (26–200 miss.)	167	11,515	4.52±0.13			

Figure 7-12

Since these statistics reflect percentages of money, the OSC will still have spent many more dollars than the NSC, although the amount is reflected as a smaller percentage of their overall budget. A further study which actually considers this variable in terms of dollars and time per missionary may be more revealing.

What Training and How Much?

The PAR of agencies that have a certain kind of training entry requirement was compared with those which do not have it. We find clear correlations between requirements for candidates and the PAR. Let us focus again on the group of agencies with 26–200 missionaries.

In this agency size group, there is a clear correlation between individual

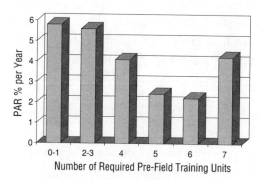

Figure 7-13. PAR of All Missionaries as a Function of Required Pre-Field Training Units (Out of a List of 7 Partially Overlapping Items)

types of training requirements and PAR (Figures 7-12 and 7-13). In fact, there is also a correlation between these training requirements and unpreventable attrition (data not shown).

In general, the number of requirements for candidates increased with the

PAR AND CANDIDATE SCREENING
Agencies with 26–200 missionaries (168 agencies with 11,550 missionaries)

Screening Area	Evaluation Made			Not Evaluated		
	# Agencies	# Miss.	PAR %	# Agencies	# Miss.	PAR %
Doctrinal statement	150	10,325	4.47±0.14	18	1,225	5.14±0.51
Clear calling	160	10,885	4.42±0.13	8	665	6.56±0.74
References/character	64	4,550	4.44±0.23	104	7,000	4.61±0.17
Previous mission exp.	161	11,130	4.61±0.13	7	420	2.70±0.70
Previous church work	125	8,155	4.44±0.16	43	3,395	4.80±0.28
Health	147	10,325	4.24±0.14	21	1,225	7.07±0.67
Communication and relationship skills	123	8,225	4.69±0.16	45	3,325	4.19±0.27
Leadership/pastoral	93	6,230	4.30±0.18	75	5,320	4.83±0.21
Family status	132	9,170	4.37±0.15	36	2,380	5.20±0.32
Limit on family size	31	2,450	5.04±0.34	137	9,100	4.41±0.15
Psychological tests	101	7,070	4.47±0.17	67	4,480	4.65±0.23
Firm financial support	104	7,140	4.11±0.17	64	4,410	5.24±0.23
Ordination	39	2,380	4.11±0.30	129	9,170	4.66±0.16

Figure 7-14

agency size, particularly in the areas of missiology, theological training, and cross-cultural orientation. Short-term experience only figures more prominently in smaller agencies. With the strong positive relationship between size and the reduction of attrition, the pre-field training factor is one to keep in mind. The group of agencies with lowest PAR had on average 50% more training requirements than those with highest attrition of the same agency size group, particularly in the fields of missiology, cross-cultural experience, and missionary training programs.

What Screening and How Much?

Does thorough screening of candidates reduce attrition? Agencies were subdivided according to whether or not they screened candidates in specific areas as part of their selection, and PAR was correlated with these screening areas. Figures 7-14 and 7-15 give the results for agencies with 26–200 missionaries.

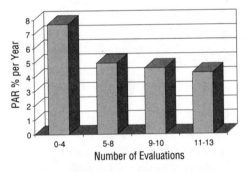

Figure 7-15. PAR as a Function of the Number of Evaluations (Out of a List of 13 Items) Applied During Candidate Screening

When taken individually, a positive effect was found for doctrinal statement (negative effect in the other agency size groups), calling (all size groups), previous church work (all size groups), health (all size groups, especially in NSC), family status (all size groups), firm financial support (all), and ordination (NSC). These areas, when taken individually, seem to be quite important in contributing to a lower PAR. Other screening elements presented a mixed picture. Keeping in mind that the 26–

200 group provides our statistically most reliable sample, we are challenged by these findings to examine some of our most cherished screening practices.

Again, since the amount of requirements increases with agency size, we are led to believe that more is better. It is wise, however, to note that adding certain elements may be inconsequential to preventing attrition. Indeed, the agencies with lowest PAR had the same number of screening areas as those with highest PAR—but they focused more on the areas mentioned above, at the expense of screening references, communication skills, leadership skills, number of children, and doctrinal

agreement (NSC). So the kind of requirement seems to be much more important than the number of requirements.

DIGGING A LITTLE DEEPER

PAR cannot be attributed to a single factor. No doubt, combinations of variables come into play. In order to begin to understand the effect of these combinations, cross-correlations were run between PAR, the number of areas checked in candidate selection, the number of pre-field training measures, the number of support provisions, and the percent of total finances used for member care (see Figure 7-16). For this purpose, the data base was sorted ac-

CROSS-CORRELATIONS BETWEEN CANDIDATE SELECTION, PRE-FIELD TRAINING, SUPPORT ON THE FIELD, AND PAR							
AGENCIES WITH 1–10 MISSIONARIES							
Selection Criteria		# Agencies	PAR %	# Evaluations	# Training	# Provisions	Financial Care %
Number of evaluation measures	1–5	24	20.28±2.71	4.13	1.82	4.21	18.30
	6–8	55	16.97±1.61	7.04	2.56	5.04	13.00
	9–13	42	11.59±1.47	10.17	3.26	5.88	14.80
Number of pre-field training measures	0–1	27	13.80±2.00	5.88	0.74	3.92	11.70
	2	25	11.20±1.87	7.68	2.00	4.76	13.00
	3	33	21.82±2.42	8.03	3.00	6.12	16.80
	4	26	14.36±2.11	8.12	4.00	5.62	14.30
	5–7	8	15.00±3.90	8.88	5.63	5.25	20.10
Number of support provisions	1–3	30	10.44±1.64	6.59	2.13	2.50	15.00
	4–6	61	17.50±1.55	7.31	2.78	5.05	14.70
	7–10	29	18.16±2.30	8.86	3.07	8.17	14.80
PAR	Low	29	6.66±0.70	7.52	2.55	5.10	14.70
	Average	34	16.10±1.00	7.65	2.68	5.44	14.60
	High	19	33.70±4.30	7.58	3.06	5.68	17.90
Financial care	0–5%	33	15.76±1.98	7.42	2.21	4.76	2.37
	6–20%	42	16.35±1.80	7.83	3.00	5.57	10.50
	21–40%	33	15.96±2.00	7.03	2.94	5.03	32.58
Total		121	15.70±1.04	7.51	2.68	5.17	14.80

Evaluations = Number of areas assessed during candidate selection.
Training = Number of pre-field training measures.
Provisions = Number of support provisions.
Financial Care % = Percent of total finances used for member care.

Figure 7-16

CROSS-CORRELATIONS BETWEEN CANDIDATE SELECTION, PRE-FIELD TRAINING, SUPPORT ON THE FIELD, AND PAR (cont.)

AGENCIES WITH 11–25 MISSIONARIES

Selection Criteria		# Agencies	PAR %	# Evaluations	# Training	# Provisions	Financial Care %
Number of evaluation measures	1–5	17	6.62±1.03	4.35	2.53	4.41	20.50
	6–8	43	8.19±0.74	7.19	2.70	5.33	13.00
	9–13	39	7.80±0.76	10.28	3.28	6.05	14.70
Number of pre-field training measures	0–1	14	8.47±1.33	6.92	0.57	5.21	14.90
	2	23	6.61±0.89	8.26	2.00	4.52	13.20
	3	33	7.51±0.80	7.58	3.00	5.42	15.80
	4	18	7.52±1.09	8.17	4.00	6.61	17.00
	5–7	11	10.41±1.72	9.36	5.64	6.19	15.30
Number of support provisions	1–3	24	7.37±0.93	7.17	2.35	2.21	14.00
	4–6	34	8.94±0.89	7.58	2.85	4.97	15.30
	7–10	42	6.84±0.67	8.62	3.24	7.67	15.50
PAR	Low	28	3.05±0.38	8.39	2.57	5.57	15.40
	Average	26	7.44±0.46	7.73	2.77	5.85	12.20
	High	24	13.53±2.02	8.04	3.38	5.29	16.50
Financial care	0–5%	22	5.11±0.78	8.00	2.81	4.36	2.23
	6–20%	37	8.62±0.83	7.76	2.84	6.03	10.33
	21–40%	30	7.92±0.87	7.96	2.97	5.57	30.33
Total		100	7.68±0.47	7.92	2.90	5.44	15.10

AGENCIES WITH 26+ MISSIONARIES

Selection Criteria		# Agencies	PAR %	# Evaluations	# Training	# Provisions	Financial Care %
Number of evaluation measures	1–5	25	5.04±0.42	4.28	1.95	5.98	10.90
	6–8	56	4.14±0.23	7.42	2.50	6.94	16.00
	9–13	111	4.21±0.17	10.07	3.59	7.38	16.00
Number of pre-field training measures	0–1	32	5.11±0.39	7.08	0.80	6.17	15.70
	2	50	4.71±0.27	8.02	2.00	7.84	13.90
	3	46	5.73±0.35	8.72	3.00	6.58	13.10
	4	40	3.36±0.25	9.58	4.00	7.37	17.40
	5–7	23	2.22±0.21	9.45	5.70	6.73	12.80
Number of support provisions	1–3	24	2.36±0.27	7.97	2.81	2.46	16.80
	4–6	74	3.70±0.19	8.01	2.39	5.54	10.80
	7–10	94	4.89±0.20	8.96	2.91	8.59	16.40
PAR	Low	61	1.14±0.09	8.36	3.80	6.12	12.70
	Average	72	3.79±0.18	8.62	2.92	7.46	16.10
	High	60	9.17±0.46	8.70	2.43	7.49	13.70
Financial care	0–5%	53	4.45±0.25	8.44	3.33	6.17	2.73
	6–20%	67	4.14±0.22	8.83	3.07	6.79	11.50
	21–40%	51	4.33±0.26	8.71	3.23	6.43	32.10
Total		193	4.27±0.13	8.56	3.06	7.08	14.40

Figure 7-16 (cont.)

cording to one (independent) variable, and the other parameters were calculated accordingly. This procedure was followed for the various agency size groups separately.

1. Candidate Selection

Sorting the data sets according to the number of areas assessed during candidate selection, we find a clear positive correlation with PAR for small agencies (1–10 missionaries) and a weaker one for larger agencies. There are also clear correlations between candidate selection and pre-field training, as well as provisions on the field, i.e., agencies that carefully screen their candidates do also invest more in pre-field training and provisions on the field and are rewarded with lower PAR. Yet they do not invest more finances in member care.

2. Training Requirements

When sorting the data base according to the amount of pre-field training, we find also a clear correlation with PAR for agencies with 26+ missionaries (90% of the global missionary force). The subset with lowest PAR (<2%) corresponded with 3.8 areas of pre-field training, compared with 2.43 for the subset with high PAR (>5%).

For small agencies, however, we find the opposite trend, yet small agencies have much higher PAR in general, so that any positive effect of training is apparently offset by other factors. We also find a clear correlation with candidate selection, but the number of provisions on the field remained constant (while increasing with agency size), as well as the percentage of finances used for member care.

3. Field Support and Supervision

Sorting the data base according to the number of provisions for field support clearly correlates with candidate screening and pre-field training, yet PAR also increases, so an increase in field support and supervision appears not to be a useful tool in and of itself to reduce preventable attrition.

When the data base is sorted according to the percentage of finances used for member care, PAR remains constant (above 5% finances used for member care). While the percentage of finances invested in member care increases by an order of magnitude, candidate selection and number of provisions on the field increase only insignificantly (5%), while pre-field training remains constant. In almost all cases, finances for member care are well above the saturation level of 5%, below which indeed PAR will rise.

Our conclusion is that a large investment in candidate selection and pre-field training is useful in reducing PAR, whereas a high number of provisions for field support and supervision may actually influence attrition negatively. This investment may come too late unless it was preceded by thorough candidate selection and pre-field training.

WHICH AGENCIES DO THE BEST?

In this section, we list some findings which may help you to draw your own conclusions.

1. Agencies with low PAR also have a lower unpreventable attrition. The unpreventable, preventable, and total attrition rates all fall with agency size by a factor of more than 5.

2. Large agencies with low PAR lose more single women (NSC and OSC) and single men (NSC), and the percentage of couples who leave is lower. In small agencies the trend is the opposite. This may reflect a difference in ratios between singles and couples in large and small missions or, perhaps, the importance given to the family in their respective mission forces.

3. Agencies with low PAR have a higher percentage of team and work-related attrition and a lower percentage of "other" and family reasons.

4. Agencies with lower PAR are more involved in foreign countries than in their own and particularly in cross-cultural work. Workers in their own country are more prone to attrition.

5. Smaller agencies have lower PAR when working with churches, while larger agencies do best when church planting.

6. In the screening of their candidates, agencies with low PAR put a higher emphasis on (a) a firm calling, (b) references (agencies with 25 or fewer missionaries), (c) previous church work (small agencies), (d) health, (e) marriage, (f) firm financial support, and (g) ordination, but they put less emphasis on (a) previous mission experience (agencies with more than 10 missionaries), (b) communication skills, (c) leadership skills (agencies with more than 25 missionaries), (d) psychological tests, (e) restrictions on family size, and (f) other areas. Agencies with low attrition do more evaluation in the area of family.

7. Agencies with lower PAR have higher training requirements, particularly in missiology (degree courses and other courses), theology (small agencies), and cross-cultural living. Generally, more training means less attrition.

8. Agencies with lower PAR provide relatively fewer field support services, particularly in the areas of team support, field leadership, schooling for children, and annual leave. This is the only negative trend which also correlates to agency size (more means worse). The number of provisions on the field increased with agency size by 50%, reflecting their infrastructure, policy, and management. Agencies from OSC give more provisions than those from NSC, particularly in the fields of pastoral care, annual leave, schooling for children, team support, field conferences, and others. Agencies from NSC as a whole provide more for field leadership, job description, on-the-job training, yearly visits, and letters and telephone calls. The only consistent winner was letters and phone calls.

9. Agencies with a low PAR spend the same amount of time and finances (10–20%) on member care, which increases with agency size by 60%. In addition, agencies from NSC spend 50–100% more time and finances on pastoral care than agencies from OSC. (Does this reflect their face to face-oriented societies?) Yet the lowest PAR agencies of OSC and NSC do not spend more resources on care than the average agency.

10. Those agencies with the lowest PAR believed that among the most important factors for staying on the field are the ability to cope with stress, good relationships with supervisors and the mission agency, and regular financial support. Those who rated contact with supporters at home, regular supervision, and regular training among the

most important reasons had a higher than average PAR.

SUMMARY AND RECOMMENDATIONS

The most striking result of this study is the enormous dependence of preventable and unpreventable attrition on agency size, falling by a factor of 5-6. It appears that a "critical mass" (number of missionaries) is necessary to keep workers on the field. This may encourage us to seek closer cooperation and perhaps organizational mergers in some cases. Yet beyond a size of 200 missionaries, we did not find further benefit to size. Is this the optimum size of an agency, maintaining personal relationship and confidence as well as efficient preparation infrastructure and administration?

There is an important correlation between candidate selection, pre-field training, and amount of care (up to 6%) in reducing PAR. Yet each factor taken individually shows a smaller improvement than one would expect from the vast diversity of attrition values. Multiple factors including "other" appear to be involved. The intrinsic limitations of this study call for additional investigation in this area.

Individual variables of field support and supervision in general did not have a positive effect. Does this reflect the characters of the individualistic, hardy boosters and boomers who still dominate the global mission force? This is an enigmatic result which merits further study.

The analysis of agencies with lowest attrition did not give a clear-cut character profile, as one would expect, but indicated only diffuse trends. This fact demonstrates that there is not a single way to lower attrition. Different strategies, means, structures, and ways which reflect the home culture or that of the country of service may be most appropriate for each situation. Apparently, success has many faces and does certainly depend on God's grace, guidance, and provision in order for each agency to address this important question.

APPENDIX A: MATHEMATICAL PROCEDURES

The following logical and arithmetic operations have been used with the data base. Refer to pages 363–370 for a copy of the questionnaire used in the research.

1. Elimination of Data Sets

Data sets without numbers for total attrition (Q3 of the questionnaire) or size of agency (Q4) were eliminated. This left us with 411 data sets. In some questionnaires, not all of questions Q1 to Q12 were answered, so some tables may have a slightly lower total.

2. Consistency Check

A check was made for consistency of data entry in Q2 and Q3, and correction was made where possible. The total loss 1992–1994 must not be negative. If Q2b-d was answered, the sum must be correct and equal to the sum in Q3, etc. In a few cases there were obvious entry mistakes, either by the person filling in the form or during data entry into the computer. These were corrected.

3. Number of Missionaries

An average number of missionaries was attributed to each data set as the best guess for the actual number of missionaries of this agency. Q4 gives the agency size in certain ranges: 1–10 missionaries (30% of the questionnaires), 11–25 missionaries (23%), 26–50 missionaries (19%), 51–100 missionaries (11%), 101–200 missionaries (9%), 201–500 missionaries (4%), >500 missionaries (2%). It is obvious that there are more smaller missions than larger agencies, particularly if we keep in mind that the ranges of the grouping are not equal. Thus it is expected that there are more agencies with a number of missionaries below the arithmetic average of the upper and lower limits than above it, and the following average numbers of missionaries per agency were used: 5 for agencies with 1–10 missionaries; 16 for agencies with 11–25 missionaries, instead of the arithmetic average of $(11 + 25)/2 = 18$; 35 for agencies with 26–50 missionaries, instead of the arithmetic average 38; 70 for agencies with 51–100 missionaries, instead of the arithmetic average 76; and 140 for agencies with 101–200 missionaries, instead of the arithmetic average 150. For agencies with >200 missionaries, the actual number of missionaries was taken from the *Missions Handbook* or *Operation World* by Patrick Johnstone. If the figures were not available for agencies from NSC, a best guess of 314 was assigned for agencies with 200–500 missionaries (instead of the arithmetic average 350), and 600 was assigned for the >500 group.

These average numbers had been derived from the "density distribution" of data points. The number of agencies in an agency size group was divided by the width of the size range (10 – 1, 25 – 11, 50 – 26, etc.), and this "density distri-

bution" of agencies was plotted against the (arithmetic) average agency size. A straight line was found only in two segments: (1) density = 52 times the number of missionaries per agency to the power of (–0.8) (for agency size <100 missionaries), and (2) density = 824 times the number of missionaries per agency to the power of (–1.6) (for agency size >100 missionaries).

This density distribution was then integrated over the agency size range (Q4), resulting in the average size given above, which is somewhat smaller than the arithmetic average.

The total attrition loss, including both unpreventable (Q3a) and preventable (Q2 last column minus Q3a), was divided by 3 in order to have the loss per year. It was divided by the average size of the agency (the best estimate available for the actual number of missionaries) in order to give the annual attrition rate. The attrition rate of an agency has an error of typically 50% because of the uncertainty of the number of missionaries (e.g., in the agency size group 11–25 missionaries, the number of missionaries was assumed to be 16, whereas the actual number could possibly have been 11 or 25). Yet by summing the attrition numbers over a larger number of agencies, overestimations and underestimations will offset each other, and the error will be reduced. The precise mathematical treatment is the integral over the "density function" and is explained below.

4. Accuracy of the Results

One major inaccuracy is due to the estimation of the agencies' number of missionaries on the field and the limited sample size. In statistics, this inaccuracy is expressed by an uncertainty range (variance) which follows an empirical value as ± uncertainty. This uncertainty is defined as that range of a variable in which 63% (= 1 − 1/e) of all actual results will fall, i.e., 63% of the results will be between the average minus the uncertainty and the average plus the uncertainty. In the agency size group 11–25 missionaries, an average value of 16 was assigned, and the maximal scattering of the data points was ±8, which is 50% of the average number. Assuming an equal distribution of the data points (density distribution), variance of a single data set will be 50% x 0.63 = 31.5%. (For the group of smallest agency size (1–10 missionaries), an average value of 5 was determined, and the maximal scattering of the data points was ±5, which is 100%, resulting in a variance of 100% x 0.63 = 63.0%.) The uncertainty of an average value is determined by the formula: sigma equals variance divided by the square root of the number of data sets. For example, in a subset of 28 agencies, the relative uncertainty due to the sample size will be 31%/5.3 = 6%.

The second source of uncertainty is the (low) number of attrition cases. In a given organization there may be 5 cases one year and 7 cases the next. The actual numbers have only limited value as a prognosis for the following year. Thus, missionary loss is a stochastic process (like radioactive decay or casting a die), and it was mathematically treated as such. This gave a second component to the uncertainty of attrition, which is 1 divided by the square root of the number of events (i.e., total loss, preventable loss, or unpreventable loss within the three years 1992–1994).

Both components together (limited sample size and stochastic nature of attrition) give the total uncertainty as follows: uncertainty = square root (0.1/number of agencies + 1/number of attrition cases) for agencies with >10 missionaries, or uncertainty = square root (0.3/number of agencies + 1/number of attrition cases) for agencies with 1–10 missionaries). For example, in a subset of 28 agencies with altogether 26 preventable attrition cases, uncertainty = square root (0.1/28 + 1/26) = square root (0.00357 + 0.03846) = square root (0.0420) = 20.5%. Multiplied with a PAR of e.g. 3.7%, this gives 0.205 x 3.7% = 0.76%, so that the result is given as 3.7± 0.76%, which means that the true value for the total group (not just the limited sample covered by the study) is somewhere between 2.9% and 4.5%.

The uncertainty is strongly dependent on the number of data sets and the number of actual missionary losses. It can vary by a factor of 40 and is given with the data as number ± uncertainty.

The subset of agencies that meet a certain criterion was selected, and the number of lost missionaries was summed up and divided by the total number of missionaries represented by these agencies. Thus the attrition response is inevitably proportional to the number of missionaries represented by the organizations. We have used the same procedure also for other questions—e.g., in studying the selection of candidates, pre-field training, or provisions on the field—by multiplying the response with the number of missionaries of that organization, and dividing the sum over the subset through the total number of missionaries represented in this subgroup. By this procedure, the response of, e.g., Wycliffe Bible Translators weighs 1,000 times more than that of a mission with only four missionaries, as Wycliffe constitutes a much larger percentage of the total mission force.

Applying this procedure, various subsets were selected, and the number of agencies, percent of agencies from NSC, total number of missionaries with these agencies, total attrition rate, PAR, and UAR were calculated and scanned for significant differences in the PAR.

APPENDIX B:
CORRECTION FOR
RAPIDLY GROWING AGENCIES

The proper procedure for attrition studies is to monitor which percentage of missionaries sent out in a certain year are still on the field after five or 10 years of service. This is tedious work, how-ever, and often the necessary data are not available, so that attrition is often approximated by the number of losses per number of missionaries on the field in a certain year. (In this study, the average of the years 1992–1994 was taken.) Computer simulations have proved that this procedure is a valid approximation for slowly growing agencies, but for rapidly growing agencies corrections need to be made. Rapidly growing missions have a high fraction of young missionaries who have not yet persevered on the field and undergone the risk of attrition. In Figure 7-17, the apparent attrition rate (number of losses per year divided by the number of missionaries on the field) was divided by the actual attrition rate, giving a correction factor C, for various agency growth rates and attrition rates.

CORRECTION FACTOR C FOR RAPIDLY GROWING AGENCIES									
Annual Growth Rate	Actual Attrition Rate								
	1%	2%	4%	6%	8%	10%	15%	20%	25%
−10%	1.0073	1.0249	1.0599	1.0934	1.1246	1.1523	1.2017	1.2247	1.2323
−7.5%	0.9981	1.0138	1.0442	1.0721	1.0966	1.1171	1.1502	1.1636	1.1676
−5%	0.9844	0.9979	1.0229	1.0446	1.0627	1.0769	1.0979	1.1054	1.1075
−2.5%	0.9658	0.9767	0.9960	1.0119	1.0244	1.0337	1.0464	1.0506	1.0517
0	0.9423	0.9505	0.9646	0.9756	0.9838	0.9896	0.9970	0.9993	0.9999
2.5%	0.9145	0.9204	0.9301	0.9373	0.9507	0.9460	0.9502	0.9515	0.9517
5%	0.8836	0.8876	0.8940	0.8986	0.9017	0.9038	0.9062	0.9068	0.9070
7.5%	0.8510	0.8536	0.8577	0.8605	0.8623	0.8635	0.8649	0.8652	0.8633
10%	0.8179	0.8195	0.8220	0.8237	0.8248	0.8255	0.8262	0.8264	0.8264
12.5%	0.7850	0.7861	0.7876	0.7886	0.7892	0.7896	0.7900	0.7901	0.7901
15%	0.7532	0.7538	0.7547	0.7553	0.7556	0.7558	0.7561	0.7561	0.7561
20%	0.6934	0.6936	0.6940	0.6942	0.6943	0.6943	0.6944	0.6944	0.6944
25%	0.6397	0.6397	0.6398	0.6399	0.6399	0.6400	0.6400	0.6400	0.6400
30%	0.5916	0.5916	0.5917	0.5917	0.5917	0.5917	0.5917	0.5917	0.5917
35%	0.5487	0.5487	0.5487	0.5487	0.5487	0.5487	0.5487	0.5487	0.5487
40%	0.5102	0.5102	0.5102	0.5102	0.5102	0.5102	0.5102	0.5102	0.5102
50%	0.4444	0.4444	0.4444	0.4444	0.4444	0.4444	0.4444	0.4444	0.4444

Figure 7-17

It becomes clear that at an annual growth rate of 20% (C = 0.69), the actual attrition rate is underestimated by 45% (1/C = 1.45). It is underestimated by a factor of 2 at an agency growth rate of 40% per year.

Corrections for this artifact can be made by multiplying by the correction factor C, giving an effective number of missionaries on the field (usually lower than the actual number of missionaries), which is the correct denominator for the annual loss. Dividing the number of missionaries lost in a certain year by this effective number of missionaries gives the proper annual attrition rate.

APPENDIX C:
NATIONAL ATTRITION VALUES

For each country that participated in the ReMAP study, the national average preventable attrition rate over all missions of a certain agency size group was calculated. For each old sending nation, this figure was compared with the average PAR of all of the old sending countries, including correction for agency growth. For each new sending country, the national average PAR value was compared with the average PAR of all of the new sending countries, including correction for agency growth. The results are shown in Figure 7-18 on this page and the next.

In some countries, only a small number of agencies of a certain size took part in the study. This resulted in a large statistical uncertainty as given in the table, in which the systematic error due to an uneven selection of the sample is not included.

The agency size distribution differed greatly from one country to another. For example, 95% of the USA missionaries belonged to agencies with 26+ missionaries, but only 27% of Danish missionaries were in this group. Since smaller agencies in general had a much higher attrition rate, differences in the national agency size distribution of the sample had a large bearing on the national average PAR.

No data are available on the agency size distribution of the national missionary force, so it is not known whether the sample of the study is an appropriate match of the overall national missionary force. Thus the national PAR average does not necessarily reflect the actual national attrition rate.

NATIONAL PAR VALUES			
Agencies With 1–10 Missionaries			
Country	# Agen	Avg PAR %	Rel PAR %
Australia	15	17.33±3.12	129±23
Brazil	2	0	0
Canada	5	16.00±5.14	91±29
Costa Rica	4	11.70±4.78	68±28
Denmark	3	0	0
Germany	5	10.67±4.06	109±23
Ghana	27	20.49±2.57	145±18
India	3	66.67±17.20	385±99
Korea	16	5.42±1.56	27±8
Nigeria	4	31.67±8.82	183±51
Philippines	6	15.56±4.62	67±20
Singapore	1	33.33±18.26	192±105
UK	8	7.50±2.64	56±20
USA	22	14.24±2.29	109±18
Total	121	15.80±1.00	100

Avg PAR % = National average preventable attrition rate over all agencies in a given size group.

Rel PAR % = National preventable attrition rate (corrected for national agency growth) relative to the overall PAR of NSC or OSC, respectively, including uncertainties.

Figure 7-18

NATIONAL PAR VALUES (cont.)					
	Agencies With 11–25 Missionaries			Agencies With 26+ Missionaries		
Country	# Agencies	Avg PAR %	Rel PAR %	# Agencies	Avg PAR %	Rel PAR %
Australia	9	6.71±1.43	83±18	16	6.01±0.62	143±15
Brazil	7	6.85±1.65	79±19	13	7.34±0.80	151±16
Canada	3	7.64±2.69	97±34	7	3.44±0.65	84±16
Costa Rica	2	2.08±1.55	35±26	1	1.90±1.48	56±44
Denmark	4	12.50±2.64	156±33	1	3.81±2.25	91±54
Germany	7	7.44±1.73	94±22	9	4.47±0.64	109±16
Ghana	11	9.28±1.59	177±30	14	3.48±0.51	114±17
India	4	10.42±3.29	116±37	12	5.20±0.57	103±12
Korea	13	7.21±1.25	95±16	17	1.81±0.26	43±6
Nigeria	6	8.33±2.01	100±24	5	3.59±0.63	77±14
Philippines	3	6.25±2.38	72±27	6	7.71±1.29	158±26
Singapore	3	2.08±1.26	28±17	2	0.48±0.49	11±11
UK	5	14.58±3.20	180±40	22	4.78±0.44	114±10
USA	22	5.97±0.85	75±11	68	3.75±0.19	91±5
Total	99	7.69±0.47	100	193	4.27±0.13	100

Avg PAR % = National average preventable attrition rate over all agencies in a given size group.

Rel PAR % = National preventable attrition rate (corrected for national agency growth) relative to the overall PAR of NSC or OSC, respectively, including uncertainties.

Figure 7-18 (cont.)

NATIONAL UAR VALUES			
	UAR % for Agency Size		
Country	1–10 Miss.	11–25 Miss.	26+ Miss.
Australia	7.56±1.93	4.86±1.18	4.49±0.50
Brazil	0	1.79±0.76	1.14±0.21
Canada	5.33±2.77	5.56±2.21	2.64±0.54
Costa Rica	3.33±2.42	1.04±1.07	1.90±1.48
Denmark	26.67±9.11	9.72±2.23	8.57±3.94
Germany	5.33±2.77	1.49±0.69	0.70±0.19
Ghana	0.74±0.43	2.08±0.66	0.30±0.13
India	4.44±3.25	2.78±1.48	0.34±0.09
Korea	1.25±0.73	0.96±0.40	0.63±0.14
Nigeria	1.67±1.69	1.39±0.72	1.70±0.35
Philippines	8.89±3.35	2.08±1.26	1.13±0.34
Singapore	0	1.39±1.01	0.95±0.71
UK	4.17±1.92	6.67±1.91	2.46±0.27
USA	5.15±1.30	0.95±0.31	2.16±0.12
Total	4.30±0.50	2.60±0.25	1.87±0.07

Figure 7-19

Figure 7-19 shows the national unpreventable attrition rate (UAR) for each of the 14 countries that participated in the study. Figure 7-20 gives the national PAR, national UAR, and national total attrition rate. The values in Figures 7-19 and 7-20 represent the number of missionaries who leave missionary service per active missionary on the field. They are not corrected for agency growth.

TOTAL NATIONAL PAR AND UAR VALUES		
Country	National PAR %	National UAR %	Natl Total Attr Rate %
Australia	6.67±0.52	4.69±0.40	11.36±0.76
Brazil	7.24±0.66	1.19±0.20	8.42±0.75
Canada	4.42±0.64	3.03±0.50	7.45±0.92
Costa Rica	4.21±1.37	1.92±0.89	6.13±1.70
Denmark	9.13±1.71	11.19±1.95	20.32±2.96
Germany	4.99±0.54	0.92±0.19	5.91±0.61
Ghana	6.90±0.57	0.69±0.16	7.59±0.61
India	5.85±0.55	0.44±0.10	6.29±0.58
Korea	2.72±0.27	0.71±0.13	3.42±0.31
Nigeria	4.65±0.55	1.66±0.28	6.31±0.70
Philippines	8.06±1.01	1.73±0.38	9.79±1.16
Singapore	2.44±0.87	1.08±0.56	3.52±1.08
UK	5.23±0.41	2.67±0.26	7.89±0.56
USA	3.96±0.17	2.15±0.11	6.12±0.24
Total	4.85±0.11	1.99±0.06	6.84±0.15

The national PAR and UAR values are calculated over all agency sizes, weighted by the number of missionaries. Because the average agency size varies from country to country, the national attrition averages cannot be easily compared.

Figure 7-20

Detlef Blöcher *was born in 1953, is married, and has three children, ages 6–12. A graduate physicist, from 1976–1984 he was a research scientist. From 1976–1981 and 1984–1985, he studied theology and missiology, and from 1986–1990 he worked as a tentmaker in the Middle East. Since 1991, Blöcher has served as deputy director of the German Missionary Fellowship in Sinsheim, Germany. He is a WEF Missions Commission Associate.*

Jonathan Lewis *was born in Argentina of missionary parents. He and his wife have been cross-cultural missionaries in Honduras, Peru, and Argentina. He has served as a church missions pastor in the USA. He authored the three-volume* **World Mission** *(1987, 1993) and edited* **Working Your Way to the Nations** *(1996). Currently, he is on staff with the Missions Commission of the World Evangelical Fellowship as a missionary training consultant and director of publications. He is married to Dawn, and together they have four children.*

Part 3

National Case Studies

Missionary Attrition in Korea: Opinions of Agency Executives

Steve Sang-Cheol Moon

Missionary attrition is not a new problem. It is one that existed in Paul's missionary band in the early church. Members of the apostolic band such as Timothy, Titus, Luke, and Crescens remained faithful to the end (2 Tim. 4:10-11). However, there were also people on the team like Demas, who later deserted Paul "because he loved this world" (2 Tim. 4:10). Mark also left the missionary team but was later recovered to the harvest force. The focus of attention in missionary attrition is not only to find ways to prevent attrition and recover some workers, but also to help the whole harvest force in our time to continue to serve the Lord where they are called to be.

Missionary attrition is not merely a theoretical problem. Missionaries who return home from the field may think primarily about the genuineness of their calling, but attrition also involves loss of personnel and financial resources. Unlike most of the other missionaries from the Two-Thirds World, most Korean

missionaries serve across the national boundary. For this reason, a returning missionary may mean a bigger loss of resources and of previous investment to the Korean churches. Missionary attrition undermines the emerging missionary movements by the younger churches in many ways. A study of the disappearing missionaries may serve to promote better missionary care, which is most significant to the younger missionary movements.

REMAP IN KOREA

Missionary attrition as a research problem was surveyed in Korea with the participation of the Korea Research Institute for Missions,[1] as part of ReMAP (Reducing Missionary Attrition Project) by the World Evangelical Fellowship Missions Commission. A standard questionnaire form prepared by the ReMAP team was translated into Korean and circulated around Korean mission agencies in April 1995, to explore the reality of missionary attrition for the

---

1. The Korea Research Institute for Missions (KRIM) is the research arm of Global Missionary Fellowship, Inc., which is an umbrella organization for seven different agencies.

three-year period 1992–1994. The questionnaire forms, which were mostly answered by mission executives, were collected by September 1995. Data processing and analysis took another six months beyond the data gathering. The results of the survey are displayed in this report.[2]

While the research process was being conducted in Korea, limitations of the research design became apparent. Since the survey was not asking for success stories from the missions, there were some barriers to understanding, cooperation, and communication with the busy mission executives. Some of these barriers were foreseen at the time the questionnaire was designed,[3] but others were not detected until the data gathering process was under way. These weaknesses (detailed below) point out the difficulties of an international research project.

Firstly, the research design was quantitative. It asked the mission administrators for numerical data. A qualitative research project conducted through interviews and observation may be desirable in the future as a supplement to this present study. The greater resources and commitment would be offset by the possibilities for in-depth probing for the reasons for attrition. The researcher tried to compensate for the quantitative limitations of this design by reflecting on some of his previous interview experience with returning missionaries during the process of interpreting findings.

Secondly, there were misunderstandings of the questions and accordingly wrong answers made. Part of the problem was inherent in the questionnaire design. Busy people found it difficult to answer complex questions. Fortunately, the most confusing item was supplemented by another similar question. The researcher's background knowledge about the mission agencies enabled him to clarify some of the ambiguous answers. However, a pilot project before the main research would have provided more clarity and accuracy in data gathering.

Thirdly, there was the potential danger, not unique to any one culture, of "impression management" by the respondents to the questionnaire. Mission administrators filled out 78.1% of the questionnaire forms. The responses could suggest a defensive mentality on the part of some of the agencies. However, efforts were made to remind the respondents that the contents of individual answers would be treated with strict confidentiality.

Fourthly, data gathering was done through a convenience sample rather than a random sample, thus precluding the use of statistical methods based on

---

2. The statistics presented in this chapter may differ from those given in other chapters. There are three reasons for the variations: (1) The calculations done by Peter Brierley (chapter 6) were based on the first examination of the data. (2) Detlef Blöcher and Jonathan Lewis (chapter 7) had additional data from which to work. They examined the data from a different perspective, asking different questions. (3) Some of the statistics in the national case studies reflect new surveys and different ways of reading the numbers.

3. The author participated in the whole ReMAP process, beginning with the questionnaire design through the debriefing, for which he shares responsibility for the weaknesses of ReMAP in terms of validity and reliability.

probability theory and the generalization of the findings to all mission agencies in Korea. However, of the 78 missionary sending agencies targeted in this survey, 64 agencies responded organizationally, representing over 90% of the total Korean missionaries. Logically, if not statistically, the findings may be assumed to be generalizable.

In this report, some background information about Korean missionaries and mission agencies is provided, followed by a statistical summary of the status of missionary attrition in Korea. Then an in-depth analysis of the causes of attrition is presented, and an attempt is made to interpret the various causes. The locus of the problem is identified, and overall guidelines for remedies are suggested. Finally, the policies of mission agencies are carefully examined.

MISSIONARY MOVEMENT IN KOREA

The issue of missionary attrition must be understood in the context of each missionary movement. The problem is all the more negative if the missionary movement is in a declining mode. The Korean missionary movement maintains its vitality as the fastest growing movement in the world, notwithstanding the fact of missionary attrition. In this section, up-to-date data from the *Korean Mission Handbook* (Lee & Moon, 1996) were used in addition to ReMAP data.

Missionary Expansion

According to the *Korean Mission Handbook* (Lee & Moon, 1996), the missionary movement in Korea has grown to 47.3 times its original size since 1979 in terms of the number of missionaries. Presently, at least 4,402[4] Korean missionaries are working scattered across 138 countries of the world (see Figures 8-1 and 8-2). The churches in Korea now send as many missionaries as the churches in Australia (3,598) and Germany (3,524), following the lead of the USA (59,074), India (11,284), UK (7,012), and Canada (5,336).[5]

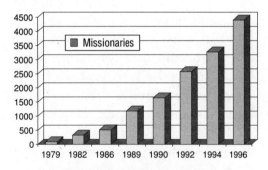

Figure 8-1. Increasing Number of Korean Missionaries

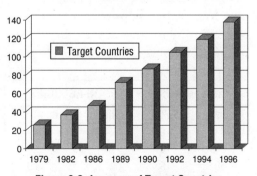

Figure 8-2. Increase of Target Countries

---

4. This number was ascertained after eliminating duplicates. A couple was counted as two in this figure (Moon, 1996, pp. i-ii).

5. These numbers of missionaries from other countries are 1993 figures, taken from Johnstone (1993).

Korean missionaries were channeled through 21 agencies in 1979, but the number grew to 113 agencies in 1994. It has been reported that 78 agencies of the 113 have at least one member on the mission field. No increase has been reported since 1994 in terms of the number of mission agencies. However, existing mission agencies are expanding rapidly in size due to the recently joining members.

Mission Agencies

Korean mission agencies are growing in size, but the majority are still small (see Figure 8-3). There are two agencies with over 500 members, and another two agencies have 201–500 members. Twelve mission agencies are known to have more than 100 missionaries. However, 83.6% of the agencies have 100 or fewer members, and 69.9% have 50 or fewer members. Approximately half (49.4%) of the mission agencies have 25 or fewer member missionaries (Moon, 1996, p. iii).

Korean mission agencies are younger in age for their size than mission agencies from other countries. It was observed in the ReMAP survey that 71.9% of the Korean agencies are 1–10 years

AGE OF KOREAN MISSION AGENCIES			
Age (yr.)	Value	Valid %	Cum. %
1–2	1	1.6	1.6
3–10	45	70.3	71.9
11–25	15	23.4	95.3
26–50	1	1.6	96.9
51–100	2	3.1	100.0
Total	64	100.0	
Valid cases, 64; Missing cases, 0			

Source: *Korean Mission Handbook* (1996)

Figure 8-4

old, and 95.3% of them are 25 years old or younger. Only two agencies (both denominational) have been sending missionaries for over 50 years (see Figure 8-4). Being young can be both a strength and a weakness, since the agency may be interpreted to be both energetic and immature at the same time.

Ministry of Korean Missionaries

During the early development of the Korean missionary movement, a majority of Korean missionaries worked among *Diaspora* Koreans. Now 91.7% of Korean missionaries are involved in intercultural ministries in other countries, leaving only 3.9% in purely *Diaspora* ministry (Moon, 1996, p. iv).

Mission executives in the ReMAP survey reconfirmed that a majority (79.7%) of Korean missionaries are involved in traditional types of ministry, including pioneer mission work among unreached people groups (45.3%), regular evangelism and church planting (26.6%), and helping the national church (7.8%). Eight agencies (12.5%) reported that they were doing relief and development, and three agencies (4.7%) were in other supportive service for missions (see Figure 8-5).

SIZE OF KOREAN MISSION AGENCIES			
Members	Value	Valid %	Cum. %
1–10	18	24.7	24.7
11–25	18	24.7	49.4
26–50	15	20.5	69.9
51–100	10	13.7	83.6
101–200	8	11.0	94.6
201–500	2	2.7	97.3
>500	2	2.7	100.0
Total	73	100.0	
Valid cases, 73; Missing cases, 0			

Source: *Korean Mission Handbook* (1996)

Figure 8-3

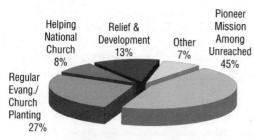

Figure 8-5. Ministry Types Of Korean Mission Agencies

One thing noticeable is that 45.3% of the respondents perceived that their missionaries are involved in pioneer mission work among unreached people groups. Surprisingly, in a 1996 survey for the handbook, 41.2% of Korean missionaries were categorized to be in frontier mission work among the unreached (see Figure 8-6). Misconception of pioneer work and a tendency toward exaggeration could have affected the ratio to some degree. Another important indication of the present missionary deployment is that 47.7% of Korean missionaries are serving in countries in the 10/40 window.[6]

Figure 8-6. Regular vs. Frontier Missions

These statistics all show that at least pioneering work among the unreached is highly regarded among Korean missionaries. Recent emphasis on reaching unreached people groups seems to be the dominant factor in selecting areas of service.

In summary, Korean missionaries in general are engaged in a difficult and demanding work of serving one of the most rapidly expanding mission thrusts in the history of Christianity. The never-easy-going way of the Koreans may possibly characterize both the missionary movement and the patterns of missionary attrition.

MISSIONARY ATTRITION IN KOREA

The focus of attention is: How many missionaries have left the mission field during the three-year period 1992–1994, terminating their ministry before the expected time? Looking at the overall picture of missions work in Korea will describe the status and recent trends of missionary attrition.

Status of Missionary Attrition

The 1994 *Korean Mission Handbook* (Lee & Moon, 1994) reported that 696 persons were added to the Korean mission force for the two years from 1992 to 1993. From the annual increase rate of 16% since 1994 which was reported in the 1996 *Korean Mission Handbook* (Moon, 1996, p. ii),[7] it can be estimated

---

6. This figure came out of the writer's calculation based on the 1996 handbook data. The number of Korean missionaries in the 10/40 countries was calculated according to the list by Luis Bush. The majority of Korean missionaries (49.3%) are in Asia. In addition, 13.1% are in Eurasia (mostly Central Asia), 7.9% in Africa, and 6.1% in the Middle East. The number of Korean missionaries in the two largest 10/40 countries of China (413 missionaries) and former USSR (Russia, 339; Central Asia countries, 577) alone reaches 1,329 (Moon, 1996, pp. iv-v).

7. This annual increase rate came out of the biannual increase rate of 34.5% (1,130/3,272 x 100) for the two-year period 1994–1995.

that the Korean missionary force increased by 523 in 1994. These figures indicate that an estimated 1,219 missionaries or 731 missionary units were added during the three-year period 1992–1994.[8]

A summary of the attrition cases in Korean mission agencies is shown in Figure 8-7. Thirty-five units (families or singles) terminated missionary work in 1992, followed by 71 cases in 1993 and 79 cases in 1994. Taken together, these numbers would tentatively indicate that 185 families and singles left the mission agency for some reason during this period, but the findings must be adjusted to compensate for overlapping memberships in mission agencies and cases of transfer of membership to other missions.

The 1994 *Korean Mission Handbook* reported overlapping in the number of missionaries due to dual memberships (239) and triple memberships (7), with the total overlapping cases equalling

253 (Moon, 1994, pp. 1-2). In other words, 7.7% of the total of Korean missionaries overlapped. If we apply this duplication ratio to the attrition cases, it could be estimated that 14 units (185 x 7.7/100) should be deducted from the grand total.

Cases of membership transfer are more difficult to estimate, as there was no question in the ReMAP survey directed to this particular concern. It is probable that about 10% (18 units) of the attrition cases could be accounted for through membership transfer.[9] The total number of attrition cases for the years 1992–1994 then becomes 153 units (185 – 14 – 18). The above figure means that approximately 833 units (731 + 153 – 51) went out within the period, but the net increase is 731 units with the disappearing missionary units counted.[10]

From the question about the preventable and unpreventable causes of loss among missionaries, the percentage of unpreventable losses was found to be 34.1% (72/211 x 100), and thus estimated preventable losses will amount to 101 cases (153 x 65.9/100).

This closer look at the reality of missionary attrition reveals several things. First, roughly 833 units (new families/singles) went to the mission field during the period 1992–1994. Secondly, roughly 153 families/singles came back home during the same period. Thirdly,

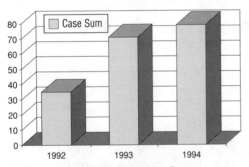

Figure 8-7. Increasing Cases Of Missionary Attrition

---

8. Since single missionaries make up 20.0% (656/3,272 x 100) of the total Korean missionary force, 243 of the 1,219 could be singles, and the remaining 976 missionaries or 488 units are married. The increase in units during this three-year period is then 731.

9. This is a subjective estimate arrived at by cases and factors the author became aware of during his research for the *Korean Mission Handbook*.

10. This figure assumes that there were 102 units that went out during the period and that 51 of the units that had been sent out before the period began returned.

roughly 101 units came back home for preventable reasons. This means that each mission agency lost an average of 2.4 missionary families (or singles) for the period. The attrition rate of the 153 units out of the 833 units is 18.4%, implying that if 100 missionaries go out, 18 will come back early. Twelve of these would come back for undesirable reasons.

If we estimate the annual loss of the missionaries to be 65 units,[11] the estimated annual attrition rate for the year 1994 becomes 3.6%.[12]

Increasing Trends

A sobering aspect of the explosion of the missionary movement is that more and more missionaries are coming back home before the expected time, and more and more mission agencies are experiencing missionary attrition. In 1992, 23.4% of the Korean mission agencies experienced missionary attrition. But that number grew to 42.9% and 43.7% in 1993 and 1994, respec-

tively. All together, 37 mission agencies (58.7% of the responding missions) experienced at least one case of missionary attrition, for preventable or unpreventable reasons, during the period 1992–1994.

Twenty-three mission agencies (35.9%) experienced at least one case of single female missionary attrition during the three-year period. Twelve mission agencies (18.7%) lost at least one single male missionary during the same period. In 28 mission agencies (43.7%), at least one missionary couple returned from the mission field.

The missionary attrition rate is higher among single missionaries than among missionary couples (see Figure 8-8). The attrition rate of the single missionaries is 45.9% (78/170 x 100) of the total returned missionaries. It is also to be noted that single female missionaries are more likely to return than single males (Figure 8-9). In Korea, 63.3% (415/656 x 100) of the single mission-

Figure 8-8. Attrition of Single Missionaries

Figure 8-9. Attrition of Female Single Missionaries

---

11. The annual loss of missionaries in 1994 equals 79/185 x 153 or 65.3.

12. The annual attrition rate equals the total loss of missionaries divided by the total number of missionaries, times 100, or 65 units/3,272 x 100 = 117 persons/3,272 x 100 = 3.6%.

aries are female, but 73.1% (57/78 x 100) of the total returned single missionaries are female. One typical reason for the higher attrition rate among single female missionaries might be parental pressure toward marriage, which often results in marriage outside of missionary commitment.[13] Korean mission agencies seem to lack specific policies for caring for single males and females.

Older and larger agencies lost more missionaries than smaller ones. This may be due to the need for more professional managerial skills and capacities within missions as they are rapidly growing.

The probability of missionary attrition was lower in international agencies, with 7.9% of the total attrition cases happening among them, whereas roughly 12% of the total Korean missionaries are with international agencies (Moon, 1994, p. 7).[14] Other factors along with the international membership may have played a part in the lower attrition rate. However, a more careful screening process in two steps (first by the home council office and then by the international office abroad), together with systematic pre-field training and expertise in member care in international agencies, may have contributed positively, notwithstanding the additional burden of cultural adjustment to the English-speaking society of the missionaries.

CAUSES OF MISSIONARY ATTRITION

Another focus of the ReMAP survey was to identify the locus of the problem in missionary attrition. To do this, reasons for attrition as perceived by agency executives were first explored. Then the actual reasons for leaving the field were considered.

Perceived Reasons

From a list of 26 reasons for attrition, respondents were asked to select the seven most important items and prioritize these according to the degree of importance. The major causes of attrition that emerged were problems with fellow missionaries, health problems, change of job, lack of call, weak home support, disagreement with the sending agency, and poor cultural adaptation (see Figure 8-10). Among the seven

A: Problems with peer missionaries
B: Health problems
C: Change of job
D: Lack of call
E: Lack of home support
F: Disagreement with sending agency
G: Poor cultural adaptation

Valid Answers: 30

Figure 8-10. Most Important Causes of Attrition

---

13. The author is indebted to Dr. Lois McKinney for this interpretation, as it was first suggested by her and was clarified through discussion with her. Additionally, her brief comments aided in the whole process of data interpretation and writing.

14. This analysis of the attrition rate in an international agency as compared to an indigenous agency was first prompted by Dr. Greg Livingstone's inquiry and advice at the Conference on Missionary Care at All Nations Christian College in April 1996.

items, "problems with peer missionaries" was considered the most serious by responding agencies. A typical example of this conflict might occur between a senior missionary and a junior. A senior missionary who has spent a longer time on the mission field might be more traditional and authoritarian in his or her leadership style, whereas a junior missionary might think a more independent spirit is needed in the life and work of a missionary. A conflictual relationship will probably develop, which will need to be resolved if the two are to work together under sound leadership.

"Health problems" was considered another important reason for the attrition of Korean missionaries. This rating may be an indication of the task-orientation of Koreans, which is both a strength and a weakness at the same time. Part of the problem may lie in the tendency of Koreans to think that ill health should not be a problem if they are called by God. It could be that Korean agencies do not pay as much attention to health issues at the time of screening as Western mission agencies do. Further, most of the Korean missionaries may feel uncomfortable spending time and money on a vacation. Many health issues could be overcome with a better balance between work and rest.

"Change of job," "lack of call," and "lack of home support" may reflect problems in the screening process. Perhaps Koreans are somewhat emotional, not only in personal decisions, but also in the group selection of missionaries. Missions zeal is a strength of Koreans, but it must not be allowed to get in the way of a careful selection process.

"Disagreement with sending agency" further indicates potential weaknesses in relational skills among Korean missionaries. It also reminds us of the importance of good interpersonal relationships as a prerequisite to intercultural competency. However, the problem of "poor cultural adaptation" also underlines a potential weakness of Koreans, who grow up in monocultural and monolingual backgrounds.

In summary, problems leading to missionary attrition appear to be more relational than work-related. Interestingly, this weakness is well perceived by mission executives and administrators.

Actual Categories of Reasons

Figure 8-11 displays the breakdown of causal categories of attrition. The questionnaire responses revealed that 72 attrition cases (34.1%)[15] were caused by unpreventable reasons, including normal retirement, political cri-

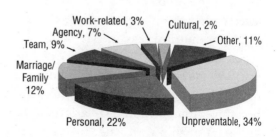

Figure 8-11. Causal Categories of Attrition

---

15. In answering the question in the ReMAP survey about the actual reasons or categories of reasons for attrition, some respondents counted a couple as two units. Even though agencies were repeatedly reminded to count a couple as one unit, some adopted different ways of counting the total cases of attrition. Inaccurate answers might erode the reliability of the research to some degree. However, additional steps were taken by the author to correct and clarify the answers to the best of his knowledge about the individual agencies.

sis, death in service, marriage outside the mission, and change of job. "Transfer to another agency" was often put in this category. Also, "outside marriage" could be interpreted as a preventable rather than an unpreventable cause of attrition, depending on the specific case involved.

Personal reasons included immature spiritual life, health problems, inadequate commitment, personal concerns, lack of call, immoral lifestyle, problems with peer missionaries, and problems with local leaders. In the perception of the mission administrators, it turned out that 21.8% (46/211 x 100) of the cases of attrition were considered to be caused by weaknesses in this category.

"Marriage and family problems" is another large category of causes (11.8% = 25/211 x 100). If the problem of an "outside marriage" of single missionaries with non-missionary spouses is included in this category, the attrition rate due to marriage and family issues is even higher.

Team reasons (9.0% = 19/211 x 100) and mission agency reasons (6.6% = 14/211 x 100) also confirm that the locus of the problem lies at a relational level, rather than being related to work (3.3%) or cultural reasons (1.9%).

In summary, at least 49.2% of the attrition cases were caused by relational problems, including intrapersonal relationship, interpersonal relationships, and relationship with God, rather than by work-related issues. This percentage is probably even higher, since many of the "unpreventable" reasons are most probably preventable in actuality and would fall into one of these relational categories. This summary in perspective coincides with the previous one about mission executives' perception of the locus of the problem.

INVESTMENTS AND MISSION POLICIES

Missionary attrition definitely has to do with an agency's willingness to care for its members. This willingness is not an abstract one, but it must find expression in actual investment. Willingness alone does not eradicate the problem. Policies of the agencies should be examined carefully to find answers to the problem.

Investments of the Agencies

Korean mission agencies spend a lot of financial and time resources on missionary care. Figure 8-12 shows that 36% (23/64 x 100) of the mission agencies spend over 30% of their financial resources on missionary care.

However, the agencies' responses show that they spend less of their time in caring for their missionaries than they do in investing funds (Figure 8-13). There was no mission agency that reported spending over 30% of its time on missionary care, although 19 agencies

FINANCIAL INVESTMENT OF KOREAN MISSION AGENCIES			
Investment of Finances (%)	Value	Valid %	Cum. %
0	12	18.8	18.8
<1	2	3.1	21.9
1–5	7	10.9	32.8
6–10	10	15.6	48.4
11–20	8	12.5	60.9
21–30	2	3.1	64.0
>30	23	36.0	100.0
Total	64	100.0	
Valid cases, 64; Missing cases, 0			

Source: *Korean Mission Handbook* (1996)

Figure 8-12

TIME INVESTMENT OF KOREAN MISSION AGENCIES			
Investment of Time (%)	Value	Valid %	Cum. %
0	12	18.8	18.8
<1	7	10.9	29.7
1–5	10	15.6	45.3
6–10	10	15.6	60.9
11–20	6	9.4	70.3
21–30	19	29.7	100.0
Total	64	100.0	

Valid cases, 64; Missing cases, 0

Source: *Korean Mission Handbook* (1996)

Figure 8-13

(29.7%) indicated that over 20% of their time is given to caring for their missionaries. Some agencies granted less than 1% of their time for missionary care. It appears that mission agencies have a willingness to spend money and time to care for their missionaries, but they do not know how.

Problems of Mission Policies

Since Korean mission agencies are willing to care for their missionaries, they may find that the problems and solutions of missionary attrition lie in policy making. As Figure 8-14 shows,

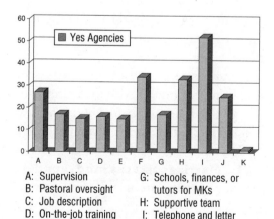

A: Supervision
B: Pastoral oversight
C: Job description
D: On-the-job training
E: Annual leave/holidays
F: Yearly visit
G: Schools, finances, or tutors for MKs
H: Supportive team
I: Telephone and letter
J: Local/area conferences
K: Other

Figure 8-14. Available Means Of Missionary Care

most of the agencies (82.5% = 52/64 x 100) provide pastoral care through telephone calls or letters at least on a quarterly basis. More than half of the mission agencies (54.0%) pay a yearly visit to the missionaries and have supportive team structures (52.4%) that may be used for missionary care. Supervision by a field leader is available in 42.9% of the agencies.

Yet Korean agencies are weak in their provision of a detailed job description or annual leave/holidays (both 23.8%); planned, on-the-job training (25.4%); pastoral oversight by someone other than a supervisor (27%); schools, finances, or tutors for missionary children (MKs) (27.4%); and local/area conferences for mission personnel (39.6%).

Types of Training Required

Almost all of the Korean mission agencies require some sort of training prior to the ministry in the mission field. However, completion of theological or professional training (62.5%), intercultural orientation (57.8%), and the organization's own courses on missions (51.6%) were more often emphasized than non-formal missionary training programs (39.1%), non-degree programs in missiology (32.8%), and short-term intercultural experience (29.7%).

These data show where the missionary training programs need to be strengthened. The importance of the - informal and non-formal aspects of missionary education cannot be overemphasized in the current Korean situation.

Weak Areas of Screening

It has often been pointed out by mission executives that efforts to maintain quality control through pre-field training have often been fruitless, because much of a person's character is determined much earlier in life.[16] So screening is more important than training, more often than not, because short-term training cannot suddenly transform the whole person.

The screening process seems to be one of the weakest areas of management in the missionary movement. Of the agencies that responded, 63.5% (40/63 x 100 of the valid answers) answered that they did not require psychological and/or personality tests in the screening process. Ages and numbers of children and other family restrictions were not considered significant among 58.7% of the agencies. Strong communication and relationship skills were not pursued by 46.0% of the agencies. Leadership and pastoral skills and the candidates' married or single status were not included among the important factors in 44.4% of the agencies. Experience in church work was not required for application to 41.3% of agencies. Another extremely serious weakness of the screening process is that 39.7% of the agencies do not require personal character references for the missionary candidates. These findings reveal that qualitative concerns and emphases are very weak or missing among many of the Korean mission agencies.

Neglected Elements Of Missionary Care

In answer to a question about insignificant areas of missionary care, 25.0%

Supportive Family/Spouse

No, not important, 25%

Yes, important, 75%

Regular Contact With Friends, Church, and Partners

No, not important, 25%

Yes, important, 75%

Figure 8-15. Most Neglected Elements Of Missionary Care

of the agencies indicated that a supportive family/spouse is not significant. Another 25.0% considered "regular contact with friends, church, and partners" to be insignificant (see Figure 8-15).

CONCLUSION

Not all missionaries should remain in the ministry. Some of them should not have been sent as part of the harvest force. But there are Marks who should be recovered. Our task is to do our best to prevent undesirable attrition and maximize the manpower of the harvest force in both a quantitative and a qualitative sense.

Analysis of the cases and causes of attrition provides us with some insights for policy making in missions, which will be used at each level of a missionary society.

1. Marriage status and gender. Mission policies should be formulated to

---

16. The author is especially indebted to Dong-Hwa Kim, director of Global Bible Translators, for this perspective. His valuable insights on quality control of Korean missions were extremely helpful.

reduce missionary attrition resulting from marriage status or gender. Ways to maximize the opportunities of single-ness should be suggested. More careful care is required in selecting and caring for single women missionaries.

2. Communication skills. Missionaries should be equipped with interpersonal communication skills before going to the mission field. The fact that more problems were seen in the relational area rather than related to work suggests that interpersonal skills are more desperately needed than intercultural competency, although the areas are intimately connected.

3. Marriage and family issues. These issues should be carefully dealt with. Awareness of the importance of family should be raised. Commitment to the ministry should not be an excuse for neglecting family concerns. Cultural norms surrounding this issue should be corrected in such a way that there can be a balanced emphasis on commitment to the task and on family care. Korean missionaries need to learn to take time to rest.

4. On-field care. Ongoing missionary care should be provided for missionaries on the field. To prevent conflict between senior and junior missionaries, detailed job descriptions and on-the-job training should be made available. Area conferences for mission personnel can be encouraged and promoted with the cooperation of mission agencies.

5. Education. Informal and non-formal aspects of education, rather than formal theological education, must be stressed in missionary education. Short-term intercultural experience is desirable because of the monocultural background of Koreans.

6. Screening. More rigorous instruments need to be developed and applied in the screening process. Personal character references, psychological and/or personality tests, and tests of communication styles should be utilized.

7. Quality control. More than anything else, awareness of and ethos for the quality control of missions should be generated and raised. Churches and agencies alike must be aware of the price that must be paid to maintain the quality of missionary work. This is not merely to prevent or reduce missionary attrition, but also to help all missionaries live and work fruitfully.

Wrapping up a lifetime of ministry, the Apostle Paul stated: "I have fought the good fight, I have finished the race, I have kept the faith. Now there is in store for me the crown of righteousness, which the Lord, the righteous Judge, will award to me on that day...." This glorious victory and promise were promised "... to all who have longed for his appearing" (2 Tim. 4:7-8). Let us strive to finish well in the task of reaching the world with the gospel.

REFERENCES

Johnstone, P. (1993). *Operation world.* Grand Rapids, MI: Zondervan.

Lee, D. T. W., & Moon, S. S. C. (Eds.). (1994). *Korean mission handbook.* Seoul, Korea: Global Missionary Press.

Lee, D. T. W., & Moon, S. S. C. (Eds.). (1996). *Korean mission handbook.* Seoul, Korea: Global Missionary Press.

Moon, S. S. C. (1994). Who are the Korean missionaries? In D. T. W. Lee & S. S. C. Moon (Eds.), *Korean mission handbook* (pp. 1-7). Seoul, Korea: Global Missionary Press.

Moon, S. S. C. (1996). Acts of the Koreans: Status and current trends of the missionary movement in Korea (1996). In D. T. W. Lee & S. S. C. Moon (Eds.), *Korean mission handbook* (pp. i-v). Seoul, Korea: Global Missionary Press.

*Steve Sang-Cheol Moon was born in Korea in 1962 and is married to Hee-Joo. Together, they have two children, Lottie Choeun and Chris Nameun. Moon has served with the Korea Research Institute for Missions (the research arm of the Global Missionary Fellowship) as chief researcher since 1990. One of his ministry obligations has been to observe and analyze the phenomenal growth of the missionary movement in Korea. He has edited the **Korean Missions Handbook** since 1990. Moon is currently finishing advanced work in intercultural studies at Trinity International University, Deerfield, Illinois. He serves as a WEF Missions Commission Associate.*

9

Brazilian Missionaries: How Long Are They Staying?

Ted Limpic

Something special is happening in Asia, Africa, and Latin America. The evangelical church is not just growing; it's exploding! Patrick Johnstone (1993) confirms that the growth of the church has been so strong that there are now more evangelicals in these non-Western regions than in North America and Europe.

Expectations have also been high that these mission *fields* would indeed become significant mission *forces*, sending out their own missionaries to join the ranks of traditionally Western-based cross-cultural workers serving around the world. Larry Keyes (1983) first talked about this "third wave" in 1983.

In Latin America, missions seemed to "come of age" in 1987, when a continent-wide missions congress called COMIBAM attracted 3,000 Latins to São Paulo, Brazil. For six days, delegates dreamed, discussed, and strategized about how to contribute most effectively to world evangelization and missions.

But just how well has the Latin missions enterprise gone since COMIBAM? Now that 10 years have passed, this seems an appropriate question to ask. How many missionaries are really being sent out? And even more importantly, how long are they staying?

THE BRAZILIAN MISSIONS MOVEMENT

Background

Although data for Latin America as a whole are still being compiled and will be presented at COMIBAM '97, another continental missions congress scheduled for Acapulco, Mexico, we do have significant information on Brazil which can help us get an idea of what's been happening.[1]

---

1. The statistics presented in this chapter may differ from those given in other chapters. There are three reasons for the variations: (1) The calculations done by Peter Brierley (chapter 6) were based on the first examination of the data. (2) Detlef Blöcher and Jonathan Lewis (chapter 7) had additional data from which to work. They examined the data from a different perspective, asking different questions. (3) Some of the statistics in the national case studies reflect new surveys and different ways of reading the numbers.

NUMBER OF CROSS-CULTURAL BRAZILIAN MISSIONARIES*						
	1989	1990	1992	1993	1994	1995
Active	856	945	1,192	1,213	1,500	1,640
On Furlough	24	20	34	54	115	124
Total	880	965	1,226	1,267	1,615	1,764
* The researcher was unable to obtain data in 1991 about Brazilian missionaries.						

Figure 9-1

Brazil is the largest country of Latin America. In terms of population, there are more people living in Brazil than in all the other countries of South America combined. This creates the curious fact that Portuguese, the language of Brazil, is the language most spoken in South America.

The growth of the evangelical church in this, the largest Roman Catholic country of the world, has been so strong that Brazilian evangelicals now make up 16% of the nation's population (up from 10% in 1985) and are growing at *twice* the rate of the population. For every baby born today in Brazil, two Brazilians are "born again."

How Many Brazilian Missionaries?

Since 1989, the number of Brazilian missionaries serving in cross-cultural contexts (both inside and outside Brazil) has grown from 880 (1989) to 1,764 (1995) (see Figure 9-1). That's an average growth of 9% per year.

It would be good to include here a brief note on definitions. In Brazil the word "missionary" does not necessarily imply "cross-cultural" involvement. Most full-time Christian workers, other than pastors, are called "missionaries." The numbers above only include Brazilian cross-cultural missionaries.

The other observation here is that 1994 and 1995 showed much higher increases in the number of missionaries than in previous years—on the order of 20% increase per year! Here we may be seeing the help of a more stable economy. Whereas prior to 1994 inflation averaged 30% per month, starting in 1994 the inflation has been reduced to 2-3% per month.

Where Are They Serving?

A look at the list of the countries where Brazilian missionaries are serving (Figure 9-2) provides an interesting insight into one facet of Brazilian missions. Most of Brazil's missionaries serve in countries where they can use either Portuguese or Spanish. The linguistic and geographical proximity of most of the countries on this list makes sense. New missions want to "get their feet wet" in safer, more familiar contexts. This should not surprise us.

TOP 15 RECEIVING COUNTRIES OF BRAZILIAN MISSIONARIES	
Country	Number of Missionaries
Brazil (among Indian tribes)	463
Portugal	104
Paraguay	82
Mozambique	78
Argentina	66
Bolivia	66
USA	59
Ecuador	51
Uruguay	47
Guinea-Bissau	45
Angola	40
Spain	37
England	34
Peru	33
Chile	29

Figure 9-2

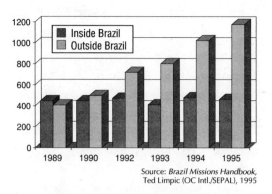

Source: *Brazil Missions Handbook*,
Ted Limpic (OC Intl./SEPAL), 1995

**Figure 9-3. Brazilian Missionaries
Serving Inside and Outside Brazil**

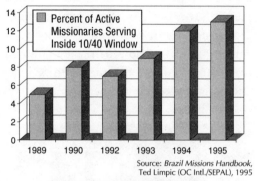

Source: *Brazil Missions Handbook*,
Ted Limpic (OC Intl./SEPAL), 1995

**Figure 9-4. Brazilian Missionaries
and the 10/40 Window**

What *has* surprised us are two significant changes that have taken place since 1989. The first has to do with the number of Brazilians serving outside Brazil. In 1989, there were more Brazilian cross-cultural missionaries serving *inside* Brazil than *outside*. Those serving inside Brazil were primarily working among Brazil's 237 different Indian tribes. But today there are nearly three times the number of workers serving outside Brazil as inside! In fact, the number of Brazilians serving in cross-cultural contexts within Brazil has remained fairly constant. No growth (see Figure 9-3)!

The second change has to do with *where* the Brazilians serving outside Brazil are going. The last few years have

made a big difference in Brazil's interest in the "10/40 window," that resistant part of the world which includes the Muslim, Hindu, and Buddhist worlds. This has been a big surprise. In 1989, just 5% of all Brazilian missionaries (including the cross-cultural missionaries within Brazil) were serving within the 10/40 window. In 1995, that percentage was up to 13%, as Figure 9-4 shows. More and more Brazilian missions are sending their workers into these very resistant areas. This certainly has implications relative to the issue of missionary attrition.

Who's Sending Them?

Although there are many respected international missions that have established offices in Brazil and are sending out Brazilians as missionaries (e.g., YWAM, OM, WEC), they account for only 31% of all the missions sending out Brazilians. The other 69% are Brazilian missions—either denominational boards or non-denominational agencies (see Figure 9-5).

When counting the missionaries themselves, we discover approximately the same breakdown. Only 30% are sent out by the *international* missions, with the rest being sent out by *Brazilian* agencies.

Source: *Brazil Missions Handbook*,
Ted Limpic (OC Intl./SEPAL), 1995

**Figure 9-5. Brazil Sending Structures:
Types of Agencies Sending Brazilians
Into Cross-Cultural Ministries**

The theological position of Brazil's sending agencies is of interest when contrasted with the strongly Pentecostal nature of Brazil's evangelical church. Estimates suggest that at least 70% of Brazilian evangelicals are Pentecostal or charismatically oriented. However, only 18% of Brazil's missionaries are sent out by agencies or boards of Pentecostal persuasion. The majority are traditional or interdenominational (see Figure 9-6).

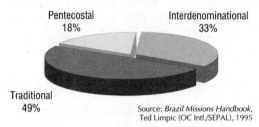

Figure 9-6. Brazilian Missionaries:
Theological Position of Sending Agency

Married or Single?

Could marital status be an issue in addressing the problem of attrition? If a strong percentage of Brazilian missionaries were single, one could suspect that a large number might feel an inclination to leave the field in order to find a suitable mate. However, as Figure 9-7 shows, more than 70% of Brazilian missionaries are married, and that percentage has tended to increase over the past several years.

Figure 9-7.
Brazilian Missionaries: Marital Status

Who's Holding Down the Fort?

One trend in Brazilian missions over the past years has been an increase in the number of Brazilians working in support or administrative capacities. In earlier years, there were very few Brazilians whose ministries were "behind the scenes." Today, things have changed dramatically.

Back in 1989, only 9% of the entire Brazilian missions enterprise served in administrative or support roles. By 1995, that percentage had nearly tripled (see Figure 9-8)! As the Brazilian missions movement matures, the need for responsible attention to financial details and more complete missionary care seems to be keenly sensed.

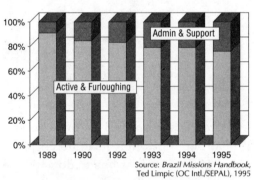

Figure 9-8. Brazilian Missionaries:
Active & Furloughing x Admin & Support

How Long Do They Stay?

Prior to the 1995 special survey on attrition sponsored by WEF (and addressed in the next section), the only data related to Brazilians and their "longevity" on the field were gathered via our yearly *Brazil Missions Handbook*. That information did not reveal anything particularly worrisome. In spite of many Brazilians participating in short-term projects with OM and YWAM, most Brazilian missionaries (55%) have been on

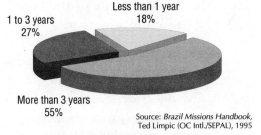

Figure 9-9. Brazilian Missionaries:
Number of Years on Mission Field

their field of service more than three years.

The percentages shown in Figure 9-9 are from 1995 and have remained fairly stable through the previous three years. The percentage of those on the field more than three years would be even higher if the short-termers were factored out.

BRAZILIANS AND THE ATTRITION ISSUE

Missions euphoria was running high in Brazil in the early 1990s. Churches all around this continent-sized country were putting on missions conferences with increasing frequency. Articles in Christian publications stressed reaching the unreached around the world. New agencies were being birthed and new fields opened, especially in the more resistant areas of the world. Interest in the Muslim world was especially high. And the initial success stories added even more fuel to the missions fire.

Shocking Statistics

But suddenly a report began circulating among Brazil's missions leaders which had the effect of a bucket of cold water. The report suggested that Brazilian missionaries were "deserters," giving up quickly when the going got rough

and heading back home. Attempts to discover the source of this sobering "research" were unfruitful. Nevertheless, the numbers cited began to be spread with increasing frequency, even being quoted at a plenary session of Brazil's national missions congress in Caxambu in October of 1993.

The numbers, though unconfirmed, were chilling: three out of four Brazilians give up before completing five years on the field. Out of 5,000 missionaries sent out, only 1,000 were still on the field five years later. In terms of attrition rate, that's a 75% loss over five years—15% per year. Not a happy statistic!

Obviously, many questions arose about the numbers. Is this possible? Where did the "research" data come from? Why doesn't this fit the numbers in the *Brazil Missions Handbook*? What about short-termers and missions summer projects? Were those workers being improperly counted, since they really did not *abandon* the field? Clearly some kind of special study needed to be done.

Going After Some Answers

The WEF Missions Commission's interest in coordinating a worldwide study of missionary attrition could not have come at a better time. In February of 1995, Brazil joined with Korea, Nigeria, Ghana, UK, Canada, USA, Australia, India, Philippines, Singapore, and others who entered later, in conducting a joint research project, ReMAP, aimed at ascertaining the causes (and possible cures) of missionary attrition.

Attrition was defined broadly as "leaving missionary service." From that perspective, some reasons for attrition are clearly acceptable: political crisis, death in service, or even normal retirement. Our intent was to identify and quantify *"undesirable attrition."* This would include problems related to (1) the missionary's marriage or family, (2) the missionary's sending body, (3) the missionary's own personal life, (4) the missionary's adaptation to the culture or language in his or her field of service, and (5) the missionary's actual work.

At a joint meeting in London, a survey form was drafted. That form was later translated into Portuguese and was then completed by 24 different Brazilian missionary-sending structures—seven denominational boards, nine non-denominational agencies, and eight international missions (most with Brazilian leaders).

Our strategy was to maximize the completion rate by conducting personal visits to each mission. Although each mission had already received the questionnaire by mail, we utilized the visit to emphasize the importance of the survey and to express face-to-face our appreciation for the agency's cooperation. We also affirmed our commitment to maintain confidentiality to whatever degree they felt comfortable. This was important, as we were dealing with issues which many of the missions considered to be pretty sensitive.

The bulk of each interview consisted in simply moving question by question through the survey questionnaire. In that way we could avoid misunderstandings and assure ourselves that we were using standard definitions and were really able to "compare apples with apples."

From the outset, we realized that there were two basic weaknesses in this process that we would have to live with.

First, the primary focus of the survey was the "sending structure," rather than the missionary. Knowing that there are always two sides to the same story, we recognized that we might only be hearing one side. Second, very few Brazilian mission agencies keep detailed records—especially as it relates to why their missionaries leave the field or their mission. In many cases, this survey served to motivate many agencies to begin keeping more detailed statistics.

What We Found Out

Copies of each completed survey form were sent to England, where they could be included in the "worldwide" ReMAP tabulations. Results of that global calculation are detailed by Peter Brierley in chapter 6.

The results shown below differ only slightly from Brierley's calculations, and any differences are due to two forms being received after the deadline. We have chosen to include the late surveys in the study presented here.

1. Real Attrition Rate

We found that the real attrition rate for the Brazilian agencies we surveyed is 7% per year. While still not good news, this is way below what we feared and about the same as in many other missionary-sending countries.

What has surprised us is the breakdown according to marital status (see Figure 9-10). As discussed above, the breakdown of the total Brazilian missions force is: married, 70%; single women, 20%; single men, 10%. When it comes to missionary attrition, the breakdown is: married, 47%; single women, 39%; single men, 14%. We are losing way more single women than we should!

**Field Breakdown
1992–1994**

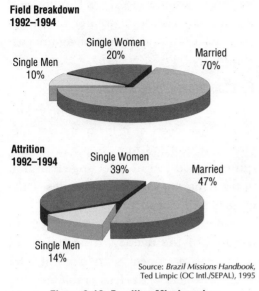

Single Women
20%

Single Men
10%

Married
70%

**Attrition
1992–1994**

Single Women
39%

Married
47%

Single Men
14%

Source: *Brazil Missions Handbook,*
Ted Limpic (OC Intl./SEPAL), 1995

**Figure 9-10. Brazilian Missionaries:
Marital Status and Attrition**

2. Greatest Single Cause of Attrition

Brazilian agencies cite "lack of financial support" as the greatest single cause of missionary attrition. In a country which has struggled through the 1980s and early 1990s with economic instability and inflation rates which have hit 40% to 50% per *month,* this attrition is more than understandable.

(American churches might find it difficult even to imagine having to adjust their missionary budgets upward by 50% per month, just to maintain their foreign workers with the same buying power in their country of service!)

Other causes cited as big contributors to Brazilian missionary attrition were:

✦ Lack of commitment.
✦ Problems with colleagues.
✦ Inadequate training.
✦ Self-esteem, stress, and other personal issues.
✦ Marriage.

3. Other Problem Areas

Outside of financial support, we found that the main problem areas are more related to character than to skills.

The third question in the survey asked the agencies to count the number of missionaries who left their mission from 1992 to 1994 and then to categorize those who left according to the reason that prompted their resignation or dismissal. Here we were not just asking agencies for their impressions. We actu-

	BRAZILIAN MISSIONARIES: REASONS FOR LEAVING MISSION	
Category	**Examples**	**% Resigned/ Dismissed**
Unpreventable	Normal retirement, political crisis, death in service, outside marriage, change of job	16
Marriage/Family	Child(ren), elderly parent, marriage/family conflicts	4
Society (Agency)	Home support, disagreement with sending agency, theological reasons	19
Personal	Immature spiritual life, health problems, inadequate commitment, personal concerns, lack of call, immoral lifestyle	26
Team	Problems with peer missionaries, problems with local leaders	5
Cultural	Poor cultural adaptation, language difficulties	3
Work-related	Dismissal by agency, lack of job satisfaction, inadequate supervision, inappropriate training	10
Other (Misc.)		17

Figure 9-11

ally gathered specific numbers. When we pooled this data, the picture represented in Figure 9-11 emerged.

The main surprise here was the discovery that the primary problem area was "personal"—reasons which related more to the missionary's character (or health) than to anything else. This finding has major implications for our training programs, some of which tend to emphasize the technical aspects of language acquisition and/or cultural adaptation over character development. We are also reminded of the importance of character formation prior to missionary service and the very important role of the local church. The importance of on-field pastoral care is also highlighted.

4. Effect of Agency Size

Only a few Brazilian agencies could be described as large (with 201-500 missionaries on their rosters). The rest are small. For the agencies we surveyed, their sizes broke down as shown in Figure 9-12.

When comparing attrition rates to agency size, there appears to be no meaningful relationship. The size of Brazilian agencies seems not to affect attrition. Both small and large agencies seem to struggle with similar issues.

SIZE OF BRAZILIAN MISSION AGENCIES	
Number of Full-Time Career Missionaries	Percent of Agencies Surveyed
1–10	9
11–25	29
26–50	22
51–100	22
101–200	9
201–500	9
>500	0

Figure 9-12

Neither a smaller agency's "family feel" nor a larger agency's greater resources provide automatic protection against attrition.

5. Older Brazilian Agencies

Some of our Brazilian sending structures have been at it for quite a while. Others are brand new. Some are doing quite a good job at selecting, training, and caring for their missionaries. Others are still learning.

When comparing attrition rates to the *age* of the agency, a pretty direct relationship appears. In general, the older the agency, the less problem it has with attrition. Our agencies seem to be learning as they grow older (see Figure 9-13).

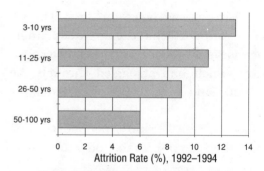

Figure 9-13. Brazilian Mission Agencies: Agency Experience and Attrition Rate

6. Place of Service

Most Brazilian agencies are sending their missionaries into contexts with high potential for attrition: different countries, different cultures, and pioneer church-planting ministries.

The agencies were asked to rank from 1 to 4 the types of missionary situations into which they send their workers (where 1 represents the area in which they have the most missionaries). We weighted their answers according to the 1–4 ranking and then compared the

BRAZILIAN MISSIONARY CONTEXTS		
Rank	Description	Estimated % of Involvement
1	People in foreign countries of a different culture and language	35
2	Ethnic groups within your own national boundaries who are of a different culture	25
3	People in foreign countries who are culturally similar and speak your national language	21
4	People within your own national boundaries who speak the national language and are culturally similar	19

Figure 9-14

1992–1994 attrition rate. The results are shown in Figure 9-14.

Due to the additional challenges of cultural adaptation, language acquisition, and (in the case of #1) geographical distance from home, we would imagine that contexts #1 and #2 would present higher potential for field losses. In fact, the actual attrition rates for agencies sending workers primarily into these contexts are indeed higher.

Brazilian workers also tend to concentrate on pioneer mission work among unreached, unchurched people groups where there is little or no evangelical presence. Such ministries might also be considered by some to present higher potential for attrition due to their distance from the support structures available where the evangelical church is present.

7. Types of Support Provided

Brazilian agencies are reasonably strong in the types of support they offer, but they are uneven in how much of their time and finances they apply to support.

We were actually quite surprised to see how active most Brazilian agencies are in the intentional support they give to their workers. Maybe this should not have surprised us, since Brazilians are by nature a relational people. Person-to-person involvement is important and is reflected in the responses we received when we asked the agencies to indicate what types of support they currently provide for their missionaries.

From Figure 9-15, it's apparent that the two weakest areas are planned, on-the-job training and provision of schools, finances, or tutors for missionary children. The other areas seem quite adequately covered. Our mission agencies give highest attention to yearly visits from the home office, quarterly

TYPES OF SUPPORT PROVIDED BY BRAZILIAN MISSION AGENCIES	
Type of Support	% of Agencies Providing
At least a yearly visit from someone in your home office	83.5
At least a quarterly telephone call or letter from your home office	83.5
Local/area conferences for mission personnel	83.5
Supervision by a mission field leader	75.0
Detailed job description	62.5
Provision of annual leave (holidays)	62.5
Supportive team structure	62.5
Pastoral oversight by someone other than a mission supervisor	54.2
Planned, on-the-job training	29.2
Provision of schools, finances, or tutors for missionary children	29.2
Other types of support	37.5

Figure 9-15

TIME AND MONEY PROVIDED BY BRAZILIAN MISSION AGENCIES		
% of Time and Financial Resources	% of Agencies Providing Specified Amount of Time	% of Agencies Providing Specified Amount of Money
<1	8.3	12.5
1–5	20.8	41.7
6–10	12.5	8.3
11–20	4.2	4.2
21–30	8.3	4.2
>30	20.8	12.5
No Response	25.1	16.6

Figure 9-16

telephone calls or letters, and local or area conferences for mission personnel.

When we look at how much time and money agencies put into this support area, we gain an additional insight (see Figure 9-16). Overall, most Brazilian agencies apply between 1% and 5% of their finances. When it comes to their investment of time, a different situation exists. Some agencies invest more than 30% of their time. On closer examination, we discovered that these were primarily the *larger* missions that have more personnel available for this kind of support.

What's the optimal investment of time and money in "member care"? That's hard to say. If those who invested more time and money showed consistently less attrition, we might have a basis for affirming that "more support equals less attrition." But this is not the case. Some of the Brazilian agencies investing the most time are still presenting the highest attrition rates! Why? Maybe these are recently-begun initiatives to correct ingrained problems. Or maybe it's not just a question of "how much time" or "how much money," but

rather a question of the *quality* of that support.

It should also be noted that our personal interviews with the agencies showed that this question was one of the most difficult to answer. Most agencies do not keep statistics in this area, and therefore they were having to make educated guesses in order to answer the question.

8. Missionary Training Required

When asked to indicate the types of training their career missionary candidates were required to complete before active service, responding Brazilian agencies answered:

- ✦ Organization's own course in missiological studies (58%).
- ✦ Cross-cultural orientation (50%).
- ✦ Short-term cross-cultural experience (42%).
- ✦ Non-degree missiological studies (42%).

The missionary training most required in Brazil is a course provided by the sending agency. Only one agency (among the 24 surveyed) requires a degree course in missiological studies. More surprising is the fact that four agencies require *no training* at all.

9. Screening Issues

When screening missionary candidates, Brazilian agencies give most importance to the candidate's personal character references, statement of God's calling, and acceptance of the mission's doctrinal statement (see Figure 9-17).

In light of the fact that missionary attrition problems most often center on personal issues, it is encouraging to see the strong value given to personal character references. The emphasis on God's

ISSUES CONSIDERED IMPORTANT BY BRAZILIAN MISSION AGENCIES

Issue	% of Agencies That Consider Issue Important
Personal character references (e.g., from candidate's church)	87.5
Clear statement of God's calling for missionary service	79.2
Acceptance of mission's doctrinal statement	70.8
Evaluation of candidate's marriage or singleness	66.7
Firm promises of financial support	62.5
Evaluation of health	58.3
Evaluation of communication and relationship skills	54.2
Previous experience in church work	45.8
Evaluation of leadership and pastoral skills	37.5
Psychological and/or personality testing	29.2
Ordination or equivalent	29.2
Previous experience in missionary work	20.8
Limits on the age or number of children; family restrictions	16.7

Figure 9-17

calling also makes sense when we remember that most Brazilian missionaries are moving into pioneer ministries where the evangelical church is either non-existent or very weak. A personal sense of God's directing hand is very important.

What is also interesting is to see what appears at the bottom of the list. What issues do Brazilian missions just not consider that important? For Brazilian mission agencies, what seems to count least is the size and age of the candidate's family. Previous experience in

missions is less important than previous experience in *church work*. Less importance is also given to ordination, one's personal call being more important than a church or denominational attribute. There is not much interest yet in psychological and/or personality testing. Not only are such tests not as accessible in Brazil, but there is also a sense that character references might provide more practical help.

10. Ways to Prevent Attrition

In preventing attrition, many Brazilian mission agencies feel the most important factors are related to the person of the individual missionary rather than the agency.

When asked to list the three factors they believe to be the *most important* in minimizing missionary attrition, Brazilian mission agencies said:

+ A clear calling to mission work from God.
+ Regular supervision, pastoral care, and support.
+ Ability to maintain a healthy spirituality without external support.

When asked to list the three factors they believe to be the *least important* in minimizing missionary attrition, the top three answers were:

+ Regular contact with friends, home church, and prayer partners.
+ Provision of appropriate and regular training.
+ Good relationship with supervisors and the mission.

While it is encouraging to see the recognition of the importance of regular supervision, pastoral care, and support, one might detect a tendency on behalf of the Brazilian missions to place a very strong emphasis on the individual: individual calling, ability to maintain a healthy spirituality *without external support*, and ability to minister without regular contact with friends, church, and prayer partners.

It surprised us to discover that *none* of the mission agencies in Brazil with the *best* attrition rates cited "ability to maintain a healthy spirituality without external support" as one of the most important factors in minimizing attrition, but *all* of the agencies with the *worst* attrition rates did! The latter place much responsibility for the missionary's success on his or her own abilities, while perhaps minimizing the agency's responsibilities.

WHERE TO FROM HERE?

After completing the study on missionary attrition and attempting to cross that information with the yearly data we've gathered on Brazilian missions and missionaries, we learned much that will be of value for the future. Besides the observations made above, certain practical needs stand out:

1. The need for Brazilian agencies to keep better statistics. For many agencies, this attrition survey was the first time they had stopped to count how many missionaries had actually left their mission. Many have indicated their desire to maintain better records and continue monitoring how they are doing in the attrition area.

2. The need to hear from the missionaries. The survey form we used was aimed exclusively at the mission agency. It's probably time to hear now from the missionaries themselves.

3. The need to keep alert to trends and keep asking questions. What happened in 1993 which resulted in the huge jump in attrition? Why are there so many single women leaving the field early? These questions and others might lead us into new insights.

4. The need to focus more attention on the local church. The top single reason for Brazilian missionary attrition is lack of financial support. The top problem area is personal: issues related to character formation and spiritual maturity. Both the financial faithfulness of the missionary "senders" as well as the character formation of those who are sent are issues tied directly to the local church.

5. The need to learn from our mistakes. The Brazil missions movement is young. We have precious few retirees. As more veterans return *successfully* from the field, they will be able to add a depth of insight to the training of newer missionaries. Today in Brazil the mission agencies that have the most experience have the least attrition. It is hoped that this reality bodes well for the future as we struggle and learn together.

REFERENCES

Johnstone, P. (1993). *Operation world.* Grand Rapids, MI: Zondervan.

Keyes, L. E. (1983). *The last age of missions: A study of Third World missionary societies.* Pasadena, CA: William Carey.

Ted Limpic is a missionary with OC International/Sepal in Brazil, where he has served since 1985. He has been a prime researcher of the Brazilian evangelical church as well as its missions movement. Prior to going to Brazil, Limpic ministered for eight years as Club Director with Youth for Christ in San Diego, California, and then 10 years as Program Director at the Forest Home Christian Conference Center. Married to Claudia since 1971, he has two sons, Jeremy and Joel.

10

Attrition in the United Kingdom

Stanley Davies

S tatistics on mission agencies have been compiled and published in the UK for more than 30 years. Figure 10-1, assembed from numbers taken from the 1996-97 *UK Christian Handbook*, gives the lie to the assumption that mission is of declining interest to the younger generations.

| UK MISSIONARIES, 1980–1995 ||
Year	Number of Missionaries
1980	8,152
1982	8,225
1984	8,095
1986	7,935
1988	8,247
1991	8,058
1993	8,742
1995	8,907

Figure 10-1

Since its inception in 1958, the Evangelical Missionary Alliance (EMA) has provided a meeting point for evangelical missions in the UK. The EMA now represents within its membership approximately 60% of all missionaries sent from the UK. In 1996, there were 120 agencies in the EMA, 56 of which are involved in sending out British expatriate missionaries to other parts of the world. Other member agencies are involved in other types of world mission activity, such as the financial support of national leaders, literature programmes, scholarship programmes, specialist support ministries, world prayer movements, and research programmes.

In the ReMAP study, 37 agencies from the UK completed the attrition questionnaire. While this response comprises only two-thirds of the EMA agencies which send missionaries, most of those participating were the larger agencies. It is therefore estimated that the UK statistics represent over 80% of all UK missionaries from EMA member societies.[1]

---

1. The statistics presented in this chapter may differ from those given in other chapters. There are three reasons for the variations: (1) The calculations done by Peter Brierley (chapter 6) were based on the first examination of the data. (2) Detlef Blöcher and Jonathan Lewis (chapter 7) had additional data from which to work.They examined the data from a different perspective, asking different questions. (3) Some of the statistics in the national case studies reflect new surveys and different ways of reading the numbers.

THE UK COMPARED WITH OTHER OSC

The "Big Four"

Four reasons for attrition are common to almost all of the old sending countries (OSC). These are normal retirement, children's needs, change of job, and health needs. In each of these cases, the UK figure stands higher than the OSC average (Figure 10-2).

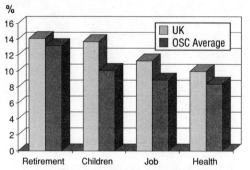

Figure 10-2. Main Reasons for UK Attrition, Compared With OSC Average

These "big four" issues account for 49% of all UK missionary attrition (compared to the OSC average of 41%). By contrast, they account for only 18% of new sending country (NSC) attrition. As such, they reflect the existence of an older missionary force in the older sending countries. Children's needs, especially education, become more pressing as secondary school age approaches. Health problems, while not confined to any one age group, become more common as one gets older. Retirement is definitely not a young person's activity!

Strengths and Challenges Specific to the UK

In order to develop the analysis of the issues in relation to the UK, it is instructive to compare the areas in which we are strongest and those in which we are

weakest with other OSC (Figure 10-3). This exercise may help highlight areas in which the UK can contribute to and also learn from other countries in the task of reducing missionary attrition.

It is encouraging to note that the UK suffers less than other countries in problems with fellow missionaries, disagreement with the sending agency, and inappropriate or inadequate training. These statistics suggest that the UK has strengths in areas such as careful screening and orientation, structural openness, provision of training, and the ability to "cope" with other missionaries!

Of more concern are the areas in which the UK comes out poorly by comparison. These are issues which require reflection and work in order to see improvement. They are areas in which we may be able to learn from others. The needs of elderly parents are a significant and perhaps unavoidable factor in all OSC attrition. The issues of job satisfaction, problems with local leaders, and change of job, however, may be related and will be examined together.

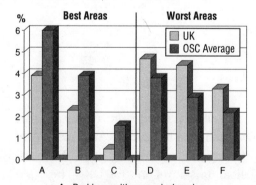

A: Problems with peer missionaries
B: Disagreement with sending agency
C: Inappropriate training
D: Elderly parents
E: Lack of job satisfaction
F: Problems with local leaders

Figure 10-3. Best and Worst UK Attrition Factors, Compared With OSC Average

Blaming the "Corporation"

Kath Donovan and Ruth Myors (chapter 4) have identified job and career issues as being of particular concern to members of the baby boomer generation (those born between 1946 and 1964). A study conducted by Ray Sanford of OC International showed that when people are dissatisfied with their job, their dissatisfaction manifests itself as concern about the work environment. Boomers tend to work according to the assumptions of a professional service-sector society, in which there are no uncontrollable elements. They solve personal struggles and problems by looking to the environment (i.e., the management) for change, such as better supervision, pastoral care, administration, and policy-making. If the problems cannot be resolved, a change of environment (i.e., a new job) becomes the only alternative.

There is increasing recognition in the UK of the need to take job issues seriously. At a conference held in June 1996, arranged by Care for Mission, a ministry specialising in the pastoral care of missionaries, several speakers referred to the need for better training of managers. They also urged that more attention be given to reducing stress caused by inadequate organisation.

One group that is striving to be responsive to such needs is People in Aid, which is a forum comprised of the major UK aid and development agencies, including Oxfam, British Red Cross, Save the Children Fund, and EMA member TEAR Fund. As a result of the experience of working in Rwanda and in the Goma refugee camp in Zaire in recent years, People in Aid is in the process of developing a Code of Best Practice for the human resource management of their field staff. Their goals are to provide the best possible support and to increase effectiveness in the use of limited resources.

UK missionaries enter service with high expectations. They have their own internal pressures, which are compounded by external pressures such as a heavy work load. It is only fair to these workers that procedures and processes be implemented which will facilitate their work and support them in their ministry. More attention needs to be given to better supervision, including job descriptions, work appraisal, and good management. Pastoral care is also important. Since pastoral care is more than "firefighting," opportunities for personal, spiritual, and career development would play a useful role in preventing attrition, as well as in helping missionary personnel to grow in their discipleship.

Culture Wars

It might be argued that there is a need for boomer and buster missionaries to develop a sacrificial ethos similar to that which characterises the older booster generation. Giving less attention to personal needs and rights would probably benefit most of us. However, the boomer concern for personal effectiveness in present and future ministry is also valid. We have to accept that there is good attrition as well as bad attrition. There have been cases of expatriate missionaries who have remained in their sphere of service far longer than necessary, prolonging dependency, stifling growth, and hindering the development and maturation of those among whom they work.

Donovan and Myors make the telling point that the idiosyncrasies of each generation are valuable in the contribution they bring to the work of mission in their time. The sacrificial and flexible ethos of many boosters was vital for the pioneering work they undertook. The boomer instinct for effectiveness and personal growth fits well with the contemporary context of partnership with national churches. It also keeps people from staying in a given position longer than necessary. The expectation is that workers will remain only as long as they are being effective. There is an acceptance of the likelihood of moving to a different locus of service at a future date.

It must be acknowledged that booster values still define the culture, expectations, and procedures of a considerable number of UK mission agencies. This can be illustrated by those senior leaders who speak of the "mission family" (which implies a long-term commitment to the same people and organisation). Another example is the idea that marriage outside the mission requires leaving the service of a given agency.

Most boomers and busters are probably more comfortable with concepts such as being part of a mission "organisation" or "movement" or being in a group of like-minded individuals. As such, the relationship is task-oriented (especially for boomers). The difference can be illustrated in the change of terminology from missionary "society" to mission "agency." Busters can accept the concept of a mission "family" if the focus is on support and relationships. If, on the other hand, the term is used to suggest a life-long relationship or conformity to booster norms and values, then the term "family" can be filled with negative connotations.

Is All Attrition Really Attrition?

The purpose in outlining the above is to illustrate that some attrition may not be attrition at all. Attrition may be caused by the way an agency operates and by the expectations communicated to its staff. For example, job change may not be attrition at all. An individual or couple may instead be moving to a different sphere of service, perhaps with another agency. From a booster point of view, this is attrition, since the missionaries are leaving the mission. But from the point of view of those making the move, they are simply moving on to a new stage in their ministry. Since most attrition is recorded and defined by the agency, this move is classified as attrition.

Differences in understanding often surface relative to what constitutes missionary service, the meaning of a call to service, the work that will be done, job supervision, and pastoral care. These differences between younger missionaries and senior staff of an older generation, who are part of the "culture" of a given mission agency, can be a contributing factor both in the increase of "real" attrition and in the inflation of attrition figures.

ACTION PLANNED IN THE UK

The EMA Council, which is made up of senior mission leaders in the UK, has begun to discuss issues of missionary attrition and generational differences. It is agreed that the analysis carried out by Donovan and Myors can assist in understanding oneself and others, as well as in identifying possible avenues for change. Areas which require acknowledgement of the differences across generations include an understanding of calling, expectations regarding pastoral care and job supervision, leadership and management styles, and organisational ethos.

While the generational distinctives are valid and are seen to be generally applicable, we need to think theologically as well as sociologically. Each area needs to be subjected to a biblical critique, so that we may all increasingly reflect the saving and transforming work of Christ. For example, it must be recognised that a life-style of sacrifice and a commitment to holiness are not simply booster characteristics. Rather, each generation may understand and translate these biblical callings differently.

It is recognised that the ReMAP study spoke primarily with mission agency leaders about reasons for missionary attrition and that different perspectives may be provided by talking to returned missionaries. A study of 41 returned missionaries who were former students of Glasgow Bible College has recently been completed by Susan Chalmers, personnel manager at Action Partners. This study provides a useful model for other colleges to adopt for their graduates. Similar studies on former students have been undertaken by Bob Hunt, Vice Principal of All Nations Christian College. The EMA Executive considers it vital that the views of former missionaries be obtained, in order to complement those of agency leaders.

The EMA will continue to examine issues relating to missionary attrition through its Personnel Officers' Group, a group run jointly with the Churches Council on Mission (the non-evangelical equivalent of EMA). The EMA recognises that it is vital that lessons be learned and procedures be improved to lessen the pain, frustration, and disappointment caused by any premature return from missionary service.

In today's rapidly changing world, we cannot lock the current generation into older ways of thinking. It is important to go on a journey together to find out what mission commitment and involvement might mean in the future. An increasingly fragmented world is not an attractive context for long-term commitment. However, God's abiding purpose in history is still to reconcile His world to Himself, and this purpose will continue to invite our commitment to mission involvement.

Stanley Davies *was born in 1939 in India of missionary parents. He is married to Margaret, the mother of their four children. A cartographical surveyor by profession, Davies traveled extensively in Africa and Asia in his work, prior to undertaking study at the Bible Training Institute, Glasgow, Scotland, to prepare for missionary service. Davies served with the Africa Inland Mission in Kenya from 1965–1980. From 1980–1983, he was Director of Missions Studies at Moorlands College, England. He is a WEF Missions Commission Associate, and since 1983 he has served as General Secretary of the Evangelical Missionary Alliance (UK). He is also Secretary to the European Evangelical Missionary Alliance, as well as TEAR Fund.*

11

Attrition in Ghana

Seth Anyomi

The Ghana Evangelical Missions Association (GEMA) took on the assignment of conducting a survey to identify specific reasons that missionaries leave missionary service. Ghana was chosen for a case study in the global project, ReMAP, of the World Evangelical Fellowship (WEF) Missions Commission. The task was assigned to GEMA's Research Commission under the leadership of Rev. Edward Arcton, General Co-ordinator of GEMA.[1]

A two-step approach was adopted for effectiveness and accuracy. First, a questionnaire prepared by the WEF Missions Commission was sent to each of the 51 missionary churches and parachurch mission organizations that comprise GEMA. To ensure that all those chosen for the survey received their questionnaire, the team traveled the length and breadth of the 10 regions within Ghana, and Rev. Arcton took pains to explain the mechanics of the survey personally to each participant.

After serving the participants with the questionnaire, the team waited for about a month before launching the second step of the project. This phase involved revisiting each of the survey recipients, in order to supervise and encourage those who had not yet filled out the questionnaire, as well as to pick up the forms that had been completed. For those who did not complete the survey during the follow-up visit, a third visit was arranged, at which time the remaining forms were collected and returned to the office for data compilation.

This approach to the survey was highly successful. Every one of the questionnaires was filled out and either mailed back or picked up by Rev. Arcton and his team. Visiting the respondents encouraged them to elaborate verbally on some of their responses, thus providing an affective dimension to the survey. GEMA's primary goal in adopting this method was to gain a new body of knowledge, insights, and challenges

---

1. The statistics presented in this chapter may differ from those given in other chapters. There are three reasons for the variations: (1) The calculations done by Peter Brierley (chapter 6) were based on the first examination of the data. (2) Detlef Blöcher and Jonathan Lewis (chapter 7) had additional data from which to work. They examined the data from a different perspective, asking different questions. (3) Some of the statistics in the national case studies reflect new surveys and different ways of reading the numbers.

which would help promote the Association's work among various churches and missionary agencies operating in Ghana. The comments that follow reflect not only the objective responses to the questionnaire, but also the experiences of missionaries, mission executives, and churches that are struggling to determine their role in the context of missions in general and Ghanaian missions in particular.

SURVEY PARTICIPANTS

The survey participants included 24 mission agencies, 6 denominational sending bodies, and 21 local missionary sending churches, making a percentage representation of 47%, 12%, and 41%, respectively. The participants may be divided broadly into churches planted by old sending (Western) mission agencies and those falling under the new mission/church category. They include recruiting agencies, training institutions, and sending agencies. Five organizational groups are present:

+ Christian Council of Ghana Churches.
+ Ghana Pentecostal Council Churches.
+ Council of Charismatic Churches.
+ Local and international parachurch organizations.
+ Indigenous independent Ghanaian missionary organizations.

To understand Two-Thirds World missions within the Ghanaian context, one needs to examine each of the above groups in relation to the causes of missionary attrition, the extent of missionary losses, and historical factors which contribute to attrition.

Christian Council Of Ghana Churches

The Christian Council of Ghana Churches includes the old mainline denominations such as Presbyterian, Methodist, Anglican, AME Zion, and the Evangelical Presbyterian churches. These churches trace their roots to the great Protestant movement that swept across Europe and later extended to America.

The beginning of the missionary movement in Ghana coincided with the Portuguese exploration of the 15th and 16th centuries. History records that the Portuguese landed on the shores of Ghana (then called Gold Coast) in 1471. Eleven years later, in 1482, they began construction of the St. George de la Mine Castle (now known as the Elmina Castle) at Elmina. After King John ascended to the throne in Portugal in 1521, he determined to teach the natives of Elmina and its surroundings the Christian faith. He therefore instructed Captain Estervao da Gama, "Command the sons of the Negroes living in the villages to learn how to read and write and how to sing and pray while ministering in the church."

The Methodist Church began its missionary work in the early part of the 19th century, followed by the Presbyterians from the Basel Mission in Switzerland and the Evangelical Presbyterians from the Bremen Mission in Germany. These groups were followed by the Anglican Church (Church of England), the AME Zion Church, and others.

The Protestant movement was very successful during its initial phase. Missionaries from Europe and later America poured in to carry out the task of spreading the gospel and planting churches after the tradition of their sending mission bodies. These early missionaries distinguished themselves in the area of endurance. The word retreat was not part of their vocabulary. With them came substantial financial support to take care of all their financial needs.

In 1957, Ghana broke away from the colonial rule of the British and became an independent nation. Political protection was no longer guaranteed for expatriates. This factor caused many missionaries to pull out of the young nation just after her birth. Thanks be to the Lord God, the national denominational churches were already in place! The new church leaders were, however, confronted with many challenges, ranging from theological issues of doctrine to financial responsibilities for the congregations to personnel salaries. Would they be able to continue to promote outreach programs so vital to the expansion of the church? Indeed they would. The WEF survey showed that there has been no significant dropout among missionaries attempting to continue the spread of the denominational churches.

Ghana Pentecostal Council Churches

The Pentecostal movement in Ghana began shortly after the close of World War I. Germany's defeat in the 1914–1918 war cost that nation her place not only in the political arena, but also in spiritual/church mission leadership. New Pentecostal movements looking for outlets took advantage of the political confusion in the large sending countries and began to move into the colonies to spread their faith.

Missionaries of the Apostolic faith arrived from Scotland to establish the Apostolic and Church of Pentecost. Later, the American Assemblies of God and Foursquare Church also initiated church planting activities in Ghana. These churches are still expanding due to the zeal passed on by their founding fathers. A few foreign missionaries continue to operate in the country, but most of the work is now carried on by nationals, who have answered the missionary/apostolic call in large numbers.

In 1937, the Apostolic Church of Bradford, Scotland, sent a missionary family, Pastor and Mrs. James McKeown, to Asamankese, in the southern part of Ghana. The McKeowns were sent in response to a request by a group of Faith Tabernacle correspondents who had experienced the baptism of the Holy Spirit with its accompanying manifestation of speaking in tongues, healing, and prophecy. A misunderstanding occurred between the McKeowns and the group that had invited them. Pastor McKeown therefore moved his headquarters to Winneba under the name Apostolic Church. The old group took the name Christ Apostolic Church under the leadership of Apostle P. N. Anim.

Pastor McKeown vigorously undertook the work of evangelism, and his denomination soon became a vibrantly growing church with assemblies along the coast and a few in Ashanti. Later the Apostolic Church suffered two more splits. The faction which Pastor McKeown led assumed the name Church of Pentecost. This denomination is today well organized as a church and has branches all over Ghana. It is perhaps the fastest growing church in Ghana, following in the tradition of the vigorous evangelism of its founder.

Charismatic Movement

The charismatic movement, characterized by healing and by the casting out of demons, has been present in Ghana since the early 20th century. The torch-bearer of this movement, William Wade Harris of Liberia, appeared in southwest Ghana in 1914, manifesting these gifts of the Spirit. There are also records of charismatic activities in some prayer groups which sprang up after World War I. These activities were said to be a response to the influenza epidemic which broke out after the war. Many of the present indigenous churches, popularly known as spiritual churches, have their roots in the charismatic revival of this period between 1914 and 1937.

In recent years, the charismatic movement in Ghana has, in effect, burst at the seams. Several thousand fellowships, churches, prayer groups, and camps have sprung up since the late 1970s among the rank and file of society. The downside of this explosive growth, which has emerged from the baby boomer/buster generation with great zeal, is that it is sometimes difficult to sustain.

Parachurch and Indigenous Independent Organizations

Most of the parachurch and indigenous independent organizations in Ghana have roots in the charismatic faith. Many members of these organizations were disciples of Scripture Union, Campus Crusade for Christ, and The Navigators from the UK and USA. Prayer, Bible study, and evangelism form the foundation of these ministries—disciplines which together can give rise to mighty revivals. Despite financial and material limitations, these groups are moving ahead by faith, and for now, their momentum seems to be sustained.

FAILINGS OF EARLY MISSIONARIES

The efforts of the early missionaries from the West in spreading the gospel resulted in the planting of the church in Ghana. However, these dedicated servants of God fell short in several critical areas. First, they failed to raise up more church planters like themselves. Unlike missionaries from the Pentecostal/charismatic movement, the early workers from the mainline denominations failed to pass on their missionary zeal, which had compelled them to leave their home countries, travel thousands of miles on rough seas, and face illness and death in an inhospitable environment in order to bring the gospel to the heathen on the continent of Africa. Because the early missionaries failed to instill this missionary fervor in their congregations, the churches that they started expanded slowly after the Westerners left.

Second, the early missionaries failed to impress upon their converts the absolute requirement of holiness, without which no one shall see God (Heb. 12:14). The result has been moral decay, illegitimate children, and general complacency in the church down to the present day. The evangelistic zeal which characterized reformers such as Martin Luther and John Wesley has been sadly lacking.

Third, the earlier missionaries were often accused of serving the interests of the nations they represented. They were charged with magnifying the power of the West and promoting capitalism. Rather than introducing a good servant-leadership example, these early workers appeared to exploit the poor. Mission education gave the impression of serving and creating a privileged elitist class, whose members were stooges of Western capitalism, exemplifying its greed, violence, and intellectual darkness.

A fourth poignant issue relates to culture. It must be the aim of missionaries to *lead people to Christ* and not to change the culture. Once people become Christians, they are bound to abandon the pagan beliefs and practices to which they had previously been enslaved. Over time, the culture may change as Christianity takes root in the area, but missionaries should not be the ones to press for such changes. To their discredit, the early missionaries were often instigators of cultural change. Even today, some conflicts which have resulted in missionary attrition may be traced to this issue.

CAUSES OF ATTRITION IN GHANA

The ReMAP study on missionary attrition identified the seven most important reasons for leaving missionary service.[2] In the Ghanaian context, personal problems appear at the top of the list of reasons missionaries leave the field, accounting for 36% of all attrition. This area includes immature spiritual life; health problems; inadequate commitment; personal concerns such as low self-esteem, stress, and singleness; lack

of genuine spiritual call to missionary work or loss of such call; and immoral lifestyle.

Societal reasons are in second place in problems of missionary attrition in Ghana. Prominent among the societal factors is lack of home support, including inadequate financial, prayer, and other support from the home church or family, together with a high rate of inflation.

Third are work-related factors. Here, inadequate or inappropriate training and preparation for missionary work is the most significant factor. There is also the problem of inadequate supervision of a missionary's work, resulting in mistakes on the job. Lack of resources to carry out the missionary task has played a part in some missionaries' early departure from the mission field.

Unpreventable reasons are in fourth place, including change of job, normal retirement, political crisis, death in service, and outside marriage.

Team factors fall into fifth place in relative seriousness of attrition factors.

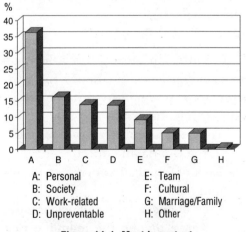

Figure 11-1. Most Important Causes of Attrition in Ghana

---

2. Refer to the survey instrument reproduced on pages 363–370 for a complete listing of the various attrition factors by category.

The greatest problem area seems to come from local church leaders who are not mission minded. Resistance from local/traditional leaders may frustrate missionaries, resulting in attrition.

Cultural reasons occupy sixth place on the chart of missionary attrition. Among the cultural reasons are the inability to adapt to a new culture and self-deception that there are no differences between one's home culture and the culture of the mission field. Where the spoken language is different, inability to learn the new language quickly may result in frustration leading to attrition.

Marriage/family reasons are in seventh place. Of particular note are the family responsibilities of a missionary in the extended family setting of Ghana. It is the responsibility of a Ghanaian adult to care for aging parents and other close relatives of the extended family. Where adequate financial provision is lacking, the missionary is compelled to drop out.

These categories of attrition factors are charted in Figure 11-1.

THE ATTRITION SURVEY AND GEMA

The attrition survey threw light on areas of deficiency in Ghana's missionary enterprise. Four areas in particular were highlighted:

+ The need for missionary awareness in the Ghanaian church.
+ Lack of financial support and commitment.
+ Lack of missionary call, vision, and objective among the mainline rich churches.
+ The need for education on resource management to yield optimal support, i.e., how to link the missionary to missionary support.

The need for missionary awareness had been previously demonstrated in 1990, through a survey conducted under the auspices of the Ghana Evangelism Committee (GEC). The purpose of the survey was to determine the scope of the unfinished missionary task in Ghana. When the findings were made public, representatives of churches and parachurch organizations were surprised at how little they knew of the mission opportunities in the country.

The Ghana Evangelical Missions Association (GEMA) was born out of this meeting specifically to tackle the missionary challenge in Ghana. GEMA sought to bring into its membership all churches and organizations, both local and international, that were operating within the country. Three main objectives were formulated:

+ Foster co-operation among the membership by holding regular seminars and workshops for fellowship.
+ Share human, financial, and material resources in order to make maximum use of these resources.
+ Tackle the task of reaching the unreached together.

So far, GEMA has helped organize seminars and workshops in select parts of the country. It has co-operated with one of its members, the African Christian Mission, and with Western partners to develop Ghana's first truly indigenous missionary training institution, the Ghana Evangelical Missionary Institute or GEMI. Through sharing of resources, GEMA has also supported worthy projects such as the work of Sports Evangelism in Ghana.

◈

In an effort to reach all unreached parts of the country, GEMA is adopting a strategy to regionalize its operations so that chapters of the Association will be present in every district in Ghana. These local bodies will provide moral support to missionaries working in these areas in an effort to reduce attrition.

In the area of finance, GEMA provides combined bargaining power and credibility for the member missionary groups. Individual member organizations and churches have benefited from overseas donor support because they belong to a larger group. For example, a church of the AME denomination received funds from TEAR Fund Switzerland as part of the foundation's assistance to the furtherance of the gospel in Ghana.

Another asset of the Association is its collective wisdom. As noted above, a prominent reason for missionary dropout is lack of missionary call, vision, and objective for individuals and some local churches. The leadership of GEMA has the resources for dealing with this situation.

AREAS FOR FURTHER STUDY

Missionary Education

There is an urgent need for a closer look at the education of national missionaries and their dependents. In the early days, the majority of graduates from the schools established by mission agencies belonged to mainline denominations. They generally became either chaplains or teachers and not missionaries. The subjects taught included Latin, mathematics, art, history, religion, and music. One might say that the primary aim of education was to facilitate the reading of the Bible and participation in church life. The overall philosophy of mission education was determined by the tenets of the church.

Unfortunately, in many mission schools, education appeared to aim at producing Ghanaians divorced from their culture, rather than individuals who understood the cultural beliefs and practices in a way that would enable them to contextualize the Scriptures in that culture. Mission schools ended up producing an elitist class who would have nothing to do with the pagan illiterate local society. This attitude persists today. Is this the kind of education to be considered for the emerging national missionaries, who have an obligation to pass on the missionary tradition to succeeding generations?

It is very true that church planters may find themselves in a primitive area where formal education does not exist. But since they are on the mission field for the primary purpose of opening the eyes of the nationals to the truth about Jesus Christ and His redemptive work, the educational tools for accomplishing this objective must form part of the missionary plan. Missionaries should include the education of the nationals with the education of their own children. The curriculum should not be limited to the three Rs; rather, it should include disciplines which promote the appreciation of all humans as being made in God's image. The highest human goal must be to restore dignity to fallen man through the message of the gospel.

Perhaps the greatest challenge faced by mission schools today is secularization. State control of education has meant less and less emphasis on the ideas, values, and perspectives that shaped the mission-controlled schools in earlier times. Even a casual look at the denominational church schools today reveals that the church has lost its grip on the theory, content, and methods of teaching that used to prevail.

Young people today are indoctrinated early into the secular philosophy of education. They are taught to pursue knowledge and to focus on outward things, rather than on the inner spiritual nature and on appropriate responses to both secular and spiritual things in a rapidly changing world. Secular education in mission schools and seminaries has robbed students of the concept of an absolute being in an absolute world with an absolute destiny. Instead, the emphasis is on relativism and nihilism, which reduce man to a nonentity drifting along in a universe of nothingness, without a purpose or a definite destiny. How can missionaries who have graduated from such schools maintain consistency on the mission field, where a lifetime of total commitment is called for?

Literature and Audiovisual Aids

Another area that needs attention is curriculum materials. To enhance education, literature that is both culturally appropriate and Christ centered is called for. With the aid of such literature, missionary education should focus on producing graduates having Christian qualities of love, compassion, humility, sacrifice, and the like. We must develop an educational perspective that includes biblical educational principles, objectives, and curriculum materials.

In the area of audiovisual aids, emphasis should be placed on materials that will serve as mission awareness tools for the next generation of missionaries, not on tools which only bring us up to par with secular educational development.

Social Development

A third area for study in the indigenous missions context is social development. Too often church planters seem to be more concerned with church buildings and musical instruments than with the living stones that make up the church or the unbelievers who are potential candidates for the church. What about the orphans, the street children, and the sick in the society? What would it take to provide for these neglected individuals? Research is called for in order to understand the task of social development and to propose ways to meet the needs that exist.

The goal of any serious Christian leader and indeed the leadership of the WEF Missions Commission must be to revive the inculcation of the ideas, values, and perspectives which produced David's men of valor (2 Sam. 23) and the heroes of faith who decorate the New Testament (Heb. 11). If attrition is to be reduced in Ghana or elsewhere, missionaries and would-be missionaries must be presented with models of fortitude, sacrifice, and daring faith in missions of men and women who "did not love their lives so much as to shrink from death" (Rev. 12:11).

CONCLUSION

The missionary attrition project brought new knowledge to the Ghanaian church and mission family. It brought to public awareness forgotten missionaries working in some of the darkest and most difficult parts of Ghana. It also threw light on the resources available to help speed up the efforts to reach the 15,000 villages in Ghana that still need the gospel of Christ. Four main challenges emerged:

1. The need for cultural training. The survey findings brought home the urgent need for cultural training as a way to forestall attrition and increase effectiveness in reaching the culturally diverse groups in Ghana. It is apparent that missionaries need to learn the local language if they expect to be effective in a new mission field. With language learning skills and tools in place, their work would not be impeded by language barriers. The same applies to other cultural variables, such as food and local customs.

2. The need for spiritual training. Spiritual emphasis in missionary preparation is a must. Indeed, some missionaries have dropped out because the spiritual warfare became too intense for them. Others have left because they were totally ignorant of the existence of the wicked spirits that scheme against us, as Ephesians 6:11-12 declares: "Put on the full armor of God so that you can take your stand against the devil's schemes. For our struggle is not against flesh and blood, but against the rulers, against the authorities, against the powers of this dark world and against the spiritual forces of evil in the heavenly realms."

3. The need for church involvement in funding. The survey showed how little Ghanaian missionaries and the church at large know about the church's role in funding missions work. The thinking of the average church member must be changed from a mentality of poverty to one of liberality. Christians must learn to depend upon the Lord's promise to supply all their needs according to His riches (Phil. 4:19). They must recognize that the church is the local representative of Christ through which the needs of others are to be met.

4. The need for Christ-centered education. The education of the next generation of missionaries must be made truly Christ centered. The principles of the Bible must supplant the principles of secular education and contemporary humanist philosophies. The importance of a Christ-centered education cannot be over-emphasized, since education defines and interprets history and life in general. The challenge is to develop a model of Christ-centered education for both missionary children and other children on the mission field.

Missionary training must present missions as more than just a call to professionalism. Missions involves total surrender to a cause worth dying for—a cause which provides purposefulness and hope beyond this life. A missionary education that is Christ centered produces a sense of usefulness in God's hands and in God's world, regardless of circumstances, hardships, or threats to life.

Finally, mission awareness and education must awaken Christians to a new social order patterned after the kingdom of God which Jesus talked about. Such a social order produces political responsibility that surpasses nationalistic tendencies. Economic possibilities are tied not to a world system having limited resources, but to God, who created, shaped, and controls the world.

It must be the prayer of every mission leader that the knowledge and new insights gained through this survey on missionary attrition will become part of the thinking of the church and will pass from there to the mission field, where missionaries labor with Christ for the salvation of the lost. It must also be the prayer of every Christian that those who are called will be totally obedient to the call and will be found faithful in fulfilling their mission. The harvest must not wait because the harvesters vacate their place of calling and lose their sense of mission!

Seth Anyomi and his wife, Christiana, have four children. Trained as a teacher in Ghana, Anyomi later did further undergraduate and graduate studies in the USA in educational administration. He and his wife pioneered the work of the African Christian Mission in Ghana. They have planted six churches and run a day care center, a Christian school, a vocational school for girls, a missionary training institute, and two medical clinics in Ghana. Since 1990, Anyomi has served as President of the Ghana Evangelical Missions Association. He is a member of the Executive Council of the TWMA, is a WEF Missions Commission Associate, and is Chancellor of the World Link University for Africa.

12

Attrition in the USA And Canada

Phillip Elkins

A few months ago I saw a news story on Jason Summon. He is a high school student whose school was experiencing a 25% dropout rate. It seemed that parents, faculty, and school administrators were concerned about attrition, but Jason made it his mission to reduce attrition to zero. He said he was creating a dropout patrol, ready to work with anyone considering dropping out. He declared zero tolerance for dropping out, and the school was destined to become "dropout free." He and his dropout patrol are dramatically impacting students' lives, because they are focused on the causes and solutions for unnecessary attrition.

MONITORING MISSIONARY ATTRITION

The single most startling discovery in my survey effort among North American mission agencies and churches was how few have "Jasons" who have created an internal structure to monitor attrition and its causes and have planned a pathway toward solutions.

There were some exceptions. Jim Slack with the Foreign Mission Board of the Southern Baptist Convention (SBC)

has been a "Jason" for over 10 years. Even before he stepped in, a "dropout" monitoring system was in place. But he has struggled over what the cause of attrition was in each case, whether it was preventable, and what can be done to prevent attrition among other missionaries. Similarly, the Christian and Missionary Alliance (CMA) has set up a very intentional system for trying to detect problems on the field, together with specific courses of action to resolve them before they blossom into premature departure. The same system is able to provide highly accurate information about the reasons for attrition for those who do depart, and it seeks corrective action when a case is determined to have been preventable.

At the opposite end of the spectrum are agencies, even among the larger ones, that have no "Jason" at work, no system to track the causes of attrition, no intentional path to correct the preventable cases. Between these two poles lie the vast majority of agencies. They have no appointed "Jason," but they believe they have a handle on their attrition causes. Some feel that the causes are disturbing but that the situation is acceptable. "We are, after all, in a war with Satan, and casualties are to be expected." These agencies have no readily available statistics tied to causes, no detailed annual or five-year or 10-year review process of how their attrition breaks down into non-preventable and preventable cases. There are even fewer agencies that have detailed analyses of what action steps to take to correct preventable attrition.

Churches were included in the survey because many larger churches in North America are taking an aggressive role in the recruitment and sending of missionaries. They justifiably want to be full partners with agencies, but I found that few have even begun to look at the effectiveness of their efforts. The question, "Do your missionaries drop out more frequently?" or, "Do they have longer, more effective ministries?" does not even appear on their agenda. When churches get heavily vested in the sending process, does it make any difference in the longevity and effectiveness of their missionaries? Currently, this cannot be measured, because there are no "Jasons" in these churches working on the issue.

I received numerous responses from agencies stating that the database on attrition that they had been keeping did not provide responsible answers to our survey questions. Translation: "We have to guess at the real causes of attrition. We have no annual, systematic method for going beyond what missionaries or a staff person gave as the reason for leaving." One well-known agency said, "We have done no analysis for 15 years. We have few answers."

One of the largest agencies in North America called and said, "Thank you for asking these questions. They are the kinds of questions we should have been asking ourselves but have not been asking. We have kept lots of data and statistics, but because we were not aggressively searching for the real causes and solutions to unnecessary attrition, we have no concrete answers. We have taken the survey as our wake-up call and are now modifying how we deal with attrition." My sincere hope is that every agency/sending church in this position would be similarly *awakened*.

We looked into the past and found that the last significant, broad-scale study on attrition was published by the Missionary Research Library in 1965 (Bailey & Jackson, 1965). That study involved 4,970 missionaries serving with 36 agencies from 1953 to 1962. At the time, there were 213 agencies altogether with 23,432 missionaries. Today, there are 360 sending agencies in the USA. Of these, 160 agencies with 18,845 career missionaries responded to our survey. In addition, 77 churches from the USA responded and 25 out of 67 Canadian agencies (see Figure 12-1).[1]

Unfortunately, the 1965 report did not give an annual attrition rate for all causes. It did rightly divide "withdraw-

---

1. The statistics presented in this chapter may differ from those given in other chapters. There are three reasons for the variations: (1) The calculations done by Peter Brierley (chapter 6) were based on the first examination of the data. (2) Detlef Blöcher and Jonathan Lewis (chapter 7) had additional data from which to work. They examined the data from a different perspective, asking different questions. (3) Some of the statistics in the national case studies reflect new surveys and different ways of reading the numbers.

SURVEY STATISTICS (USA AND CANADA)				
	Number of Surveys Sent	Number of Surveys Determined Not Applicable	Number of Usable Surveys	Percent of Surveys Completed
USA agencies	360	13	160	46
Canadian agencies	67	1	25	38
USA churches	277	11	77	29
Canadian churches	1	0	1	100

Figure 12-1

als" into two categories: "presumably-avoidable" withdrawals and "normally-anticipated" withdrawals. The latter category included retirements, deaths, short-term missionaries completing contracts, and career missionaries with 20 or more years of service. These four classifications were not regarded as casualties and therefore were not included in the study. Casualties included only those who were described as "presumably-avoidable" withdrawals.

The avoidable attrition for the decade 1953–1962 was 28% or 2.8% per year. The annual avoidable attrition rate in the current study for the USA was 3.96%; for Canada it was 4.42%. The unavoidable rate for the USA was 2.15%; for Canada, 3.03%. For all reasons, the USA had a 6.12% annual attrition rate, and Canada had a 7.45% rate.

A tribute to the Christian and Missionary Alliance is that their avoidable attrition rate has been a mere 1.3% per year for the last decade. Similarly, in 1995 the Assemblies of God had an avoidable attrition rate of 2.33%.

One has to look closely at how attrition percentages are determined by different agencies in order to make comparisons between agencies. For the decade 1984–1993, the CMA had an annual overall attrition rate of 6.3%. But 87% of the staff were career missionaries, and their attrition rate was only 3.8%. If we exclude acceptable reasons for withdrawal, the number drops to 1.3%.

The Foreign Mission Board of the Southern Baptist Convention did a study for the period 1980–1991 that showed an annual attrition rate of 3.84%. This attrition rate does not include (1) retirement at a regular age, (2) termination of journeymen and associates after contract time, or (3) special assignment after the completion of their assignment (Bridges, 1982). It does include death, however, as an attrition factor. Thus, a clear comparison between the SBC and CMA reports cannot be made, because they do not have the same "acceptable" and "non-acceptable" categories. Since they do keep extremely detailed records, however, equivalent comparisons could be determined, if needed. It is our hope that a concerted effort might be made by the missions community to arrive at commonly defined and accepted categories of attrition in order to facilitate the collection and analysis of data for the good of the movement.

For our current study, we chose to divide attrition into two major categories: "preventable" and "unpreventable." It seems obvious, from an agency perspective, that preventable attrition requires effort in the area of "prevention," while unpreventable attrition requires a very different emphasis, perhaps on "replacement." Under the category of unpreventable attrition, we listed five reasons:

+ Normal retirement.
+ Political crisis.
+ Death in service.
+ Marriage outside the mission.
+ Change of job due to completion of assignment or move to a new post.

Preventable attrition included six major categories:

+ Marriage/family reasons.
+ Agency reasons.
+ Personal reasons.
+ Team reasons.
+ Cultural reasons.
+ Work-related reasons.[2]

CONDUCTING THE NORTH AMERICAN SURVEY

Our first task was deciding which agencies to include in this kind of survey. The most helpful listing was that contained in the *Mission Handbook* produced by the Missions Advanced Research and Communications Center of World Vision International. From this list, we selected the 360 USA and 67 Canadian agencies that send career missionaries. A list of sending churches was provided by ACMC, a national association of church missions committees. Figure 12-2 summarizes the statistics on the agencies that responded to the survey.

MISSIONARY DEMOGRAPHICS (USA AND CANADA)		
	USA Agencies	**Canadian Agencies**
Income for overseas ministries	$941,199,283 (138 of 160 reported)	$41,924,814 (24 of 25 reported)
Expecting to serve more than 4 years overseas	18,845	923
Expecting to serve 1–4 years	1,961	92
Expecting to serve 2–11 months	438	49
Serving less than 2 months	12,981	872
Fully supported nationals	2,615	7
Partially supported nationals	6,001	50
Nonresidential mission personnel	223	37
Non-USA/Canada sent to other countries	913	14
Tentmakers	478	31
Home ministry and office staff	4,520	262
Total years of service	8,537	1,280
Average years of service	56	53

Source: *Mission Handbook*

Figure 12-2

---

2. For details, see the survey instrument, which is reproduced on pages 363–370.

SURVEY RESULTS

The survey listed 26 reasons why missionaries leave mission service. Figure 12-3 lists these reasons in order of perceived importance.

It is no surprise that "normal retirement" (an unpreventable cause) would top the list. That "child(ren)" ranked second should alert us to where corrective energy should be placed. As part of

Reason	Worldwide %	N. American Agencies %	N. American Churches %	Rank Order		
				All	Agencies	Churches
Normal retirement	9.4	9.3	12.6	1	1	1
Child(ren)	8.1	8.5	7.3	2	2	2
Change of job	7.4	7.7	5.9	3	3	4=
Health problems	7.2	7.5	5.9	4	4	4=
Lack of home support	6.2	6.4	5.9	5	5	4=
Problems with peers	5.9	5.8	6.4	6	6	3
Personal concerns	4.9	5.0	3.9	7	7	10
Disagreement with agency	4.7	4.7	4.7	8	9	8
Inadequate commitment	4.4	4.8	3.0	9	8	16=
Lack of call	4.1	4.3	3.7	10	10	11
Outside marriage	3.6	3.7	0.9	11	11	25
Immature spiritual life	3.3	3.4	3.2	12=	12	13=
Marriage/family conflict	3.3	2.8	5.3	12=	15	7
Poor cultural adaptation	3.1	3.0	4.4	14	13	9
Problems with local leaders	2.9	2.9	2.6	15=	14	20
Elderly parents	2.9	2.7	3.0	15=	16	16=
Inappropriate training	2.7	2.3	3.0	17	18	16=
Lack of job satisfaction	2.6	2.6	3.1	18	17	15
Political crisis	2.4	2.1	3.3	19	19	12
Inadequate supervision	2.1	2.0	3.0	20	20	16=
Death in service	1.6	1.6	1.1	21=	21=	23=
Dismissal by agency	1.6	1.6	1.8	21=	21=	22
Immoral lifestyle	1.4	1.1	3.2	23	24	13=
Language problems	1.3	1.2	1.9	24	23	21
Theological reasons	1.0	1.0	1.1	25	25	23=
Other	1.9	2.0	0.6			

TOTAL WEIGHTED REASONS FOR LEAVING MISSIONARY SERVICE (USA AND CANADA)

Figure 12-3

the solution to this significant problem, Mission Training International and Los Angeles Missionary Internship offer pre-field training programs for the children of missionary candidates. The trauma of leaving friends, family, and school for the sake of their parents' choice to become foreign missionaries should be dealt with extensively prior to departure to the field.

"Problems with peers" also appears as a major concern. The churches perceive this reason as the third most significant cause, and agencies rate it sixth. It is an area that pre-field preparation frequently misses. We would not think of sending missionaries without adequate biblical training. Nor would we send them out without language preparation. But we often fail to help them develop adequate interpersonal and team communication skills. Among Western sending nations, team reasons accounted for 8% of all attrition. North Americans also have a high number of withdrawals because of marriage and family reasons. There are special issues here which deserve more pre-field screening and training and on-field attention.

"Health problems" is high on the list of causes as well. The Southern Baptists, who have an excellent attrition tracking system, noticed that missionaries in areas where malaria is endemic were consistently leaving for health reasons around the 10-year mark. When they analyzed these data, they found that after about 10 years the malaria preventive medication failed to work. The solution was to anticipate the problem and relocate the missionaries to a non-malaria area to prevent permanent attrition. Similar solutions may be found to prevent permanent loss arising from other health issues.

THE TRAINING PICTURE

Perhaps the most disturbing result of the survey to me as a missionary trainer was the apparent lack of value placed on training in many areas. The percentages in Figure 12-4 reflect the agencies that require no training in certain categories.

Analysis of the overall data collected for the 14-nation attrition study demonstrated that there exists a significant relationship between attrition and the kinds and amounts of training that candidates receive. Interestingly, doing a half-hearted job of training may be associated with higher attrition than having no training requirements at all! Thorough training isn't a cure-all, but it is one important factor in reducing attrition.

MISSION AGENCIES AND TRAINING (USA AND CANADA)	
Training Category	Percent of Agencies Requiring No Training In This Area
Cross-cultural orientation	38
Theological/professional training	42
In-house orientation	72
Non-formal training	52
Short term in cross-cultural setting	67
Missiological studies (non-degree)	86
Missiological studies (degree)	93
Other skills	73
Any training	8

Figure 12-4

SOLVING THE PROBLEM

Part of the answer to the attrition problem is found in asking the right questions. Every agency and sending church should be asking itself the following questions:

+ What is our annual attrition rate?
+ How much of this attrition is due to preventable causes?
+ What can we do to lower this attrition?

Currently, few sending agencies or sending churches have a well-designed plan for doing systematic studies of missionary withdrawal. It takes forethought and planning to create a tracking system that will produce accurate information, upon which management can base decisions for needed changes in the selection, preparation, sending, and field care process.

When someone resigns or is released from the mission, what information do we want to have that might contribute to an understanding of the causes of that attrition? Sometimes, how that information is gathered is an important part of reducing attrition. In the course of this research, two highly commendable systems for tracking attrition were identified. The first is used by the Foreign Mission Board of the Southern Baptist Convention; the second, by the Christian and Missionary Alliance.

In the SBC, identical forms are filled out separately by the missionary husband, the missionary wife, the field supervisor, and the area director. The last two individuals are asked to review the missionaries' response and also give what they consider are the true causes for the attrition. The area director makes the final determination of the causes and records this information.

The forms are then sent to the medical department and finally to the research and planning department. There, they are entered into a *blind file*, and all forms are shredded to protect the identity of the missionaries involved.

Each year a statistical analyst looks at all of the attrition data, prepares a report, and combines the data with prior study for analysis. From the analysis, recommendations are made for possible changes in selection procedures, training, leadership, deployment of personnel, etc. These analyses are conducted in many different ways. For example, the profile of attrition in a particular country may be examined to see if after X number of years an unusually high number of workers are leaving. This may point to a lack of quality leadership and pastoring by the field supervisor. Attention is also paid to unusually high numbers of departing missionaries in a particular region to see if there may be a unique medical, leadership, political, or other reason contributing to attrition. Profiles are done on kinds of job assignments most prone to attrition. Not long ago, the SBC found that there is a higher resignation percentage in open versus restricted access countries.

The second methodology comes from the Christian and Missionary Alliance. I greatly appreciate the intentional way the CMA tries to prevent attrition by closely monitoring the efforts of each field missionary. Their first step in monitoring is to have the field director (or in very small fields, the regional director) prepare an Annual Progress Report and give it to the missionary two months prior to a scheduled interview. After the interview, the review is shared with the field leadership team and regional director. If there are signs that the missionary may be heading down the road of attrition, corrective plans are made.

Toward the end of each third year of service, each missionary completes a Three-Year Self-Evaluation of Field Experience. The field director reviews the evaluation, meets with the missionary, and then consults with the field leadership team and regional director. The field team does a Term Evaluation of Individual. The regional director receives a copy of the completed form, as does the national office of the missionaries' sending church. Therefore, there is a concerted effort to monitor each person's ministry and possible signals that he or she needs corrective assistance to prevent becoming an unnecessary attrition factor. This approach also assists in helping pinpoint the actual cause of withdrawal when it does occur.

CONCLUSION

During our research, we noted that those agencies that work hard to track and analyze their attrition achieve and maintain relatively low rates of attrition. Our conclusion is that as agencies and churches take up this discipline, they will see their own attrition statistics improve. Every agency needs its "Jason"— someone who will passionately track attrition and its causes and aggressively work to discover ways to prevent it. Only in this way can we hope to stem this problem with its terrible waste of resources and attendant human agony. If your church or agency needs someplace to start, a suggested tracking form is provided as an appendix in this book.

REFERENCES AND SUGGESTED READINGS

Allen, F. (1986). Why do they leave? Reflections on attrition. *Evangelical Missions Quarterly*, **22**, 118-122.

Arndt, J. R., & Lindquist, S. (1976). Twenty to fifty percent fail to make it: why? *Evangelical Missions Quarterly*, **12**, 141-148.

Bailey, H., & Jackson, H. C. (1965). *A study of missionary motivation, training and withdrawal (1953–62)*. New York, NY: Missionary Research Library.

Bridges, E. (1982). Missionary resignations down but reasons still complex. *Foreign Mission News*. Richmond, VA: Richmond Southern Baptist Convention.

Britt, G. W. (1983). Pretraining variables in prediction of missionary success overseas. *Journal of Psychology and Theology*, **11**, 203-212.

Cummings, D. (1987). Programmed for failure: Mission candidates at risk. *Evangelical Missions Quarterly*, **23**, 240-246.

Cureton, C., & Kliewer, D. (1983). Service effectiveness at home and abroad: An annotated bibliography. *Journal of Psychology and Christianity*, **2**, 45-51.

Dye, S. F. (1974). Decreasing fatigue and illness in field work. *Missiology*, **2**, 79-109.

Gardner, L. M. (1984). *Preventive care of mission personnel*. Doctoral dissertation, Conservative Baptist Seminary, Denver, CO.

Gardner, L. M. (1989). *A case study examination of missionary terminations: Study of predictability and preventability factors by using the case method*. Doctoral dissertation, Fuller Theological Seminary, Pasadena, CA.

Hanscome, C. (1979). Predicting missionary drop-out. *Evangelical Missions Quarterly*, **15**, 152-155.

Herndon, H. L. (1980). How many "dropouts" really are "pushouts"? *Evangelical Missions Quarterly*, **16**, 13-16.

Howard, E. (1985). *Personality strengths and temperament traits: Factors in continued and discontinued missionaries*. Doctoral dissertation, University of Alabama, Tuscaloosa, AL.

Iwasko, R. (1986). Danger in the parsonage: Why missionaries and ministers fail. *Proceedings of the Seventh Annual Conference on Mental Health and Missions,* Angola, IN.

Kennedy, P., & Dreger, R. (1974). Development of criterion measure of overseas missionary performance. *Journal of Applied Psychology,* **59**, 69-73.

Link Care. (1981). *The use of psychological assessment in the evaluation of missionary candidates: A handbook.* Fresno, CA: Author.

Mission Handbook (15th ed.). (1993). Monrovia, CA: MARC.

Nanfelt, P. N. (1991). *A restructuring of the administrative procedures governing the missionary program of the Christian and Missionary Alliance.* Unpublished master's thesis, Fuller Theological Seminary, Pasadena, CA.

Nelson, T. R. (1985). *Critical cross-cultural adjustment skills needed by overseas missionary personnel: A preliminary study of missionary preservice training programs.* Doctoral dissertation, New York University, New York, NY.

Parshall, P. (1975). A "dropout syndrome" you can overcome. *Evangelical Missions Quarterly,* **11**, 223-227.

Reyburn, W. D. (1966). Perspective on missionary loss. *Evangelical Missions Quarterly,* **2**, 84-90.

Studies of attrition by four mission agencies. (1986). *Evangelical Missions Quarterly,* **22**, 122-129.

Tippett, A. R. (1960). Probing missionary inadequacies at the popular level. *International Review of Missions,* **49**, 411-414.

Tucker, M. (1981). *Factors influencing cross-cultural adjustment.* Paper presented at the Society for Intercultural Education and Research, Long Beach, CA.

Williams, D. (1983). Assessment of cross-cultural adjustability in missionary candidates: Theoretical, biblical and practical perspectives. *Journal of Psychology and Christianity,* **2**, 18-24.

Williams, K. (1973). Characteristics of the more successful and less successful missionaries. *Dissertation Abstracts International,* **34**, 1786B-1787B.

Phillip Elkins *is Executive Director of the Paraclete Mission Group, a team of colleagues who bring consultive solutions to strategic issues facing mission agencies and churches. He also is the director of the experience-based training program of the Mission Training and Resource Center in Pasadena, California. In the early 1970s, with a team of five families, he planted churches among the unreached Tonga of Zambia and later worked for many years as a tentmaker missionary in Liberia. Elkins was the first director of the Intercultural Studies program at Fuller Seminary. He has also pastored, taught, and was CEO of several businesses in the USA and Africa.*

Part 4

Thematic
Chapters

13

The Selection Process And the Issue of Attrition

PERSPECTIVE OF THE NEW SENDING COUNTRIES

Bertil Ekström

The missionary movement from the Two-Thirds World is growing fast. We all know that. The contribution to the evangelization of the world from countries such as Korea, India, Myanmar (Burma), the Philippines, Ghana, Nigeria, Kenya, Zimbabwe, and Brazil—and many others on a smaller scale—is one of the most positive facts of the last two decades. From being traditional receiving nations, these countries are now sending bodies.

The theme of COMIBAM '87 in São Paulo, Brazil, "From mission field to sending body" (*de campo misionero para cuerpo misionero*), was not only a dream, but also the description of a reality. Latin America had been impacted by a missionary awakening from the Spirit that nothing could hinder. And the same was occurring in other parts of the Two-Thirds World.

In many cases, sending agencies have sprung up in traditional receiving countries. The situation in Brazil is a good example. Denominations such as the Baptist Convention, the Assemblies of God, and the Presbyterian Church have participated in the worldwide missionary movement since the start of the century. Almost from their beginning, these denominations have sent out missionaries to other Latin American nations and to Portugal.

However, it was not until the 1970s and '80s that the movement had its breakthrough. In the case of Latin America, mission agencies working with young people (for example, YWAM and OM), together with mission conferences held by the Lausanne Movement, COMIBAM, and others, had an enormous impact on the church. Especially among students and youth leaders, an increasing interest in missions could be seen.

With the new missionary candidates that presented themselves to their churches and to the denominations, the need for sending structures was actualized. In some cases, the churches already had a denominational board for missions and could take care of the candidates. In other situations, there was no such structure, and there was very little comprehension of the need of it. In still other cases, the need for a sending structure was clearly recognized. Many mission agencies were started, and they have been a major force in the sending of missionaries during the last two decades.

We can now see, if we still talk about Latin America, that both local churches and denominations are awakening to their responsibility with regard to missionary work and are taking a more active role in the sending process.

One of the key issues in this reality of missions in the new sending countries is the selection process. From having few candidates and a limited possibility of sending missionaries, mission organizations, both parachurch and denominational, now daily receive new people who are asking for an opportunity to serve overseas. "Shouldn't we send out every candidate that knocks on our door?" asked one mission leader. "Is it right to hinder people from going out to serve the Lord?" was the reaction of one candidate.

In this context, we are concerned with the high attrition rate among missionaries from the Two-Thirds World. So the question is: How important is the selection process in preventing dropout from the mission field? In dealing with different aspects of selection in the new sending countries, our focus will be on maintaining missionaries in their ministries as long as possible.

Two statements are basic here. First, we believe that the ideal is a long-term commitment in missions, although we recognize that short-termers can give a good contribution and are also important, especially in situations where practical jobs are performed or where there is no possibility of staying for a

longer period. Second, we are convinced that good selection of candidates can minimize attrition and prevent many difficulties on the field.

WHO ARE THE CANDIDATES?

It can be difficult to identify common characteristics of missionary candidates in the new sending nations, but perhaps we can find some elements to help us understand their situation.

As in the whole world, it is mainly young people who search for cross-cultural ministries. There are some cases of middle-aged couples who, after a long service in a local church, want to experience the mission field, but they are exceptions.

The variety of backgrounds among candidates is truly amazing—from well-educated people to almost illiterate, from traditional churches to new charismatic communities to no local involvement, from all kinds of social environments and conditions. Each candidate has his or her own story and needs individual treatment. The background in itself cannot be decisive for selection. Good missionaries have come from all situations. The questions we must ask are whether there are grounds for believing that the person has a real call from God to missions and whether the candidate is suited for the task.

One of the weak areas in the new sending nations is their lack of mission tradition. The churches have received missionaries from other nations for a long time, but they have not been educated to reflect on their own responsibility. Missionaries are not automatically mission-minded in their work, so the churches founded by them, in many cases, are not aware of their role in world evangelization.

This means that many of the candidates come from contexts in which they have never heard about missions and know very little about what is involved. They often have erroneous ideas of what a cross-cultural ministry implies, and they tend to reflect the values of foreign missionaries working in their own country. Expectations regarding type of work and economic support are often related to the old sending structures.

On the positive side, it is important to say that the emerging missionary force, both active and potential, is a tremendous gift from God to the missionary movement. The contribution that missionaries from the Two-Thirds World can give and are giving is crucial for the advance of the gospel and for reaching the unreached peoples.

THE ROLE OF
THE LOCAL CHURCH

From a Latin American point of view, the local church plays an important role in the selection and sending process. There is very little real participation in missions apart from the local communities. Even the parachurch agencies understand, after a while, that the basis for the support of their mission work is the local church. There are no funds or easy money from central organizations that can substitute for the provision from the church.

The selection process must have its beginning in the local community. We agree with Rudy Girón's statement: "Unquestionably, the best entity to authenticate the missionary call of a given person is the church" (see chapter 3). It is in the local church that candidates grow up spiritually and in some cases even physically. The pastor and some members probably know them well and are the best suited to decide if they have a real call for the task. Of course, even a pastor and a local church can make mistakes, but an agency should think three times before accepting candidates who do not have the recommendation of their local community.

There can be a difference here between old and new sending nations. In the new sending countries, for the most part, candidates come almost directly from the local church, often with poor secular and theological backgrounds but with a burning heart and practical experience from church work. The pastor knows them quite well, and the applicants have a good relationship with their church. In contrast, in the old sending nations, it seems that more often people come from a university or a seminary. They have been away from their home town for several years. They have attended different churches during their studies and do not have a close relation to a local church. Sometimes they come from a short-term program or several short-term experiences, and their local church does not know much about them anymore.

In the ideal situation, the local church functions as a living body in which every member is known by the community and is followed up by the leaders. Discipleship in the church is needed to give missionary candidates the orientation and support they must have.

But even if this ideal is not reached, that cannot be an excuse for leaving the local church out of the selection proc-

ess. People who have followed applicants during past years can give a good
description of them and can share important insights that the agency or the
mission board should know.

Looking at the matter from another
point of view, we can see a great number
of benefits from the church's involvement in accepting missionaries. In
shouldering its responsibility for selection, the church can give candidates an
excellent platform for practicing their
gifts and skills, along with the basic
training they will need for their coming
tasks. The church can present candidates to the other members as future
missionaries. Individuals can then follow the candidates' growth and can have
a part in their ministry from the beginning. This will make a difference in financial support and intercession later
on when the missionaries are on the
field. Weaknesses in character and
spiritual needs can be dealt with. Candidates' families can be prepared.
Through candidates' testimonies, other
young people can be motivated to become involved in mission work.

Certainly we could make a long list
of advantages of having the local church
involved in the selection process, added
to the biblical basis that the church is
the real sending agency, called for missions "in Jerusalem, and in all Judea
and Samaria, and to the ends of the
earth" (Acts 1:8). Generally speaking,
the churches in the Two-Thirds World
are concerned about what happens to
their young people and have a strong
desire to take part in missionary work.

USING THE STRUCTURE OF A MISSION AGENCY

Notwithstanding the advantages
outlined above, the local church has its
limitations when it comes to doing missions. For such a task, a broader and
cooperative structure is called for,
which can help the church do its missionary work. The structure can be a
denominational mission board that co-
ordinates the mission effort of its member churches or a non-denominational
mission that has the participation of
churches from a variety of ecclesiastical
backgrounds. In Latin America, the second type of agency has been predomi-
nant, but in recent years there has been
an increase in the number of denominations that are forming their own sending
structures.

Every agency has its own standard
for selecting missionaries. In Brazil, the
Brazilian Association of Cross-Cultural
Agencies (Associação de Missões Trans-
culturais Brasileiras, or AMTB) has a
recommended standard for screening
and sending missionaries, but not all
organizations can fully follow the proposed level. Among the reasons for the
discrepancy are mission leaders' lack of
field experience and their insufficient
understanding of the necessary requi-
sites. Economy, lack of personnel, and
a wish to do the screening in their own
way are other factors.

A growing number of agencies are
participating in AMTB and are trying to
reach a higher quality in their work.
Nevertheless, the "holes in the screen"
vary a great deal, depending on the
number of applicants, the resources
available, and the demands of doing a
good job.

Getting through the screening process in the old sending countries may be more difficult because of a decreasing interest in utilizing sending structures, long experience with selection, developed criteria for accepting people, and the fact that many churches do not have room for new missionaries in their budgets. Meanwhile, in the newer sending countries, where there is a growing sending structure, almost all candidates can find a way to go out. If they are stopped by one board or agency, there is always some new agency searching for missionaries that will take them on.

What this exaggerated picture shows is that the selection process is very important in the new sending agencies, even if it signifies fewer missionaries going to the field over the short term.

CRITERIA FOR SELECTION

In the Two-Thirds World, the criteria for a good missionary may differ from the standards set in the North, at least in certain areas. Perhaps the differences are a way of contributing to a holistic view of mission work. In other words, missionaries from the Two-Thirds World can serve in areas where workers from other nations are not skilled or well trained. Again, we are talking in general terms, knowing that there are all kinds of missionaries both in the North and in the South. But there are, without doubt, differences in how we are educated and in the emphasis given to special skills. There are also differences in the way the local churches function, giving future missionaries opportunities to train in different areas.

We can ask the question: What criteria for selection in the Two-Thirds World

might help prevent attrition and promote the possibility of reaching a high level of success in mission work? In the screening process done by the church or by the agency in dialogue with the local church, the following are some basic criteria for selecting candidates for the mission field:

1. Born-Again Experience

Experience has shown that a personal commitment to the Lord is not always a matter of course and is not always obvious for the applicant. Coming from a background, especially in Latin America, Africa, and South Asia, where the emotions are stressed and conversion often involves feeling rather than understanding, the candidate may not have had a real experience of new birth.

2. Right Motivation

There are many reasons a person might want to become a missionary. In many cases, the vision of mission work and the idea of a missionary's lifestyle are inaccurate. In other situations, the chance to see the world and the status of being a missionary are attractive. The candidate's motives should be examined carefully before the person is accepted for service.

3. Genuine Call From God

This is closely tied to the right motivation. Does the candidate have a real call from God? Obviously, it can be hard for a mission leader and even for the local pastor to decide if a person is called by God or not. But in some sense, there must be evidence of the vocation in the applicant's life. A missionary call begins with a deep personal conviction, but it also needs the confirmation of people who know the applicant.

4. Christian Character And Spiritual Maturity

For all kinds of leadership and service in the kingdom of God, it is important to analyze a person's character. There are no perfect people, but we seek committed Christians who have subordinated their whole lives to the Lord, including their personalities. Mission work requires people who are humble, servant-hearted, faithful, honest, team-minded, cooperative, generous, etc. The list can go on and on. A good basis for testing the candidate is to compare the person's character with the list of the fruit of the Spirit in Galatians 5:22-23 and with the requirements for church leadership in 1 Timothy 3.

These aspects of Christian character cannot be achieved in a one-year or even a four-year seminary course. Rather, they must be developed in the local church before the training program of an agency begins. Any weaknesses in character must then be dealt with during the period of theological or missionary training.

Here is one of the key points for the situation in Latin America. The double standard preached by the old religious tradition and by society in general produces people who put great stress on superficial and visible things but who have little concern for deeper and internal life. The mentality is, "If you look Christian, it is enough to be a member of the church." A change is occurring in this attitude, but the problem still exists. The Latin *malicia* (malice) is not an illness, but a way of making a joke with life, saying one thing and meaning another, often with sexual connotations. The mentality of Brazilians, for example, with their tendency to make jokes with Portuguese people, is in many cases a barrier. Brazilian missionaries in Portugal do not take the Portuguese people seriously, and the Portuguese don't accept Brazilian workers.

Devotional life with willingness to pray and read the Bible is basic for all disciples of Christ and especially for missionaries. Only a good intercessor for the nations can feel passion for lost people and have real empathy with members of a new culture.

5. Good Relationships With Others

Relational problems are among the most serious in the daily work on the mission field and are one of the most common causes of attrition. To work alongside peers who are from other backgrounds and who have different ways of seeing things requires a lot of patience and humility. Few situations offer a place for "lone rangers." Typically mission work is done in close relationship to both nationals and missionary colleagues.

Most people in the Two-Thirds World are relationship-oriented. It is puzzling for them to observe expatriate missionaries working alone and not in a team. Especially in leadership, the models that candidates have are more of a "one man show" than of teamwork.

6. Ability to Cope With Stress

Mission work is not a game but a war. The spiritual battle is a reality, while at the same time all sorts of tensions occur in daily life. A missionary needs perseverance and the ability to cope with stressful situations, sometimes without external help. For a Latin American, who is generally impulsive and emotional, perseverance can be a great challenge.

Lack of family relationships on the field can be a source of stress for many candidates from the Two-Thirds World. Young people are used to living with their parents as long as they are single. After marriage, couples still maintain a close relationship with relatives. On the mission field, loneliness can be difficult to bear, especially for single workers.

7. Good Biblical Knowledge

Candidates need good training in the Bible in order to be prepared for future ministries on the field. Sadly, the experience in many countries of the Two-Thirds World is that the Bible teaching in local churches is far from what would be desirable. A candidate once asked why Jesus did not use the New Testament in His teaching but only the Old!

In the selection process, the willingness to study the Bible and take a theological course should be one of the requirements, if the person does not already have this foundation. The idea that "spiritual fire" is enough and that the Lord gives His word when we need it does not work in long-term ministry, even if it does teach dependence on the Holy Spirit.

8. Missiological Training

We have seen a growing number of mission courses in our sending countries, so in most cases there are options for missiological training. Especially among young people who have not had the opportunity to travel worldwide and to confront other cultures, the study of fundamental principles of cross-cultural encounter and adaptation is

necessary. But the time of reflection and of confrontation with key issues in missiology is also helpful for those who live in multicultural societies and who have traveled to other parts of the world. All applicants for missions need to be prepared to take time to complete such a course.

In this matter, we may have a different view from local churches that send their missionaries directly to the field without using an agency. It is crucial that such groups understand that missionaries will do a much better job if they have had the opportunity to deal with questions relating to cross-cultural life and ministry before they leave their own country.

Some churches and agencies have their own mission course; others utilize the courses given by seminaries and theological faculties. If the teachers of these courses are involved in the screening process of missionary candidates, probably the standard will be raised and the courses will be more adaptable to the needs felt by the church, the agency, and the missionary.

The training should include the entire missionary family. The reason is that the missionary unit is not an individual, but the family as a whole, at least in cases in which both parents are involved in the work. It should, therefore, be required that both husband and wife complete the missiological training. Something for the children would also be desirable.

9. Professional Skills

In today's missions, the demand for people with professional training is increasing. To reach most of the hidden peoples and unreached people groups in the Muslim world and Central Asia, mission workers must have a secular profession in order to get a visa. Often the local situation demands involvement in both evangelistic work and social concern. Education, health programs, agriculture, etc., go hand in hand with the proclamation of the gospel.

A growing number of candidates in the Two-Thirds World possess professional training in a technical or even an academic discipline. Their willingness to sacrifice their career in the homeland for missionary service is commendable.

10. Recognition as Being Human

We must be aware that expectations placed on missionaries are constantly rising. When we look at the preceding list of qualifications, the question arises: Who is sufficient for all these things?

Agencies, churches, and missionaries have to realize that missionaries are first of all human beings, with all the imperfections that are due to their humanity. Competence comes from the Lord (2 Cor. 3:5). In advising, in pastoral care, in ongoing training, etc., we must remember that every mission worker has a combination of strengths, personal needs, and human weaknesses.

RECOMMENDATIONS FOR THE SELECTION PROCESS

Every missionary sending group must develop its own selection process. We are becoming more and more suspicious in the South about "canned formulas" and "how-to-do-it packages." We must find our own ways of doing things according to each cultural setting, but at the same time we can benefit from the long experience of the old sending agencies. Following are some fundamental aspects of the selection process that need to be taken seriously.

1. Teach About The Missionary Vocation

The foundation for understanding the call from God to the specific task of being a missionary is the Bible teaching given in the local church. The pastor is the first person responsible for giving candidates an accurate idea of the missionary vocation. The teaching also has the benefit of inspiring and motivating for missions. Many candidates receive their "call" in missions conferences or youth camps, because only there do they hear about the missionary vocation. The tendency, therefore, is to search for sending structures outside the local church first. If candidates hear about missions and are well taught in the local church about the challenges mission work offers, the natural consequence will be to involve their community in the process of preparing for the mission field.

2. Think Over The Selection Process

We easily fall into a routine and do things the same way we have always done them. We need to ask: What are the criteria for our selection today? We know that the demands upon missionaries have increased both in terms of cultural adaptation and in terms of professional ability. The understanding of the missionary calling has also passed through a change. Today's candidates think of their involvement in a different way from the generations before them. Short-term commitment and a disposition to change fields more often are characteristics of the new missionaries.

Therefore, the selection process needs constant revision in order to reflect current trends in missions.

One such trend is "tentmaking." The number of tentmaker missionaries is increasing, and it is necessary to fit these workers into the selection procedure, as well as into the training programs. There are specially designed courses for prospective tentmakers, and the WEF Missions Commission has excellent material on the subject.

3. Raise the Standards Of Selection

The objective of a higher standard is not to hinder people from going to the mission field, but to strive for better quality in our missionaries. Steve Moon, in his analysis of the Korean situation (chapter 8), has stated, "The screening process seems to be one of the weakest areas of management in the missionary movement." Raising the standards of selection will help alleviate this deficiency.

As noted earlier, the enthusiasm of now being a part of the missionary movement can result in "too big holes in the screen," where all candidates are accepted without major requirements. In the end, we will probably profit from being more restrictive and careful.

4. Tell Candidates The Whole Story

If one of the reasons for attrition is missionaries' difficulty in coping with the problems they meet on the field, it is essential that candidates know beforehand the reality of mission work. One mission leader from India has affirmed, "In most of the training, as I see it, the missionaries were not taught that suffering is part and parcel of a believer's life. When I came as a missionary after my theological studies, I thought that missionary work was a bed of roses. But soon in the mission field, I learned that I was wrong." A good way to give applicants realistic information about the mission field is to recommend short-term experience in some part of the world.

In the mission courses in the Two-Thirds World, we have a lack of experienced teachers. Few of them have their own missionary practical training. They have not been missionaries themselves. Time will change the situation. In the meantime, we can always listen to active missionaries and learn from their personal experiences.

5. Use Several Methods To Get to Know Candidates

Interviews, psychological tests, medical tests, etc., are useful means for getting a picture of candidates. Along with the evaluation done by the pastor, teachers, and employers, the tests help to analyze applicants' suitability.

Psychological tests can help identify emotional problems, increase candidates' self-awareness, give insight into strengths and weaknesses, and cast light on other areas that need to be dealt with. Marjory Foyle, in writing about a survey she did among 121 missionaries, observed: "Fifty-four percent of the missionaries I saw complained of problems that were present long before they entered the selection process. Either they were not asked about these or over-spiritualized. Only about one-quarter of those who had problems prior to their selection received any help—and that was usually minimal." If candidates do not have a chance to work through their problems and wounds before leaving their secure home, there is a great risk that a deeper crisis will appear on the field.

There is also a positive side to the screening tests. These instruments give both applicants and the agency the means of identifying the tasks for which candidates are best suited and the types of support that will be needed in order for them to function well.

6. Develop a Selection Process In Cooperation With Others

We do not need to have the same system everywhere, but if mission agencies can find a common standard for selection, that will strengthen the national movement as a whole. To work together in a concrete project gives understanding and rich learning. In addition, candidates know that in all agencies they will be faced by equal requirements. There will always be agencies working in their own way, and God in His mercy can use them too. But in the long run, cooperation is more productive.

We can also ask if the participation of the receiving church, when there is one, in the selection process would not be desirable. If the plan for the applicant is to work in cooperation with partner churches in another culture, what would be more reasonable than to let the recipients also have a word about the candidate? There are barriers and problems with this approach, but in the globalization and internationalization of missions, we must accept new ways of doing things and comprehend the importance and richness of sharing responsibilities.

7. Train Church Leaders To Do Selection

Because of the limited participation that church leaders, including the pastor, have had in the selection process in the new sending countries, there is a need for training. If possible, the church should have a selection committee to assess those who feel the call. Perhaps agencies could offer a training program for pastors and other people involved in selecting candidates.

8. Depend on the Holy Spirit

We are part of a holy enterprise that cannot be dealt with in only a human way. We can do our best, using our logical thinking and the gifts God has given us in the selection and sending process. But ultimately it is God who gives growth and prosperity. In mission work, we are constantly challenged to depend on the guidance and the power of the Holy Spirit. So also in the screening of candidates. It is not wrong to pray for and with applicants nor to inspire others to do the same!

As we look at mission history, we must recognize that the human way of evaluating people and situations has not always been the right one. So, we must humble ourselves before the Lord and ask Him for wisdom and mercy when we face a screening process with a young person who is ready to serve in missions. At the same time, we must believe that the Lord has oriented those who take part in the establishing of standards and the evaluation of candidates.

CONCLUSION

Selection of people for missionary service is not easy. An objective evaluation of candidates is almost impossible, and we need concrete steps to follow in order to forestall injustice.

The selection process takes time, and rightly so. A good example is the Apostle Paul, who was called to minister among the Gentiles when he met Jesus on the road to Damascus. However, he had to wait some years before he was definitely selected by the Holy Spirit and the church in Antioch to the specific job of being a missionary. The waiting period was, of course, also a time of training and of practical experience in local churches and maybe even in a pioneer work in Tarsus.

Today, candidates may be in a hurry to get to the field, but it is important to give them and, if necessary, to force them to take time for preparation and maturation. In Latin America, in particular, the tendency is to send individuals out before they are ready, rather than keeping them waiting and training them as long as necessary.

In the different models for selecting people, some agencies have chosen to let candidates work for a short time in a culture that is near their own. If they can adapt well and do a good job during that experience, they will be accepted for a long-term commitment and will work in a more advanced field, after a deeper missiological course and after having worked through any personal problems.

A common rule in seminaries and missiological schools in the Two-Thirds World is to give the final diploma to students only after they have proved themselves capable of founding a church or of working in a team. In other words, the formal education goes hand in hand with the informal and non-formal.

Missionary work needs the best people we have! In the business world, companies that want to prosper in their selling search for the best-skilled and best-suited people who, with passion and faithfulness, can stand for their product. In the same way, local churches and mission agencies should seek keen Christians who have a passion for the unreached and who are willing to be molded by the Lord. Finding suitable candidates can be done through the screening process and through the instruments given to the missionary movement to train and prepare the missionaries of tomorrow.

There is no doubt that the starting point of avoiding attrition is good selection! And good selection starts in the local church!

Bertil Ekström *was born in 1953 and is married to Alzira. They have four children: Cristina (16), Denise (11), Erik (7), and Felipe (2). Ekström is a missionary kid with Swedish background who has lived in Brazil since he was five years old. A Baptist pastor and seminary teacher, from 1991–1995 he was president of AMTB, the Brazilian Association of Cross-Cultural Agencies. He serves on the executive committee of COMIBAM International and the WEF Missions Commission. Currently he works with Interact, a Swedish Baptist mission, and with Convenção das Igrejas Batistas Independentes (The Convention of the Independent Baptist Churches of Brazil).*

14

A Call to Partnership
In the Missionary Selection Process

PERSPECTIVE OF THE OLD SENDING COUNTRIES

Daryl Platt

During the World Evangelical Fellowship (WEF) Missions Consultation held at All Nations Christian College, England, in April 1996, a committee was assigned to examine the relationship between missionary attrition and the candidate selection process. This chapter reflects the issues discussed and the conclusions reached by that committee. There is an underlying foundational endorsement by the committee of the plenary document presented by Rudy Girón (see chapter 3), which outlined an integrated partnership for the selection, preparation, and care of missionaries.

This chapter is presented as a challenge to Christian leaders of the older sending nations (Europe, North America, Australia) who are concerned about the loss of career workers for reasons other than ministry completion. An urgent appeal is made for Christian leaders to give careful and prayerful consideration to the theology of missions which guides their selection processes. In addition, procedures are outlined for developing clear candidate

selection guidelines which are based on authoritative biblical standards and which allow for a development of partnership between local churches and mission agencies.

INTRODUCTORY ISSUES

Generational Confusion

In a day of increased opportunity among the nations of the world, mission structures of the older sending nations are facing obstacles and issues that go right to the heart of effective missionary ministry. A measurable malaise about missions in the older sending nations is compounded by generational issues facing potential candidates. Discussions among mission and church leaders regarding selection and attrition issues indicate that there is widespread confusion concerning an adequate theology of missions which is applicable to today's generations.

This type of confusion was expressed in picturesque language by several participants at the All Nations WEF conference. One person suggested, "Boomers

and busters [generational group desig-
nations] are guided by the Parable of the
Talents, not the Parable of the Plow, as
the boosters have been. These newer
generations are concerned about not
wasting God-given talent and resources." In other words, long-term
commitment without results is unac-
ceptable to the present generations. Another leader observed, "Many busters
are choosing to be missionaries as a
profession, but not because of God's call
on their lives." Meantime, it was reported that one in six missionaries already on the field is being totally lost to
missionary service in the first term, for
preventable reasons.

Selection and Attrition

The recent research project of the
WEF Missions Commission highlighted
the primary factors involved in missionary attrition. Many of these factors were
related to an inadequate candidate selection process. Causes of premature
return from the field included fundamental matters such as doubt or confusion about personal conversion,
indifference to a clear vocational call,
inadequate preparation, and spiritual
immaturity. These attrition factors were
particularly evident among the older
sending nations, whose mission leaders
seem less willing to submit to the
authority of scriptural criteria for the
selection process. The committee discussions revealed the conviction that an
adequate selection process would have
been alert to these foundational needs
prior to the deployment of missionaries.

The WEF research, which was conducted among missions from 14 sending nations, showed that similar factors
are impacting mission agencies of all
types. The patterns related to undesirable missionary attrition apply to all of
the sending structures; none is exempt
from the generational issues and the
pressures of the day. Consequently,
personnel issues are coming under
scrutiny by mission leaders, beginning
with the basal selection process for missionary candidates.

Competition or Cooperation

Perhaps influenced by the social,
cultural, and religious changes that are
impacting today's generations, both
mission agencies and local churches are
incorporating subtle changes into long-
standing selection policies. This practice is resulting in the tacit disregard
of a biblical theology of missions, in
which interdependence and partnership throughout the missionary endeavor are clearly evident. In place of
such a theology of missions, conflicting
trends are developing within mission
circles.

Among mission agency leaders, there
is a growing trend to look for help in
processing the issues which are influencing the younger generation. In their
search for solutions, many leaders are
increasingly turning to extrabiblical resources. Regardless of the type of mission agency, the trend toward the use of
tools and techniques from the modern
social sciences, such as psychological
and personality testing devices, is becoming more prominent. These tools are
being employed throughout the process
of selection and preparation of candidates. As agencies increasingly encounter candidates who have little or no
affiliation with a local church, the use

of these tools has become more wide-spread as an aid to screening and selection. However, there is growing evidence that the use of such tools does not lessen the attrition rate.

At the same time, there is a parallel but contrasting trend developing among local churches. Younger church leaders are reexamining ministry structures, including the biblical missionary mandate, and they are seeking to have a more active role in missions. There is a growing movement in which local churches are bypassing mission agencies completely and are assuming full responsibility for the selection, preparation, and deployment of their own missionaries. Increasingly, a selective theology of missions is being implemented among such churches. All too often, the result is that personnel with monocultural perspectives and little ministry experience are thrust into leadership positions in cross-cultural situations.

These two trends reveal a growing polarity between local churches and mission agencies concerning the selection and sending out of missionary workers. Frequently, a spirit of competition rather than cooperation develops. Such competition is contrary to basic New Testament missiology and is proving to be detrimental to missionary outreach at the close of this century. The differences in outlook and approach between churches and agencies are seriously impacting the deployment of qualified personnel and have become contributing factors to missionary attrition.

RECOVERY OF A BIBLICAL BALANCE

The polarization of positions within the body of Christ does not reflect a true picture of the biblical missionary mandate, nor does it accurately portray the practice of New Testament outreach. The mission enterprise requires a solid commitment to partnership throughout the entire process. Local churches and biblically oriented agencies have complementary functions—the church as the mediating body and the agency as the implementing structure. In the face of challenges presented by an increasingly secular world, there is a critical need to recover a foundational understanding and biblical balance.

The neglect of biblical principles regarding missions has caused churches and agencies alike to look for other solutions to missionary attrition. The focus of the WEF consultation was to urge responsible Christian leaders to measure their current practices by a review of key passages that mark the pathway of development for missionary ministry in the New Testament.

Throughout the narrative flow of the New Testament, two components of missionary activity are evident—one corporate, the other individual. When the development of each of these components is traced, it becomes expressly clear that cooperation rather than competition was the foundation for New Testament ministry. Cooperation provided the sense of holistic partnership which characterized the entire process of formation, selection, and deployment of missionary personnel.

PATTERNS OF MISSIONS OUTREACH

The book of Acts shows that from its birth, the church displayed a missionary nature, which was expressed in a multitude of activities. Some of these activities can be considered normative for every generation, while others were unique to the New Testament era. There are four discernible stages of outreach in the history of the early church.

Spontaneous Outreach

Spontaneous outreach is evident in Acts 1–7. The euphoria of Pentecost immediately propelled the church into outreach. By means of spontaneous occurrences, the church filled Jerusalem with the gospel and even carried the good news to Judea and Samaria during this initial stage.

Forced Outreach

This second stage of mission outreach is described in Acts 8–11. It bore little resemblance to the first stage. Under severe persecution, the church in Jerusalem was scattered throughout Judea and Samaria. Some of the disciples made their way to Antioch, where the results of their ministry are recorded in Scripture. Like the first stage of spontaneous outreach, this forced outreach was not a permanent part of the corporate mission thrust of the churches.

Planned Outreach

The first missionary commissioning by the church leaders at Antioch (Acts 13:1-4) marked the beginning of the period of planned outreach. Under the guidance of the Holy Spirit, the church provided the context and became the conduit for the first planned cross-cultural mission undertaking from Antioch. However, this occasion was not the beginning, but rather the third stage of corporate mission effort.

Partnership Outreach

The fourth stage of mission outreach involved partnership between missionaries and the local church. This focus becomes evident following the completion of Paul's first missionary journey (Acts 15:36ff). From this point on, partnership patterns form the framework of the New Testament Epistles. The missionaries and the church were in partnership together to accomplish the ministry.

It is important to notice that, unlike the earlier stages, this pattern of partnership is continually repeated. Paul's plea to the church at Rome was for their assistance in continuing his missionary ministry (Rom. 15:22-24). In a similar manner, Paul's commendation to the Philippian church was based on their partnership commitment to missionary outreach through his ministry (Phil. 4:10-20). Finally, at the close of the New Testament era, the Apostle John underlined the need for a continuing partnership and commitment among those involved in missions, as he instructed the churches that "we ought therefore to show hospitality to such men so that we may work together for the truth" (3 John 5-8).

Through the deliberations and conclusions of the Jerusalem Council, guidelines for missionary ministry were established by a representative body, and creative cross-cultural missionary service was officially endorsed (Acts 15:6-32). As a result, individual missionary outreach went forward, as evidenced by references to various missionary teams. The names of the team members appear in nearly every Epistle. In addition, individuals were often sent by the churches to assist the missionaries on a short-term basis (Acts 18:1-4; 2 Cor. 8:19).

MISSIONARY PREPARATION STANDARDS

Biblical references to these early missionaries consistently depict a close relationship with a local congregation, where personal discipling and development took place. The basic qualifications displayed by these early outreach workers were a transformed life, obedience to the Spirit, and adequate equipping for their assigned tasks (1 Tim. 3; 5:17-25; 2 Tim. 1:6-7; Tit. 2).

Glimpses of the preparatory stages of the Apostle Paul's life provide further insight concerning missionary qualifications (Acts 9–15). No other New Testament character has such a detailed record concerning his personal preparation for ministry. Paul's missionary commissioning by the church was the culmination of years of progressive formation, which took place in the real-life context of the day. There were some supernatural encounters, but apart from these, numerous leaders and various congregations were used by God to mold the essential qualities into Paul's life.

Not only was the local church instrumental in sending Paul out on his missionary ministry, but the centrality of the local church is unmistakable in Paul's preparation. In a day of growing attrition, competition, and confusion, leaders of both churches and mission agencies can gain valuable insights through a careful review of these preparatory stages as seen in the life of Paul. They present a biblical pattern that can serve as a template for the preparation of missionaries today. A closer examination of the component stages of the process will give a clearer understanding of the biblical qualifications indicated.

COMPONENTS OF THE PREPARATION PROCESS

There are four stages through which Paul passed in preparation for cross-cultural missionary service:

+ Development of spiritual life.
+ Formation of Christian character.
+ Acquisition of ministry-related skills.
+ Understanding of basic relational patterns.

1. Spiritual Life

Both subjective and objective references indicate the kind of formative process which was taking place in Paul's life. Subjectively, he had key personal experiences which shaped his life and indicated God's particular calling for service. Objectively, the Christian community benefited from his service and testified to the fruitfulness of his ministry.

Conversion

The Damascus Road encounter with Jesus changed Saul's life permanently (Acts 9:1-6; 22:6-13). His good family, excellent education, and zealous good works were all disqualified at the moment of conversion (Phil. 3:3-8). There is no substitute for a genuine personal conversion experience, regardless of a person's background. All other qualifications flow from this foundation.

Convictions

Paul's previous set of personal values and religious convictions as a Pharisee needed to undergo a radical transformation in order for Paul to understand the simplicity of the gospel. Immediately following his baptism and initial instruction from the disciples at Damascus, Paul began to proclaim the message of Jesus. Later, the warmth of Christian fellowship and the consistent teaching of the apostles' doctrine in the Jerusalem Church during Paul's short stay there gave formation to his new convictions (Acts 9:19-31). The fundamental understanding about the centrality of Jesus and the uniqueness of biblical revelation enabled Paul to declare later that the gospel is not a commodity to be marketed nor a philosophy to be accommodated to diverse cultural interpretations (2 Cor. 2:17; Col. 2:2-15).

Call

Paul knew personally and the church knew corporately about God's missionary call upon his life. This call was first revealed to Ananias, the early discipler of the newly converted Saul. Ananias shared this word from the Lord with Paul prior to his baptism (Acts 9:15-17). The divine purpose was later confirmed personally by the Lord as Paul was praying at the temple in Jerusalem (Acts 22:17-21). Finally, while Paul was ministering at the Antioch Church, the Holy Spirit called for him and Barnabas to be publicly set apart for cross-cultural ministry to the Gentiles (Acts 13:1-4). Although there was a significant time lapse involved, both a subjective and objective confirmation of the call were a

part of the preparation process (Gal. 1:15-16).

Commission

As the mediating agency, the local church played a unique role in the deployment of the first missionary team. The team's commissioning was a pivotal point for the congregation and for the missionaries as they were set apart for that specific "work" ordained for them by the Holy Spirit. Because their testimony was known and their ministry trusted, the local church could joyfully send Paul and Barnabas out as ambassadors from their congregation to a lost world, with a message of reconciliation to God through Christ (Acts 13:2-3).

For the second missionary journey, the local church commissioned their missionaries anew, commending them to the grace of the Lord (Acts 15:40). Clearly, the Holy Spirit was the prime mover in the calling and sending of missionaries. The church was used as an instrument of preparation and commissioning (2 Tim. 2:15). In each generation, the commissioning of cross-cultural workers by the local church continues to affirm the divine-human nature of missionary service.

2. Christian Character

In spite of commendable personal traits, the newly converted Saul did not automatically display a mature Christian character. The New Testament reveals that he had to overcome several outstanding personal obstacles related to his socio-religious heritage and his former acts of terrorism against the church. An examination of Paul's spiritual growth shows the development of key qualities, including a good reputation, trustworthiness, and a servant heart, which are needed by every generation of missionary workers.

Good Reputation

Under the tutelage of more mature Christians, Paul learned the importance of matching the life of the messenger with the message of the gospel. The care and concern shown by Ananias during the first days after Paul's conversion became a permanent part of Paul's testimony (Acts 22:12-16). Barnabas also staked his reputation on the new convert, caring for him and modeling the character qualities Paul needed (Acts 4:36-37; 11:24-25). Later, Paul could invite others to follow his own example as a standard for what a good reputation should be (1 Cor. 11:1; Phil. 3:17; 1 Tim. 3:2).

In the New Testament, the local congregation is the primary source of confirmation of a good reputation. Special care is required in affirming missionaries, since the reputation of the church and the reputation of the gospel in a new culture are dependent upon the character of the messengers (Acts 20:18-21; 1 Cor. 2:1-5).

Trustworthiness

The quality of trustworthiness at every level of life and service was modeled by the church from the very start of Paul's Christian life. Paul learned about the proper attitude toward possessions from the testimony of Barnabas among the brethren (Acts 4:36-37). The infamous results of Ananias and Sapphira's duplicity would have been an unforgettable lesson concerning the honest handling of finances (Acts 5:1-11). Within the church, the faithful service of the newly appointed deacons set the tone of servanthood in ordinary daily things

(Acts 6:3-7). Paul personally witnessed Stephen's martyrdom as the price of faithfulness to the truth of the gospel (Acts 7). Later, Paul's willingness to return to Tarsus for further training demonstrated humble obedience to godly counsel and showed that he was acquiring trustworthiness himself (Acts 9:30; 1 Cor. 4:1-2).

Servant Heart

Before his conversion, Paul moved in the highest circles of influence and political power. His associations put him in a position of authority, not a place of service. But prior to being sent out as Christ's ambassador, Paul had to surrender personal ambition and develop a servant heart. He learned to serve by doing acts of service. Particularly noteworthy was the assignment by the church to accompany Barnabas in taking the offering from Antioch to Jerusalem. This was a practical task needing to be done (the text calls it a "mission"). It was assigned and completed well (Acts 11:29-30; 12:25).

Having been proven through practical service, Paul could be entrusted with delegated authority to lead in the ministry of cross-cultural outreach. Paul's use of the word "servant" to refer to himself in the Epistles demonstrates his heart attitude. He was not a ruler of the churches, but their servant for Jesus' sake (2 Cor. 4:5).

3. Ministry Skills

Every missionary candidate must be equipped with a minimum set of learned skills which will serve as the foundation of life and service. Some of these skills are acquired through formal training programs; others are gained through informal or seminar training processes;

still others are added through non-formal, discipling-type activities. Regardless of the nature of the training, missionary selection must make certain that adequate skills have been acquired in the primary areas of biblical knowledge, communication ability, teamwork, and servant leadership.

Biblical Knowledge

During his formative years, Paul was trained in the formal educational processes of his generation (Phil. 3:5). In addition, he received advanced training at the feet of Gamaliel, who was the best teacher of the Old Testament Law of that day (Acts 22:3). By Paul's own testimony, however, this educational background, far from being an automatic asset, produced a legalistic righteousness which had to undergo a radical transformation after Paul's surrender to Christ on the Damascus Road.

Initially, Paul's spiritual understanding as a new Christian was shaped by the Jerusalem Church, being nurtured by the daily, consistent teaching of the doctrine of the apostles. Paul was further equipped through his three years in the "seminary of the desert," where his understanding of the Christian gospel was clarified and defined (Gal. 1:17-18). Paul's ongoing belief in the need for training in biblical knowledge was demonstrated during the two years he systematically taught the disciples at the Lecture Hall of Tyrannus in Ephesus (Acts 19:9-10).

Communication Ability

While the early churches may not have had a defined candidate selection process, they recognized that the ability to articulate the truth of Scripture was essential for ministry. Paul's life demonstrated that no training is wasted. His communication ability utilized both written and oral skills. These were first evident as he disputed with the Jews in Damascus soon after his conversion (Acts 9:20-22). Eventually, Paul's public ministry style of reasoning, disputing, and evangelizing revealed his ability to make use of his secular knowledge as well as theological truth. He employed skills in logic, languages, literature styles, and writing to communicate the Christian message effectively. In addition, his multinational citizenship provided an innate understanding of and respect for cross-cultural realities. Paul was able to move freely among different people groups in order to present the gospel through communication bridges which he recognized and utilized (Acts 19:8).

Teamwork

The concept of interdependent team function is so basic to New Testament ministry that it is imperative that teamwork be part of the missionary selection and preparation process. Theological and practical truths underscore a team approach to ministry. From the beginning of his Christian development, Paul was placed in a team context by the repeated interventions of the Lord. Conspicuous examples included his conversion follow-up experience with Ananias (Acts 9:10-17), his introduction into the Jerusalem Church by Barnabas, where he witnessed the modeling of apostolic team functions (Acts 9:26-28), and his personal participation in the ministry team of the Antioch Church (Acts 11:25-26). As part of his missionary commissioning, Paul was paired with Barnabas by the explicit instruction of the Holy

Spirit (Acts 13:1-3). Even the discussions, decisions, and follow-through actions of the pivotal Jerusalem Council were done jointly, not by the unilateral action of one individual (Acts 15:1, 19, 22). Besides the Pauline teams, there are numerous references to other missionary teams throughout the New Testament Epistles, providing evidence of the modus operandi of the early congregations.

Servant Leadership

The kind of leadership taught and demonstrated in the New Testament cuts across the social patterns of the nations of the world. The Lord Jesus rejected the Gentile pattern of strong man leadership for His followers. In its place, He taught and modeled a servant leader approach (Matt. 20:25-28; Mark 10:42-45). Through firsthand experience, Paul learned about the character and servant leadership of his mentor, Barnabas (Acts 4:36-37; 11:22-24). The purpose of Barnabas' life was not to be served but to serve. As a result, possessions, power, and position were nonissues with Barnabas, making it easy for him to help others grow. He even saw his pupil exceed him in leadership by the time the first missionary journey was completed (Acts 14:23-28). Paul's ability to live with plenty or want, to be esteemed or repudiated, to suffer or stand firm, to exercise authority or be engaged in earnest pleading for change grew out of the servant leadership perspective he had observed and emulated (Phil. 4:10-13).

4. Relational Patterns

Personal relationships form the heart of cross-cultural ministry. In the final analysis, ministry requires person-to-person, face-to-face, life-to-life contacts. Perhaps no aspect of ministry demands more grace, tolerance, and goodwill than relationships. Lack of adequate equipping too often leads to the kind of anomaly described by one national church leader, who observed, "Often missionaries we have seen love souls but hate people." As in many other aspects of the missionary preparation process, the local church frequently plays a determining part in the development of relational patterns through its ministries of incorporation, formation, participation, and accountability.

Incorporation

In every generation, the sense of nurturing and acceptance experienced by new believers goes a long way toward determining their balanced Christian development. Paul began to grow in his Christian life within a fellowship of other believers. Steps in his experience indicate a pattern of progressive incorporation. First, acting upon inspired instruction from the Lord, Ananias performed the service of a "spiritual big brother" until the new convert received his baptism (Acts 9:10-19). Next, Barnabas became Paul's advocate and discipler, introducing the awkward new believer into the fellowship of the church (Acts 9:26-30). Thus, from his earliest experience as a believer, Paul understood the importance of relational patterns for the establishment and extension of the church. His frequent appeals for unity and harmony between believers, found throughout the New Testament Epistles, underline the importance of incorporation into a local congregation as a normative standard (Rom. 14:1, 13; 15:1-7).

Formation

The discipling process of a believer has corporate as well as individual aspects to it. Practices which are emphasized publicly form the standard for belief and conduct. During the formative period of Paul's Christian life, two local congregations provided a determinative influence. Ministering largely within a monocultural context, the Jerusalem Church emphasized the importance of the public teaching of doctrine, daily close fellowship among believers, and the supernatural nature of the church (Acts 2:42-47). The Antioch Church emphasized multiple leadership, teaching, worship, and cross-cultural outreach (Acts 13:1-3). Still, within each setting, individual Christian responsibilities for life and service were not diminished but were placed within the context of the corporate Christian community.

Participation

There is no adequate substitute for participation in ministry prior to the cross-cultural deployment of a missionary. Involvement in the full circle of ministry within the home church and home culture provides an important filter for the selection process. By conviction, preparation, and personality, the newly converted Paul was an active participant in the life and ministry of the local congregations where he received his nurturing. Significantly, he was not barred from ministry participation until he had received special training. In God's plan, he was under the caring eye of older believers during those early days, while his attempts at ministry caused difficulty for himself and the congregation of believers at Jerusalem

(Acts 9:28-31). Later, in the Antioch congregation, Paul was given a significant leadership function within a familiar context. There his skills were honed before he was thrust into a cross-cultural setting (Acts 11:25-26; 13:1-3).

Accountability

The biblical pattern reveals that accountability involves responsibility for the correctness of doctrinal teaching, the handling of resources, and the eventual result of the ministry. The value Paul placed on personal accountability within the ministry is evident at several points. In spite of the unique missionary call which guided his life, Paul made it a point to be accountable to other leaders prior to starting his missionary ministry. After his three years of further preparation in Arabia and Damascus, he felt responsible to review with the apostles at Jerusalem the content of the gospel message he was preaching (Gal. 1:17-21). In the area of finances, Paul felt accountable for the safe delivery of the offering sent from Antioch to the elders of the Jerusalem congregation during a time of severe need (Acts 11:29-30). At the end of his first missionary journey, Paul returned to his sending congregation to give full account of how the Lord had used him and Barnabas to open the door of faith to the Gentiles (Acts 14:26-28). Significantly, even the declared motive for the second missionary journey was the sense of responsibility and accountability felt by the missionaries (Acts 15:36).

CONCLUSION

In its simplest description, missions is a divine-human endeavor. Consequently, the basic question regarding missionary selection simply asks, "Who should be sent as a missionary?" Ultimately, selection involves determining those whom God has designated for missionary service. These are the ones who should be recognized, prepared, and deployed into cross-cultural ministries.

Selection is the foundation of most other basic personnel issues. When the complex factors of attrition are reduced to their simplest components, the evidence undergirds the importance of a careful selection process guided by standards that are bound neither by culture nor by time. Through conferences, consultations, and publications, a solid biblical foundation for selection must be renewed and widely disseminated to all concerned. A suggested check list for selection is included below. This check list recognizes the fundamental importance of both the divine and the human elements involved in the careful selection and preparation of missionary personnel.

In summary, there are four corrective recommendations relating to missionary selection and deployment from the older sending nations:

1. Partnership. There must be a recognition by Christian leaders, mission agencies, and churches that the normative New Testament model for missions is one of genuine partnership by all involved. The partnerships should include local congregations, training institutions, and implementing agencies.

2. Selection. There must be an understanding that the existing confusion about selection contributes to the problems of attrition. The proper response is to emphasize the development of a biblical theology of missions, which gives priority to continual cross-cultural mission outreach by the whole Christian community.

3. Standards. Mutually accepted, authoritative standards for the selection and preparation of missionaries must be adopted. These standards should certify the requisite qualifications of genuine spiritual life, Christian character, ministry skills, and relational abilities.

4. Communication. Greater interaction and communication must be promoted among leaders at all levels relative to cross-cultural outreach. For the sake of the unreached, congregations, training institutions, and mission agencies that represent compatible ministries must find ways to dialogue about standards for selection, rather than remaining in isolation or opposition to each other.

APPENDIX:
SUGGESTED CHECK LIST FOR THE SELECTION OF MISSIONARY CANDIDATES

Rating Scale: 1 = Yes
2 = No
3 = Doubtful

A. Spiritual Life

____ 1. Gives a clear testimony of personal conversion.

____ 2. Regularly practices the foundational Christian disciplines of prayer, Bible study, etc.

____ 3. Has a clear conviction concerning a personal call to missionary ministry.

____ 4. Demonstrates objective evidence confirming a call to missions.

____ 5. Shows evidence of firm understanding regarding basic Christian doctrines.

B. Christian Character

____ 1. Clearly manifests a life of mature Christian character and discipline.

____ 2. Manifests joy and humility while serving others.

____ 3. Has a teachable spirit and good reputation with coworkers and leaders.

____ 4. Is considered to be trustworthy in all relationships.

____ 5. Has a reputation of honesty and integrity in all financial matters.

C. Ministry Skills

____ 1. Has completed a recognized course of biblical studies.

____ 2. Demonstrates a proven record of effective ministry and service at various levels.

____ 3. Is trained and experienced in effective leadership activities.

____ 4. Demonstrates an eagerness to serve others within his or her abilities.

____ 5. Has experienced fruitful cross-cultural service.

D. Relational Patterns

____ 1. Is known for the harmony and integrity of his or her family relationships.

____ 2. Understands and practices the role of servant leadership.

____ 3. Is committed to involvement with the life and ministry of a local church.

____ 4. Shows evidence of ability to work harmoniously with others in service and ministry.

____ 5. Demonstrates a willingness to be accountable to leadership.

NOTE: Those items marked with a rating of 2 or 3 indicate areas needing further preparation prior to commissioning the candidate for missionary service.

Daryl Platt has over 30 years of ministry experience in North and South America, Southern Africa, and Eastern Europe. Personal involvement has provided opportunities for him to know the missionary enterprise as a pastor, missionary, observer, leader, and ministry advisor. He and his wife, Carolyn, have four grown children, all of whom have been raised in cross-cultural settings and are committed to Christ. The Platts have served with OC International for 22 years. They are currently members of the International Ministry Team based in Colorado Springs, Colorado.

15

Formal and Non-Formal Pre-Field Training

PERSPECTIVE OF THE NEW SENDING COUNTRIES

Margaretha Adiwardana

Pre-field training aims at preparing missionaries to live and serve effectively in cross-cultural situations. All of the stakeholders in missions—the local church, the school, the agency, and the missionaries themselves—are jointly responsible for a successful and fruit-bearing mission effort. They need to work together during the various stages of selection, formation/training, sending, on-field ministry, and reentry. We can see a clear picture of this interaction in the model presented by Rudy Girón (chapter 3).

In any training program, curricula and teaching styles should be tailored to develop in candidates the abilities and character traits they will need in order to adapt and survive on the mission field and to minister in a relevant way to the people. In most cases, having a productive ministry means staying for several years among the people served. Mission attrition reports and surveys should therefore be taken seriously, so that as information comes in from the various fields about failures that have occurred, pre-field training can be ad-

justed to help reduce the numbers of missionaries returning home.

MAJOR REASONS FOR ATTRITION

This chapter is based on Peter Brierley's report (chapter 6), which was presented during the 1996 WEF Missions Commission workshop on missionary attrition in England. It also reflects some of the comments made by Kath Donovan and Ruth Myors (chapter 4). In addition, it sets forth the conclusions reached by a workshop discussion group which considered issues related to pre-field training.

According to Brierley's report, inappropriate training ranks 17th overall among 26 reasons for missionary attrition. It ranks 20th for the old sending countries (OSC), ninth for the new sending countries (NSC), but first for Brazil! Although it may seem at first glance that inadequate pre-field training is not one of the major reasons for attrition outside Brazil, it is one of the top 10 reasons for the NSC, and it contributes to several of the other attrition factors listed. Areas linked to pre-field training may be grouped as follows:

1. Lack of support. Lack of home support is the number one attrition factor in the NSC. This problem may seem to be unrelated to training, but having an integrated, church-oriented pre-field training program should help reduce attrition from this cause, as will be discussed later in this chapter.

2. Spiritual qualities. This category includes lack of call (second in rank for NSC), inadequate commitment (third), immature spiritual life (tied for ninth place), and personal concerns such as problems related to low self-esteem, stress, anger, unrealistic expectations, singleness, and loneliness (ninth).

3. Relationships. Under this heading are disagreement with the sending agency (fourth in rank), problems with peers (fifth), and problems with local leaders (12th).

4. Inappropriate training. In addition to inadequate training programs (ninth in rank), this category includes poor cultural adaptation (15th) and language problems (23rd).

ATTITUDES, VALUES, AND BEHAVIOR

Kath Donovan and Ruth Myors (chapter 4) have made the following observations regarding reasons for attrition:

+ Today's missionaries are so different from those of 30 years ago that they no longer fit traditional missionary models.
+ There is a cultural gap between the booster generation and the post-boosters. The latter tend to collide head-on with the mission agencies.

+ Significant changes have occurred in the last 70 years in the attitudes, values, and behavior of people.

Although the terms referring to the various generations and the studies carried out are from the OSC, the world is increasingly becoming a global village. What happens in one country affects other societies. This is especially true of values in the economically and technologically powerful OSC and their influence upon the developing NSC. Most of the NSC have been sending missionaries only since about 1980. Thus their workers are mostly from the post-booster generations. We would expect that there would be no cultural gap between the generations involved in missions in the NSC. We would also expect missionary models to fit the current situation. These conclusions are incorrect. Due to historic events and societal changes which occurred after World War II, there have been attitude and value changes among the post-boosters in the NSC, just as in the OSC.

These new attitudes, values, and behaviors are in many ways the real causes underlying attrition. For example, with reference to call and commitment, Donovan and Myors noted that boomers are willing to move to a new position in another location if they believe the new setting may be more fruitful for ministry. The older generation of boosters generally committed themselves to stay in one place for their entire career. Busters tend to make only short-term commitments, because they don't know what the future holds. These characteristics of the younger generations in the OSC relate to lack of call and inadequate commitment in the NSC, which rank second and third, respectively, as reasons for attrition.

Donovan and Myors predicted that relationship issues would be one of the causes of attrition in post-booster missionaries. In the NSC, relationships with fellow missionaries, the agency, and local leaders are indeed significant attrition factors.

Donovan and Myors' comments that busters are vulnerable to emotional problems on the field and that their self-esteem is easily eroded relate to personal concerns as the ninth-ranking reason for attrition in the NSC.

PRE-FIELD TRAINING CONSIDERATIONS

In the NSC, the preventable reasons for attrition, listed in order of weight, are as follows:

✦ Church (lack of home support).
✦ Spiritual qualities (lack of call, inadequate commitment, immature spiritual life, personal concerns).
✦ Relationships (disagreement with agency, problems with peers, problems with local leaders).
✦ Inappropriate training (inadequate training, poor cultural adaptation, language problems).
✦ Family (children's needs, marriage conflicts, elderly parents).
✦ The underlying factor: a paradigm shift in the post-boosters' culture.

Let us consider each of these areas more thoroughly.

1. Church

Pre-field training should be carried out cooperatively by the local church, the school (Bible school, theological seminary, or cross-cultural institution), and the sending agency. The local church is vital because it provides a setting for self-preparation by prospective missionaries, and it helps candidates confirm their call to missions. Rudy Girón (chapter 3) refers to this process as discipleship at the local church level, asserting, "We cannot overstate the value of church experience."

Since lack of home support is the primary reason for attrition in the NSC, the church urgently needs to be involved in training. A church which disciples its missionaries knows them well. It can accompany candidates through the process of pre-field training and can offer suggestions specifically tailored to each candidate's program. In their church environment, candidates can put into practice what they are learning. This practical experience, in turn, provides the basis for assessment and improvement in training at the institution.

By the time pre-field training ends, when candidates are ready to leave for the field, the church will be ready to send them. If the church has been involved during the training period, its leaders and members will know the missionaries well and will love and take care of them once they are on the field. Home support, even to the point of financial sacrifice (as is needed in some of the new sending nations) will be the result.

2. Spiritual Qualities

The discussion group on pre-field training considered eight spiritual qualities: character, attitude, walk, call, commitment, theology (biblical basis), spiritual warfare, and expectations. The following statement was formulated:

We believe that the church needs to rediscover a biblical theology of the cross which not only considers its historical significance, but which will impinge realistically on our daily living. We are called to be ambassadors of Christ, so we should reflect the nature of the True Ambassador, Jesus Christ. We recognize at the same time that Christ came as The Servant, and He gave us the example that we should follow. He said, "Learn from Me, for I am among you as one who serves.... The servant is not greater than his master."

The whole thrust of missionary training is to ensure that missionary candidates are being conformed to the image of Christ. From this level of being servants, Jesus Christ wants us to become His friends and, finally, the bride elect. We are not here to produce "workers," but our goal is to train candidates to be prepared for suffering and hardship as good soldiers of Jesus Christ. The reason for the need of such emphasis is that it goes against the present flow of our culture, which encourages self-indulgence and which is oriented to aspirations of success. There are continual expectations that we will be cushioned from hardship and suffering if we are faithful to Christ (see 1 Pet. 4:12; Jas. 1:12).

All training should therefore focus primarily on the development of our "being," anticipating that "doing" and "knowing" will facilitate that development.

We recommend that special attention in training be given to development of character, having the right attitudes, maintaining daily relationship and walk with Christ; emphasizing holiness of life; understanding what call and commitment really mean. We also believe that candidates should be prepared and trained for spiritual warfare with regard

to demonic oppression in all its manifestations.

3. Relationships

This area includes relationships with fellow missionaries, the sending agency, and local leaders. The discussion group identified two aspects of training that affect relationships: interpersonal factors and intrapersonal preparation. Interpersonal factors include social flexibility toward the various cultures represented (the host culture, the missionary's own culture, and the culture of other missionaries), interactional skills, and people-oriented communication. Intrapersonal preparation includes internship in the mission agency office to learn the interactions that take place there; identification of groups holding expectations of the missionary; introduction to the nature of tensions; mentoring; experiential aspects besides skills; and the initiation of regular communication and prayer with supporters.

4. Training for Cross-Cultural Readiness

Here again is the conclusion of the discussion group:

Although in the report on attrition, the cross-cultural adaptation factor is not the most important reason for attrition (it ranked 15th in the new sending countries), a suitable cross-cultural readiness prepared in pre-field training will help a lot in cultural adaptation. In turn, this reduces the stress on field and bolsters psychological strength. Adaptability also increases effectiveness in communicating the gospel in another culture.

Therefore we propose that:

a. Training in cross-cultural adaptability should be perceived as an on-

going process, not only pre-field but on-field as well.

b. *Training in cross-cultural issues should aim at the preparation of heart and mind, to develop attitudes of openness and willingness to learn and to identify with people.*

c. *The contents, which include language-learning skills and techniques, cultural anthropology and related issues, and cross-cultural communication skills, should prepare trainees for cross-cultural competency know-how.*

d. *Knowledge may be imparted in formal, non-formal, and informal manners—i.e., theory, information, simulation, exposure, debriefing, and practical ministry in the community of the field culture, whenever possible—with a view toward preparing trainees culturally, mentally, and spiritually in personal discipline to cope with stress and frustrations, with a more realistic expectation of the on-field situation.*

e. *This training should be carried out in conjunction with sending churches, mission agencies, and the receiving church, in order to facilitate the continuous development of the cross-cultural competency for the servant of God and thereby reducing the possibility of attrition.*

5. Family

In the OSC, children's needs are the top preventable reason for missionaries' leaving the field, but in the NSC this area ranks eighth. Marriage/family conflict ranks 16th in the NSC. Remarkably, elderly parents rank 24th in the NSC, whereas this area ranks ninth in the OSC. This finding is surprising, because some new sending nations are culturally obligated to care for elderly parents. In fact, some candidates to missions may not be allowed by their parents to go abroad. Perhaps the reason for the low ranking in this area is that most NSC mission agencies and missionaries are young and have not yet had to face the dilemma of taking care of elderly parents.

David Pollock (chapter 23) deals with the issue of missionary children. Regarding marriage conflicts, Donovan and Myors have observed that some cases of attrition occur because of wives' dissatisfaction with their ministries. Unlike their booster predecessors, boomer women have very often had professional training. Many of them expect to assume roles in keeping with their background, instead of just supporting their husbands and fitting into whatever role is available.

To help reduce marriage conflicts, training should be completed by the whole family. David Harley (1995, p. 89) has noted, "All but one of the training centres studied expect married couples to be trained together for their future work. Some wives suffer from a low self-image and think they will be of little use in ministry. During a period of training they can discover previously unrecognized gifts, as well as be encouraged to practise their gifts of hospitality, listening or caring. Well-educated wives may feel especially frustrated if they are not trained along with their husbands."

6. Post-Boosters' Culture

Changes in attitude, values, and behavior are inevitable, but as Donovan and Myors have affirmed, attitudes that are not biblical should not be accepted. We need to study the changes that have occurred and ask what the present generation's cultural values are and how they measure up from a biblical point of view. In the language of contextualization, we need to reflect, contextualize, and confront in order to find out what needs to be developed and cultivated and what needs to be decontextualized and rejected.

Following are the responses of the pre-field training discussion group to some of the issues raised by Donovan and Myors.

Characteristics in Need Of Tempering

Donovan and Myors listed several characteristics of boomers and busters which are in special need of tempering with the wisdom of booster leaders, including the sense of entitlement, the temptation towards professional development for selfish reasons, lack of respect for experience and authority, and outspokenness. The statement given above under the heading "Spiritual Qualities" speaks to these areas.

Devotional Life

Donovan and Myors noted that today's younger missionaries find it difficult to discipline themselves to a regular devotional time. The busters especially welcome assistance in maintaining their devotional lives.

Our response is that pre-field training needs to address this problem area. One viable solution is seen in the training given at the Chinese Mission Seminary in Hong Kong, which specializes in training missionaries for China. During their first year at the seminary, students are trained mostly in spiritual life and devotional discipline. They also learn to cope with loneliness, as this may be needed in their future ministry. Only

after they have received this foundation, starting in the second year, do students undertake theological, academic, and practical subjects. They also get on-the-job training in teams. Such teamwork meets their need for support and pastoral care and alleviates the fear of isolation in mission, another concern mentioned by Donovan and Myors.

Listening Skills

Donovan and Myors observed that participants at missionary orientation courses often seem unable to hear much of what is taught in lectures. Our response is that more stress needs to be put on listening skills and not just speaking proficiency in communications subjects.

Monitoring and Mentoring

Donovan and Myors recommended that more effort be put into support, monitoring, and mentoring during the first year on the field. In Brazil, Kairos, Antioch Mission, and the Baptist Convention regard the first one or two years on the field as part of training. New missionaries are sent to "near culture" fields for this initial period before beginning their main assignment. During the introductory period of service, workers are under the close supervision of seniors, so that guidance can be given and any problem areas can be dealt with quickly.

Emotional Vulnerability

Donovan and Myors noted that busters are quite vulnerable emotionally, because many have had a great deal of pain in their backgrounds. To deal with this situation, both formal and non-formal pre-departure courses should include segments on identifying and curing wounds. The selection process must be flexible enough to accommodate those who may need a more intensive and longer time of care before being accepted to go to the field.

In October 1995, the Association of Missions Agencies in Brazil, the Association of Brazilian Missions Professors, and the Association of Brazilian Church Missions Committees held a joint consultation regarding the current situation of Brazilian missionaries. One of the findings that emerged was that personal concerns due to character and spiritual problems were the leading reason for attrition among Brazilian workers. This finding underscores the need to focus on developing character and spiritual qualities in candidates during training. Such development should take place in all of the training arenas—church, school, and mission agency.

A specific problem for some new sending countries is that we lack trainers. Those who possess training skills, academic qualifications, and field experience are filling needed roles on the field and are often not available for home assignment as trainers.

FORMAL AND NON-FORMAL PRE-FIELD TRAINING

It is widely accepted that a combination of formal, non-formal, and informal training is the best model. These three methods of missionary development should form an integrated curriculum which is implemented by the church, the school, and the agency.

Formal instruction sees to it that candidates are equipped not only with knowledge, but also with a biblical understanding of the what, why, and how of missions. With the shift in cultural

values and the ensuing changes in attitudes and behavior, an understanding of the biblical basis for being is urgently needed. Students need to see their present culture in light of eternal biblical principles, so they can judge wisely what to conform to and what to confront. More than just imparting knowledge, formal training leads to being.

The social and cultural sciences can study the changes that have taken place, along with why and how these changes have occurred. In the NSC, the political and social changes since World War II have been great: independence from colonialism, a fledgling period, dictatorship and the struggle to get free from such rule, bridging the gap between rich and poor, etc. We need to ask, What historical roots form the foundation of the present culture? Each country or culture group should study its own cultural context.

In Brazil during the last three decades, there has been an increase in the practice of what is called *jeitinho* (literally, "a way or manner"). This practice is used in everyday life to solve any problem in an unofficial—and often illegal—way. It is also used to resolve relationship problems in an impasse. One of the roots for *jeitinho* is the need to bridge gaps, whether social, educational, economic, or power gaps. Another determinant is the mixed racial origin of Brazilians. *Jeitinho* can be innocent, creative, and friendly, or it can be dishonest and law-breaking. It is considered by sociologists to be a core element of Brazil's culture today. It permeates the whole society. Its influence extends to Brazilian missionaries, who may automatically act in the *jeitinho* way in solving problems. On the mission field, in relationships with an international team or with nationals, the *jeitinho* way often shocks people. It seems disrespectful or even unbiblical.

Special attention must be given to this area during training in order to make missionary candidates aware of this cultural characteristic and of how it affects their relationships and behavior. Courses in cross-cultural communication and missionary anthropology are useful foundations for enlightenment and discussion. The historical roots and origin of the *jeitinho* can be explored, along with the influence of the social, economic, and political contexts. Biblical and theological subjects can be structured to include studies on how each trait of the *jeitinho* is seen under the light of God's Word. Case studies are useful for group discussion and self-reflection. Sherwood Lingenfelter and Marvin Mayers (1986) include an exercise on the six areas of tensions in their book *Ministering Cross-Culturally: An Incarnational Model for Personal Relationships*. This exercise can help students discover for themselves how they relate to other people. Another resource is the grid model presented by Lingenfelter (1992) in *Transforming Culture: A Challenge for Christian Mission*. This model assists students in seeing their culture in relation to other cultures. Most students in seminary or pre-departure courses become aware of their own cultural characteristics for the first time through such exercises.

Non-formal training allows candidates to practice the things they have become aware of through their formal training. This phase may consist of practical work or apprenticeship in Bible institutions, or it may include training in missionary training centers and/or in agency orientation courses. Non-formal training should also be the setting in which trainers reflect on what improvements they can make in their training programs.

Some pre-departure courses emphasize daily living, including group living, teamwork, hard work, discipline, a tight schedule, and different kinds of food. This rigorous program serves as a perseverance exercise for candidates and allows trainers to verify decisions made in the selection process. Such non-formal experiences comprise a "hidden" curriculum, which contributes to the development of character and spiritual qualities.

CONCLUSION

If we examine the preventable reasons for attrition in the new sending countries, it is apparent that over half are spiritual and character factors. This means that formal and non-formal pre-field training needs to emphasize the formation of the being.

Instruction that focuses primarily on the development of being, with doing and knowing facilitating, is a discipleship kind of training. This is the approach Jesus used with His disciples—teaching, preaching, explaining, correcting, doing, and sending. Knowing leads to being, resulting in doing. Doing provides input for correcting. The process can be accomplished successfully only as the church, school, and mission agency work together. In the body of Christ, all the members need to exercise their spiritual gifts for the body to function properly. In like manner, the church, the school, and the agency must all contribute to the process of equipping missionaries. Trainers need to be living examples as well (Phil. 2:1-11). Then missionary workers will be able to go to their fields of service fully equipped and able to overcome the factors that commonly cause attrition.

REFERENCES

Harley, C. D. (1995). *Preparing to serve: Training for cross-cultural mission.* Pasadena, CA: William Carey Library.

Lingenfelter, S. G. (1992). *Transforming culture: A challenge for Christian mission.* Grand Rapids, MI: Baker Book House.

Lingenfelter, S. G., & Mayers, M. K. (1986). *Ministering cross-culturally: An incarnational model for personal relationships.* Grand Rapids, MI: Baker Book House.

Margaretha Nalina Adiwardana is a Brazilian missions leader born in Indonesia. She serves on the faculty of the missions department of the Baptist Seminary in São Paulo and helps to train missionaries for other Brazilian organizations, including Kairos, Antioch Mission, Horizons, and the Missionary Training Centre of the Church of God. She is first vice-president of the Association of Missions Professors of Brazil and is also a WEF Missions Commission Associate.

16

Formal and Non-Formal Pre-Field Training

PERSPECTIVE OF THE OLD SENDING COUNTRIES

Bruce Dipple

Y ou have to experience it to understand it" is a maxim that has circulated in mission circles for many years. The element of truth in this statement is not to be ignored, but it does not negate the fact that effective and appropriate pre-field training can make a major difference in the "experience." To take time for preparation is a biblical concept, and it is certainly one that must be taken into account when considering the reasons that cross-cultural missionaries conclude their time of service earlier than originally planned.

The research data gathered by the WEF Missions Commission Task Force identify a number of reported reasons for missionary loss that ought to be addressed in pre-field training. It is recognised that some of the areas of concern have implications for other approaches to the problem of missionary loss. For example, conflict with peers could be related to inadequate selection processes or inadequate field supervision, as much as to inadequate pre-field training. Most frequently, such conflict is probably due to a combination of these factors, which underlines the necessity of trainers' giving consideration to these reasons for early withdrawal.

The Task Force research drew together a number of reasons for missionary loss that could be related to the quality of pre-departure training received. The initial analysis by the Task Force includes certain factors that could be described as unpreventable, such as retirement or death. When these reasons are removed from the total equation, the percentages listed in Figure 16-1 emerge for the 13 areas in the analysis that can be identified as being relevant to pre-field training.

This analysis suggests that 73.8% of the reasons given for missionary loss by agencies from old sending countries could be addressed and corrected to some degree by more adequate and appropriate pre-field training. This unequivocal demonstration of the value of pre-field training is endorsed by the fact that some two-thirds of the agencies involved in the research reported having cross-cultural orientation and some kind of theological or other professional

REASONS FOR MISSIONARY LOSS THAT HAVE RELEVANCE TO PRE-FIELD TRAINING	
Reason	Percentage of Total Reasons
Children's adjustment, education, health, behaviour	14.4
Problems related to mental or physical health	11.6
Relationship problems with field leaders and missionaries	8.5
Personal problems—self-esteem, stress, expectations, etc.	8.4
Disagreement with sending body on theological issues	5.5
Poor adaptation to culture and living conditions	4.8
Marriage or family conflict	4.1
Immature spiritual life, unmet spiritual needs	4.0
Lack of understanding of cost and commitment	3.7
Inadequate or inappropriate training and preparation	2.9
Relationship problems with church leaders and colleagues	2.5
Lack of genuine spiritual call to missionary work	2.2
Inability to learn the country's language adequately	1.2
Total	73.8%

Figure 16-1

training as prerequisites to cross-cultural service.

In response to one research question, the agencies indicated that they perceived "provision of appropriate and regular training" as the least useful factor (out of 11 items) in preventing missionary loss. This at first appears to contradict the other findings concerning the importance of training, but probably the discrepancy is due to the fact that the question sets training apart from other factors, such as a clear calling to mission work, good relationships with other missionaries and colleagues,

and the ability to adapt to different cultures and to learn languages, all of which could be related to training, as indicated above. The exclusion of these aspects of missionary life from the concept of training has the effect of making "provision of appropriate and regular training" refer primarily to academic study, which may explain why it is seen as less important in preventing missionary loss.

SPIRITUAL FORMATION

The Apostle Paul asserts that step by step we are being changed so that we conform more closely to the image of Christ. He affirms repeatedly that in Christ we find the strength, wisdom, and purpose we need for life. Those responsible for the training of missionaries are obligated to ensure that their training program facilitates the process of being conformed to Christ and of discovering His adequacy for the challenges of life. While only 4% of the respondents made direct reference to their spiritual life in the list of causes in Figure 16-1, there is little doubt that spiritual difficulties would have been a contributing factor to many of the other reasons for attrition. The spiritual nature of mission work guarantees this outcome.

The current prominence given to accredited programs, educational goals, and measurable outcomes has tended to reinforce the existing emphasis in Western society on spirituality as a private matter. An aspect of modernity, this viewpoint has resulted in a limitation in the degree to which training programs see themselves as responsible for spiritual formation. Spiritual development does not lend itself to a credit-hour system, and it is difficult to include on an official transcript. Therefore, it tends to appear as an appendage to the "real" program. Yet there are few personnel involved in missionary training programs, formal or non-formal, who would not agree that spiritual maturity is the key to perseverance and effectiveness in Christian ministry. The attrition research gives its own endorsement to this conviction.

Spiritual formation has to find its place in the core subjects of each program. The theologian should emphasise a theological understanding of spirituality and the relationship of the doctrine of the Holy Spirit to the life of the missionary in the midst of spirit worshippers. The church historian should consider the history of spirituality and the spiritual character of effective servants of God down through the years. The biblical exegete can look at servanthood and sacrifice and God's expectations for holy living. Spiritual development is relevant to every discipline and adds a spiritual growth element to much that is labeled academic. Unless an emphasis on spiritual formation is manifested across the range of disciplines, future missionaries will develop the false assumption that the training per se will make them effective, rather than their spiritual capacity to use that training.

The training institution does not stand in isolation with this responsibility. The local church retains its biblical role as the location of worship, teaching, practical equipping for ministry, and growth in spiritual maturity. Training institutions and local churches need to maintain a climate of interaction and cooperation in order to ensure that they are pulling together in the same direction. Practical spiritual disciplines being taught at the institution need reinforcement and opportunity for expression in the local church. At the same time, processes need to be in place for the training institution to hear from local churches concerning areas of spiritual formation that appear to be lacking in the training program. The institution and church together can provide experiential training in developing skills in areas such as how to build trust relationships with colleagues, how to encourage one another, how to share and to benefit from sharing, how to develop relationships with difficult people, and how to grow through mentoring. Many training programs include such topics in one course or another, but frequently there is no opportunity given to experiment with the skills learned until the student has arrived at the ministry location.

An increasing number of missionary candidates from old sending countries have come out of a dysfunctional family background and broken, painful homes. Such a background often leaves them vulnerable to emotional problems and susceptible to the erosion of their personal self-esteem. Opportunity has to be provided within the training process for these areas of potential need to surface and to be dealt with within the context of spiritual growth. Christian counsellors and psychologists may be the best ones to give input at this level, but those responsible for training missionaries must ensure that such input has a place in the program and that it is not left as an optional extra for the candidates to follow up if they so desire.

Cross-cultural missionaries frequently find themselves in isolated locations, as far as contact with other Christians is concerned. This requires the development of a different set of skills for the maintenance of spiritual vitality—skills that need to be introduced and exercised during the training period. Hermeneutics takes on new meaning when there is no Bible teacher or preacher to give biblical input, just as the sufficiency of God becomes critical when there is no colleague or pastor to provide encouragement. Residential training institutions can easily make candidates' spiritual life dependent upon the vitality of the group and the stimulation of the interaction. Training situations need to be devised that will initially impress upon candidates the necessity of these spiritual survival skills, as well as provide candidates with practical responses through such things as spiritual journals and personal retreats. This area of instruction needs to focus on continued growth in the future, rather than being perceived as another pre-departure requirement.

INTERPERSONAL FORMATION

Even a cursory review of Figure 16-1 reveals the importance of relational issues in missionary life. To move into a cross-cultural environment requires a significant level of social flexibility for any person, but even more so for missionaries who desire to communicate a distinct message through social relationships. Missionaries are confronted with the necessity of reinterpreting their Christian lifestyle in terms of the host culture. To make the situation more complex, they also have to do the same

thing to a certain degree with respect to the cultures of their fellow missionaries.

For this reinterpretation to be undertaken, missionaries must have developed the ability to be active listeners and learners, willing to take the time necessary to understand and appreciate the cultural and social milieu within which they must now live. This is a skill that can be developed during the pre-field training period, particularly with the multicultural makeup of most modern Western cities. It is imperative, however, that training programs do not leave this as an optional extra to be included by trainees in their out-of-class hours. It is an area of preparation that needs time allocated in the program for both theoretical input and practical experience. Too few graduates from training institutions have been guided through the process of identifying those aspects of their own life and experience which are totally cultural, those which are gospel essentials, and those which are a cultural interpretation of a gospel principle. Without a skill set and basic experience in this area, cross-cultural workers will struggle in their understanding of the host society and its pattern of social relationships.

Many courses exist at training institutions on the subject of interpersonal relationships, yet this area continues to be a major source of concern in any discussion on missionary stress or attrition. This has to suggest that the need exists for these courses to be reviewed and revised in some way, so as to increase their effectiveness when the principles are translated into practice in a cross-cultural environment. Any such review needs to take into account the fact that anecdotal evidence strongly supports the assertion that the rate of interpersonal difficulties with fellow missionaries is inordinately higher than with the national people being ministered to. Missionaries are clearly going to their field of service with false assumptions and unrealistic expectations with regard to their fellow workers. There is need for these assumptions and expectations to be exposed and corrected during the training period, through planned activities that demand interaction and cooperation within a team context.

College mission teams that minister in a cultural environment different from that of the team members can be helpful, although it is essential that such an activity be an integral part of the curriculum, with appropriate preparation and debriefing, to make it a truly educational experience. Such activities would increase in training value if the mission team were composed of students from several different training institutions, each college group thus having to encounter and adjust to the patterns and ethos of the other groups with which they must work.

The increased use of teams in mission work in recent years has highlighted the fact that the concept of a team is culturally defined as far as leadership, member participation, and decision making are concerned. Trainers need to be alert to these differences and, possibly through appropriate simulations, should expose their students to the differences to the degree possible. Private research by this author revealed that a number of missionaries who had quoted "administration difficulties" as their reason for leaving the field had actually run into difficulties because of

disagreement between team members as to what it meant to be a team.

These latter missionaries ended up in a situation of conflict, which brings into focus the need that exists for cross-cultural personnel to be trained in the area of conflict resolution. There appears to be a reticence on the part of many training institutions to include conflict resolution skills in the curriculum, possibly because of a lingering idea amongst Christians that conflict is inherently bad and that failure is inevitable once conflict arises. Yet the need for such skills is undisputed, and many valuable texts are available on the subject. Since conflict is a phenomenon in all of life, it is an area in which the skills taught can easily be practiced, providing a good basis for subsequent discussion on the effectiveness of their implementation.

In recent years, a lot of thought has been given to the impact of generational differences within the missionary force. The generational cycle is becoming smaller, and the fundamental difference between the generations is becoming greater. Work therefore needs to be done to prepare missionaries from the different generations to work together in harmony and understanding. To put it another way, today's missionaries have need of cross-generational as well as cross-cultural understanding and coping skills.

PERSONAL PREPARATION

The Mission Agency Or Sending Church

A number of the reasons for termination listed in Figure 16-1 can be seen to relate to some aspect of the mission agency, which could include the agency's theological position, financial system, leadership structure, personnel care, or general ethos. The majority of mission agencies require their candidates to complete some form of orientation course, at which these topics are presented and discussed. This element of pre-field training could be made much more effective, however, if the training institutions and mission agencies worked together to identify the areas of potential stress and conflict that need to be addressed. This step would enable the training institutions to schedule time for looking at the different structures and processes employed by various agencies, which would in turn help future missionary candidates to recognise those areas where they need to ask particular questions of the mission agencies. At one training institution, the graduating missions class prepared a questionnaire for candidates to submit to a mission agency, along the lines of those sent by the agency to applicants. The candidates were also encouraged to obtain references for the mission, in the same way that the mission obtained references for the candidate, all in an attempt to remove the unknowns concerning the agency. A further possibility would be for agencies to require candidates to participate in a short-term internship in the mission home office as part of the application process.

This kind of approach does presume on the agency leadership and staff being receptive to such inquiries and willing to be open concerning all aspects of the agency's structure and procedures. Such open communication before new missionaries commence their ministry will bring a level of understanding that has two particular benefits. Firstly, it could assist missionary candidates in discovering a seemingly minor disagreement that they may have with the agency, which could escalate into a major problem once they arrive on the field. Further discussion might resolve the issue, or alternatively, it might prove necessary for the candidate to consider a different agency. Secondly, familiarity with agency policies and procedures would enable new missionaries to integrate into the missionary team more effectively and rapidly. This would have a positive impact on their total cross-cultural adjustment and would increase their sense of belonging to the agency.

The Issue of Expectations

It is difficult to estimate the degree to which false or conflicting expectations contribute to missionary loss, but any experienced mission administrator is aware of the frequency with which this topic arises in discussion with missionaries concluding their service. Expectations concerning missionaries and their ministry come from a wide range of sources, including the missionaries themselves, family members, supporters, sending churches, mission home leadership, mission field leadership, receiving church, other missionaries, and professional peers. During the pre-departure training period, missionary candidates need to be made aware of these different sources of expectations and the tensions they can create. This will help candidates understand that one of the significant educational tasks they have before their departure is to help family members, supporters, and sending churches to have realistic expectations for the future ministry.

Before others can be educated, however, it is essential that candidates themselves have expectations that are realistic and that are in harmony with those of the sending church and mission society. Opportunity can be provided in the pre-departure orientation program for the mission home staff and candidates to discuss their understanding in this area. Whatever agreement is reached at this level, however, can be jeopardised by the fact that the expectations of the field leadership have not been taken into account. In an attempt to deal with this complication, one mission agency, SIM International, recently introduced a process whereby expectations in the major areas of cross-cultural life and ministry are clarified prior to departure through consultation with new missionaries, the mission home leadership, and the mission field leadership. The resulting document is known as a Newcomer Development Plan. A process of this nature will go a long way toward reducing one area of potential conflict for first-term missionaries, as well as alerting each participant to areas that could be overlooked or pushed aside, such as the need for planned rest and recreation, for spiritual refreshment, or for professional development.

Before this process begins, missionary candidates can be taught how to prepare and evaluate a personal growth and development plan. This will equip them to clarify expectations for each stage of their missionary career, with their pre-departure program being used as the first example. As they bring together in their plan each aspect of the pre-departure period, they will not only develop an increased understanding of the necessity and relevance of each part, but will also gain competency in using such an essential process for the future. Any pre-field language learning programs can be written up and evaluated in the same way, thus developing the skill even further.

Physical Readiness And Health Care

There is no question that a significant percentage of the health problems referred to in Figure 16-1 would have occurred even if the individuals concerned had been in their own culture. The assertion can also confidently be made, however, that some of the problems could have been avoided if more adequate and appropriate preparation had been given in the area of health care. While the current data are insufficient to speak with certainty, it is also possible that health issues, particularly chronic tiredness, could have been a contributing factor to some of the other attrition causes highlighted by the research.

Pre-field preparation in this area could include an introduction to the biblical teaching and its implications with regard to our responsibility for the care of the physical body God has entrusted to us. In addition, candidates should be made aware of the health issues that can arise when moving to a new cultural environment, particularly where the understanding of hygiene and medical care are less developed. Candidates should be familiarised with basic health issues and the responses to them, including medications and other items that could be taken from the home country. Finally, they should be urged to participate in a fitness program, since such a program demonstrates the foundational relationship between keeping fit and all other health issues.

A question that immediately arises in this area of preparation concerns who should take responsibility for its inclusion in the pre-field training program. Training institutions that have adopted a totally academic model for their programs would probably hesitate to go beyond the biblical teaching area. Mission agencies that offer pre-departure orientation would see some of these issues as too complex for inclusion in a two- or three-week program. The answer must surely lie in cooperation among all those involved in pre-field preparation. Mission agencies and training institutions need to talk to each other and to specialist groups that could have input at this level, including Schools of Tropical Medicine and similar bodies. Health concerns are having too great a negative impact on missionaries for them to be left to individual missionaries to follow up.

The missionary application process invariably involves a full medical evaluation, but the attrition research data suggest that this evaluation needs to be undertaken in a broader context of training missionaries to remain healthy in difficult environments. If the mission agency is serious about reducing attrition, then health care training must be made obligatory, like the initial health evaluation. Not to do this reveals a very short-term focus in the agency's thinking.

Family Readiness

Given that factors relating to children claim first place on the chart in Figure 16-1, questions must be asked concerning the amount of time and effort being given to the preparation of the children for the cross-cultural adjustments that are demanded of them. Every area of preparation referred to in this chapter needs to be considered in relation to the children of missionaries, and appropriate training strategies must subsequently be developed that will ensure the complete family unit is as well prepared as possible for the cross-cultural encounter.

Many training institutions would probably see this focus of training as being outside their area of responsibility, although a brief but effective course could usefully be put together on the Christian family in a cross-cultural environment. And would it really be so radical if the school-age children were invited to accompany their parents to an appropriately scheduled session in the course? Not only would it be good for the children to attend, but they would probably raise a different set of issues from those raised by the parents.

The use of children with cross-cultural experience as instructors should also be given consideration. While in their teenage years, the children of this writer effectively handled a session with missionary candidates, many of whom later recorded it as the most useful of the course. This latter strategy may be more appropriate for a pre-field orientation course, but mission agencies and training institutions need to collaborate so as to ensure that the preparation of children is seriously addressed at some stage in the pre-field training process.

This is also an area in which the mission agency can profitably involve the local church. So many families preparing for cross-cultural service are surrounded by a church membership that does not understand the pressures and difficulties they are going to face, a situation that is probably even more acute for the children. By involving the church members, the agency will be able to educate them concerning the future needs of the children and how the church will be able to help through informed prayer, letters, and the sending of appropriate materials.

The educational needs of the children remain a major reason that many missionaries return home. This is an issue that is far from being solved amongst missions from the old sending countries, in spite of the number of years that the matter has been before them. It is an area that demands continued creativity and flexibility on the part of mission agencies. It is also an area that is subject to changing generational values and expectations. The resurgence of nationalism in Western countries also comes into play, translating into strong ethnocentrism in all areas at the mission field level. From a training perspective, the formal training institutions have a major role to play, because they can so easily communicate the message, as much by methodology as by course content, that there is only one acceptable educational model.

Once again, this is an area in which mission agencies and training institutions need to sit down and talk to each other, along with their alumni, so as to be certain that they are not repressing the very flexibility and understanding that are demanded of missionary parents with regard to the education of their children. With the broad range of educational options available for mis-

sionary children around the world, it is essential that the pre-field training process provide an opportunity to become familiar with the strengths of each option. New missionaries must have the same broad awareness and capacity for adjustment in this area as in all the other aspects of missionary life.

The research data make it clear that, if we are serious about reducing attrition, the children of missionary candidates cannot be ignored or treated as a side issue in the training process. Children need to be as aware as their parents of the pressures of cross-cultural living and need to know that the reactions they will experience are normal. It is not only the parents who need to understand that the children will grasp the language and culture at a faster rate and with less stress. The children need to know how to deal with slow-learning, high-stress parents!

Children also need to understand that God is granting them the privilege of understanding and experiencing in a fuller way the world He has created, rather than punishing them by taking them away from the smaller world with which they are familiar. They must know they are active partners in a family that God has chosen to use in the world, and to this end, time and opportunity must be given for some evaluation of the readiness of the whole family unit for cross-cultural service. This is a difficult area, because ideas on husband/wife and parent/child relationships are intensely personal and, in many people, culturally determined. The importance of this area cannot be ignored, however, and some opportunity must be given in the training process for all missionary candidates, married and single, to be alerted to the kinds of pressures in a cross-cultural ministry environment that can weaken marriage and family relationships. The missionary family is itself a valuable expression of the gospel and demands careful preparation for cross-cultural living.

Cross-Cultural Readiness

The research data would appear to suggest that there remains a need for new missionaries to be more aware of the proactive steps they can take in adjusting to a new cultural environment. This need exists in spite of the number of courses offered in this area at most missionary training institutions. (This assumes that all new missionaries will have had some kind of formal training for cross-cultural service.) The reason for the continuing need for training in cross-cultural living may be that too many of the existing courses are restricted to classroom instruction and do not include any opportunity for experiential learning. With the growth of multiculturalism in most old sending countries, it is hard to justify any missionary training program that does not have a practical component which demands some level of cross-cultural interaction and understanding. Such activities need to be an integral part of the learning program, with appropriate supervision and evaluation to give students a clear understanding of how they are coping with the situation.

Training institutions also need to consider the possibility of introducing a level of flexibility to the content and structure of their programs that will permit a measure of customisation for each student. The diversity of ministry approaches being employed around the world demands a parallel diversification in the training being offered, reflecting the pattern already observable in other areas of professional training.

Where the institution is not able for some reason to provide an adequate cross-cultural ministry experience as part of the program, the sending body (agency or church) must accept responsibility to seek the assistance of local churches serving communities of different language and cultural orientation. A cooperative program could be developed that would contribute to each church's own understanding of and involvement in world mission, as well as meeting the needs of missionary candidates. In today's world, the first term of new missionaries should never be their first exposure to the pressures of cross-cultural life and ministry.

TRAINERS

Up to this point, we have primarily discussed the content of pre-field training and the methodologies that could be employed in its delivery. To complete the picture, we also need to give some thought to the question of the trainers themselves. To put it within the context of this book, we must consider the question of the relationship between missionary attrition and those who train the missionaries in the first place. To what degree are missionaries today being trained by those who have a personal awareness and understanding of the pressures of cross-cultural ministry that underlie the attrition causes listed in Figure 16-1? Academic qualifications must not be disregarded, but unless they are balanced by a personal experience of the nature of the future service environment of the trainees, then there will be a sterility in the teaching that will leave missionary candidates poorly prepared. Prior experience as a missionary would be an excellent prerequisite for anyone training missionaries, but whether this is possible or not, our fast-changing world obligates every missionary training program to provide for the regular exposure of its trainers to the field environment in which the graduates are serving. It is at the point of field service that true accreditation occurs for any missionary training program. All those involved in missionary training need such exposure, including those teaching the biblical and theological subjects. Without such exposure and understanding, the trainers in these disciplines will not be providing their students, as comprehensively as they might, with the resources needed to facilitate their effectiveness and survival in cross-cultural ministry.

The involvement of missionary trainers on the boards and councils of mission agencies would give added breadth to the trainers' understanding of the issues their graduates will need to confront. This would also provide the initial forum for the interaction between institution and agency that has been advocated elsewhere in this chapter.

The effectiveness of missionary trainers is a key element in the fight against attrition, and it is an area that needs to be brought under the microscope as much as any other. It is essential that these trainers have in their purview an accurate profile of pre-field readiness for missionary candidates and a relevant understanding of the cross-cultural competencies that will make missionaries effective.

CONCLUSION

In this discussion of pre-field training in the context of missionary attrition, several issues have surfaced that demand a place on the agenda of missionary training groups in old sending countries. They are issues that need to be explored within the context of each training program. They should be approached with a desire to reduce the loss through attrition by improving the appropriateness and personal relevance of the training process.

1. Collaboration. There must be a high level of collaboration among the institutions providing the training, the agencies with which the missionaries serve, and the local churches that send and support the missionaries. And this partnership needs to be constantly evaluated and improved.

2. Balance. Regular review must take place of the balance being maintained in the overall training process between theoretical input and evaluated practical experience.

3. Cross-cultural competencies. While profiting from academic accreditation whenever possible, the training program must constantly consider the cross-cultural competencies needed by its graduates to effectively carry out the task for which they are being prepared.

4. Relevance. With so much that is changing in the nature of missionary work around the world, all training programs need regular review of their relevancy in content and structure to the needs of the missionaries of the next decade.

5. Trainers. Given the diversity of instructors who have a part to play in the training of missionaries, there is need to evaluate regularly, first of all, the degree to which trainers are aware of the environment for which they are preparing their students and, secondly, what can be done to increase that awareness.

6. Spiritual effectiveness. Taking the Word of God to the world is in its essence a spiritual task, demanding that each aspect of the training process be evaluated for its contribution to the spiritual maturity and spiritual effectiveness of the graduates. The goal of all that is undertaken should be the glory of God.

*Previously a Baptist minister in Australia, **Bruce Dipple** has served with SIM for 20 years— eight years as Principal of the SIM French Bible College in Niger, two years as a student worker in Sydney, and 10 years as Australia National Director. From 1992–1996, he was Chairman of Missions Interlink. In 1997, he was named the inaugural Director of the Graduate School of Cross-Cultural Mission at Sydney Missionary and Bible College, one of the two major missionary training institutions in Australia. Dipple is married to Sylvia and has four adult children and three grandchildren.*

17

Mission Agency Screening and Orientation And Effect of Attrition Factors

PERSPECTIVE OF THE NEW SENDING COUNTRIES

Seth Anyomi

Traditional mission fields in Africa, Asia, and South America are fast becoming active mission senders themselves. The church in these nations thus inherited the missionary task, as well as the mechanics for success in missions. Of particular interest to this discussion is the role of mission agencies in screening would-be missionaries. Kath Donovan and Ruth Myors (chapter 4) have delved into the process that puts a missionary on the mission field. They have pointed out, "The conservation of missionaries begins with selecting the right people and identifying those who are not suited to cross-cultural ministry before they are too far down the assessment track."

Church and mission leaders must know what to look for in missionary candidates in order to do a good job of screening the right people. This means that leaders need a basic understanding of the essential qualities and traits of those called to cross-cultural mission. African missionaries must be equipped with the qualifications of church plant-ers. They must be apostles who can train people in the ways of God and who can bring salvation, healing, and deliverance to the people through the application of the shed blood of Jesus.

In his book, *The Growth of the Church in Africa*, Peter Falk (1979, p. 441) observed, "The early workers came from within the life of the church." If this ideal is to continue to be fulfilled and if the selection process is to be legitimate, there must be a close partnership between mission agencies and the church.

A NEW MISSIONARY CHALLENGE

The missionary movement in Africa today is a mighty force to reckon with. Although certain parts of Africa were Christianized long before Western Europe (i.e., Egypt, Carthage, and Numidia in the first three centuries of the church), modern missionary activity in Africa traces its origins to the 15th century exploratory zeal of Henry the Navigator. But Africans themselves did not become actively involved in cross-cultural missions until about three decades ago. This period coincided with the collapse of colonialism on the African continent and the need for Western mission agencies to hand their work over to the national churches which they had previously planted.

Once the baton of leadership was passed on to Western-trained Africans, there came the responsibility of maintaining and expanding the work of Western mission agencies. African church leaders were ill prepared for this challenge, because during the colonial era the work of missions was generally the exclusive privilege of Western missionaries.

The responsibility of maintenance of the church implied that the national church must now be self-supporting in personnel and finances, self-governing, and self-propagating. Even in recent times, some of the denominational churches in Africa continue to depend on financial support from the West. A case in point happened about six years ago in Ghana. There was a church split involving one of the main denominational churches. Since most of the "enlightened" and big financial contributors went with the breakaway group, the main denomination was hit hard with the loss of its local source of income; then the Western supporters also withdrew their support. The effect was felt immediately. Payment of salaries went into arrears, and vehicles were parked due to lack of funds for maintenance.

In parts of northern Nigeria, Sudan, and Chad, the departure of the Western missionaries resulted in a leadership vacuum, in spite of the fact that there were a few educated local church men. These few had never been given the chance to exercise leadership skills during the reign of the Western missionaries, because all of the key positions had been taken by the missionaries. Thus these local church men were barely able to keep the churches running, much less put in place any missionary programs to expand the church.

But while denominational churches were struggling with their new responsibilities, the independent African Christian movement began to sweep across Africa, ignited by the Pentecostal and charismatic fires from America and other parts of the West. Many young Christians were caught by this mighty missionary wind and were driven to their local and surrounding communities and people groups, some of which had never heard the gospel.

After the initial enthusiasm had subsided, the questions which had nagged at the old established churches in the West began to knock on the doors of the African churches: Weighed down by the burden of supporting and governing themselves, did these churches have the energy or the human and financial resources to multiply themselves in other places where there was no witness? Should they follow the example of the Western world, where mission agencies were established to attend to the task of missions, leaving the church to care for its other needs? What should the African church do with the thousands of young people who, because of evangelical movements like Scripture Union, Youth for Christ, Campus Crusade for Christ, and YWAM, had become aware of the church's obligation to do missions and were bursting to launch out into mission fields? How should the church determine those truly called to cross-cultural missions? Where would these missionary candidates go for training, since there were no missionary training institutions at the time? After training, where would their support come from? What about the care of families and the education of the children?

The parachurch missionary movement in Africa emerged as a direct response to the dilemma the churches faced regarding the above questions. The Nigeria Evangelical Missionary Association and the Ghana Evangelical Missions Association are two examples of parachurch organizations that have answered the churches' far cry for missions.

Now that missionary organizations have accepted the challenge of missions, they are faced with the task of determining what the ideal relationship with the local church should be in the areas of missionary screening and orientation. Who affirms the missionary call? Who determines the type of preparation and orientation appropriate for missionary candidates? How are missionaries funded and provided with pastoral care? And the big question: How should solutions to the above issues be co-ordinated so as to reduce attrition?

Africa is part of the new sending continents and shows a lower rate of attrition for unpreventable reasons. In the recent research conducted by the WEF Missions Commission, the old sending missions scored a higher percentage here for reasons which mainly include retirement due to old age and death. The cause of death is often a result of a hostile environment and disease-infected mission fields. Many of

the early Western missionaries to Africa died from malaria. Missionaries of African origin have not lived on the field long enough to retire due to old age, nor do they face disease or death threats in other areas of the continent. The most common reason given by new sending agencies for missionary dropout is lack of finances.

FACTORS TO CONSIDER IN MISSIONARY SELECTION

Marriage/Family Issues

The marriage/family factor is highly significant in the African context. This is due to the tradition of the extended family. Every male in the African society, including every male missionary, is expected to provide for his extended family, i.e., parents, younger siblings, nieces, nephews, etc. Recently, a missionary training institute with which this writer is associated lost one of its most brilliant students when family needs compelled the young man to drop out. In selecting African missionaries, mission agencies must make adequate provision for the upkeep of the extended family.

Worldview

A narrow worldview has contributed to problems that African missionaries have encountered on the field. Some new missionaries have little education and no exposure to the world outside their own locality. The result is that they often find it hard to settle in a new area. One young missionary graduated from a missionary training school and was invited to work in a suburban part of Accra, Ghana. He was always homesick and made frequent visits to his home town. Because he did not stay on the task consistently, he lost some of his converts and failed to achieve his desired goals.

Level of Support

Christian workers in Africa are generally viewed as belonging to the class of the poor. The African church has for over a century been a dependent church. Key personal and financial resources came from the home mission. When Western mission agencies began to pull out of their mission fields, they also took away their money. This move was in keeping with the plan to grant independence to the African church and to encourage the church to be self-supporting, self-governing, and self-propagating. The policy was supported by a declaration drafted at the historic 1974 congress at which the Lausanne Covenant was enacted. The statement read, "A reduction of foreign missionaries and money may sometimes be necessary to facilitate the national church's growth in self-reliance and to release resources for unevangelized areas."

Movement toward independence is desirable, but it should be accompanied by education and orientation of African Christians regarding their responsibility to make financial contributions and pay their tithes. In this way, money will be available to pay personnel, to run the church, and to engage in missions outreach.

Support for new missionaries is critical. Since people do not support a cause with which they are unfamiliar, the sending agency should attempt to determine the level of awareness of and support for missions in the sending church during the selection process.

Reasons for Opposition

Harold Cook (1971) pointed out four basic reasons that many nominal Christians in Western cultures do not support missions. These reasons may apply to churches in the new sending nations as well.

1. Lack of Personal Experience With Christ

Many who profess to be Christians lack a personal and vital experience with Christ. They may have joined the church because their parents were churchgoers. Some go to church because their parents or the society expect them to. Such people find it hard to understand missions and may oppose those who desire to pursue missionary work.

This author faced such opposition when, after studying for a secular degree overseas, he returned home to announce that he had been called into Christian mission. The displeasure of the family was obvious. They had expected that the financial burden of the family would lighten when their son entered the job market and started to bring home a good monthly pay cheque. To them, missionary work would not provide the financial rewards they desired.

2. Lack of Vision

African Christians must look beyond their horizons and show concern for others who need the gospel of Jesus Christ. Because many Africans are not interested in what lies beyond their area, they feel no strong obligation to support missionaries who have gone out from among them to reach pagan people beyond.

3. Misunderstanding

The Western world is generally referred to as the Christian world, while Africa and other non-Western parts of the world are referred to as pagan. The assumption is that only the Western church and Western missions have the mandate and qualifications to reach the rest of the world with the gospel. Other continents and nations are considered to be *receiving mission fields*. Unfortunately, this thinking has been passed on to the churches which the Western missions have planted and nurtured. Vigorous education is necessary to undo such a dangerous mind-set.

4. Liberalism

Liberal theology puts Christianity on a par with other religions. It assumes that Christianity is just *one* of the ways to God and that other religions are roads to the same end. African traditionalists contend that Christianity is a white man's religion and that it should not be allowed to replace the ancestral religion. To these people, Christian missionary work is wrong, because it attempts to replace the pagan way of life. The process of missionary selection must make certain that candidates understand different belief systems and know how Christianity stands out among all other religions.

Missionary Calling

Lack of call and lack of commitment are perceived to be major attrition factors in the new sending countries (lack of call, 8.0%; inadequate commitment, 7.3%), as shown by the WEF Missions Commission study on missionary attrition (chapter 6). The first task facing any mission board committee or agency in the selection of a missionary candidate is to determine whether the person has a call to missions. To a large extent, the success of missions depends on the wisdom with which missionaries are selected.

There are several propositions on the subject of missions. The four main viewpoints are outlined below. It should be noted that standards of selection set by a selection body are very much influenced by the proposition that dominates the thinking of the group.

1. The Job of the Church

The first proposition stipulates that missions is the job of the Christian church. This proposition is not referring to denominations and local churches. Rather, it refers to the body of believers in Christ who make up the church. Missions, therefore, can never be just a private affair; it always involves the church. This is true even of missions undertaken by those referred to as *independent missionaries*. Such missionaries may not be controlled by any mission society, but almost always they are sent out and supported by one or more groups of Christians. It is important for missionaries to grasp the fact that they are carrying out a task that Christ gave to the whole church. This understanding does not always exist in the African Pentecostal and charismatic context. Some young missionaries contend that they receive their call directly from the Holy Spirit. They launch out without the support and the blessings of other members of the body. It is no surprise that such people do not last long on the field.

2. Serious Effort to Win Others

A second proposition is that missions is the Christian church trying to win others. This implies that missions calls for serious effort. Missions is not simply making the gospel available. It is not just saying, "Here it is; you can have it if you want it." It entails selling—convincing people that the gospel is worth paying the price to get it. A true missionary knows that mission work is not fanfare or emotional hype. Such seriousness is sometimes missing among young Pentecostal/charismatic Christians, who jump at the opportunity to serve in missions because it seems exciting and adventurous. But then the dust settles, and they find themselves packing bag and baggage on a homeward journey.

3. Evangelism vs. Proselytism

A third proposition is that in missions the church is attempting to win others to faith in Christ through evangelism. However, what an evangelical Christian may term evangelism may be seen as proselytism by many others. Missionary evangelists may be branded as *sheep-stealers* or as engaged in *cultural aggression*. In many Muslim parts of Africa, social services of Christian missions are appreciated. Medical missions and even the establishment of hospitals staffed with Christian doctors and nurses are accepted, as long as no deliberate attempt is made to convert the Muslims to the Christian faith. Doing missions in some other way may draw harsh persecution, which may lead to attrition.

4. The Work of Missionaries

A fourth proposition is that the work of missions is normally carried on through a group of selected workers called missionaries. Although a vast amount of missionary work is accomplished voluntarily by members of the Christian church, these workers often do not consider themselves to be missionaries. They see themselves as personal witnesses to the transforming power of the gospel (Acts 1:8). History has proven that the work of missions could hardly be carried on without the aid of these voluntary workers. There must be a place for these while we screen for full-time missionaries.

Perhaps in the absence of adequate financial support, volunteering may be encouraged, although economic hardships may leave little room for volunteering in certain African nations. In these situations, the sacrifice that goes with missionary commitment must be stressed.

MISSIONARY PREPARATION
Spiritual Disciplines

There is a direct correlation between missionary success and appropriate missionary training. This is partly because missions generally crosses cultures. More importantly, though, missionary work is fraught with spiritual issues such as spiritual warfare, spiritual counseling, and providing guidance for immature Christians. Once missionary candidates are selected, they must be grounded in the spiritual disciplines of prayer, Scripture memory, meditation, and fasting. These disciplines bring a release of spiritual knowledge, wisdom, and power as missionaries minister to the spirit in other people and war on behalf of that spirit to bring salvation and deliverance.

Cross-Cultural Training

In addition to spiritual disciplines, cross-cultural training is necessary for missionary candidates. Students need to learn as much as possible about the people they will be working with, including demographic information, socioeconomic standards of life, etc. They should become familiar with societal norms and values. A good understanding of the culture aids in the presentation of the gospel in a culturally appropriate context. Candidates must also acquire skills for learning the language of the target group in order to facilitate communication.

Leadership Training

Early church workers in the non-Western world were trained in Western seminaries and Bible colleges. Home mission societies and agencies provided financial aid packages to key national leaders so they could train in the West and then return to help in their local church. Unfortunately, some of these individuals never returned to their homelands.

Now such scholarships are not as readily available from Western missions. The national church lacks the resources to provide adequate training opportunities for its workers, particularly those engaged in the work of missions. Church leaders are reluctant to spend their scarce foreign exchange in training their workers, because some do not fit in well when they return. Writing on the topic, "Toward Indigenization of Christianity in Africa: A Missiological Task," Zablon Nthamburi (1989, p. 116)

remarked, "Western-trained clergy do not have time for the *real problems* that haunt people, since they have been taught that such problems do not exist." Africa is going through rapid social, political, cultural, and spiritual changes. Every missionary on the continent must understand these dynamic forces and how they translate into the real-life situations of the local people.

Curriculum Development

Mission agencies would do well to develop a curriculum which will help missionaries execute their tasks among a given target group effectively. Agencies must make missionary training a top priority in planning and budgetary allocations. They must aim at training that is relevant, affordable, and culturally contextual. This calls for curriculum research, leading to the development of appropriate materials and library resources. Consulting experts are needed to provide training and guidance. Finances must be secured to enable agencies to implement research findings and to establish missionary training centers all over the continent.

In addition to the need for information on the practice of missions, there is also a great need for administrative expertise in order to manage mission funds and resources. Culturally contextual Bible studies should be developed on the topics of indigenous forms of worship, the art of spiritual warfare, and the exercise of spiritual gifts. Knowledge and wisdom are needed in the enforcement of moral requirements, in pastoral care, in community living, and in spiritual fellowship. Corporate prayer, opportunities for service and ministry, inductive and authoritative

Bible teaching, personal faith, and spiritual experience are also essential. And over all, there must be emphasis on the supernatural power of God.

People Profiles

African missionaries are pioneers on the mission field. They move in uncharted territory. They cross into new cultures and devise methods of ministry about which Westerners know nothing. They are now on the front lines. They are sending rather than receiving. They are self-governing rather than being governed, multiplying the seed of faith rather than remaining dormant. But they need a map to guide them—a profile of the target people to lead them on. Missionary orientation must therefore include mission mapping skills and the preparation of people profiles.

A little over a decade ago, the Ghana Evangelical Committee (GEC), under Ross Campbell, set the pace for Africa. The GEC provided case studies of different people groups. It also provided the impetus for beginning local congregations based on ethnic groupings and language, enhanced by literacy work.

Learning From Old Sending Nations

New sending agencies need to tap into the history, experience, and expertise of the old sending nations. This should be done in accordance with New Testament patterns. Paul's tradition of settling in places where churches had already been planted, in order to train his converts and prepare them for leadership, is worth looking at. Paul taught the people to take responsibility for the churches they inherited. He encouraged them to be self-supporting, self-governing, and self-propagating with the goal

of attaining independence. African missionaries must adhere to this New Testament model in order to produce New Testament results!

FACTORS AFFECTING ATTRITION

Funding

Adequate funding is crucial for the survival of missionaries on the field. Unfortunately, obtaining such funding seems to be a universal problem. This writer hosted a Western missionary a few years ago who had dropped out of missionary work after less than a year because his funding situation had changed and he had no alternative plan for surviving without the donations from his home country.

In the New Testament, the local church provided the funds for missions. The Apostle Paul took the weekly collection from the local church to use for missions outreach (1 Cor. 16:1-3). He worked to support himself through tentmaking. In the case of African missionaries, it may be necessary to investigate the level of financial commitment from any sponsors. Often African missionaries have little or no support from their local church. They therefore must work at some income-producing occupation such as farming, fishing, weaving, carpentry, masonry, and the like.

Mission agencies would do well to incorporate vocational training into their missionary training effort. They also must teach their churches to raise money for missions. This is critical for the future of missions on the African continent and, for that matter, in the rest of the Two-Thirds World. There is an urgent need to set apart funds specifically for missionary work, as Paul advocated in 1 Corinthians 16:1-3. Partnership between old and new sending countries is crucial, but attention must be paid to the sustainability of such relationships, especially in the area of finances.

Personal Traits

The strengths and weaknesses of each missionary are significant determinants of how long the person will remain on the mission field. Factors such as worldview/perspective on missions, spiritual maturity, personality traits, character, and intelligence all contribute to a missionary's longevity on the mission field.

Marriage/Family Issues

As noted earlier, marriage and the family are frequently contributors to attrition, since marriage in Africa is rooted in the extended family. The economic strength of the husband is important to the extended family. Relatives might bring pressure to bear on the missionary and force him to quit if he fails to measure up to his family obligations. In addition to providing for his wife and children, the African male is expected to provide for aging parents, nephews and nieces, and even cousins, aunts, and uncles. The mission agency and local church would do well to make financial provision for significant dependents of a missionary, unless the missionary has other sources of personal income. Failure to make this provision could lead to attrition.

Cross-Cultural Skills

Lack of cross-cultural skills and wrong assumptions regarding other people groups have been a pitfall for some African missionaries. Each Afri-

can tribe differs in many ways from the others. Workers who are not prepared for the differences may experience cultural shock and non-acceptance, which can cut short their missionary career.

REDUCING ATTRITION

After agencies have identified the factors which contribute to attrition, they have the responsibility to prepare their people—senders, receivers, and the sent—in order to minimize attrition. The consultation on attrition held at All Nations Christian College in UK in April 1996 recognized the following four dimensions that agencies must tackle:

✦ Interaction between church and agency.

✦ Agency policies and systems.

✦ The concepts of call and commitment.

✦ Agency preparation/orientation.

Relationship With Agency

The WEF Missions Commission study on attrition showed that there is a 3.9% attrition factor in old sending countries as against 6.1% in new sending countries in the area of conflicts with the sending agency. The difference in rates may be due to the stronger role sending agencies in the older countries play in recruitment and sending of missionaries. The majority of missionaries in Africa are self-supporting and do not feel a strong sense of belonging to the sending agency, so any disagreements with the agency are more likely to result in attrition. When church involvement in missionary recruitment, orientation, and dispatch of missionaries increases and also includes more financial support, we may see a decrease in conflicts with the sending agency.

Preparation/Orientation

The pre-field orientation should aim at vital contact with candidates commencing in their teen years, before a long schooling process begins. Efforts should be made to maintain such relationships throughout candidates' years of training.

It is necessary that sending agencies give clear instructions to their missionaries both before and after departure regarding what is expected of them. When new missionaries arrive at their destination, they should be instructed by the receiving church leader, rather than by the field leader. Arrangements may be made for the missionary family to live with a family from the receiving culture in order to foster relationships with the nationals.

African missionaries must be encouraged to learn the local dialect rather than using English or French, as the case may be. Mission agencies may need to provide separate orientation programs for singles and couples. Families may require more time because of the involvement of children.

A key activity that safeguards missionary success and extended stay is spiritual emphasis. New missionaries should be instructed in the spiritual norms and values of the receiving church. Such instruction will help mitigate potential conflicts on spiritual matters.

Leadership

Good field leadership is perhaps the biggest deterrent to attrition on the field. Mission agencies may get more for their money if they focus on leadership training instead of on recruitment. A common reason for burnout in field leaders is insufficient training in delegation and conflict resolution. The problem may start with the chief executive officer's not having the requisite leadership skills himself. It should be noted that experienced missionaries are not necessarily the best people to put into leadership positions. Some find leadership like babysitting. In Africa, the approach is more directed to mentoring. While being given a clear job description, missionaries must be allowed room for creativity. This type of leadership allows freedom in the choice of operation strategies and projects, with the missionaries serving as guides for their agencies.

CONCLUSION

The African missionary movement is gaining momentum. Christian leaders across the continent report that there is escalating interest in missions. Among the youth, especially in the independent Pentecostal and charismatic churches, hundreds, even thousands, are answering the call to missions. But the number of those stepping out who will remain after a few years on the field will correspond to the methods of screening and orientation employed by the sending agencies.

In sending countries, the responsible agencies must look for more than a call. They must also pay heed to the tools, the climatic factors, and the relational factors which may prolong or curtail the duration of stay on the mission field.

REFERENCES

Cho, D. (1986). *World mission and world peace.* Seoul, Korea: AMA.

Cook, H. R. (1971). *An introduction to Christian mission* (15th ed., rev.). Chicago, IL: Moody Press.

Falk, P. (1979). *The growth of the church in Africa.* Grand Rapids, MI: Zondervan.

Ghana Evangelism Committee. (1986). *Greater Accra regional church/evangelism survey.*

Ghana Evangelism Committee. (1986). *Regional congress on evangelization resource book.*

Harley, D. (1995). *Preparing to serve: Training for cross-cultural mission.* Pasadena, CA: William Carey Library.

Nthamburi, Z. (1989). Toward indigenization of Christianity in Africa: A missiological task. *International Bulletin of Missionary Research,* **13**(3), 112-118.

Seth Anyomi and his wife, Christiana, have four children. Trained as a teacher in Ghana, Anyomi later did further undergraduate and graduate studies in the USA in educational administration. He and his wife pioneered the work of the African Christian Mission in Ghana. They have planted six churches and run a day care center, a Christian school, a vocational school for girls, a missionary training institute, and two medical clinics in Ghana. Since 1990, Anyomi has served as President of the Ghana Evangelical Missions Association. He is a member of the Executive Council of the TWMA, is a WEF Missions Commission Associate, and is Chancellor of the World Link University for Africa.

18

Mission Agency
Screening and Orientation:
A Personal Journey

PERSPECTIVE OF THE OLD SENDING COUNTRIES

Brent Lindquist

This chapter focuses on attrition in relation to the mission agency's screening and orientation of the missionary, from the perspective of the old sending nations agency. The author is a clinical psychologist by training, but for the last 15 years he has had the delight of being mentored by a linguist/anthropologist, so he does not bring a purely clinical/counseling dimension to this discussion. At his counseling center, Link Care, it is said in a somewhat humorous fashion that the psychologist thinks deeply about feelings, and the linguist feels deeply about thinking. The humor arises out of the fact that there is more truth to this dichotomy than one cares to admit.

The title of this chapter is significant in that the discussion, to a large extent, reflects the author's personal journey through the areas of selection, training, and attrition. Due to the personal nature of the account, the first person pronoun will be used from here on.

I have been in the missionary endeavor at Link Care Center for 32 years,

first in the background and later in the forefront. For the past 22 years, I have been a part of the orientation of missionaries for many mission organizations. For the past 16 years, I have been engaged in intense psychological assessment of missionary candidates. The comments, ideas, hypotheses, and prejudices reflected in this chapter arise out of my work over these years with three kinds of missionaries: the **candidates**, before they are accepted by their organizations; the **rookies**, before they go overseas; and the **"restorees,"** those who have experienced personally the tremendous effects of primary attrition—what I choose to call the first stage of leaving. I make a distinction between primary and secondary attrition only in order to note that people come to Link Care as "potential attrition victims"—to use a 1990s popular term—but about 65% of them consistently end up "unattriting" and reentering the missionary force, often in the same tasks they were in before they stumbled. Their attrition does not progress to the secondary stage, which would be coming home and staying home. Through a combination of sensitivity to the Spirit, professional counseling, pastoral care, common sense, and group comparisons, the "primary attrits" and their organizations discover that there is a place for them back in their previous ministry or service on the mission field. Through all of these activities, I have been on an intensive journey: Where do I fit in? Where does what I know fit in? Where does Link Care fit into this vast and complex issue of people carrying the good news outside their home contexts? What is the "power" of the psychological part of the equation of missionary selection, training, service, and attrition?

OLD HELPING NEW

Throughout this book, attempts have been made to pair leaders of old sending nations with leaders of new sending nations to discuss particular topics. Looking back over the past 30 years of the missionary endeavor, I have attempted to understand some of the pitfalls of the present position of the old sending countries and how they relate to the new sending countries.

Some of our strategies of selection and orientation have become, or are in danger of becoming, technologically dependent. The same can be said of the economics of missions. We need a realistic appraisal of what is useful from the old sending nations that can be shared with the new, not in a paternalistic or colonialistic manner, but in a way that will empower the new sending nations to carry on their task so as to benefit both themselves and the old sending nations. The objectives of this chapter, then, are (1) to analyze the trends that

have become apparent through the Re-MAP research; (2) to enlarge on that analysis from the perspective of 30 years of working with missionaries in training and healing ministries; (3) to look at the impact that the identified trends have had on missions; and (4) to set forth some ideas that may be more technologically or culturally independent, so as to be considered by both the old and the new sending agencies as points of departure on the journey toward improving the process of selection and orientation.

FORCES SHAPING MISSIONS

I am taking a great risk in simply identifying the trends shaping missions in the old sending nations' spheres of influence, because I will mainly gloss over these trends in order to draw out a few points. We are living in a context molded by the forces of modernity and post-modernity. We are shaped to a great extent, whether we like it or not and whether we have good scientific data to support the conclusion, by the forces of advertising, materialism, and media communications. The result is a population of potential missionary candidates who see the world in small terms, in sound bites. Much of the younger generation's information about the state of the church around the world has been derived from the secular media. International and educational cable channels make it possible to keep up to date with the vast array of social, political, and religious changes going on in the world today. Many young people today have a pluralistic attitude and readily accept diversity. Their theology does not necessarily impinge on their diverse viewpoints.

Some North Americans, particularly, have come to expect that any venture they pursue will have a larger number of "givens" than past generations of missionaries had. This checklist includes things such as security, health plans, pension plans, retirement plans, educational needs of children, opportunities for continuing personal growth and development, leisure and recreational aspects, and unspoken guarantees regarding financial, physical, and emotional security. One young person I know indicated that a mission prospect needed to be "fun," "easy," "now" (as opposed to later), and "me" oriented. That is, it must benefit him in some way. My friend was being facetious as he tried to describe what he saw in his peers, but he may not have been far from the truth. Missionary applicants are becoming more and more accustomed to a self-centered approach to missions, as opposed to a more traditional, other-centered approach.

In addition, missionary recruits are coming out of a wide variety of ethnic and family backgrounds which, when put into the mix of cross-cultural ministry, have many consequences. The background issues relative to the dysfunctional family system have had a tremendous impact on the state of the missionary family today. Many problems in field missionaries can be traced to these issues.

In North America, generational factors, such as the differences among baby boomers, baby busters, the X generation, and the silent generation, are all affecting the way missionary work is done. These factors also influence the way organizational climates are developed or attacked and the way relationships are developed. American individualism has created people who have a different sense of history and a different sense of identity from people in most other places in the world. Unfortunately, because of the exportation of economic and technological strength, the problems associated with American cultural development are showing up in other areas around the world, with associated breakdowns in family systems and community identity.

ATTRITION CAUSES

The ReMAP research report (chapter 6) encompasses the data from many mission organizations and is a good first step in understanding the nature and causes of attrition. Care needs to be taken not to assume too much from the numbers, but to look more at the process that occurs. I will stay in the process aspect as well, in looking over my 32 years of restoring missionaries who are in danger of "attriting" for a wide variety of reasons. I have identified four major arenas in which missionaries who come to Link Care Center need intensive psychological and pastoral care. These areas are not necessarily listed in order of frequency of occurrence.

1. Background Issues and Cross-Cultural Contexts

All too often, a person comes to service from a problematic background. Sometimes the vulnerabilities are identified, and the individual is redirected through the use of psychological tests. Sometimes appropriate steps are taken to remediate problem areas, and the applicant goes on to service. Sometimes the background issues are ignored in an attempt to be sensitive to the Spirit's leading. The problem with all three of these courses of action is that they ignore the potential impact of background issues when the person is under the stress and strain of cross-cultural living. Although little is understood in this area, a general trend can be identified, i.e., small things tend to be magnified in new contexts. Issues that were well taken care of, well addressed, and well protected in the home culture have a tendency during the period of adjustment to a new cultural context to become more major and even to become terminal issues for attrition.

2. Unrealistic Expectations

A common occurrence at Link Care, both in the training and in the restoring aspects of the center's ministry, is to have missionaries report that they went overseas with expectations that were unrealistic with regard to being accepted in the culture, being able to minister, and understanding what the place of service would be like. Many people report that they thought they could minister immediately, without taking language differences into account. The insights shared in pre-field programs may help some people to avoid this negative impact. Others learn these things only in the middle of some crisis, or in discovering that they were mismatched with the situation, or over the course of becoming burned out.

3. Conflicts in Relationships

The third cause of attrition has to do with the conflicts that develop with the mission organization, with other missionaries, with the national Christians, and with the community at large. The consequence of these conflicts can be external, degrading the quality of inter-personal relationships, or it can be internal, producing psychological and other emotional and spiritual symptoms. Many of these symptoms are coping strategies to help the person adjust to the developing problems on the outside.

4. Destructive Symptomatic Responses

The fourth attrition cause really arises out of the third one. Everyone has to cope. The coping strategies some people use are more destructive than those of others. Coping strategies in and of themselves are neutral, but they can have either positive or negative effects. Chronic stress that is seen as unmanageable can produce major destructive symptomatic responses. Acute traumatic situations, such as being the victim of violence or revolution, can trigger preexisting vulnerabilities for destructive symptomatic responses, or these situations can cause all new responses in people who may have shown no indication of destructive potential responses.

The above four attrition causes point to the extreme complexity of the problem and the difficulty of finding solutions in the screening and orientation processes.

SCREENING PROBLEMS

Screening and selection procedures are uniformly fairly well developed among a majority of old sending nations. The procedures go through regular reviews, and a lot of time and energy are invested in trying to make sure that issues being screened for are relevant for missionary service. Unfortunately, many screening procedures focus on items that are assumed to be separate and independent, when, in fact, many of the issues are continuous and inter-related. Not enough effort has been spent on integrating the information. To use a metaphor, too many still pictures are taken of a candidate and not enough video.

A major problem I struggle with, as a psychologist and as a bit player in the whole screening/selection/assessment area, is that psychological assessment is often compartmentalized. There is such a concern about identifying dys-functionality or pathology that psycho-logical assessment is relegated to playing only a small part of what it could play. Because of the complexity of the impact of cross-cultural issues on the individual and on his or her personality and psychological makeup, it is very difficult to identify particular factors that may be predictive of future pathol-ogy. Most long-term studies are not completed, and most psychological re-sources are snapshots of particular as-pects or concepts. For the most part, mission agencies do not pay enough attention to how they can integrate psy-chological assessment into the larger picture.

Psychological assessment could fo-cus on making specific predictions about an individual's personality and about the impact of the personality in the new cultural context. Follow-up contacts with the individual could focus on practical aspects of adjustment and the development of competencies in daily living, based on that person's par-ticular psychological makeup.

Outside the area of psychological as-sessment, it appears that while refer-ences are used in the screening process, they are typically underutilized or util-ized in ineffective ways. Oftentimes mis-sion agencies could gain additional information by moving on to secondary references. For example, references are typically gathered about a missionary candidate's abilities on Sunday, but lit-tle information is gleaned regarding the person's conduct on Monday through Saturday. Yet we find that most prob-lems occur not on Sunday; they happen on Monday through Saturday. What I'm getting at here is that too often we don't make the effort to understand how a person manages daily living situations. Is the individual being a person of influ-ence in a daily way? Are references from neighbors, coworkers, friends, and ac-quaintances being sought? It would be useful, as well, to try to get references from people who may not like the mis-sionary candidate very much. Maybe the characteristics for which the person is disliked are the very ones that could help him or her to manage and even thrive amidst the difficulties that will be encountered on the mission field.

I also wonder about screening in the area of health. To what extent are we really paying attention to the physical needs of people and how those needs might be impacted on the mission field? I come from a family in which asthma has played a prominent part. Therefore, I often marvel at people with pulmonary problems who reach the final candidacy stage of psychological assessment with-out having had anyone ask them how they expect to function in an extremely polluted environment, when they have not been able to function well in a cleaner environment in their home country. Such problems should be ad-dressed early in the screening process.

ORIENTATION PROBLEMS

The vast number of agencies from the old sending countries understand the relevance of orientation and some training in preparing their missionary candidates for service. A surprising number have not looked carefully at the different kinds of orientation that may be necessary. For example, numerous organizations confuse entry orientation, which is entry into something (the organization, for instance), with exit orientation, which is exit from something (the home culture). Most in-house programs present entry into the organization intermixed with exiting from the home culture. The result is confusing and needlessly complicates the whole process. In addition, many old sending organizations are only now developing strategies to enhance the entry orientation into the new culture. They feel pretty good about what they're doing or what they're having other organizations do for them with regard to leaving the home culture. But they are recognizing that there are deficits in terms of facilitating the entry and continuing development of the missionary into the new context of cross-cultural ministry.

What is missing is practical instruction in how to develop daily living skills in the new cultural context. Theories are wonderful. But the practical aspects of those theories as applied to specific situations are generally lacking.

A SELECTION AND ORIENTATION MODEL

The challenge for agencies from both the old and the new sending countries is that agencies can't all do the same things. Many of the models or programs developed by old sending countries are simply inappropriate for the new sending nations. They are inappropriate because of cultural distinctives, they are inappropriate because of economic realities, and they are inappropriate because of technological or personnel concerns. If we really want to bring together the old and the new sending nations to address the issue of attrition, then we need processes of selection and orientation that arise out of similar principles, which can then be worked out in productive ways relative to each sending agency.

The following is a preliminary sketch outlining some basic ideas and principles. It will be up to the reader to flesh out this skeletal framework and up to the author to continue to develop it, in order to provide some of the practical applications to daily living that have been critiqued elsewhere.

Person

We have to start somewhere, and we might as well start with the person. Certainly many cultural structures in various parts of the world don't start with the person; they start with the community. The understanding here is that both the community and the person need to be taken into account. Person here has to do mostly with selection. The following questions serve as a guide in ferreting out some of the basic principles of selection.

1. What kind of person do we see?

2. What are the person's strengths and weaknesses, assets and vulnerabilities?

3. In what context has this person grown up?

4. In what context is the person now living?

5. What inter-ethnic experiences has the person had? How have these experiences influenced the person, both positively and negatively?

6. How has the person maintained stability in unstable situations in the past?

7. What skills, gifts, and strengths has the person used in the past?

Presence

Presence has to do with the relationship of the individual to the present context. This area addresses the community/family mindset of other cultural contexts.

1. How does the person see himself/herself in relation to the context, both the home context and the mission field context?

2. In what ways does the person develop relationships with others? Is there evidence of positive relationships over the years? What has happened in any relationships that ended?

3. How do others see the person as a member of the community and as an individual who is doing things that are related to the assigned task?

4. What information can be obtained from the various interpersonal communities in which the person operates, such as the neighborhood in which the person lives, the environment in which the person works, the relationships in which the person socializes, and the various believing communities in which the person operates?

Purpose

Purpose looks, to some extent, at the kinds of things the person wants to do or feels called to do and at the kinds of things the agency has available that need to be accomplished. Purpose also looks at what, where, and how these things can be accomplished relative to the expectations of the person, the organization, and the receiving entities—including other missionaries, the national church, and the community at large.

1. What knowledge, skills, and insights does the person bring?

2. How do these qualities match with what the organization is looking for?

3. What expectations about purpose does the person have? What expectations come from the sending church or churches? What expectations come from the receiving bodies, including the on-field missionary organization, the local church, and the larger national community? Do these various expectations match with the organization's purpose?

Possibilities

The term "possibilities" refers to the challenging step of faith that mission leaders must take. There must be an understanding that God is in the middle of the picture and that decisions are made, not just on the basis of the best possible theory about organizational development or personnel management, but also with a sense of the leading of the Spirit. The term "possibilities" also recognizes that there is never a perfect fit between a missionary and the mission organization. The fit varies from person to person and place to place.

1. What evidence do you have that the person has the ability to manage critical issues in his or her future?

2. How well do you manage the idiosyncrasies of workers within your mission organization?

3. What steps of faith could be taken? Are these steps possible?

4. As a mission organization, do you have coaches, cheerleaders, shepherds, encouragers, and helpers available to assist the new missionary in his or her journey with your organization?

USING THE QUESTIONS

To use the preceding questions, each agency could look at its current practices. Do these practices answer the above questions? Old sending nations could ask their consultants to respond to the questions directly, if the information is already gathered, or they could change the selection process to include the information requested. New sending nations could develop forms or interview processes to ensure that the information is gathered.

One of the basic areas of information addressed here is community-based assessment. By this I mean that the focus is on gathering information about the person in the community in which the individual is living. Old sending nations generally place too little emphasis on specific references from the "Monday through Saturday" networks. New sending nations could utilize such resources with a minimum of expense or technology.

If I were to devise a reference form, I would first ask myself what I was expecting of the applicant. I would want applicants who have experience being members of neighborhoods, interacting in non-Christian social networks, and working among non-Christians. I would want to know how the person is per-

ceived by the members of those networks. Is the individual a good neighbor? How do other parents at the applicant's children's school, for example, perceive the applicant? Is the applicant a person of influence in his or her various arenas? Not necessarily a leader. I believe a person can be influential and not have to be a leader.

I would want to get information from primary references (people whose names were provided by the applicant) and also from secondary references (names provided by the primary references). I would want critical references from people who might not particularly like the applicant. I have learned so much from people who don't care for me!

All this information would be quite useful—perhaps more useful than a test report that states only that no pathology is present. Such information would help me do more than merely select or de-select the applicant. It would help me work with the applicant in developing an individualized program for managing rough edges and overcoming problem areas.

There are other issues that could be addressed, and they will be as I continue on my journey of discovery. However, they are not developed enough for this chapter and will appear in subsequent articles. I would welcome responses to the above questions and suggestions for additional ones.

CONCLUSION

This process of analysis must go on. We must keep looking for ways in which the old sending nations can help and learn from the new sending nations. The ReMAP project has been a good start. A commitment on all parts to continue this process is necessary in order to get beyond the opinions to actual facts and measurable results. We are paving the way to effectiveness for our sons and daughters in the missionary endeavor—what could be a greater commission?

As I look to the future, as far as attrition goes, I don't see a positive picture. The fact is that attrition will always be with us. We can't simply do away with it by coming up with perfect or even simply better selection and training programs. If you think about it, even Jesus had around an 8% attrition rate in His original missionary organization! Perhaps the major point in all of this is that analysis is good. We need to be constantly on the alert for what we as agencies are doing with and to God's people. Are we being good stewards of the vineyard? We need to remember that there are seasons of birth, growth production, harvest, pruning, and dormancy in the

vineyard. How are we managing each phase? Do we learn from our mistakes? Are we faithful to the cause? Do we adjust where necessary? Are we sensitive to our "failures" as well as our "successes"? If we are, then we are doing what we should be doing. May God grant us the insight to know and do the above.

Brent Lindquist *is a psychologist and is the President of Link Care Center in Fresno, California. He is a member of the Board of Directors of the Evangelical Fellowship of Mission Agencies (EFMA) and consults with numerous mission organizations on member care and other organizational issues. Together with Donald N. Larson, Lindquist runs an orientation program for new missionaries and a consultation process for organizations seeking to enhance their on-field effectiveness. He has been married to Colleen for 21 years and is the father of Sarah and Benjamin.*

19

Missionary Attrition Issues: Supervision

PERSPECTIVE OF THE NEW SENDING COUNTRIES

Sung-Sam Kang

In the research carried out by the WEF Missions Commission as part of their Reducing Missionary Attrition Project (ReMAP), 26 specific reasons for leaving missionary service were investigated. Nineteen of these 26 attrition factors can be seen to fall under the broad heading of pastoral care and supervision. These causes of attrition are itemized in Figure 19-1, weighted according to their frequency of occurrence. The listing focuses on the new sending countries (NSC), which included Brazil, Costa Rica, Ghana, Korea, Nigeria, India, the Philippines, and Singapore.[1]

The table reveals that inadequate pastoral care and supervision is responsible for nearly 80% of all attrition in the NSC. It is apparent that if pastoral care and supervision can be improved, then missionary attrition should be reduced. To promote this end, this chapter explores the following aspects of supervision:

✦ The scope of supervision.

NSC ATTRITION RELATING TO PASTORAL CARE AND SUPERVISION				
Category		**Attrition Factor**	**%**	**Total**
F A M I L Y		Health problems	5.1	22.5
		Children	4.8	
		Personal concerns	4.5	
		Outside marriage	4.0	
		Elderly parents	1.3	
	S P I R I T U A L	Marriage/family conflict	2.8	36.7
		Lack of call	8.0	
		Inadequate commitment	7.3	
		Immature spiritual life	4.5	
		Immoral lifestyle	2.2	
		Problems w/ peers	5.7	35.4
	M I N I S T R Y	Problems w/ local leaders	4.0	
		Lack of job satisfaction	2.2	
		Dismissal by agency	2.5	
		Inadequate supervision	2.3	
		Poor cultural adaptation	3.0	
		Language problems	1.5	
		Lack of home support	8.1	
		Disagreement w/ agency	6.1	
Total			79.9	

Figure 19-1

✦ Guidelines for the provision of supervision.

✦ Strategies for supervision.

---

1. For a listing of all 26 attrition factors broken down by country, see chapter 6.

THE SCOPE
OF SUPERVISION

Rudy Girón (chapter 3) has outlined how selection, training, sending, and pastoral care and supervision of missionaries can be integrated into an effective missions model. The supervision element should include three areas: family, spiritual life, and ministry. These areas are outlined briefly in this section and then are discussed more fully further on.

Family

As Figure 19-1 shows, six attrition factors make up the family category: health problems, children's needs, personal concerns, marriage outside the mission agency, elderly parents, and marriage/family conflicts. Together, these factors account for 22.5% of all attrition among NSC missionaries. In other words, more than 1 in 5 NSC missionaries who return home prematurely do so because of various personal or family problems.

It is encouraging to note that not all missionary attrition caused by family problems is permanent. Recently a missionary couple from the Missions Board of the Presbyterian Church in Korea (Hapdong) had to return home from Russia after three and a half years of service, because their child suffered from autism. The youngster is currently under special treatment and is improving. The parents are committed to their work and are planning to return to Russia as soon as the child has adequately recovered. Two other couples working in St. Petersburg and Tashkent under the same mission agency have 12-year-old daughters who are experiencing the same problem. Both couples decided to remain on the field and asked us to pray for their children. Over five years have passed, and we rejoice that both girls are getting better.

How should family problems on the field be addressed? Should we just disregard them for the sake of the kingdom of God? Should families with difficulties be advised to leave their mission field? What about family supervision in restricted access countries? Missionaries in these regions need pastoral care and practical supervision for family matters, but how can these needs be addressed? All of these issues must be resolved if we expect to maintain an effective missionary force.

Spiritual Life

If we group the attrition factors that relate to spiritual life (allowing some overlap with the family and ministry categories, as shown in Figure 19-1), we can see that the spiritual element is responsible for 36.7% of the missionary attrition in the NSC. Supervision of missionaries' spiritual life is vital, because spiritual life tends to affect emotional well-being. A broken spiritual life will likely cause family conflicts and relational problems, and it may eventually lead to an immoral lifestyle. Ministry is also affected. In fact, there is a direct link between ministry success and spiritual life. Ultimately, a missionary whose spiritual life has deteriorated becomes ineffectual on the mission field. It is up to mission supervisors to help workers maintain their spiritual identity in the Lord.

Ministry

The third area of supervision is ministry. According to the ReMAP research, the top ministries of missionaries from

TOP MINISTRIES IN THE NSC		
Country	Top Ministry	% of Miss. Engaged in This Ministry
Brazil	Pioneer work	24
Costa Rica	Church planting	25
Ghana	Church planting	24
India	Pioneer work	29
Korea	Pioneer work	23
Nigeria	Pioneer work	36
Philippines	Pioneer work	23
Singapore	Pioneer work	28

Figure 19-2

the NSC are pioneer work and church planting (see Figure 19-2).

If we refer back to Figure 19-1 again, we can see that the ministry-related causes of attrition from the NSC make up 35.4% of all NSC attrition. Ministry-related causes include problems with fellow missionaries, problems with local leaders, lack of job satisfaction, dismissal by the mission agency, inadequate supervision, poor cultural adaptation, language problems, lack of home support, and disagreement with the sending agency.

It is likely that almost all agencies, old and new alike, experience some problems between peer missionaries as well as with local leaders. Ministry in limited access countries is even more difficult, because workers in these countries experience more kinds and degrees of stress than those who are in areas with free access. Supervision in restricted access countries is more difficult as well. In addition to everything else, there are generational gaps within the missionary agencies.[2]

How then can we help our workers do a better job in the various fields, despite the different generational and cultural gaps, in order to reduce the attrition rate?

GUIDELINES FOR THE PROVISION OF SUPERVISION

In this section, a few more relevant questions will be raised. Who should supervise? How often should supervision be done? What are some specific guidelines for supervising the family, spiritual life, and ministry? How can supervision be provided in countries with restricted access?

Who Should Supervise?

Qualified Missionaries

The primary principle guiding supervisory selection is that it should be field-oriented. That is, supervisors should all be missionaries themselves. However, as Denis Lane (1990, p. 38) points out, "In a small and emerging mission, little pastoral care can be provided by the mission itself. Someone has to be the first worker in a country or area, and that person has to be able to find his own place and face all the necessary adjustments alone in reliance upon the Lord. He needs a very deep conviction that he is meant to be there, and the best possible preparation for facing the situation."

Some missions in the NSC do have a considerable number of senior missionaries who have had over six years of field service. For example, the missions board of the Presbyterian Church in Korea (Hapdong), which has 90 years of

---

2. See chapter 4 for a discussion of the generational differences.

history, has 235 senior workers among 780 missionaries, serving in 77 countries. For a field council to be formed under this mission, there must be at least five units of missionary families in a country of service. If fewer than five units are serving, a team is made. The field leader or team leader has to be elected by the bona fide members in order to become a field supervisor.

Although supervision should be done by experienced missionaries, not all experienced field missionaries should supervise. Certain additional qualifications are needed. There must be ability in leadership, counseling, problem solving, handling interpersonal conflicts, relational skills, and evaluation. The character qualities of integrity and spiritual sensitivity must also be present. On some occasions, a field leader plays a pastoral care role. But administration and pastoral care do not mix very well, because the person to whom missionaries tell their problems is also the one who performs evaluations. Serious difficulties then tend to be left unmentioned (Lane, 1990).

Itinerant Missionaries

In the case of a limited access country, an itinerant missionary who is qualified can serve as a supervisor. He may reside either in the same country or in a nearby country. In either case, he should take care that the nationals do not see him very often, so that the security of missionaries working in the country will not be jeopardized.

Older Agencies

What kind of supervision should be done in a small and emerging mission? As Lane (1990) suggests, missions with experience should assist emerging ones

in these situations. This is a third alternative for providing supervision. By allowing new missionaries to work under the pastoral care of an older and larger mission, workers may be able to receive much needed help. Some emerging missions have cooperative agreements with older international mission agencies to enable their missionaries to have dual membership. In this case, cooperation between missions and missionaries from various agencies is necessary. However, the older agencies should not directly recruit or accept individual missionaries in the home country of the emerging mission. If a candidate from the Two-Thirds World happens to apply directly to an older agency, resulting in competition with an emerging mission, the agency should advise the individual to go through the proper channels.

Field Fellowships

A fourth way that missionary supervision can be provided is through a missionary field fellowship under the indirect leadership of agencies at home. Each group of missionaries in the field must have approval from the home authority and must then have their delegations join the field fellowship. For example, all of the Korean missionaries in the various fields have formed a missionary fellowship or association. Each fellowship belongs to The Korean World Missions Association (KWMA). This is an autonomous group which is recognized by the mission agencies at home and which meets every two years. In some countries, even church planting has been done cooperatively under the auspices of the fellowship. The church is usually named "The Evangelical Church of (country name)."

An example of a denominational fellowship in the Philippines is the General Assembly of the Presbyterian Church of the Philippines (GAPCP). This association was inaugurated in 1996 through the efforts of five Presbyterian missions from Korea and the Presbyterian Church of America. The church planting ministry had begun in 1976 in the name of the Presbyterian Church of the Philippines (PCP) and was initiated by the Evangelical Presbyterian Mission (EPM). Later on, four other groups of Presbyterian missionaries joined in the project. After 19 years of cooperative efforts by the five groups in the Philippines, the Lord blessed them to form the GAPCP.

An interdenominational fellowship exists in Central Asia. There, Korean missionaries from various backgrounds and denominations got together and agreed that any churches established in the area would be called "The Evangelical Church of (country name)" instead of bearing denominational names.

Nationals

In general, few missionaries in the field want to be supervised by nationals. Why? The reasons may vary. First, there may be feelings of superiority and ethnic prejudice. Secondly, selfishness might be in operation. Ignorance of the host culture and worldview could be another reason. Finally, missionaries may be operating under an outdated, colonialistic mission strategy that lies subconsciously in their minds.

From my own experience in Africa, having intimate fellowship with national friends always brought me joy. We would fellowship through shared meals and celebrations at my home. To be invited to the home of national friends was not uncommon, and it was always an affirmative experience for my family. Occasionally we had our frustrating moments with the local leaders when it came to matters of use of foreign funds. It seemed that the local leaders had a different agenda for the use of the funds. Other than that, we have fond memories of the friendships we shared with local leaders and people.

Several methods can be cooperatively used to involve nationals in the supervision of missionaries. First of all, most **language learning** may be done under the supervision of national language teachers. Very often, living with a local family for the first year or two is the best way to learn a field language. Second, nationals can offer culturally appropriate information to new missionaries as part of their **field orientation**. Third, nationals can be good coworkers in a **church planting team** and can contribute contextual feedback.

Fourth, national leaders can participate in **evaluations** for missionaries. Nationals' involvement in evaluations can be valuable, because missionaries may thereby gain a true feedback of their work. I have seen some missionaries who were almost not invited back for the next term of service due to their insensitive cultural attitudes.

Fifth, some national Christians or leaders can become **safeguards for missionaries** in limited access areas. To have a reliable national Christian friend in a restricted access country may sometimes be far better than having a missionary supervisor who is always struggling for visa status. Whether a country is open or restricted, close per-

sonal relationships are always beneficial. Loving-kindness and time are the
cost to develop and maintain such relationships.

How Often Should Supervision Be Done?

The ReMAP research showed that
agencies from the NSC invest more time
(21%) and resources (20%) than those
from the old sending countries (OSC)
(13% and 12%, respectively). Three possible factors are thought to contribute
to this difference. The first is the experience and know-how already attained
by the OSC. Usually the OSC agencies
have a longer history of missionary supervision and more senior leaders who
know the ins and outs of supervision, so
supervision requires less time. Second,
the OSC generally have an extensive
written manual which includes detailed
job descriptions for their missionaries.
Most NSC agencies have only brief
written policies and do not include job
descriptions. Third, there are fundamental differences in the culture and
thinking patterns between the OSC and
the NSC. Kang (1995, pp. 41-42) quotes
Plueddemann on this subject: "The
most fundamental influence on culture
and thinking is the degree of people's
sensitivity to their context. High context
people pay special attention to the concrete world around them. Low context
people, on the other hand, pay special
attention to words, ideas, and concepts." In general, the OSC are considered to be low context, while the NSC are
considered to be high context. For example, most Orientals are much more
interested than a Westerner would be in
knowing someone's age, belongings,
marital status, and number of children,

and they are more group oriented in
regards to decision making. Most Westerners are individualistic and are interested in words, concepts, logic, etc. All
of these differences affect the supervision of missionary personnel.

Current Practices

When we met in a small group at the
attrition consultation in England, we
briefly shared what the agencies represented were already doing in terms of
on-field supervision. The following activities were noted:

WEC: The field leader debriefs new
missionaries every six months for the
first two years.

FEDEMEC (Costa Rica): Team
members on the field team show their
weekly chart of notes. Supervisors from
Costa Rica review the notes when they
arrive.

OMF: An annual supervisory retreat
is held. Every three years a training
seminar for supervisors meets. The field
leader meets four or five times a year
with supervisors.

Frontiers: An outside coach visits
every 90 days; 50% are non-Frontiers
resource persons who report their findings back to the field director after re-
viewing their perceptions with the team
leader. The team leader distributes a
questionnaire to the team members to
evaluate the team and team leadership.

Ghana: Some African agencies plan
spiritual renewal gatherings with
anointed prophet/teachers, plus relax-
ing fun times.

GAPCK (Korea): An annual assembly of bona fide members of a field council is held with all the members in the
field. They alter their by-laws, if necessary, and hold elections for their field

leadership to fill officer vacancies. A general election is held every two or three years. Very often, older leaders are replaced by newly elected ones. Other activities in an annual gathering include fellowship, prayer, the sharing of experiences, and discussions of important matters or issues as introduced by the members.

The field officers and team leaders meet regularly (quarterly or monthly) to deal with the matters brought from the teams or individual members. Informal gatherings of a team are held weekly or biweekly to have fellowship and pray. Once every four years, a large regional field gathering is held for spiritual renewal, supervision, and auditing initiated by the home office. At this time, many supporting churches and individuals visit to see the field ministry and to encourage their missionaries.

Two evaluation forms are used. One is filled out by the team supervisor and is treated as confidential. The other is completed by the missionary.

Supervision in restricted access countries is very limited. Most ministries are performed under the form and in the name of a non-governmental organization (NGO). Supervision and evaluation are carefully performed in the same pattern. An annual gathering for renewal and discussion is held outside the country. Leaders from home meet with the missionaries at this location.

Pastoral Care and Supervision

Missionary supervision is pastoral care. Such care should be a continual process, but it should especially be given during the first two years of a missionary's life in another culture, since this period may possibly be the most difficult period of the person's life. Emotional and physical adjustments pour in like a flood to overwhelm a novice. At such a time, pastoral care can make the critical difference as to whether new missionaries stay or quit. After a term of service, workers normally want to return to the mission field even before completing their first home assignment, because they have adjusted to the host culture and have learned the language fairly well. From this stage on, supervision can be done periodically. Later, after over two terms of service, missionaries should be mature enough to assume the role of a helper or caretaker, if necessary, at differing levels of leadership for newly arriving missionaries. Yet seasoned missionaries still need Christian fellowship with other workers in the field all year round. Pastoral care is an ongoing process.

Specific Guidelines

Let us draw attention again to the scope of supervision by more in-depth consideration of the issues mentioned earlier—family, spiritual life, and ministry.

Supervision of the Family

Supervision of the family is difficult, due to the general attitude that family life is a private affair. However, missionary life and ministry are not separate concerns but are inherently integrated. Thus, family matters come under the purview of supervisors.

The first aspect of family care is supervision of **family conflicts**. The frequency and intensity of supervision for family issues is dependent upon the soundness and spiritual life of the family. Prayer and patience need to be practiced diligently by supervisors and agencies.

Consider one case of family conflict which arose a few years ago. A certain Korean family had dual membership with an international mission agency and a Korean one. After serving a term in South America, they went to the United States to study during their furlough. When their furlough was nearly over, an emergency report came to my office from the wife and from their international mission agency, saying that the husband had disappeared over two weeks earlier. We were told that he had left after having had an exhaustive family dispute during their stay in the USA. While many efforts were being made to find him, another two weeks passed without any success. Meanwhile, we received another upsetting report from a concerned missions supervisor, informing us that the wife, who possessed a strong character, had in desperation attempted suicide. Thankfully, two months later the husband did return home. After his return, the family seemed to have reconciled their differences.

Following this incident, the mission's administrators, the main supporting church, and the cooperating mission agency had a long period of discussion over what had transpired. It was decided that the family would need to go through counseling. However, a question arose as to whether they should be called back home or not. Finally, it was agreed by both cooperating mission agencies that the family should be sent back to the field directly from the USA with our patient prayers. At present, they are successfully ministering in the field with a baby boy who is newly arrived after a 10-year gap. If they had been brought back home, it would have been necessary to report every detail of the incident to their supporters. Saving face is of great importance in the Korean culture, and disclosure of the incident would have curtailed the family's missionary work. In this family's case, all supervisors and other informed personnel kept the matter secret so that they might continue their work for the Lord.

A second element of family supervision is supervision of the **education of the missionary children** (MKs). The agency should have and should enforce a written policy covering this area. The team leader in the field must be responsible for local compliance of all children under his supervisory umbrella. On many occasions, MKs from Two-Thirds World countries are sent to Western MK or international schools with little regard for the children's future. Recently the member agencies of the Korean World Missions Association (KWMA) agreed to reconsider the policy of MK education. First, they encouraged MKs to keep their Korean identity. The children can still become world Christians by being educated in biblical foundations under the ultimate auspices of their missionary parents. Second, it was affirmed that MK college education must be done in Korea. Third, it was agreed that Korean agencies together with KWMA should try to establish Korean MK schools in the field wherever many Korean missionaries work closely together. The first Korean Academy was established in the Philippines in 1994; it now has 130 students with about 30 teachers and dorm parents. Korean missionary fellowships in other countries are applying to KWMA to establish regional Korean Academies.

Physical health is the third aspect of family supervision. The health of a missionary family needs to be checked regularly in the field and also at home during furlough.

Fourth, the matter of **entering into marriage** needs to be supervised. Occasionally, single missionaries want to marry an outsider to the mission or pursue an unbiblical union. Agencies should have written policies in these areas. Supervisors should provide help for orientation and loneliness so that critical mistakes are not made.

Fifth, supervision is occasionally needed in the area of **relationships**, such as between a missionary family and nationals, between the family and other missions families, and between the family and supporting churches. Relational conflicts may result in attrition. Thus regular contact and pastoral care need to be given. The team leader should incorporate a visitation schedule for fellowship from house to house. A single missionary may invite fellow missionaries and national friends at assorted family celebrations. Good relationships build up the ethos of missionary family ties.

Finally, an **annual retreat** will help build family unity within and among missionary families, in addition to allowing for spiritual recharging.

Supervision of Spiritual Life

How can we help our missionaries to maintain an unwavering and ever deepening spiritual life? How can we encourage them to train themselves to be godly (1 Tim. 4:7-8)? The following practices are suggested (Kang, 1996):

First, we should urge workers to be committed to a strong and regular **prayer life**. Many godly heroes such as Moses (book of Exodus), Daniel (Dan. 6–9), Jesus Christ our Lord (Mark 1:35; 6:46; Luke 3:21; 6:12; 22:44; Heb. 5:7), and Paul (Acts 16:13-25; Rom. 15:30-32; 2 Cor. 1:10-11; Eph. 6:18-20; Phil. 1:19; Col. 4:2-4; 1 Thess. 5:25; 2 Thess. 3:1-3; Philem. 22) are seen in the Holy Bible to give us examples to follow.

Second, we should urge our people to **read and meditate on the Word of God** day and night (Ps. 1:2; 119:97). The Holy Scripture opens our eyes to help us discern what God's will is. "All Scripture is God-breathed and is useful for teaching, rebuking, correcting, and training in righteousness, so that the man of God may be thoroughly equipped for every good work" (2 Tim. 3:16-17).

Third, we should encourage families to practice a regular **family altar**. The family unit is the most basic unit in God's kingdom on earth and is therefore the most appropriate place to fellowship and develop a strong spiritual life.

Fourth, we should suggest that our missionaries read and listen to godly **literature and tapes**. Throughout history, there have been many men and women of God who have left their thoughts and insights for us to read and learn from. These resources have much to offer and should be utilized to sharpen our spiritual life.

Fifth, we should initiate **annual retreats or spiritual conferences**. Spiritual life can be greatly enhanced through these times, when missionaries can be spiritually replenished and have their minds challenged.

Sixth, we need to insist that missionaries put work aside from time to time and **rest**, in order to dislodge stresses and enjoy the peace and rest that God provides. An exhausted workaholic may easily fall into spiritual as well as psychological depression. Those from the NSC especially need to learn to take rest. Sadly, some pastors in Korea who did not know how to rest abused their health and have as a result gone to be with the Lord in their 40s.

Seventh, we should encourage missionaries to practice knowing and affirming their **identity in Christ** in their daily spiritual warfare.

In addition to these seven practices, we should also urge missionaries to maintain a network of spiritual advisors, close friendships, and people who intercede for them. This kind of **support network** can be invaluable during times of testing. Supervisors may provide some of this support, but it should also be found through other believers.

Supervision for Ministry

There are several possible ministry situations for supervisors to consider. The first is **team ministry**. Here, the first order of business is to establish a clearly defined common goal, which should be agreed upon by all of the team members. Doing this will significantly reduce conflict. Second, the team members should be given proper job descriptions according to their individual gifts, skills, and talents. If this is not done, many problems will arise, and the team will break down sooner or later. The job description should include production roles that focus on a particular task or job. Myron Rush (1989) has explained that a person contributing to team production generally plays one of five roles: organizer, initiator, data collector, facili-

tator, or evaluator. An organizer works with the group to identify, assign, and schedule tasks and activities. An initiator offers suggestions and recommendations for the group's consideration. A data collector gathers facts, figures, and other information needed to assist the group with its work. A facilitator helps maintain a constant flow of communication needed in order for the team to achieve its goal. An evaluator studies results and assists in making change where needed.

The second type of ministry situation might be an individual ministry with **pioneering work** in a new field or in a limited access area. In this case, the pioneer must be an experienced missionary or at least well trained if relatively inexperienced. There are not a few cases within NSC agencies where new missionaries are appointed as team leaders because the agencies do not have experienced missionaries available. After a pioneer has established a base, others sometimes join as a team. In this case, the pioneer may assume a certain degree of vested rights while displaying an authoritarian leadership style. If proper care is not taken, the team members may experience significant frustration. Proper supervision can prevent much of this discord.

The third situation is the case of missionaries who are working in **limited access countries**. Some of the missionaries may be tentmakers or lay professionals. They may need to establish NGOs that involve various helping ministries such as development, medicine, teaching, cultural exchange, and business. In general, their spiritual work tends to be out of sight for security reasons, which creates problems for supervision. In the case of church planting in a limited access country, special attention must be given so that expatriate workers are not seen in leadership positions. Instead, nationals who are well-trained or who have promising abilities should be encouraged to lead. Meanwhile, missionaries should stay in the background, discipling promising national leaders.

Lastly, there is the case of leading a band of **short-term workers**. These individuals are usually obedient to the team leader if they have had good pre-field training. But some of them may still cause difficulties because they are excited and curious about new people, a new culture, and new circumstances. These workers need to be carefully supervised. Otherwise, two problems can arise. First, the presence of the short-term workers will not be beneficial to career workers in the area. Secondly, short-termers' recruitability and/or suitability for future career service may be jeopardized.

Provision of Supervision In Restricted Access Countries

The contexts of restricted access countries are different from those of open ones, varying according to religion, social systems or governments, and responsiveness to the gospel. Missionaries may experience frustration from lack of conversions, feelings of inadequacy, lack of status in the society, specialized tensions for the children's education, and other stresses. As mentioned above, some workers may be tentmakers or lay professionals who carry out their spiritual activities under the mantle of NGO activities.

When missionaries are doing church planting in a limited access country and are training national leadership behind the scenes, they must be very careful to select only highly committed national Christians for the work. Significant time will be spent in developing the national leadership. The missionary workers may travel home occasionally for spiritual renewal. **Home caring** or supervision may be appropriate in these cases.

Second, if all members of an **NGO** are missionaries, then caring supervision can be applied to the members within the structure, including fellowship, group Bible study (not open though), and evaluation done by the leader of the NGO. If supervision cannot be done in these ways, then care must be taken so that it is provided in other ways. Newer missionaries must not be hurt through lack of attention. Supervisors or caring pastors from home or from third countries may need to go help new workers.

Third, an **annual retreat or spiritual conference** can be held in a neutral country for purposes such as having fellowship together with all families in the field, helping to release stresses, sharing information about experiences, having informal or non-formal continuing education, receiving supervision, being refreshed spiritually, and renewing mission strategies in the same but ever-changing context. A few good speakers should be invited to encourage and challenge the attendees. Home leaders and supporters should participate as well. Then mutual understanding can be expected, and comfort and encouragement can be given to those enduring a stressful context. To evaluate team members in restricted access contexts, each person can fill out a self-evaluation form, and a supervisor in the field can then study each evaluation very carefully.

Fourth, a **traveling supervisor and a counselor** (a missionary pastor) can visit from time to time to supervise and care for workers in the field. Such personal amenities as homemade cookies, ready-to-eat dried food, and home newspapers will be welcomed greatly by those in limited access contexts. Evaluation should be performed during the visit. A self-evaluation should be considered as proportionately weightier than a supervisor's evaluation, because the supervisor is present only infrequently and only for short visits.

Fifth, how can we help those who have children get **education** in this context? Several options may be offered. Home schooling is one possibility at the elementary levels. Another choice is to send MKs to an international school. A third option is to send MKs to the national schools. In this last case, spiritual training must be diligently provided by the parents. Otherwise the children may be affected by the religious teachings and social impact of the local schools.

STRATEGIES FOR SUPERVISION

Prior to talking about strategies for supervision, let's raise some questions to help clarify the issue of supervision. What do we mean by better or quality supervision? How strong are the supervisor's shepherding skills? Is the caring system outlined in the agency's manual? Does each missionary have a job description? What issues arise from the context in which the missionaries are working? Are the missionaries in-

experienced or experienced? Are they adequately trained? What about their personalities, character, and spiritual and emotional condition? Are they truly committed as missionaries? Are the roles of both single and married women defined in the caring or supervision system? Do missionaries know how to act during various contingencies or emergencies? How can workers attain competency in the language where they are serving? How can supervisors help appropriately gifted people work together? Do the supervisors understand the cultural gap between generations? How many children do the missionaries have, and what kinds of schools are available? Is there any biblical standard for the numerical size of the supervisory umbrella? What are other agencies doing in order to offer quality supervision? Can we utilize their methods?

Traditional patterns of supervision have focused on structure and on informal fellowship. With regards to **structure**, if there are more than two or three dozen missionary units in a field, there may be full-time officers, such as a field director, a personnel officer, a financial officer, a travel coordinator if necessary, and station managers or team leaders who work with their members. Team members are given job descriptions, and they report to the leader; team leaders are accountable to the field director. The field director may have an advisory committee who can help him with decision making. The field director is accountable to the general director, who is accountable to the board of governors.

Prayer letters should be read by the team leader to make sure they would be acceptable to the host authorities. A few cases in West Africa have occurred in which missionaries were forced to pack and go home, because their letters were examined by government officials and were found offensive. This proofreading system may be utilized by the supervisor in some ways, because the proofreader may more fully appreciate what is going on in the ministry and what the needs are. Missionaries are free to send personal letters, but they must make sure that there are no words that would be offensive to the host government.

Women's abilities as leaders can be utilized in gatherings for fellowship and caring. Potluck dinner parties or picnics for all team members may be scheduled from time to time. It isn't necessary to spend much money, energy, or time in planning. Informal fellowship with each other is the main goal.

One limitation of supervision is that in most cases, the NSC do not have enough experienced missionaries to establish an elaborate supervisory structure to care for their smaller number of field workers. The supervisors often have their own ministries and are not free to function as full-time supervisors.

Should we consider focusing or limiting our missions strategy in order to offer better supervision? To answer this question, we need to be aware of the **pros and cons of unlimited expansion without adequate supervision**. If we proceed with rapid growth on the field without an adequate supervisory umbrella, we will have a higher attrition rate, and it may even be significantly higher. With a higher attrition rate comes an assortment of physical, emotional, and spiritual problems that can cause long-lasting damage to the missionaries who leave the field for less than desirable reasons. In other words,

we may have a large number of hurting people. Some who survive without good supervision may have to endure excessive stress, whereas good supervision might prevent learning lessons the hard way.

But there may be some benefits to rapid growth. We may more quickly locate those who are suitable for long-term missions and may locate greater numbers of missionaries of this type. Also, sometimes we can be overselective. Some people that we think are not good missionary candidates may in fact be very productive on the field. When we grow rapidly, we may admit some hidden gems that would otherwise be selected out.

When we limit growth to those we can adequately supervise, new missionaries have a greater chance for success, because they receive ample supervisory help. However, at times we may "carry" people because of compassion who are not really effective, and the expense of sending them to the field is unwarranted by what they will accomplish and their gifting. We would all agree that proper selection and training would ideally eliminate this problem, but we know in real life that the problem does occur.

Focusing and limiting strategy forces us to neglect certain ministry needs and opportunities, so that we can guarantee the success of a higher percentage of long-term missionaries. Effectual, productive, well-adjusted, happy, and fulfilled long-term missionaries are the critical people who do the bulk of long-lasting, survivable mission work. How can we recruit, train, and nurture the greatest number of these people? The answer probably lies in limiting or focusing the span of supervision to the gifts and ability of each supervisor. But with this decision there are some trade-offs, and it is not totally a win-win situation.

Sometimes a poorly supervised missionary is better than no missionary to the national church. The church may be in a crisis leadership situation, and so the needs of the field pressure us to send people that we know cannot be adequately supervised. Sometimes this works, but sometimes poorly supervised missionaries do more damage than good. I have seen it work both ways.

In balance, I personally prefer limiting or focusing strategy to ensure adequate supervision in most situations, but certainly there are exceptions, so that we cannot always make this an absolute rule.

REFERENCES

Kang, S. S. (1995). *Development of non-Western missionaries: Characteristics of four contrasting programs.* Deerfield, IL: Trinity International University.

Kang, S. S. (1996, Autumn). Theological foundation and reality of spiritual warfare. In E. S. Choi (Ed.), *World Missions*, pp. 17-18. Seoul, Korea: Chongshin Seminary.

Lane, D. (1990). *Tuning God's new instruments: A handbook for missions from the Two-Thirds World.* Singapore: World Evangelical Fellowship.

Rush, M. (1989). *Management: A biblical approach.* Wheaton, IL: Victor Books.

Sung-Sam Kang *since 1991 has served as Executive Missions Director of the Presbyterian Church (Hapdong) in Korea. He pastored for five years in Korea, and then with his wife and two sons served in Nigeria with GAPCK/SIM for 11 years. He is also missions professor at the Graduate School of World Missions, Chongshin University in Korea, and Associate General Secretary of the Korea Church Council.*

20

On-Field Training and Supervision

PERSPECTIVE OF THE OLD SENDING COUNTRIES

Myron S. Harrison

The fact that a growing number of missionaries are coming home for preventable reasons is cause for concern. What can be done to address this issue? Are any of the causes of missionary attrition related to on-field training or on-field supervision—areas which can be positively addressed, thus reducing the premature return of choice workers to the land of their origin?

The missionary is a significant link between those without Christ and those who come to Jesus to worship Him. Our goal is to keep new workers on the field once they arrive in their target country, not only because of the high cost of pre-field preparation and training (in terms of finances, time, and effort), but more importantly, because missionaries continue to be key workers in the task of reaching the world with the message of salvation in Christ.

SELECTED REASONS FOR ATTRITION

Lack of Further Development/Training Of Personnel on the Field

Although lack of on-field training is not often cited in survey reports as the major reason for missionary attrition, it is apparent that further development of personnel on the field would significantly help to stem the untimely flow of choice workers back to their homeland (Allen, 1986; see also Steve Moon's analysis in chapter 8). Frequently, the attitude of mission organizations is that new workers have been trained and have received proper equipping prior to their arrival on the field; thus, they should now be ready for ministry. No thought is given to further on-field training. Unfortunately, new workers often find that their preparation prior to coming to the field was inadequate or was not related to the actual ministry in which they are engaged. This realization leads to discouragement and a feeling of non-fulfillment in ministry. Before long, these once-aspiring workers retreat from the field.

Lack of Adequate Supervision on the Field

Inadequate supervision is another area of concern for those who return home prematurely. Again, the problem is not cited as the major cause of attrition, but there is evidence to suggest that more effective and efficient supervision would help greatly in decreasing the attrition flow. Surface reasons that might be given for returning home could include family issues, medical problems, and unfulfilled expectations, but in actual fact, the underlying reason may be inadequate supervision.

Let us now look more specifically at these two significant areas—on-field training of missionaries and on-field supervision.

ON-FIELD TRAINING

Issues for Consideration

The concept embodied in the word "training" needs to be considered. For some, training is an end in itself. That is, once an individual is "trained," there is no need for further training. The person is ready for ministry! Others would argue that training is a process that continues throughout life. As new situations arise in the life of the missionary, further preparation is required. At times, previous training will need to be upgraded and enhanced for greater effectiveness in ministry.

The younger missionaries of today (the boomer generation, ages 30 to 50, and the busters, under age 30) differ significantly from the older, traditional missionaries of a generation past (the booster generation, over age 50). Today, professionalism is significant among missionaries. Further development and education in order to meet the demands of the task are desirable and are often expected. In order to retain choice new workers on the field, mission agencies must address the matter of on-field training.

The concept of personnel development within an organization is also important. Such development is considered essential in secular organizations. It is also a key element in enhancing the ministry of those involved in missions. No one in a specific mission context will be fully equipped for the duration of a given task. There will be need along the way to enhance skills and gifting through training. The result will be greater effectiveness in ministry.

A positive attitude towards learning must be cultivated among missionary personnel. Certain members of the missionary force today concentrate solely on the urgent task before them of evangelizing those without Christ. They bypass the opportunity to upgrade their ministry skills—something which, if done, could greatly improve their ministry and multiply the results. It is necessary to instill in all missionary workers a sense of the value of improving in whatever ministry calling they may have, whether it be evangelism, teaching, administration, or service of another kind.

Where the missionary is functioning or will function has a direct effect upon the training program. In all cases, though, on-field training should include the family, individual spiritual needs, and obviously the missionary's personal ministry. These areas are discussed below.

Family

There are two issues to consider here. First, there is the family situation of living in a foreign culture. In order to survive in their new surroundings, of necessity the entire family must be trained in cross-cultural living. This training should not be relegated to a one-time-only session, but may require a longer-term program over a period of time. The second issue is the need for a spouse, most often the wife, to take courses with a view to upgrading ministry skills. Care must be taken that the focus is not just on whichever person in a couple is involved in the more major ministry. Not only will further on-field training provide upgrading in ministry, but it will also furnish essential personal stimulation and encouragement.

Spiritual Needs

In addition to covering family issues, training must focus on the spiritual needs of the individual, since a spiritual, biblical, and theological foundation is basic to any missionary work.

Ministry

This focus is obvious, as we seek to train missionaries on the field for more effective ministry. Courses offered should help workers upgrade their personal focus in ministry. In addition, courses should be made available to retrain personnel when there is a change in their ministry, so that they can learn new skills and concepts and possibly new approaches to their ministry. At times, the goal will be to enhance the skills of those who are already effective in ministry, so that they can do an even better job. On other occasions, training may be indicated when a new project is undertaken. For instance, the mission organization may decide to engage in a new ministry in which video is the medium of instruction. Those involved in this ministry will need to be trained in the area of video, possibly involving production, promotion, and training of others to do the actual work in time.

Need for On-Field Training

Dr. Herbert Kane (1983, p. 176) has argued that it is an act of consummate folly for anyone to proceed to the mission field without professional missionary training. The truth of this statement notwithstanding, it should also be noted that much of what is taught and learned during the preparatory (pre-field) stage is forgotten, or else the material is not understood at the time it is presented and thus is not applied, since it is not seen in context. To reinforce pre-field training, ongoing field training is indispensable. Training will be more effective in the context of the country and people to whom the missionary has gone. In this environment, greater assimilation of the matters that are studied will take place.

Workers today expect that they will receive further training as they progress in their ministry. Recently, this writer's own mission agency has begun developing a program which will affect all of the members on the field. There was a most positive response from members when they realized that the program is not designed just to train and develop potential leaders, but to involve all workers in personal development. Tentatively, the program is being termed the Life and Ministry Program or LAMP. Apart from the benefit individually, it is hoped and assumed that there will be positive results throughout the organization as workers are further enhanced in ministry and encouraged through the training.

Changing ministry roles requires retooling, which comes through further training. We live in a changing world, and the field of missions is no exception. Sometimes a missionary needs to change his or her ministry role, possibly from church planter to mission administrator. Or within the church planting situation, the individual may change focus from leading evangelistic home Bible studies to training nationals to lead home Bible studies. A course relating to training others in a specific ministry can be of great help in enhancing the changed ministry role of the individual missionary. Training can also affect the situation of missionaries who are approaching the mid-life crisis point in their ministry. As changes take place in their outlook on life, training can serve as a positive approach to help them through this period so they can avoid a premature exodus from field ministry.

The diversity of situations in which missionaries minister also suggests the need for on-field training. As nations undergo political and economic changes and upheavals, conditions that existed when the missionary arrived in the country may change dramatically over time. In such situations, there is a call for on-field training to enable missionaries to cope with the challenges of change.

Training can also help missionaries be more focused in relating to the target country or to a target people within the country. This writer has known a number of missionaries who arrived in their target country with the idea of ministering in a certain situation, only to find that that situation no longer existed, so they had to switch their focus to another people or ministry. Also, experience has shown that God may lead new missionaries to a different ministry from that anticipated prior to their arriving on the field. These situations will require possible retraining or at least some further training so that workers will be better equipped for the task. Although pre-field training is vital, it is almost impossible today to be fully equipped for the opportunities which are available in ministry. As David Harley (1995, pp. 7-8) has observed, inadequate training often leads to frustration and discouragement over the inability to relate to the target people. Unrest and insecurity are also present, and too often workers, feeling overwhelmed, make an early return to the homeland.

Types of On-Field Training

Mentoring is an effective form of on-field training, but it seems to be frequently overlooked as a valid method for training. The classroom style of training takes precedence, even though it may be a less effective form of training to use. S. Vasantharaj Albert (1996) observes dryly that the only training that the missionary and the agency know is seminary training. He goes on to say that on-the-job training (mentoring) is one solution to the need for more effective and cost-efficient training. We note in Scripture that Jesus made full use of a mentoring, on-the-job style of training with His disciples. He took this form to its ultimate expression by actually living with those He was mentoring.

Solid, positive experience by older workers is a rich resource for training younger, less experienced colleagues. In the LAMP program mentioned above, one of the basic courses has to do with mentoring—the why and how of positively mentoring others. Mentoring involves finding the right person, not necessarily someone older, but someone who will be able to share his or her God-given resources to foster life development. The effective mentor will be someone who offers positive support at crucial points along the way, is a model to follow, gives timely counsel and encouragement, and seeks to provide learning experiences in ministry which will move the person being mentored forward in life. The mentor could well be a national from the target country. In developing an on-field mentoring program, we need to consider questions such as the following: What is the expected outcome of our mentoring program? What should be the content of the program? How should we design the program? How can we involve nationals in the mentoring program?

Seminar and module type situations are popular on the mission field. There are many topics relating to missions which are being presented today through several day-long seminars. Almost any subject is available. Occasionally, there are ongoing seminars on specific topics over a period of time. These provide a cost-effective means of training, while producing minimal disruptions in missionaries' busy schedules. Often, these seminars also provide positive networking possibilities with other missionaries who are involved in similar ministries. Opportunities for challenge and encouragement are numerous.

National colleges and seminaries should not be overlooked as viable resources for upgrading knowledge and skills. In many countries today, there are educational institutions which can meet missionaries' need for further training. Not only is there the opportunity for training, but there is also the opportunity to relate through another format with the people of the target country.

Benefits of On-Field Training

The result of on-field training should be more effective and productive workers who have greater job satisfaction. However, it should be understood that the benefits will depend upon various factors related to the individual training program. The content, length, purpose, expected outcomes, and quality of trainers, among other things, will directly affect the results.

Cost issues are also included in the benefits. It is often less expensive to train personnel on location than to send them to an educational institution in another country, even if the school is in the home country of the individuals involved in the training. Also, with on-field training, several members of the same team may be simultaneously included in the training program, thus saving additional expense. The form of training can save money as well. Seminars, for example, are cheaper than individual instruction. Finally, the training program can be tailored to the actual field needs, once again cutting costs.

A decrease in attrition is, of course, the ultimate goal we seek. Training for the sake of training will not be productive. Beyond the benefits noted above, training should result in personnel remaining longer on the field, thus accomplishing the overall purpose of seeing missionaries continue in their tasks of evangelism, teaching, and establishing the church of Jesus Christ in the target country.

ON-FIELD SUPERVISION

Issues for Consideration

The urgent need for positive on-field supervision is the call being heard from various sectors of the mission field today. Whether from the old sending agencies or the new sending agencies, missionaries are searching for supervision that helps rather than hinders their ministry. They want supervision that encourages rather than curtails their personal creativity in ministry and that leads them forward rather than limits the possibilities of positive results in their ministry. If one reads through various reports, it doesn't take long to become aware of the need for good field supervisors. In spite of the obvious need, it is interesting to note that this particular item, like on-field training, is not usually at the top of the list of reasons given for attrition. Instead, relationship problems, non-fulfillment in the task, lack of pastoral support, a sense of loneliness, lack of a sense of direction in ministry, and other reasons are given. But behind all of these issues is the basic problem of inadequate supervision.

Often because of a lack of trained field personnel, roles which differ greatly in their makeup are combined, especially in supervisors. Pastoral (people-oriented) and administrative (goal-oriented) roles are frequently lumped together. The common idea in people's minds is that a supervisor is a person who relates basically to administrative matters, whether this be in areas of finance, strategy, goal setting, or agency relationships. Although these areas are important to the welfare of the missionary, the significant aspect of pastoral support and care is lacking. It is almost impossible to find the perfect individual who is able to care for missionaries from a pastoral perspective and who can also assume oversight in administrative concerns and field direction. Without adequate supervision in both areas, undue stress and pressure develop, resulting in pain, frustration, and broken relationships. Strong reasons emerge for workers to leave their field of ministry and return to their homeland.

There is a need to foster mutual evaluation (constructive criticism of both supervisors and missionaries) in on-field supervision. The issue has two sides. The most common viewpoint focuses on the supervisor and his or her relationship to the one supervised. Depending upon the approach used by the supervisor, the supervised person may react negatively, with possible feelings of being threatened. In contrast, in the second model, the supervised person is able to make constructive comments concerning the supervisor in order to enhance the supervisor's ministry as well as to relieve stress in the relationship. The comment has been rightly made that it is not so much what is said but rather how it is said. The need is to build a positive relationship which allows for mutual sharing and evaluation of one another. This relationship must be worked out in both directions between supervisor and supervised. Creating such a relationship will go far in reducing the attrition rate significantly, at least in the areas mentioned above. It should be noted, however, that care is required in certain cultural situations in which it may be difficult, if not impossible, for a supervised person to relate in this way to the supervisor.

Building harmony in team ministry among people of differing gifting and personality makeup is difficult at best. Yet experience has shown that such harmony is requisite if the team is to achieve success in ministry. Before the team is brought together, the gifting and personality makeup of the potential team members must be evaluated. Not to do so is to ask for disunity before the team even gets underway. Balance in gifting (i.e., not all members being leadership types or all administrators) and personality (i.e., not all dominant or all laid back) is central to the success of team building. Here we see the need for supervisors who possess understanding and insight into these types of concerns. Having experienced people as supervisors is crucial in bringing together any harmonious team for effective ministry.

Supervising personnel in limited access nations is another major concern today. Frequently, the situation in these nations is such that personnel are in distant locations for ministry and have no one in an adjacent location to relate to. Also, there will most likely not be a supervisor located near enough to provide regular oversight including visitation of the personnel concerned. Steps need to be taken to overcome these obstacles. One organization provides for regular visits of their personnel to some neutral location, where they can interact with mission leadership and with others involved in the same or a similar type of ministry. Although this arrangement requires personnel to travel more frequently than desired from the ministry location, it does seek to address the issue. Of course, the supervisor can also visit on location. However, in certain

circumstances, too many visits can raise questions on the part of the nationals in restricted access nations. It has been suggested that these nations be termed creative access nations rather than restricted or limited access, thus suggesting that in order to minister effectively, missionaries need to be creative in their ministries. The need for creativity also applies to those responsible for on-field supervision of personnel in these countries.

The question has been raised whether we should consider focusing or limiting our strategy and ministry in order to offer more effective supervision. There are several issues here. The first has to do with the location of ministry. In countries where personnel are located in such a way that they cannot be properly supervised, limiting ministry possibly would mean not reaching out to tribal groups or to limited access nations. If there is a clear call from the Lord to go to a distant unreached tribal group or to enter a restricted country, then obedience is important. The second issue involves the particular personnel being sent. The screening process comes into play here. Certain individuals are capable of ministering in out-of-the-way places and with a minimum of oversight, thus allowing for the expansion of ministry into remote areas. Third, there is the need to be creative in the approach to on-field supervision. The fact that a worker may be serving in a distant or difficult situation does not necessarily mean that sufficient supervision is impossible. The preceding paragraph suggests ways of meeting supervision needs in unique situations. Overall, it is important to strategize well and to move forward in ministry. However, consideration does need to be given to the various dynamics involved. Mission organizations can then move forward with care, assuring the best on-field supervision possible under the specific circumstances.

Scope of Supervision

All missionaries are part of a family. Even those coming to the field as single workers are part of a family which they have left behind in the homeland. On-field supervision must take the family into account. A much-noted reason given for attrition is "for family reasons." The various "family reasons" are numerous. Many of them could come under the preventable category if time had been taken to look at the problem from a total family perspective. Kath Donovan and Ruth Myors (chapter 4) have suggested that family systems theory be incorporated into supervision. This model looks at individuals in the context of their whole family or team. From personal experience, this writer has seen situations in which a husband and wife both had good missionary potential, but difficulties with the children compelled them to return home. If they had been seen as a family, then family issues could have been dealt with early in their ministry, and their premature departure from the field might have been prevented.

Too often, only the husband's viewpoint is considered in dealing with family and ministry issues. Input should be obtained from the wife as well. Including the children is also desirable. For single workers, understanding some of their background helps greatly in understanding current issues they may be dealing with. All in all, the family ap-

proach to supervision is a definite need. As David Pollock (chapter 23) has stated, "This delicate balancing act of 'family in ministry' requires encouragement and assistance from both authority and assistance sources in order for a person to be a good spouse, a good parent, and a good missionary."

The spiritual dimension is crucial in the ministry life of any Christian. We do not minister out of a vacuum, but rather from a source of spiritual energy and power that is unknown in the secular world. Missionaries may well be involved in teaching, administration, and various other ministries which are similar in method to the activities of secular organizations. However, within the ministry realm, the spiritual element is paramount in ministering successfully. It therefore behooves mission leadership to take note of and respond to the spiritual needs of those they supervise. Encouragement, prayer together, biblical stimulation, and spiritual counsel are all important elements in the task of overseeing the work of colleagues. Attention to spiritual needs will surely build stronger spiritual lives and result in greater ministry satisfaction.

Guidance in ministry-related matters is another area of supervision. Ministry is the basic reason missionaries go to the field. The Lord does much to develop character and cause spiritual growth through such ministry. Although most new workers have had college and some Bible school or seminary training, many are unable to take their formal training and translate it into everyday living on the mission field. Setting goals, establishing priorities, managing time, and mastering other related issues are major hurdles in the new setting.

Supervisors who recognize these difficulties and who are capable of providing positive input will be most valuable to new workers. As supervisors relate these areas to their personal experience and then help new workers apply them to their own situation, much growth will be achieved. A further concern with respect to ministry is the building of relationships. Conflicts are sure to occur. By building supportive relationships with those they supervise, supervisors will be able to mediate conflicts more effectively and maintain good working relations among team members.

Personnel Involved in Supervision

Who is best qualified for a supervisory role? This is a critical question. To insist either that older, more experienced personnel are the best or that we need the younger generation of leaders to take on supervisory roles is simplistic. The older, more mature leaders have much to offer in the way of past experience, wisdom, and knowledge of the work. However, due to the vast differences between their perspective on life and ministry and the perspective of the boomer and buster generations, harmony is often unattainable. On the other hand, younger personnel lack the qualities that supervisors need due to shortness of time in ministry, and they struggle in knowing how to respond in various situations. There is a serious need for training of mission field leadership in order to meet the demands expressed here. A mixed team of leaders including both the older and newer workers can be ideal. The older leaders need to update their understanding of today's generation, while the younger workers need to acknowledge the experience and wisdom of those who have been on the field much longer. Together, both can bring a richness to on-field supervision, resulting in satisfied personnel who enjoy the ministry to which they have been called.

The use of nationals in supervisory roles is an option that deserves consideration. Often mission leadership overlook this natural resource right at their doorstep. In most countries where missionaries are ministering today, national pastors and church leaders have come to full maturity in ministry and leadership responsibilities. Personally, this writer had a most positive experience during the first term of ministry under the leadership of a Filipino pastor. Many of the principles used throughout subsequent years of involvement in church planting were learned during that time. Training in how to relate in a Filipino manner and how best to react and respond in numerous situations was acquired both directly and indirectly from this pastor.

It is desirable that this kind of situation be repeated over and over again. However, we must also note that the national church leaders will not necessarily supervise in the same manner as those from our own sending country. Their approach to life will be different. Their understanding of scriptural principles and methods of ministry will be filtered through their own cultural grid rather than through the grid of the missionary's country of origin. These differences should have a beneficial element, in that learning takes place through the means and norms of the target country and people. Having nationals as supervisors also promotes more in-depth bonding between missionaries and those to whom they have come to minister. We must be aware, though, that not just any national will be suitable for a supervisory position. Much as a selection process is needed in determining supervisors within one's own organization, so also is this true in selecting nationals as supervisors.

Obviously, the type of training and ministry skills needed for a supervisory role are important. Our goal is not to hasten the exodus of workers from the field, but to retain missionaries in an enjoyable and satisfying ministry role. Significant time and effort should be devoted to providing correct training of those who are to be overseers of others in ministry on the mission field. As Donovan and Myors (chapter 4) have noted, movement away from authoritarian, non-consultative, task-oriented leadership is essential. There needs to be a change to more consultative leadership, with emphasis on understanding the personality traits of those to whom we are responsible. Friendship leadership is important to young people today. "Personal power" rather than "positional power" is significant. One leads through the respect that has been established through relationship, not because of any appointed position that has been assigned. The process in decision making needs to include the grassroots-level thinking if there is to be ownership of the decisions taken. Doing this will build the relationship and establish rapport between the supervisor and those being supervised. Administrative skills should also be addressed in training supervisors, although this writer has found in personal experience that this area should take second place. Relational skills in working with and overseeing personnel in their ministries are the primary skills needed by supervisors.

From time to time, supervisors need to upgrade their supervisory skills. No one is trained once and for always. With the constant and rapid changes taking place in societies today, if one is to lead effectively, there is call for upgrading through seminars and short courses that are available both in the home country and in the target country of ministry. Upgrading should be both for pastoral care of people (relational) and for administrative duties. The tendency is to cover only administrative skills in upgrading, which is insufficient. To keep those workers the Lord has sent to us, we need to do our best in keeping ourselves equipped and effective in the task of overseeing them in their personal ministry.

CONCLUSION

A senior single missionary from Thailand who has been involved with overseeing new workers for a number of years has noted that there are three significant areas of concern in the lives of missionaries. These are inner security, time management, and relationship building, especially with reference to resolving conflicts and increasing understanding. Good on-field training and positive on-field supervision will do much in the long term to promote and satisfy these three key areas. It is hoped that attention to these areas will also reduce the premature attrition flow back to the homeland. Would that we see workers remain on the field of their adoption until they have completed the task the Lord of the harvest has given them.

REFERENCES

Albert, S. V. (1996, April – June). Missionaries: Drop-outs or pushed out? *Planters Magazine*, **2**, 17.

Allen, F. (1986). Why do they leave? Reflections on attrition. *Evangelical Missions Quarterly*, **22**, 119-122.

Harley, C. D. (1995). *Preparing to serve: Training for cross-cultural mission.* Pasadena, CA: William Carey Library.

Kane, J. H. (1983). *A concise history of the Christian world mission.* Grand Rapids, MI: Baker Book House.

 *Myron S. Harrison, currently Area Director for OMF International, Philippines, has been serving in the Philippines since 1967, together with his wife, Betty. They have been involved mainly in church planting ministry through the years. Harrison has also been in administrative roles for 16 years and as Area Director for the last six years. They live in Quezon City (part of the metro Manila complex), Philippines. Harrison is an American, and his wife is Canadian. They have three adult children, one of whom is married with two children, all living in the States.*

21

Some Reflections On Pastoral Care

PERSPECTIVE OF THE NEW SENDING COUNTRIES

Belinda Ng

Pastoral care is often associated with the local church in the context of caring for the flock. However, this care must extend beyond ordinary members to include missionaries, whether they are on the field or on home soil for one reason or another. It should cover both adults and children, candidates as well as retirees, church planters as well as home office people. Indeed, pastoral care is critically important and is a lifeline for missionaries if the church seriously desires to have an effective, on-going work in Christ's Great Commission. While missionary pastoral care may mean different things to different people, it generally encompasses the following elements: understanding the special needs of missionaries, guidance, counseling, sharing, communicating, friendship, fellowship, visitation, crisis care, prayers, encouragement, and affirmation.

Cross-cultural mission is growing rapidly in Asia. Recent statistics showed an increase of 200% in the number of missionaries sent out, whereas the increase in the Western or older sending countries was only 4%. With such phenomenal expansion, heavy responsibilities are thrust upon all sending bodies in Asia. The question is: Do we fully understand the magnitude of the missionary task? The challenges facing cross-cultural missionaries are many today, and they call for empathy and sensitivity in our approach to those sent from our midst. Does our pastoral care match the expectations we have of our missionaries? How do we provide appropriate and adequate on-going pastoral care to ensure that those sent out remain on the field for as long as possible to fulfill their call to missions?

Missions is costly, involving risks, suffering, and sacrifices. To keep our missionaries effective on the field takes continuing pastoral care. Our sensitivity to their needs and well-being reflects our love, concern, and care when we send missionaries out to the front line. They are more than just our representatives. We are their partners on the home base. Therefore, as people at home, we need to be combat-fit as well, in order to be able to do our part in the missions enterprise.

Increasing attrition is affecting our young (referring to the time served rather than missionaries' age) missionary force. According to WEF's recent findings, one missionary in six never completed the first term. Therefore, recognising the critical role of pastoral care will go a long way in affirming and encouraging our missionaries. When the going gets tough, missionaries will press on instead of pulling out and returning prematurely from the field.

A PARADIGM SHIFT IN THINKING AND ATTITUDE

Before we embark on thinking about the caring task, we need to consider some misconceptions and views about missionaries and their work that exist in the Asian church today. Some of these prevailing attitudes can hurt and discourage those sent out and may hinder recruitment of new workers. After all, it is people who make up missions and who are therefore the church's resource for obeying God's command to go into all the world and preach the gospel.

1. "Real" missionaries. The first misconception relates to who the "real" missionaries are. Many churches in Asia still consider only church planting, evangelism, and training as the frontline ministries in which to be involved. Support ministries are low in rank. It is not uncommon to find that the main goal of many churches is to plant denominational churches, even at this age of missions. There is a need to understand that all types of workers are needed. Those in support roles are just as vital as any other members of the team.

2. Home assignment. It must be understood that home assignment is part of the service cycle. Too often, Christians do not understand why missionaries on home assignment need support or even a furlough. Some people prefer to continue their support only when the missionary returns to the field. Sometimes premature return home because of poor health is not understood by the home church. The person may be viewed as a failure or as being lazy. Attitudes such as these cause some Asians not to complete a full home assignment after serving a full term. They would rather return to the field early or pursue further studies away from their home country.

3. Partnership. There is a need to maximise resources through partnership. It is a growing trend for bigger churches to send missionaries out directly rather than channeling them through an agency. Missions takes more than missionaries and finances, but the value of partnership between churches and agencies has yet to be recognised to a great degree. Currently there is little cooperation and hardly any networking in pastoral care. Working in a team can bring about the synergy that facilitates mutual support, as well as the accountability that maximises limited resources. The recognition that, if possible, neither church nor agency should function independently will help missions to move forward significantly beyond this century.

4. Geographical focus. Another viewpoint that needs to be changed is the trend to focus on only one particular geographical area. Missionaries who are called to areas other than the countries selected by their home church are often not considered for church support, or they may receive less of the support dollar.

5. Vision for missions. A large number of churches still lack a vision for cross-cultural missions. These churches are often involved only in local ministries and in reaching their own ethnic people. Therefore, a person who has a calling to cross-cultural missions is not able to rally the support needed from the church.

6. Importance of senders. During the Persian Gulf War in 1991, there were nine support people backing up each soldier on the front line. How much more is such support necessary in the battlefield of missions! Missions success depends critically on logistic support from the base. Baseline people are all those in the body of Christ, from the church leadership to the lay people. No one is a spectator. Every believer is to be mobilised as either a goer or a sender.

7. Role of missionary wives. If a church's financial support policy is indicative of its overall care for its missionaries, then missionary wives in some quarters receive less recognition than other workers. There is a line of thinking that a single woman's role is very clear and warrants the church's recognition as a full missionary in terms of the support dollar. In contrast, the role of missionary wives is often unclear. Someone was heard asking, "What if she becomes pregnant and is unable to serve while on the field?" While Asians are perceived to be wholistic in orientation, this scenario shows otherwise. There is a lack of understanding of missionary life and work and of the "global" role of wives. Missionary wives who leave career, home, and country for missionary service need all forms of affirmation and encouragement from the sending church.

UNDERSTANDING MISSIONARIES' NEED OF PASTORAL CARE

The expectations placed on missionaries are sometimes unrealistic. Missionaries are placed on a pedestal, as if they have no spiritual problems and do not need pastoral help. However, they are human and are just as much in need of pastoral care as any ordinary church member. In fact, missionaries have extra needs for such care, for the following reasons:

+ Cross-cultural stresses.
+ Critical life transitions and experiences, such as facing unknown situations, having a baby on the field, sending a child to boarding school, and keeping the marriage growing and glowing under very challenging circumstances.
+ New issues which they face while on the field.
+ Crisis experiences on the field, such as civil war, political backlash, hostage, famine, robbery, intimidation, harassment, etc.

As Asian churches take up the challenge of missions, they are gradually facing the same problems that churches in the First World have experienced. Attrition, discouragement, sending the wrong kind of missionaries, discontentment, disillusionment, and many other categories of negative feelings are now surfacing and creating concerns. Pastoral care is often an after-thought, rather than part of the strategy at the outset of a church mission programme. Financial and material support are usually the main concerns, because they are more obvious and visible. Yet the truth is that, just like professional people at home needing some pastoral care, missionaries need the same generic care.

The principles of such care are similar. However, the context is different because of the peculiarities of cross-cultural missions: greater sense of isolation, distance, lack of immediacy, greater expectations by missionaries for care, being taken for granted, etc. Unconsciously, senders and sending churches often assume that someone is already doing the caring. There is also the assumption that the mission agency alone is able to give that care, without realising that there is a qualitative difference between what the agency provides on the field and what the missionaries need from their support base or home church. It is essential that missionaries feel a sense of "touch" with their home church. This is something that no agency can truly give without the involvement of the sending church.

The problem is made more difficult if a missionary is supported through many churches, with none being fully responsible for the missionary's support. This is the situation that missionaries from smaller churches may face. In these cases, the churches need to band together to provide pastoral care to their missionary. They must coordinate with all the other supporting churches, even if each group is only a minor shareholder in terms of financial support.

LAYING THE FOUNDATIONS FOR PASTORAL CARE

Pastoral care actually begins with the selection process. The moment a person shows an interest in cross-cultural missions, pastoral counseling and guidance should be provided. Of course, the support can be very general or even minimal in the beginning, but as the interest becomes serious, counseling and guidance will have to be intensified. The goal should be to present a mature candidate ready for service.

Potential missionaries must reach the stage of genuine commitment, must understand what it means to be a missionary, and must build trust and confidence with an adequate number of church members, church leaders, pastors, and friends. These are essential foundations for the missionary's future pastoral care. No amount of pastoral care from an agency can adequately substitute for what a group of caring people can provide.

Potential problems, rough edges, and weaknesses that could become liabilities should be dealt with as early as possible. Unfortunately, time for adequate pastoral care is sometimes insufficient due to underestimating the long process of missionary preparation. Many applicants take the definitive step of approaching their church or an agency only when they are on the verge of leaving for the mission field.

The missionary application process, unlike secular employment, should take into consideration the lengthy process of knowing the candidate well and of laying the foundations for pastoral care. If these things are not done and missionaries are not bonded to the active sending group (especially the leaders), then the ability or the desire to care for these workers when they have difficulties will be limited or may be entirely lacking. In such cases, without a deep relationship with the senders, missionaries are often left with less than adequate pastoral care from the home end.

UNDERSTANDING THE CONSTRAINTS

The High Cost of Missions

Asians must learn to bear with the high cost of cross-cultural missions. Because of the costs, churches are demanding greater accountability from mission agencies to justify the outlay of funds. Unfortunately, when such accountability is practised by an agency, missionaries often misinterpret the results. They tend to view the increasing pressure or demand for accountability as though they are not being cared for pastorally, even though there may be no concrete justification for this conclusion.

The problem may be exacerbated when Asians compare their situation with the ability of First World churches to provide more material incentives for their missionaries as part of their missionary care. Likewise, faith agencies are sometimes compared with denominationally supported groups or, worse, with secular agencies in terms of tangible provisions, which are then extrapolated to mean pastoral care.

Asians tend to equate (too rigidly) material provisions and other perks with pastoral care, without realising that these extras have to be balanced with their own desire and the desire of most Asian churches to control the escalating costs of cross-cultural missions. If Asian churches were required

to pay for all the benefits given to missionaries, very few workers would be sent out. On most fields, agencies could easily justify asking churches to provide a lot more support funds to care fully for all the needs of the missionaries. However, the psychological barrier to raising all these funds would repel most individual donors and churches.

The high cost of missions has given rise to the increasingly common refrain that we should make more use of nationals at US$50 per month salary, since they can function without need for furloughs, travel, costly education for children, etc. Cost constraints and pastoral care do not go hand in hand, unless we are prepared to redefine pastoral care and to provide such care in only non-material ways.

The Need for Balance And Response

Since pastoral care cannot be accomplished in purely non-material ways, nor by funds or perks that supporters/churches are unwilling to regard as essential (as shown by their hesitancy to commit their resources), agencies have to have a listening ear for both sides and must mediate between missionaries and senders. Neither extreme position (too spiritual or too material kind of care) is good. Drawing a line somewhere in the middle can be subjective and can often lead to misunderstandings and hurt feelings that are directed at the only obvious symbol of authority, the church leaders or the mission agency leaders—"they do not care for missionaries."

Ultimately, the means to provide pastoral care is the dynamic balance between genuine needs and the response of churches and donors. Agencies do not have the resources to provide everything, even if they put in writing a statement of what they would like to provide for their missionaries. Very often, the very making of such a statement can lead to expectations and demands which neither the agency nor the senders can fulfill. Many senders want to make the final decision about what they consider to be reasonable. Usually, on a case-by-case basis, they agree to whatever the agency might say on behalf of their missionaries. In all cases, the church, the agency, and the missionary need to reach a mutual understanding regarding what they consider to be balanced, cost-effective, and affordable.

There is a problem when missionaries do not have a main sending church to which they are accountable. In such cases, the sending agency may be left with no effective way to dialogue with someone who has the overall responsibility for the missionaries.

Limitations of Coverage

Agencies that have full-time pastoral ministers still suffer from avoidable attrition and face many criticisms. Pastoral needs are different for each individual. Some needs can only be met by a certain kind of minister that a missionary is open to share with and to listen to in his or her moment of crisis. For this reason, no agency can fully cover every missionary under its care to everyone's satisfaction. It is unrealistic to think that all pastoral care problems can be solved in this way. Asians also face the problem that the full-time ministers provided do not always understand the Asian culture. But if a multi-

cultural team is needed to provide adequate care, it will usually be beyond the resources of a single agency or denomination.

CRITICAL PHASES/AREAS FOR SPECIAL ATTENTION

Special attention to pastoral care is needed during the transitions of a missionary's life. Critical periods are the pre-field phase, the schooling of children either at a boarding school or through home schooling, the first term on the field, and the re-entry period.

Pre-Field Preparation

Providing adequate pre-field training demonstrates responsible caring. Training should include self-care, personal management, cross-cultural communication, basic counseling, and spiritual maintenance. Managing conflict needs to be evaluated in the context of an international team, with consideration given to the "face saving" values of the Asian culture. With increasing urbanisation, modern conveniences make it necessary that survival skills be imparted. Can a missionary going to a remote rural setting fix a meal from scratch?

In the Asian context, care should extend beyond the missionary. Before departure, it is good to establish links with missionaries' elderly parents. Many missionaries find it difficult to leave home and parents, because looking after aging parents is a filial duty that is expected in the culture. Guilt may surface and cause internal conflicts. Recently a certain field approved a missionary's request to return home to spend time with her terminally ill father. In doing so, the missionary was able to perform a loving act of providing nourishing soup for her father daily for a few weeks before his home-going. This gave her a great sense of satisfaction and comfort to be able to honour her father with her last act of duty. For missionaries on the field, expressions of care to the extended families by people on the home front go a long way in reassuring missionaries that someone is looking out for their folks at home during their absence.

Understanding Missionary Children and Their Needs

The number of Asian missionary children (MKs) is growing, and greater attention must be given to their needs. Statistics show that a large proportion of missionary families return to their home countries due to their children's needs, at a time when the parents are at their prime in their ministries. Pastoral care should include pre-field orientation of school-aged children, in either formal or informal sessions. This is very important if we want to see children adapt well on the mission field.

Proper screening must also be in place to ensure that reluctant children are not forced to leave their country of citizenship. Their non-cooperation is a sign that they need counseling and re-assurance. Proper orientation must be given to help them reach a stage where they can feel a part of their parents' calling and ministry. Only then will they be willing to go with their parents to the mission field. It is harmful to coerce or persuade children into leaving if internally they are struggling and resisting.

At present, the mission with which I am affiliated has about 50 Asian MKs, many of whom came from monocultural backgrounds and were non-English speakers at the beginning. Asian parents are concerned about their children losing their identity and mother tongue. Therefore, it is vital to assist parents in planning how to work through this issue. Parents need to know their own culture and language in order to teach their children. Keeping their own cultural traditions during the critical phase of early childhood will provide MKs with a solid foundation and will help foster strong bonds, so that they will be emotionally stable as they grow up.

MK education is another big concern. As yet, no solution is in sight. Unless the churches in Asia recognise that providing appropriate education is a part of pastoral care, the attrition of missionary families will continue to increase. For too long, education has been the sole concern and problem of the missionary families themselves. Mission leaders of sending bodies are recognising this problem and are addressing this issue more and more, but we need to confront it head-on with concrete actions. Otherwise, fewer families will present themselves for service, or we will be raising a new generation of Westernised missionary kids.

New MKs on the field who are in higher grades have the greatest struggles, due to language problems. It is painful and unnecessary for them to fall back in grades just because of the lack of English language. The dilemma is that many will not be able to return to the education systems from which they came nor enter a college in the West, because the high fees are unaffordable on missionary allowances. A significant step in the right direction is to recognise MK teachers as missionaries. Asian churches need to take responsibility to recruit such teachers for Asian MKs, to ensure that families who receive God's calling will not hesitate to take the plunge to leave country and kindred.

On the Field

Most Asian family members live together as long as they are single. Because of this tradition, single Asian missionaries are more prone to loneliness on the field than their Western colleagues. Understanding this cultural norm will assist leaders in placing singles close to other people for support. This will reduce considerable anxiety, homesickness, and insecurity. Usually in a strange new environment, Asians prefer to share housing.

Increasingly, many married couples are living on their own. However, the majority still depend on a network of support from their in-laws and siblings. Young families on the mission field tend to miss this support terribly. Missionary mothers do not have the help of their mothers or mothers-in-law at the birth of their children. Sensitivity to the needs of new mothers will help them through the vulnerable period of the baby's first month.

The church in Asia is young, and most missionaries are first-generation believers. Many have no Christian role models for parenting and therefore need guidance. As a minority nationality or culture, some missionaries may feel lonely during Christian festivals and holidays. Many do not have enough history to have traditions for celebrations. Making special efforts to include them will build bridges within international teams.

In the area of relationships, it appears that Asians and other minorities do most of the adapting in international teams. Every team member should adapt to one another. Initiative must come from all—whether top leaders or grassroots members. In the body of Christ, there should be no segregation but integration of people. The experience will be enriching. Unity in diversity is a powerful message to all, especially unbelievers. It reflects the character of our Creator God.

To help new missionaries adjust on the field, a mentoring system is recommended. No matter how thoroughly missionaries are prepared for going to their field of service, the reality is often far from their expectations. The situations on the field change rapidly. Mentoring in the initial weeks after arrival can help new missionaries adapt to the new country and culture. Such mentoring should involve coming alongside newcomers to teach them new customs, show them how to buy local food in the market, listen to them, and answer their innumerable questions about things that may seem obvious to veteran missionaries.

Understanding first termers' need for time to learn the language is also important. This involves long-term vision. Without language competence, many missionaries struggle with staying on the field and with returning for subsequent terms of service. In this age of "instant" results, many senders have no patience with this approach. The desire to see missionaries produce numbers of converts often steers churches to do missions only in places where no language learning is required. However, most of the world's population will not be reached if we do not cross linguistic barriers. The remaining unreached people groups will have a chance to hear the gospel only if missionaries are given adequate time at the beginning of their missionary career to learn the language. This period will enable them to communicate at the heart level. Experience has shown that language ability greatly facilitates the bonding of missionaries with the people to whom they are ministering.

The job of the support team at home does not end when missionaries depart for the field but continues while they are in their place of service. Pastoral care must be extended from the home base; it is not just field-initiated. Saying goodbye is painful, and it does not get easier with more experience. On the contrary, it can get worse, if not for the grace of God. Missionaries face the pain of separation more often than the average person does. Maintaining friendship is a precious gift that supporters at home can give. Asians are often poor letter writers, but if we care and are aware of how much such communication means to a missionary, we will write. There are many creative ways to communicate in this high-tech age. However, in many developing countries, letters are still the only possible means. Indeed, "snail mail" is still appreciated and will help to keep up missionaries' morale even during hard times.

A final element of on-field pastoral care is crisis care. Increasing dangers on the field should cause all of us to evaluate contingency plans for our missionaries serving in unstable areas. Is our structure adequate to provide care and debriefing in time of war, death, burnout, kidnap, or political backlash?

This area must be constantly reviewed so that missionaries are not spending all of their time and emotional energy handling these situations.

Re-entry

The more missionaries adapt to the country of service, the greater the readjustment when they return for home assignment. Most missionaries feel that re-entry is the greatest challenge of the entire missionary experience. The fact that re-adjustment is necessary, in the face of all the changes that occurred during the time away, can cause real stress and pain to returnees. The need to debrief is critical. Preparing returning missionaries for reverse culture shock will ease the stress of re-entry. Taking time to listen also constitutes pastoral care.

Since Asian missionaries are still few in number at any given time in a particular country, cooperation among sending bodies is recommended. Joint re-entry seminars for all returning missionaries and MKs can provide opportunities for returnees to share experiences of grieving, reverse culture shock, and re-integration of MKs back into the local school system. Such interaction is therapeutic and encouraging and will help to facilitate a smooth transition from life on the field to life at home. The period at home also offers countless opportunities for those on the home base to minister and play a meaningful part in missionary involvement.

CONCLUSION

Pastoral care of missionaries is an on-going concern for both the church and the mission agency. It spans a missionary's entire life cycle, from the cradle (new MKs) to the grave (retirement). To be effective, pastoral care requires continual dialogue with missionaries. Needs vary from person to person, and care calls for a caring heart. With the high rate of attrition, we want to do our best to ensure that the return is not because of preventable reasons or because we fail in adequate pastoral care. Continual and sensitive pastoral care will keep workers on the field as long as it is the Lord's plan for them to remain there to serve Him.

Belinda Ng was born in Singapore and has served as a missionary with SIM for 20 years. For 12 years she and her surgeon husband, Andrew, worked at Galmi Hospital in Niger. At the end of 1989, they returned to Singapore, where they head the SIM work in East Asia. They have two sons. In Singapore, Ng set up the Resource Library and continues to edit the East Asian edition of the **SIMNOW** magazine. Her primary role up to the present is as Personnel Coordinator, which allows her to express her pastoral gifting and concern for Asian missionaries. She is also a WEF Missions Commission Associate.

22

Member Care on the Field: Taking the Longer Road

PERSPECTIVE OF THE OLD SENDING COUNTRIES

Kelly O'Donnell

*Climb, traveler, or stiffen
slowly on the plain.*
— Irish proverb
(MacIntyre, 1995, p. 18)

When Jesus said He was sending His disciples out like sheep in the midst of wolves (Matt. 10:16), He was not kidding! The persecutions of the early church and of subsequent generations give ample testimony to His warning. Neither was He speaking lightly when He commanded us to love one another as He loved us (John 15:12). Member care is an example of such love, for it seeks to support missionaries as they face the challenging "wolves" of missionary life. Indeed, the heart of member care lies not in the specialized services of caring professionals (important as these are), but rather in the mutual support between friends who "encourage one another daily" (Heb. 3:13) in the midst of their sacrificial lifestyles. Such member care gives us strength to continue on the long road of mission life.

Member care can be defined as the **ongoing investment of resources by mission agencies, churches, and mission service organizations for the nurture and development of missionary personnel.** It focuses on everyone in missions (field missionaries, support staff, children, and families) and does so over the course of the missionary life cycle, from recruitment through retirement. Member care is the responsibility of everyone in missions—sending church, mission agency, fellow workers, and member care specialists. Another key source of member care is the mutually supportive relationships which missionaries form with those in the host culture. Whatever the source, the goal is to develop godly character, inner strength, and skills to help personnel remain effective in their work.

Member care, then, is as much about developing inner resources within the person as it is about providing external resources to support missionaries in their work. Some examples of member care for field personnel include on-field orientation, team building, crisis intervention, logistical support (help with visas, MK education, medical insurance, travel arrangements), retreats, friendships with national colleagues and neighbors, ongoing skill development (training in language acquisition and job areas), and visits from pastors for encouragement, teaching, and counseling (O'Donnell, 1997).

In this chapter, I will look at four areas of member care, with a special emphasis on field care:

+ **Patterns of member care.** An overview of significant member care trends that affect us.

+ **Parameters of member care.** A grid to help us identify our strengths and gaps in staff care.

+ **Problems in field care.** The challenge to make services acceptable/available to more people.

+ **Practical strategies.** An inquiry into some of the important ingredients of member care.

I close the article with some future directions for the long-term development of member care.

PATTERNS OF MEMBER CARE

No doubt about it: Member care is becoming increasingly accepted and mainstreamed in missions. In the ReMAP study, agencies from old sending countries used an average of 12% of their resources for pastoral care and supervision, and agencies from new sending countries used a surprising 20%! Member care has grown in prominence and is now generally viewed as both a biblical responsibility and a central component of mission strategy.

Some argue, though, that the member care pendulum has swung too far and that member care—or at least certain types—is overemphasized. Don

Larson and Brent Lindquist, for example, member care advocates themselves, have recently reminded me of the importance of developing supportive relationships with nationals and not just with fellow Christian/expatriate colleagues. Too much expatriate member care could actually hinder involvement with people in the host culture.

Social Movement

Member care can be viewed as a social movement within missions, being influenced by and mirroring a similar movement in the secular work world (e.g., Human Resource Development, Employee Assistance Programs). The main premise is that **investing in workers' personal and professional growth will result in greater job satisfaction and productivity**. Further, it is also accurate to say that member care is now a disciplinary "field" within missions. It has its own body of knowledge, research base, practitioners, and models.

Christian Health Care

I am delighted to say that a growing number of member care workers from the old sending countries are "taking the show on the road." That is, many are making cross-cultural applications of Christian health care to non-Western and mission settings. For example, there is a growing interest in the area of multicultural team life, where finding practical ways to understand each other and get along is essential. There is even a proposal now to develop contextualized Christian family and marital resources in Arabic, as a way to further disciple Arabic-speaking believers.

Member care is also being discussed and developed within mission societies from the new sending countries. There is a felt need to upgrade both conceptually and practically. One encouraging example is the India Mission Association's proposal to develop a health care team and eventually a health care facility for Indian missionaries. Another example is the pastoral care that missionary candidates receive at training centers such as the Outreach Training Institute of the Indian Evangelical Mission.

Written Materials

There continues to be a steady stream of dissertations, articles, research projects, and books in areas related to member care. One classic work is Marjory Foyle's (1987) *Overcoming Missionary Stress*. For a compilation of 50 important articles from 1974–1988, see *Helping Missionaries Grow* (O'Donnell & O'Donnell, 1988). Gordon and Rosemary Jones' (1995) recent book *Teamwork* is excellent, as is Ted Lankester's (1995) book on staying healthy overseas, *Good Health, Good Travel*. *Missionary Care* (O'Donnell, 1992a), a compilation of 25 recent articles, is another good resource. Finally, the October 1995 issue of the *International Journal of Frontier Missions* deals with member care issues in frontier mission settings (multinational teams, contingency management, brief field counseling, needs assessment, etc.). Clearly, though, there is a dearth of written materials from the new sending countries.

Conferences

The grandfather of all conferences related to member care has been the International Conference on MKs (held in Quito, Manila, and Nairobi in the 1980s). The gatherings of personnel directors/secretaries in the USA and UK are also noteworthy. The Mental Health and Missions Conference (now in its 18th year) and the Pastors to Missionaries Conference are held annually in the USA. Various mission associations and societies also have member care workshops during their conferences. Doubtless the recent WEF Pastoral Care Workshop in the UK will be seen as one of the most important (and one of the few) international, interagency member care gatherings to date.

Member Care Organizations

How I thank the Lord for the growing number of member care service organizations. Chapter 25 in this book lists more than 100 key groups, organizations, and individuals! That such a guide can now be assembled is indicative of the unprecedented number of service groups forming during the last few years. For example, two interagency member care groups have recently formed to stimulate/complement services for their respective regions of the Middle East and North Africa. People in other regions, such as Europe and New Zealand, are also considering forming similar groups to help coordinate and provide regional care services. Finally, the International Association of Christian Counselors is encouraging the development of national associations of Christian counselors, which could result in some important referral sources for missionaries.

Training

There are many workshops and courses being taught on member care and related subjects. Fuller Theological Seminary, Columbia International University, and Rosemead School of Psychology in the USA and IGNIS School of Psychology in Germany offer courses in member care for psychologists/counselors in training. In Singapore, Ron and Barbara Noll from Campus Crusade have been training Asians to counsel within the local church and missions settings. Singapore was also recently the site of an intensive workshop to train Christian leaders in the area of addiction and running support groups.

So what is the upshot of all of the above trends? The longer road: healthier missionaries, who receive and provide ongoing member care, who touch the lives of people with the love of Jesus, and who persevere over the long haul.

PARAMETERS OF MEMBER CARE

Organizations that send out missionaries are responsible to do all they can to sustain them. This assumption is almost axiomatic these days. But how best to sustain and support these workers? Let's construct a conceptual grid with four parameters: types of staff, types of stages, types of services, and types of stressors. Such a grid will help us to evaluate the strengths and weaknesses of our member care programs.

Types of Staff

We often build our member care programs around the needs of individuals, couples, and families. However, for member care to be less fragmentary, we must think more collectively and consider the other types of staff: teams, departments, regions, agencies themselves, and interagency partnerships. Our groups and corporate structures have member care needs too!

Types of Stages

A second parameter is the life cycle stages for the various types of staff. At the individual level, this parameter consists of the different stages of the missionary life cycle, including recruitment, selection, candidacy, first term, furloughs, and retirement (see Dodds, Dodds, & Kuitems, 1993; Gardner, 1987). For missionary families, the life cycle stages are the various family stages—newly married couples, families with young children, families with adolescents, launching children, and families in later life (see O'Donnell, 1987). Teams also cycle through stages—beginning, adjustment, working, ending (see Love, 1996; O'Donnell, 1992b). Organizational life can be demarcated by significant transition phases, such as Griener's (1972) model of organizational growth, which starts with a creativity phase followed by direction, delegation, coordination, and finally collaboration. There has also been some preliminary thinking done on the life cycle of partnerships by Interdev (1995), including an exploration phase of one to three years, a formation phase, and then an operation phase.

Hence it is not enough to point out a person's or group's needs. We must also identify at what life stage these needs occur—a signal for when the entity might be most at risk. Some classic examples are the first-term missionary struggling with culture shock, the missionary family with adolescents reentering the parents' home culture, the team embroiled in interpersonal conflict during the adjustment stage, and the young mission organization transitioning from founder dominance to a more participative leadership style.

Types of Services

Good field care usually includes things like on-field orientation, ongoing training, pastoral or crisis counseling when needed, logistical support from a home office/church, an occasional visit from a trusted leader, and supportive times with friends. These and other services can be grouped in four categories (O'Donnell & O'Donnell, 1992):

Prevention services decrease the incidence of problems. Examples include selecting missionaries who are free of significant personal struggles that would interfere with their work/relationships and clarifying/validating a candidate's call. Meeting regularly to discuss the quality of team life is another example. The aim is to eliminate problems before they occur.

Development services equip missionaries with the skills they need to deal with cross-cultural life and work. One key area is training team members in conflict resolution skills. Another form of development is senior staff coaching others on discipling new Christians, or missionaries taking correspondence courses.

Support services focus on encouraging missionaries during the ups and downs of life. Praying together, brief counseling, fostering family life via family retreats, pastoral visits, and helping to secure housing for new field arrivals are good examples.

Restoration services seek to remediate the effects of serious problems. For instance, a couple seeks out counseling after prolonged marital discord, or a field worker relapses with chronic fatigue syndrome, requiring medical evaluation and counseling care.

Types of Stressors

There are many ways to cut the "missionary needs" pie. The ReMAP study does this by listing 26 "reasons for leaving." Here is another way which identifies 10 types of stressors—sometimes overlapping—that are common to field personnel (adapted from O'Donnell & O'Donnell, 1995). For some people, the greatest stress results from a poor fit between one's background (vocational, denominational, cultural) and the type of agency ethos (organizational stressors). For others, the greatest stress results from the more common or anticipated stressors, such as cross-cultural adjustment or possibly conflict with colleagues. Note that in the list below I have used the acronym CHOPS to help you identify/remember these stressors.

✦ **Cultural.** Getting your needs met in unfamiliar ways: language learning, culture shock, reentry.

✦ **Crises.** Events which are potentially traumatic and often unexpected: natural disasters, wars, accidents, political instability.

✦ **Historical.** Unresolved areas of past personal struggle: family-of-origin issues, personal weaknesses.

✦ **Human.** Relationships with family members, colleagues, nationals: raising children, couple conflict, struggles with team members, social opposition.

✦ **Occupational.** Job-specific challenges and pressures: work load, travel schedule, exposure to people with problems, job satisfaction, training needs, government "red tape."

✦ **Organizational.** Incongruence between one's background and the organizational ethos: differing with company policies, work style, expectations.

+ **Physical.** Overall health and factors that affect it: nutrition, climate, illness, aging, environment, sexual harassment.

+ **Psychological.** Overall emotional stability and self-esteem: sense of identity, loneliness, frustration, depression, unwanted habits, developmental issues/stage-of-life issues.

+ **Support.** Resources to sustain one's work: finances, housing, clerical and technical help, maintaining donor contact.

+ **Spiritual.** Relationship with the Lord: devotional life, subtle temptations, time with other believers, adjustments in one's theology and understanding of God, spiritual warfare.

Now for some fun. Let's integrate all four of the parameters—types of staff, types of stages, types of services, and types of stressors—to get a clearer picture of the needs and resources for our field staff. This results is a grid of 16 matrices (see Figure 22-1).

Perhaps the best way to use this grid is to get together with a few colleagues and write down some of the stressors for each of the four types of staff. Start out with the first level, people, and discuss some of the stressors for singles in your setting. Then proceed to couples, children, and families. Do you notice any patterns and any special issues? And which issues occur at the different life cycle stages? The next step is to identify which types of services are available for each of the four types of staff. Which services need to be developed and for which life stage?

All of this might seem a bit abstract and complicated, but it really is not. Once you practice on one or two matrices, you will catch on fast. Here are some examples from the grid to show

THE MEMBER CARE NEEDS AND RESOURCES GRID (WITH FIELD EXAMPLES)					
Types of Staff	**Types of Services**				**Types of Stages**
	Prevention	**Development**	**Support**	**Restoration**	
People: singles, couples, children, families	A. Children's special needs		B. Single women		Mission, family, and individual life cycles
Small group: teams, departments		C. Relief teams		D. Church planting team	Team/group stages
Large group: center, region, agency	E. Organization quality of life		F. Retreat for agencies		Organizational phases
Partnerships: country, people group region, global		G. Partnership training		H. Partnership conflict	Partnership phases
	Types of Stressors (each stressor can affect any matrix)				
	Cultural Historical	Occupational	Physical	Support	
	Crises Human	Organizational	Psychological	Spiritual	

Figure 22-1

you just how easy it is to do this assessment of needs and resources.

A. We have pre-field assessment services by an educational specialist to screen for special needs (developmental delay, academic or behavioral problems, family tensions) of the missionary children who are going into our main region, the Middle East.

B. Half of our single women in the subcontinent are feeling isolated and sexually harassed, especially during the first term. They need more encouragement from colleagues and practical ways for dealing with harassment.

C. The three relief teams that our mission center has sent to work in a war-torn area are trained to use team-building tools to help at different stages of the group life cycle.

D. A church planting team in North Africa is going through the "differing" stage of team life and needs an outside coach to help them heal interpersonal wounds. This is not an isolated occurrence, as many of our other 18 church planting teams report similar problems.

E. The home office of our organization has developed a "mutual feedback form" in addition to the usual performance evaluation. Staff and supervisors now have a mechanism for discussing expectations and the quality of departmental life. This is in keeping with their desire to build an ethos of mutual respect and accountability and to maintain a more "collaborative" atmosphere as the organization gets bigger.

F. Six European mission centers from one organization come together for a retreat, in order to seek the Lord and encourage each other during a key organizational transition time.

G. Training in contingency planning (evacuation, hostage situations) is done at a regional partnership gathering, in an effort to prevent serious mishaps should a crisis occur in the region.

H. Partnership leaders speak with representatives from a large church denomination in an unreached area. The church members feel alienated and are concerned about inappropriate "Western" methods of evangelism.

PROBLEMS IN FIELD CARE

ReMAP identified some of the common problems that produce attrition, as reported by administrators. For the new sending countries, the top undesirable attrition factors, in order, are lack of home support, lack of call, inadequate commitment, disagreements with the sending agency, and problems with peer missionaries. For the old sending countries they are children's issues, change of job, health problems, problems with peers, and personal concerns.

Types of Issues

Some of these issues are **relational in nature** (e.g., peer relation problems, disagreement with the sending agency) and might partly stem from the different generational perspectives on how to work in missions (see Kath Donovan and Ruth Myors' analysis in chapter 4). They might also result from a poor fit between one's background and expectations and those of the organization, as well as from having limited skills in conflict management. Defusing some of these relational land mines would involve a concerted effort by agencies to build in mutual feedback times; develop community life in their various settings; encourage leaders to teach and model forgiveness; discuss the realities of different (generational) styles in leadership, self-disclosure, and decision making; and systematically train staff in culturally appropriate conflict resolution skills (see Augsburger, 1992; Elmer, 1993).

Other undesirable attrition issues seem more **personal in nature** (e.g., commitment levels, adequate call, health issues, personal problems), possibly stemming from an inadequate formation in one's family of origin and in the local church, augmented by the stressors of mission life (see Rudy Girón's discussion in chapter 3).

A third type of issue, especially for those from the old sending countries, involves **children's needs**, such as their schooling options and their overall adjustment (topics dealt with at length in literature from the old sending countries).

Team Issues

Teams in particular are vulnerable to the negative impact of relational and personal problems. The ReMAP study (see chapter 6) indicates that maintaining good relationships with other missionaries and colleagues is an important means of preventing attrition. Listen carefully to Greg Livingstone's (1993, p. 115) perceptions on some struggles in team life from his book, *Planting Churches in Muslim Cities*:

It is important that through team fellowship the problem of members' sinful nature be continually addressed. It should not be a shock but should be considered normal that there are times when various team members are ugly, unreasonable, and judgmental. It is important as well for all to be aware that,

due to being reared by sinners in a fallen world, none of us have escaped emotional damage. All missionaries, like all other Christians everywhere, have blindspots, that is, areas where we do not recognize sin, selfishness, self-centeredness, or neurotic addictive behavior and how it affects our colleagues. Thus it is vital to know how to practice reconciliation according to Matthew 5:23-24 and 18:15-17.... Experience shows that missionaries do not often follow these instructions seriously.

Teams would do well to plan team building sessions at least once a month. One good exercise is to review the various "one another" verses in the New Testament (e.g., forgiving one another, bearing one another's burdens, loving one another from the heart). Other team building ideas can be found in Gordon and Rosemary Jones' (1995) excellent book *Teamwork* and in the article, "Tools for Team Viability" (O'Donnell, 1992b).

Acceptability and Availability of Services

Another nemesis to field care is the acceptability and availability of member care services. By *acceptable*, I am primarily thinking of the need to bend over backwards to make sure we are providing and developing culturally relevant resources (e.g., counseling, books), especially for the growing numbers of those from the new sending countries (e.g., Nigeria, Brazil). And by *available*, I refer to the need to provide and develop supportive resources for the growing numbers of missionaries working in difficult, isolated, frontier locations.

Acceptability of Services

Member care means different things to different cultures. For example, would Asian members of a multinational team engage in self-disclosure about personal struggles (possibly seen as showing weakness and shaming themselves)? Or would Latin Americans on this team give their leader "honest feedback" at a group meeting about how the leader is doing (possibly seen as confronting and shaming someone in authority)? For some, such responses would be most inappropriate. So indirect approaches, like talking through a mediator/friend, or a more private approach, like seeing someone individually, are often more culturally appropriate (see Cho & Greenlee, 1995; Mackin, 1992).

Other issues pertaining to the acceptability of services are described by Barry Austin (1992, p. 62) in his article, "Supporting Missions Through Pastoral Care":

Mutual care among missionary personnel can be awkward at times. For instance, perhaps the person you want to approach for some help or advice is struggling just as much as you. Or you may be hesitant to share your real thoughts and feelings with someone because your work relationship might in some way be adversely affected. Maybe you are in a multinational setting and it is hard to communicate deeply in a second language and feel understood by others from a different culture. Or in the case where a pastoral caregiver is designated, you might just find it hard to relate together for whatever reason.

Availability of Services

I remember speaking at an international conference about the need to develop a "comprehensive range of member care services" for missionaries. Both my member care zeal and my comprehensive list were met with some blank stares by my brethren from developing countries. It was as if I were talking about life on another planet, which of course I was—the planet of abundant, Western-type resources!

Suppose a Latin American couple is physically assaulted and robbed while working in a Central Asian city. Although their friends empathically listen to them, encourage them, and provide some financial help, they are still struggling with classic "post-traumatic symptoms." Six weeks later, they still experience intrusive images of the event, are preoccupied with personal safety, stay inside most of the time, and sleep poorly at night. Is there any specialized help available in such an isolated setting? Is it provided in Spanish/Portuguese? Would they prefer to see a physician or pastor, rather than a therapist specializing in trauma? Do they and/or their sponsoring church or agency have funds to help them in this crisis? Do they feel guilt and shame at not being able to "shake off" the assault experience, go on with their work, and "walk in victory"?

For many in similar situations, pursuing personal therapy is simply out of the question for financial, geographic, and/or cultural reasons. The same can be true when trying to resolve other significant problems, such as intense marital discord, approaching burnout, hidden addictions such as pornography or eating, and major depression. Our people frankly may be stuck—there are few available resources.

Although I am fond of touting the many advances in member care, the fact is that in many isolated settings (and certainly for many of the new sending countries), many services are still seen as a luxury. Retirement packages, pension plans, therapy? Unthinkable extravagances—and perhaps not in keeping with a life of faith. In the no-frills world of missions, the new sending countries excel in making the most out of the least. Much of their member care emphasis seems to be not so much on services to receive, but on developing the inner qualities to keep a person going over the long haul. Added to this are a sprinkling of pastoral care from a visiting leader and some good times of fellowship and prayer with missionary colleagues, and you now have the main ingredients of many a member care "program." To a point, maybe such a program is not so bad after all! But in my experience, it is often not enough to sustain people on the longer road.

PRACTICAL STRATEGIES

So what other types of resources and strategies need to be developed for the longer road? This final section will look at this question.

Counseling Care

Peer and Professional Counseling

Counseling for missionaries is a fairly popular member care topic. Lindquist (1995) and Cerny and Smith (1995) take a look at the practicalities of providing brief counseling on the field. Both agree that more informal and intermittent approaches work best for field staff. Other authors discuss the use of counseling in general. For example, White (1989) emphasizes pastoral counseling for stress, Powell (1992) focuses on common missionary struggles (guilt, depression, grief, anger, crises), and Dennett (1990) explores the role of counseling for four types of personnel (candidates, first-termers, leaders, and retired missionaries). The importance of first-term counseling is often highlighted (e.g., Jones, 1993), when the realities of culture shock and personal adjustment can plague the new arrivals. Williams (1992) describes a helpful model for mutual care and peer counseling between missionaries.

One of the most fascinating studies to date was done by Robert Lugar (1995). This study surveyed 55 agencies to determine the relationship between the availability of counseling services and agency attrition during a five-year period (1988–1992). Counseling was defined broadly to also include things like debriefing and conducting a needs assessment. Roughly half of the agencies surveyed required their personnel to have regular contact with a counselor, and the other half did not. Lugar found that the average attrition rate for agencies requiring regular contact with a counselor was less than half that of the other agencies (8% over the five-year period).

Journaling

One form of counseling that can be useful for field staff—especially those with limited access to counselors—is journaling. Journaling involves taking time to reflect upon and write down your thoughts and feelings, usually in a special book and at least once a week. When done diligently, this exercise becomes a meaningful way to access your inner world, talk to God, and grow as a person. Journal writing can take some creative twists too. Husbands and wives can journal individually and then share their entries with each other. You can draw a picture representing a current life experience or a picture of a special place in your inner or outer world. Another option is writing a dialogue between your "critical" self and your "accepting" self or even working on some of your "bruises" from earlier years. For more suggestions on journaling, see *Tracks in the Sand* by Vance and Beth Shepperson (1992).

The consensus in the counseling literature is clear: Counseling, whether it is done by peers, professionals, or through journaling, can be a vital means of support and growth. Counseling is too good for only the sick; the healthy need it too!

Member Care Teams

Another field care strategy is the use of short-term member care teams. These teams can include pastors, counselors, experienced missionaries, physicians, and psychologists who provide services to missionary personnel in their field settings or at mission gatherings/conferences. These teams seem to work best when they are invited to a field, rather than inviting themselves, and when they are interested in developing longer-term relationships with field personnel, rather than one-time events. The time is ripe for forming and using such teams! Following is a description of the member care teams (MECA teams) that we in Member Care Associates organize. I offer this overview as a possible set of guidelines for other teams to consider.

Participation

Involvement on our teams is by invitation, based on an informal interview and two recommendations. In addition to their specialized skills, participants must be in good health, emotionally balanced, spiritually mature, flexible, capable of working in new situations and under pressure at times, able to work on a small team, and sensitive to cross-cultural differences. Certain graduate students may also be invited to participate.

Accountability

A team leader is designated for each MECA team. This person functions as the main supervisor and usually provides most of the orientation to the group/area where the team is going, including any basic cultural do's and don'ts. The team meets each day for mutual consultation, some training, and prayer. Team debriefing occurs at the end of the time together.

Logistics

Team members often pay for their own transportation. Lodging is usually provided by the group receiving services. Team members are cautioned about bringing any "sensitive" material with them into "restricted access" areas, and they frequently courier requested items. They usually enter into the host country as tourists, staying for only a short visit. Team members technically work as volunteers, which means that they do not solicit or receive funds for their services while temporarily residing in the host country. Honorariums may sometimes be offered and accepted.

Coverage for malpractice insurance, if desired, is the responsibility of the individual.

Preparation for Departing And Returning

We request team members to find at least five friends who will diligently pray for them. Some also ask a few of their friends or church to help cover part of the expenses. Team members will read up on the area where they are going, as well as the agencies with which they will be working. We encourage them to learn a few important phrases in the local language, travel light, bring a few "creature comforts," and be aware of health risks, the need for vaccinations, and additional health insurance. Simply describing themselves as tourists is the easiest thing to do when entering, visiting, and leaving the country.

The week before and after a MECA team can be especially hectic, so members have to anticipate this and plan to pace themselves. We suggest that they write down some of their expectations, realistically appraise the impact of jet lag on their ministry, take a break after the ministry time, and find a confidant with whom to do some additional debriefing after the trip. Readjustment can be a challenge—even after brief service overseas.

Some Ethical Notes

Our policy is that all material discussed with workers is confidential. The exception is when there is a clear danger to self and others, or child/elder abuse. Any personal struggle which significantly jeopardizes the functioning of the client, the client's agency, or the client's team is considered to be an issue bigger than the professional relationship. Hence it may have to be reported to a leader in the organization, preferably by the client and possibly in the presence of the MECA member (e.g., embezzlement of funds, moral failure, major depression, abusive leadership, serious marital problems). This confidentiality policy is clarified in advance with the agency and the missionary client.

Competency in one's home country and work setting does not necessarily generalize to cross-cultural situations. Team members must be aware of their limits and must endeavor to be as much learners as they are service providers. Team members are usually called on to provide services both informally (over a meal, while going for a walk together) and more formally (in doing a workshop, using a counseling office). This makes role flexibility very important indeed.

We caution team members about stirring up or trying to deal with long-term concerns ("bruised" backgrounds, serious character issues) within the short-term parameters. As is true of brief therapy, team members try to identify one or two problem areas, define them in manageable terms, stay focused, be supportive, cultivate cooperation, be pragmatic, and not be too concerned about coming up with the "right" answers. Missionaries really appreciate encouragement, a listening/objective ear, spiritual input, and specific advice upon request.

FUTURE DIRECTIONS FOR MEMBER CARE: PACTS

The current momentum in member care is most encouraging. We in the missions community understand the importance of developing both cross-cultural competence and godly character in our people. And we are seeing the link between staff care and staff longevity. Enough with "Kamikaze Christianity"! Yet there must be a direction for this momentum if member care is to stay on track—on the longer road—and make a sustainable mark on world missions and missionary longevity.

I believe that this direction must involve a significant shift in the way that Christian resources—including member care resources—are being developed and deployed in missions, so that every person and every generation has a valid opportunity to hear and respond to the gospel. I say this in light of the fact that only about 10% of the world's mission force is serving among the world's 2.5 billion who make up the world's least evangelized people groups. It is a sad state of affairs to note, for example, that less than 2% of the missions force is working among the 1 billion Muslims of the earth. We in the missions and member care community are thus impelled to seek out new directions which will strategically prioritize member care services on behalf of those who are serving among the least evangelized.

Here are five such directions—easily remembered by the acronym PACTS—which will help us work together and further develop member care:
+ Pioneering
+ Affiliations
+ Continuing growth/care
+ Training
+ Special projects

Please keep in mind that PACTS are as much about forming supportive, trusting friendships with member care colleagues as they are about accomplishing strategic member care projects.

They thus involve going after close relationships, along with cooperative tasks.

Pioneering

It's time to break out of some Western member care bubbles. Let's go to places with relatively few member care resources. Prioritize those working among the least evangelized peoples. Innovate! Help set up permanent member care teams, for instance, in Central Asia, India, or Africa. Sure, it would be challenging, but why not? Or how about helping to connect culturally sensitive member care workers with the many interagency partnerships ministering within the 10/40 window (Butler, 1994)?

Affiliations

Bring together member care workers for mutual projects, mutual support, and mutual consultation. Purposefully affiliate! Set up regional or organizational networks of caregivers. Form short-term teams with members from different agencies or service groups. Encourage their members to track with mission personnel over time. In addition, convene and attend strategic consultations of mission personnel and/or member care workers to discuss ways to further coordinate services. These can be small and informal or larger and more formal. Prioritize these for regions of the world where coordination is still greatly needed. Finally, consider forming a member care task force as part of one of the larger mission groups, like WEF's Missions Commission or the AD2000 Movement.

Continuing Growth/Care

Member care is an interdisciplinary field, requiring lots of work to keep on top of new developments and to maintain one's skills. Prioritize time to read, attend seminars, and upgrade. It would be helpful for some to link with a few of the secular umbrella agencies such as the World Health Organization and the International Union of Psychological Science as a way to network and stay on top of current trends (see Pawlik & Ydewalle, 1996). Also, member care can be a burnout profession. So we must maintain accountability with others, pace ourselves, find ways to "refuel" emotionally, seek God, and practice what we teach!

Training

Utilize missionaries and member care workers alike as resources via workshops at conferences. Include member care tracks at major conferences. Teach member care courses, seminars, and modules at key graduate schools and seminaries, and not just within the USA, but also at places like the Bible colleges in Africa and India, the missionary training centers in Latin America, or the European schools of Christian psychology, such as IGNIS in Germany and the Moscow School of Christian Psychology in Russia. The following areas of training are especially important: peer counseling, marriage enrichment, family life, team building, spiritual warfare, and crisis intervention. Further, help mission personnel from both the new and old sending countries to develop member care skills and programs which are culturally relevant. There could be opportunities to join with groups such as Youth With A Mission and Operation Mobilization, which offer counseling courses in different locations to train their missionaries

in helping skills, or the Operation Impact program at Azusa Pacific University in the USA, which provides various field-based courses in the area of leadership development.

Special Projects

Based on strategic needs and common interests, pursue some short-term and longer-term projects together. Some examples include maintaining and updating a global referral base of member care organizations, doing joint research/articles, and setting up an e-mail forum/bulletin board for member care. But let us also pursue some projects together where we get a bit "dirty"—and take some risks. A cutting-edge example would be to provide supportive services such as critical incident debriefing, counseling, or reconciliation seminars to people who have been traumatized by war and natural disasters. In short: be proactive; don't reinvent the wheel; pursue God's heart for the unreached peoples; and prioritize time to work on strategic, doable, field-related projects.

REFERENCES

Augsburger, D. (1992). *Conflict mediation across cultures: Pathways and patterns.* Louisville, KY: Westminster/John Knox Press.

Austin, B. (1992). Supporting missions through pastoral care. In K. O'Donnell (Ed.), *Missionary care: Counting the cost for world evangelization* (pp. 60-68). Pasadena, CA: William Carey Library.

Butler, P. (1994). Kingdom partnerships in the '90s: Is there a new way forward? In W. D. Taylor (Ed.), *Kingdom partnerships for synergy in missions* (pp. 9-30). Pasadena, CA: William Carey Library.

Cerny, L., & Smith, D. (1995). Short-term counseling on the frontiers: A case study. *International Journal of Frontier Missions,* **12**, 189-194.

Cho, Y., & Greenlee, D. (1995). Avoiding pitfalls on multinational teams. *International Journal of Frontier Missions*, **12**, 179-183.

Dennett, J. (1990). Let my people grow: Counseling as a way to maturity in Christ. *Evangelical Missions Quarterly*, **26**, 146-152.

Dodds, L., Dodds, L., & Kuitems, L. (1993). *A developmental model of disease progression: Levels of prevention and intervention and interacting dimensions of health and life process.* Paper presented at the 1993 Mental Health and Missions Conference, Angola, IN. (Available from Heartstreams Resources, 101 Herman Lee Circle, Liverpool, PA 17045, USA)

Elmer, D. (1993). *Cross-cultural conflict: Building relationships for effective ministry.* Downers Grove, IL: InterVarsity Press.

Foyle, M. (1987). *Overcoming missionary stress.* Wheaton, IL: EMIS.

Gardner, L. (1987). A practical approach to transitions in missionary living. *Journal of Psychology and Theology*, **15**, 342-349.

Griener, L. (1972, July/August). Evolution and revolution as organizations grow. *Harvard Business Review*.

Interdev (1995). *Interdev annual report.* (Available from P.O. Box 47, Ashford, England TW15 2LX)

Jones, G., & Jones, R. (1995). *Teamwork.* London, UK: Scripture Union.

Jones, M. (1993). First year counseling: A key ingredient to success. *Evangelical Missions Quarterly*, **29**, 294-298.

Lankester, T. (1995). *Good health, good travel.* London, UK: Hodder & Stoughton.

Lindquist, B. (1995). How to make the most of short-term missionary counseling. *Evangelical Missions Quarterly*, **31**, 312-316.

Livingstone, G. (1993). *Planting churches in Muslim cities: A team approach.* Grand Rapids, MI: Baker Book House.

Love, R. (1996). Four stages of team development. *Evangelical Missions Quarterly*, **32**, 312-316.

Lugar, R. (1995). *The efficacy of agency sponsored professional counseling as a deterrent to the attrition of career missionary personnel.* Unpublished doctoral dissertation, American Center for Religion/Society Studies, Oxford Graduate School, Oxford, England.

MacIntyre, T. (1995). A glance will tell you and a dream confirm. In C. Reilly & R. Reilly (Eds.), *A gift of Irish wisdom* (p. 18). New York, NY: Hearst Books. (Original work published 1992)

Mackin, S. (1992). Multinational teams. In K. O'Donnell (Ed.), *Missionary care: Counting the cost for world evangelization* (pp. 155-162). Pasadena, CA: William Carey Library.

O'Donnell, K. (1987). Developmental tasks in the life cycle of mission families. *Journal of Psychology and Theology*, **15**, 281-290.

O'Donnell, K. (Ed.). (1992a). *Missionary care: Counting the cost for world evangelization.* Pasadena, CA: William Carey Library.

O'Donnell, K. (1992b). Tools for team viability. In K. O'Donnell (Ed.), *Missionary care: Counting the cost for world evangelization* (pp. 184-201). Pasadena, CA: William Carey Library.

O'Donnell, K. (1997). Member care in missions: Global perspectives and future directions. *Journal of Psychology and Theology*, **25**, 143-154.

O'Donnell, K., & O'Donnell, M. (Eds.). (1988). *Helping missionaries grow: Readings in mental health and missions.* Pasadena, CA: William Carey Library.

O'Donnell, K., & O'Donnell, M. (1992). Understanding and managing stress. In K. O'Donnell (Ed.), *Missionary care: Counting the cost for world evangelization* (pp. 110-122). Pasadena, CA: William Carey Library.

O'Donnell, K., & O'Donnell, M. (1995). Foxes, giants, and wolves. *International Journal of Frontier Missions*, **12**, 185-188.

Pawlik, K., & Ydewalle, G. (1996). Psychology and the global commons: Perspectives of international psychology. *American Psychologist*, **51**, 488-495.

Powell, J. (1992). Short term missionary counseling. In K. O'Donnell (Ed.), *Missionary care: Counting the cost for world evangelization* (pp. 121-135). Pasadena, CA: William Carey Library.

Shepperson, V., & Shepperson, B. (1992). *Tracks in the sand: An interactive workbook*. Nashville, TN: Thomas Nelson Publishers.

White, G. (1989). Pastoral counseling: The key to a healthy missions force. *Evangelical Missions Quarterly*, **25**, 304-309.

Williams, K. (1992). A model for mutual care in missions. In K. O'Donnell (Ed.), *Missionary care: Counting the cost for world evangelization* (pp. 46-59). Pasadena, CA: William Carey Library.

Kelly O'Donnell *is a psychologist working as part of Youth With A Mission and Member Care Associates, an interagency member care group based in England. Together with his wife, Michele, he edited* **Helping Missionaries Grow** *(1988) and* **Missionary Care** *(1992). O'Donnell ministers in the areas of team building, counseling, family life, member care training, and program consultation, and he actively promotes member care in frontier missions.*

23

What About the Missionary Kids and Attrition?

David Pollock

Don't we have the right to take a believing wife along with us, as do the other apostles and the Lord's brothers and Cephas?" (1 Cor. 9:5). Obviously, from the first generation of missionaries, the issue of marriage and family was a matter of discussion and perhaps turmoil. In 1 Corinthians 7 and 9, Paul addresses the issue, but we are often frustrated by the lack of a clear conclusion. Should servants of God marry? Should they make decisions that impose sacrifice on others in the family? What of the children? In these 2,000 years of ministry and missions, marriage and family has been an issue of concern and a cause of tension.

According to the 1996 Christian Research report on mission attrition (part of the larger study by the WEF Missions Commission), marriage and family issues are the second major reason for preventable loss of missionary personnel, accounting for 13% of overall attrition. In the old sending countries researched (Australia, Denmark, Germany, UK, Canada, and USA), 17% of attrition was due to this factor. The new sending nations (Brazil, Costa Rica, Ghana, Nigeria, India, Korea, Philip-

pines, and Singapore) reported that 9% of their losses were related to marriage and family. It is important to note that personnel problems and even health problems may be related to family and children. The issues of marriage and family are serious ones that deserve careful, biblical consideration.

PERSPECTIVE

Paul addresses this very practical issue from a very basic point of view. In the middle of his discussion about singleness, marriage, and family responsibility, he says, "Keeping God's commands is what counts" (1 Cor. 7:19). Samuel told Saul, "To obey is better than sacrifice" (1 Sam. 15:22). There is no question that ministry often results in sacrifice. Jesus acknowledged this and indicated that the Father would restore and reward in multiples (Mark 10:29-30). However, the position of Scripture is that obedience to Jehovah is the key issue, not sacrifice to or for Him.

John 13–17 paints the proper picture of life and ministry for the Christian. Jesus demonstrated an obedient servanthood in many ways, including the washing of His disciples' feet. When He was done, He said, "Do you understand what I have done for you?... You call me 'Teacher' and 'Lord,' and rightly so, for that is what I am. Now that I, your Lord and Teacher, have washed your feet, you also should wash one another's feet. I have set you an example that you should do as I have done for you. I tell you the truth, no servant is greater than his master, nor is a messenger greater than the one who sent him. Now that you know these things, you will be blessed if you do them" (John 13:12-17).

After Jesus had eaten with the disciples, identified the bread and wine as symbols of His coming sacrifice, and dismissed the betrayer, He gave a new and key commandment, "Love one another," and He pronounced that love is the primary identifying mark of our being His disciples (John 13:34-35). Love is, in fact, the compelling evidence to the world that "God was reconciling the world to Himself in Christ" (2 Cor. 5:19) and that "if anyone is in Christ, he is a new creation" (2 Cor. 5:17), alive and producing the fruit of the Spirit of God (Gal. 5:22-23). The command to love is at the heart of mission strategy—by this "all men will know that you are My disciples" (John 13:35)—and it is the validation of a theology of care. The profile of the church in Acts 2:42-47 and the content of the Epistles bear this out. To seal the importance of the commandment, Jesus said, "If you love Me, you will obey what I command" (John 14:15) and, "My command is this: Love each other as I have loved you" (John 15:12).

Paul in Ephesians 5:15–6:9 and Colossians 3:15-21 is very specific in applying the principle of love to the family. Jesus in Matthew 18:1-14 is very clear in His concern for children and very strong in His condemnation of any who disregard the well-being of these little ones. The weight of Scripture forces us to recognize that the *presence* of missionary kids (MKs), whether a cause of attrition or not, is reason for specific concern for them. It is also important to recognize that *sometimes* leaving the mission field because of the needs of a family or of an individual child may be appropriate, in order to keep from making a sacrifice that is not in obedience to God. We must remember that it was Molech who required child sacrifice, not Jehovah. Proper care of one's children is not a challenge to obedience to God's call; it *is* obedience.

Unfortunately, the good missionary who is committed to being a good parent may be a loss to ministry due to the failure in the missions community of leaders, teachers, caregivers, home church pastors, and missions supporters to give the assistance needed. If the missionary *parent* is to be free to accomplish the purpose for going to the field, then all of us must take seriously the care and support of missionary children. The very important first step is for all of us to reject the extremes of "family vs. ministry" and "ministry vs. family." The family sacrificed for ministry is not consistent with the direction of Scripture. On the other hand, ministry that is rejected and sacrificed because of a "worshiping" of the family and an unwillingness to be inconvenienced is not acceptable either. **Family in ministry** is a concept that recognizes that there may be some things that can or can't be done at certain times in the ministry or for the family. It also recognizes that there are advantages to both family and ministry over the course of a lifetime.

Family in ministry is a useful frame of reference in keeping a proper balance in life and in addressing the issue of attrition. It recognizes that each member of the family is important as a subject of care, and each is also important as a caregiver and communicator of the good news. Family in ministry acknowledges that as a unit the family communicates, through model and ministry, the message that God was in Christ reconciling the world to Himself.

Our basic understanding of MK care must include an awareness that each child is a growing, developing creation of God who is going somewhere to be a mature someone. Research done on North American adult MKs revealed that 17.5% returned to be career missionaries (Duvall, 1993). Such *potential* must not be ignored. Cultivating these young people who will be better equipped for cross-cultural ministry than their parents were is part of the concept of family in ministry. Some MKs will return as missionaries, while others will carry their skills into government, business, and education, where their testimony will reach people untouched by normal mission endeavors. Proper care of MKs will not only help reduce attrition now, but will also produce greater stability in cross-cultural ministry in the future.

CONCERNS

Several years ago, I was conducting a seminar on third-culture kids (TCKs)[1] at the United Nations School in New York City. I asked why everyone had come to this voluntary seminar. All of the non-North Americans agreed that they wanted to find out how to keep their children from becoming American. I told them that I had some good news and some bad news. First the bad news: When adults decide to move from their home country and culture to a new country, they make the decision that their children will be strongly influenced by another culture and will not be the same as they would have been had they remained in Seoul, Quito, Accra, Paris, or Chicago. The children will probably never feel totally at home anywhere, but they may have many places and cultures where they can have relationships with people of other cultures and function with reasonable comfort. The good news is that the life of the young person is not ruined because of the move, and the new cultural setting may be a great advantage.

This view, however, does not and should not mask the legitimate concerns for MKs. It is important to recognize that the life of this perfectly normal person who is an MK is influenced by two extraordinary factors. First, the MK lives a very mobile life in the very mobile international community. People are always coming and going, and life is filled with separations, good-byes, and grief. The instability and grief need to be recognized and given proper support, comfort, and care.

Second, the MK experiences a variety of intercultural influences. No longer are perspectives, values, and behaviors

---

1. A third-culture kid is an individual who has spent a significant part of the developmental years (ages 0–18) in a culture other than that of the parents. A TCK/MK cannot be the same person he or she would have been apart from the cultural setting.

determined by a single cultural group. The host culture or cultures, the international school classroom, the expatriate community, and the intercultural mission team all make an impact on the development of the MK. Viewpoints, values, and behavior that would have been almost automatic to the monocultural missionary parent are questioned by the young person in the intercultural setting.

Parents who do not understand this fact are very concerned. They ask: Where will our children go after we have lived and ministered in this country far from our own? Whom will they marry? Where will our grandchildren grow up? Will our children even be able to fit into our country of passport? What will our parents, brothers, sisters, people in our church, and people in the community think about our children? Will they let them fit back into our culture? Can they fit? Will they want to fit?

The young person asks many questions as well. Where do I fit? Where do I want to fit? How can I please my parents and still be the person I have become? Who am I? Where am I from? Am I normal? Will I ever feel at home anywhere? These are questions that reflect the fact that TCKs have a sense of belonging everywhere and nowhere at the same time. The questions of identity— Where do I belong? To whom do I belong?—are part of the experience of most TCKs/MKs.

Returning to one's culture of origin is often a much greater issue than being a global nomad. The more clearly defined a culture may be, the greater the challenge to the person returning. Rules for behavior, guidelines for relationships according to age, gender, and social po-sition, and ways of doing things are especially confusing to young people who have not lived in their home cultures for a significant part of their developing years. MKs who have grown up in another part of the world with people of other cultures may not know the rules and expectations of their own culture and may not understand why it is important to care about those rules.

Another concern of parents is the extent of identity their child or children may have with the culture or cultures they have known as they grew. Children in the same family may respond in different ways to the surroundings. Figure 23-1 gives some idea of four basic levels of enculturization that may be experienced by MKs.

1. The Mirror. Sometimes a strong desire or ability allows an MK who looks like the majority of people in the host culture quickly and easily to develop thought, attitudes, and behavior like the people in the host culture. Such a compatibility allows the individual to fit in so well that he or she may never want to leave. The host culture becomes "home." An example might be a Korean young person growing up in Japan.

2. The Hidden Immigrant. Looking like the majority of people in a culture does not guarantee that an MK will think or behave like them. Because of the physical similarity, the people in the community may expect the individual to be one of them, but thoughts and values may be very different, even if the person copies the behavior. Upon returning to the passport culture (home for mother and father), the young person may look like everyone else in the community, but the deeper part of the person belongs somewhere else. An example of this

LOOK

		LIKE	DIFFERENT
THINK	**LIKE**	Look Like Think Like **MIRROR**	Look Different Think Like **ADOPTED**
	DIFFERENT	Look Like Think Different **HIDDEN IMMIGRANT**	Look Different Think Different **FOREIGNER**

Figure 23-1. Four Levels of Enculturization

situation might be a Ghanaian young person growing up in Kenya.

3. The Adopted One. This young person may be very visible in a crowd because his or her appearance is strikingly different from the majority of the people, but education, friendships, and the comfort of the culture may produce a person who thinks and acts like those from the host culture. A friend of mine born in Nigeria spent part of her childhood and youth in Canada as her parents were completing their education. She quickly adopted a deeply Canadian identity in every way except appearance. In her secondary school days, she was returned to Nigeria, but there she was a "hidden immigrant." Although she looked like others in her home culture, she thought very differently from them.

4. The Foreigner. For a variety of reasons, an MK or other TCK may think and act very differently from those in the surrounding culture. Not looking like the people in that culture may only be part of the reason for being a permanent foreigner. A young man from Ecuador living in Sweden may fit this category very well if he holds tightly to his South American identity.

Parents are often confused by the differences that they see among their own children. Not all people respond or react in the same way to the influences around them. Parents must realize that every child should be treated as an individual. The child who adjusts quickly upon return to the passport country may be praised and deeply appreciated by the people at home, including the parents. The child who adjusts slowly, who is reluctant to adopt the ways of the parents' home, or who is rebellious, especially when pressured to conform, often is the object of anger and rejection.

INSIGHTS INTO REARING MKs/TCKs

There are no formulas for rearing children in any situation and certainly not for rearing MKs. The personality differences alone are reason enough for the variety of responses to being reared outside the passport culture. Added to these differences are the variables of influences from teachers, friends, caregivers, and the associates of one's parents. The stage in the life of the young person's development and the intensity of certain experiences are other variables. Parenting is an art, not a science. There are, however, some basic considerations that are important in rearing MKs/TCKs and in easing the struggles in adjusting.

1. Accept the MK Experience

It is important to accept the reality of the MK/TCK experience. Parents, mission agency administrators, pastors, relatives, educators, and employers need to be educated regarding the significance of growing up outside one's own culture. They must be helped to understand that MKs/TCKs are normal, but they are different from what they would have been had they grown up in the community of their roots. It is helpful if the people named above can not only accept the differences, but also respect and value them.

2. Defend the MK Experience

If mission leaders would recognize the MK life experience and be the defenders to the general population of this phenomenon, it could open the door to better adjustment and greater use of the experience by MKs. At the same time, leaders must assist families and educators in preparing MKs to return to their home cultures.

3. Provide for Educational Needs

Education is a critical concern. Being able to continue one's education in one's home country is important to most MKs. Educators should be provided who can prepare young people for required examinations to qualify for education and jobs in the home/passport country. It is also important to note that education systems are changing, and parents should keep themselves and their children aware of these changes. For example, in some countries with strict entrance examination requirements, the MK/TCK may enter a university as a foreign student. Accurate information and clear perceptions for MK education are important to both the child's and the parent's sense of well-being and security in remaining away from the educational opportunities of the home culture.

The old sending countries have had time to develop schools for young people who are from those countries. Some attempts are being made to provide courses of study that will prepare stu-

dents to take exams and enter universities in various countries. Such education does not work for everyone. On the basis of Jesus' command to love each other, it is important that we care about the lifelong impact of the MK experience on our young people. The new sending countries may need to develop schools of their own, such as the Korean school in Manila. In some cases, an option is to provide a national staff of teachers to work with a certain nationality of students within a larger school. Tutors for individuals or small groups may be suitable for some.

4. Speak the Mother Tongue

It is extremely important for a child's mother language to be taught and used. Every person deserves to have a language in which he or she can express the deepest thoughts of the heart. Parents should use their mother language in the home from a child's earliest days. If parents are from different language backgrounds, each parent should use his or her language with the children so they learn to express themselves at the deepest levels of the heart and are able to communicate with grandparents and other relatives in each parent's home country. This gives freedom to the young people to choose where they will work and continue their own lives.

5. Educate Those Back Home

It is very helpful if the leaders of the sponsoring body help educate the church family and relatives in the home country regarding the needs and unique situation of the mission family and MKs. Missionaries are not in a position to be able to do this educating on their own. Books, seminars, articles, videos, audiocassettes, and the Internet are all tools that must be developed to help in this process.

6. Maintain Cultural Identity

Parents can help their children to maintain healthy family and cultural identity. Celebration of one's own national and cultural holidays, reading history and literature in one's own language, and inviting others to learn about one's culture are aids in affirming a child's cultural identity. Talking about relatives, including stories from generations past, learning genealogies, watching videos and slides of the family and friends, and keeping photos of the same in sight in one's house underline the importance of the people at home and maintain familiarity with them. Co-workers can be of help by being open and interested in others' cultures, families, and experiences. Interest shows that we value each other.

The missions community is by definition intercultural. Scripture makes it plain that equality and unity exist in our relationship to Christ. Jesus prayed for our unity in John 17, that through our oneness in Him the world might know that Jesus Christ was sent by the Father. Our oneness is demonstrated in our respect for each other. Part of that respect is for the diversity that exists in our cultural backgrounds and in the culture of the people we serve. We show this respect by learning about each other and coming to new levels of understanding of our differences.

7. Develop Cultural Awareness

The MK/TCK should be encouraged to develop awareness and sensitivity to the cultures around him or her. Language learning, intercultural friendships, observing good cross-cultural models in parents, educators, and other missionaries, and having opportunity to use this awareness to serve are important. Such cross-cultural development is valuable in affirming the MK's identity and also in developing the attitudes, knowledge, and skills that will be used for a lifetime.

The family that fears separation and rejection from their extended family and friends becomes an attrition statistic. Concerns about children's enculturization and educational difficulties are strong reasons to terminate mission service. The inability of children to express themselves in their mother language motivates many to return to their passport countries to stay.

Parents who fear that their children's education will suffer because the children are outside their own culture need help in recognizing that education is greater than school. The exposure to a larger world and the learning of other languages and cultures are additions to education that parents could not have provided if the family had not moved away from the home territory. Such exposure is a gift given to one's child that keeps giving for a lifetime. It permits a child to burst from the "bubbles" that may otherwise entrap an MK, as Bill Taylor (1991) expressed so well. Parents need to recognize, however, that the pain of moving and the struggles of identity may not be seen as positive by the young person at the time of the experience.

THE SENDING BODY, CHURCH OR MISSION: A CAREGIVER

Once again, we need to remind ourselves of the biblical perspective that our relationship to other Christians proclaims Christ's relationship to us and ours to Him. The care of MKs is not the job of the parent or the educator alone. Church leaders and mission administrators must learn to see themselves as part of the caring community of world Christians (John 13:34-35). The love demonstrated by mission leadership is, in fact, key to accomplishing the task of world evangelism, not only in minimizing attrition and enhancing performance, but also in demonstrating who we are in Christ.

Central to the care for MKs and the mission family in general is the development of a **flow of care** in each agency and across agencies. This flow of care recognizes different needs at various places in the life of a missionary, a missionary family, and each MK. There are points of intervention where the right action can make a significant difference in the success and continuation of mission personnel and the well-being of the family.

Pre-Field

Before people leave their homeland or cultural community, careful screening should be conducted to be certain that no one and no family is sent out if problems exist that predict failure or harm. In addition, seminars, resource materials, and counseling must be done to prepare each member of the family to leave right, to develop appropriate expectations, and to be prepared to learn the many new things that await. Children as well as adults should be prepared for this experience. They should be helped to feel a part of the entire process.

On-Site

Orientation programs that are coordinated with the content and approach of the pre-field programs are important if the value of the pre-field preparation is to be maximized. Schools should be assisted in providing orientation for children. Parents and educators should meet to exchange information about each child's background and education and the expectations of and for the new school.

Adults should have mentors or "culture guides"—people who will answer their questions, give information about the new culture, and introduce them to others in the community. These mentors should be the best adjusted and most mature people in the community. **Children need this same help from the best influences.**

Counselors and pastoral caregivers should be an ongoing part of the experience of the mission family. There are times when lack of money is given as the reason for a lack of care support. Is it not significant that the largest percentage of a nation's military force is not the combat troops but those who support them? Should we not be as serious about our task?

Crisis care is necessary. Traumatic experiences are reported daily in the missions community. Trained and available personnel should be on-site to help in such situations, and **don't forget the children**. What may be a minor incident to a person with adult perspective may be terrifying to a six-year-old.

Anticipation of danger may be as serious to a nine-year-old as the actual event.

Transition

As families move from field assignment to home, they need help in preparing to leave, as well as assistance in returning to their "home" country.

Leaving right involves resolving problems with others and saying farewell to people, places, pets, and possessions in satisfying ways. Children need help in these partings by having parents, teachers, and leaders provide opportunities to leave right.

Entering right requires adults and children to have realistic and positive expectations for entering. The members of the missionary family have changed, and so have the people at home. All should be helped to prepare for this shock. Knowing what takes place in transition can help people be less surprised and more patient with themselves and with others.

Often the shock of feeling like an outsider to one's family begins a process of questioning the wisdom of returning to mission service, even if this was the plan. Fearing that they or their children will never fit into their home culture pushes some parents close to rejecting the idea of returning to a mission assignment. Proper care and sensitively given information on adjustment can help missionaries to withhold final decisions until they are more rational and less emotionally motivated.

Continuing Care

Mission agencies, mission-minded churches, and mission-concerned individuals can be of particular help to the mission family when a couple is faced with leaving older children in the home country as they return to their overseas post. Homes that are provided especially for MKs, where they can live while attending school or looking for employment or where they can visit on holidays, can be a source of great help and encouragement.

Retreats, school and mission reunions, and seminars for adult MKs enable these individuals to identify areas of need, solve problems, and think through the importance of their experience while growing up as it has affected their decisions about eduction, career, and a life partner. Adult MKs from the US who are missionaries themselves have indicated that the support and care given them as young adults had a significant influence on their lives (Duvall, 1993).

It is important to note for the sake of mission leaders, caregivers, MKs, and missionaries themselves that attrition for family reasons is not always to be avoided. There are times in the seasons of family life when it is wise and proper to return to the home country for the care of children and the meeting of family needs. In such cases, colleagues and leaders need to be both understanding and supportive. An appropriate retreat may allow an individual to be involved in missions both later and longer.

Each mission community must examine its unique family needs and research the specific reasons for attrition. When the needs and reasons are identified, wise leaders will respond and not excuse the lack of care.

"By this shall all men know...."

"Now that (we) know these things, (we) will be blessed if (we) do them."

REFERENCES

Duvall, N. S. (1993, April). Paper presented at the Seventh Annual Meeting of MK-CART/CORE, Colorado Springs, CO.

Taylor, W. D. (1991). Reflections of an MK: Breaking out of the tricky bubble. *Evangelical Missions Quarterly*, **27**, 140-144.

David Pollock *is the director of Interaction, Inc., an organization committed to the support and care of interculturally mobile families and young people. He conducts seminars, writes extensively, and speaks on behalf of the "third culture" community in a variety of settings. With his wife, he was a missionary in Kenya with the Africa Inland Mission. Earlier ministry included youth ministry under Youth for Christ and the Manhattan Christian Youth Service plus seven years as a pastor in New Jersey. Coincidental to his work with Interaction, Pollock has been Director of Intercultural Programs at Houghton College in New York and presently is an adjunct professor there. He serves as a WEF Missions Commission Associate.*

24

Interview of Six Church Pastors From Five Nations: Attrition Issues

William D. Taylor

Missionary attrition is not just the problem of the mission agency. Many of the participants who came to the consultation on missionary attrition at All Nations Christian College in UK were pastors. In the following interview, six men with a pastor's heart but from different continents and contexts express their concerns and opinions.

Bill Schmidt is a veteran pastor in the USA who is now using his shepherding gifts with SIM International. Oswaldo Prado and Antonio Carlos Nasser pastor in Brazil, but both also have larger missions responsibilities in the country. Don Mckenzie pastors in New Zealand, while José Cintrón serves an Hispanic congregation in the USA. Dawuda D. Maigari utilizes his pastoral gifts with the 1000+ missionaries of the Evangelical Missionary Society in Nigeria. All six of these pastors participated in the 1996 attrition workshop. We asked these men the following questions:

EXPERIENCE WITH MISSIONARY ATTRITION

Q **Bill Taylor:** From a pastor's perspective, what has been your experience with missionaries who have returned from the mission field early or who, after home leave, have not gone back to the mission field?

A **Bill Schmidt:** As I think about this, I am amazed at the experiences as they flood back to me. Few missionaries from the two churches I pastored in my 29 years were "washouts"—folks who could not make the grade. There were other reasons.

I recall one who returned because of moral failure. He had an affair with the keenest woman in his newly planted church. He was clearly the most successful and energetic church planter I have ever met, with perhaps a dozen solid churches in his wake. What I regret is that I saw the signs of the collapse of his marriage, but I did nothing, presuming that that was "just the kind of relationship they have." I knew I could never live as they did (no evidence of affection or romance—a business relationship), but I figured, "It must be working for them." If I had it to do over, I might try to probe, but I doubt that they would have opened up. These people were members of a major mission

313

with good supervision. We all read the signs but missed our cue on that one.

I recall visiting another missionary couple in their field of service and sensing that these folks had no supervision and weren't doing anything current. Everything we saw had to do either with what they used to do or with simply surviving in that place. There was no supervised, current work. I reported the situation to the church, suggesting withdrawal of support, but I was flatly rejected due to the family's personal relationships in the church. They remained on the field for the next 20 years. They should have become an attrition statistic but didn't.

I recall another family who were removed from a country due to political unrest and revolution. The crisis opened up and exacerbated personal weaknesses in the husband, including a strange subjective mysticism about the leading of the Lord and the need for daily motivation and consolation in order to perform. The family resisted all attempts to relocate them to enable them to work under appropriate supervision. Ultimately, they withdrew from ministry rather than submit.

One missionary took his life due to chronic headaches from a war injury and a metal plate. Another died from stress-induced heart attack in Japan. Another—coincidentally, another amazing evangelistic type, by my own observation and visits on the field—has come home to educate a mildly retarded daughter.

This last reason—the education of children—has been a persistent irritant to be dealt with, but in our past experience it hasn't been the major source of lost personnel that it seems to be today.

In response to the pressures in this area, I have been preaching the biblical exhortations to a single life and the wisdom of forgoing the pleasure of children for the sake of the gospel.

Oswaldo Prado: Recent missions history in Brazil has happily seen rapid growth. In spite of that, from a pastoral perspective there has been a great concern with those who return from the field emotionally broken and, worse, who do not want to return. The work of restoration has been difficult and often without positive results, because those who return are completely resistant to emotional treatment. This may have to do with anger towards the mission.

Antonio Nasser: I had one case of a missionary who had relationship problems because he didn't understand English well. For example, when the mission leader said, "I apologize," the missionary took it to mean that he was not sincerely sorry, since he did not ask for forgiveness ("Forgive me"). The missionary also had difficulty accepting the rules of the mission in terms of the "work fund." He could not understand how something that he bought with money he raised from his donors should belong to the mission and should be available for use by other missionaries. We asked this couple to stay two years in Brazil before returning to the field in order to resolve these difficulties.

Another case was that of a woman who went out without resolving some emotional problems. The pastor of her church asked me as the mission leader to have her return to Brazil. He said that she had had an emotional homosexual relationship before being sent as a missionary. I asked her to come back to deal with this issue, and thankfully, she was later able to return to the field with everything cleared up.

I believe the missionary's home church pastor should have full knowledge of the life and background of each prospective missionary. The pastor cannot send someone without a complete knowledge of the person's situation and preparation in relation to the particular mission field where the person is being sent. I also believe that we should not "force" the sending of a missionary by trying, for example, to gather money to complete the person's support, since God may be delaying the moment of departure through this lack of resources.

Missionaries who are going to work with foreigners should know beforehand what language is most used by the mission and should be fluent in that language. Preparation for missionary service should not be restricted to formal training but should continue in the local church before new missionaries are sent out. Within the local church, everything should be well resolved and firmed up. More serious problems should be under the supervision of the sending pastor. If something is wrong, it should be dealt with before departure for the mission assignment.

Dawuda D. Maigari: The lack of educational opportunities for children is one of the major reasons some of our missionaries have left the field. Also, the need of aging parents is an issue here in Nigeria. Some missionaries have left for pastoral ministries. Some, I suspect, have left because, from the start, they were not convinced of the Holy Spirit's calling on their life for mission service.

José Cintrón: Lack of missionary training before being sent and a further

lack of supervision and care on the field have contributed greatly to the return of some of our missionaries and their unwillingness to go back to the field. Right now, I'm dealing with a young woman who has returned from the field and is still working through her negative feelings about going back.

Don Mckenzie: I have been involved with a number of people who have come home prematurely or who have not returned overseas following home leave. At our church, we see training and preparation for overseas mission lying in three distinct areas: self-preparation, theological/missiological preparation, and preparation by the home church.

In our effort to prepare people adequately for service overseas, within the home church we have erred at times by being over-protective. When the trainee fell apart, there was always someone there to scrape him off the carpet. This cushioning has not prepared some people for the rigors of service overseas, where the support structures may be nowhere near as great. In other words, if not done wisely, laudable efforts to train, prepare, and care can set people up for failure. There is a thin line between being over-protective and providing adequate pastoral care.

Another area in which we have been weak is neglecting the wife in the partnership. We have been very good at preparing the husband by providing him with opportunities for practical experience and subsequent evaluation. However, the wife has often been neglected and has been the cause of the premature return of some couples and families.

We also feel that unhealthy emphasis on the needs of children has come into play—fear of letting go of the children, over-protectiveness, paranoia about the children's needs. This situation has forced mission leaders on the field to base mission strategy decisions on parents who may exhibit these unhealthy tendencies. As a screening measure, we have learnt to investigate fully when overseas mission trainees have opted to home school their children while in New Zealand. Is it because they are not free to take risks with their children?

A fourth area we've learnt to suspect is the absence of missiological preparation. We have statistical evidence that shows that those who have received a sound missiological component with their theological training are less likely to be an attrition statistic than those whose training is purely theological in content.

REASONS FOR ATTRITION

Q Taylor: The WEF Missions Commission task force on attrition has identified 26 reasons that people leave the field. In your opinion, what are the most common reasons that missionaries you have known "give up" or withdraw from cross-cultural ministry?

A Cintrón: Perhaps the most common reason we have seen is the lack of financial and prayer support by the local church. Spiritual immaturity of the missionary may be a close second. Interpersonal problems, both with fellow missionaries and with the national leaders with whom they are supposed to work, also contribute heavily to the return of missionaries.

Prado: Our survey showed that the principal reasons for attrition in Brazil are a lack of adequate training, a lack of commitment by the sending church, the emotional immaturity of the missionary, and the lack of mutual understanding with the sending agency.

Nasser: I believe that the question of inadequate financial support is a very strong reason for attrition. The lack of real commitment from the Brazilian church is terrible. There are many who return in less than a year because they do not receive promised support. Another strong reason is the relationship with field leadership. If the mission team is international, this problem is even greater. The lack of preparation for work in teams is a serious deficiency. I think many need to learn that obedience is necessary to be able to work as a team on the field and that humility is a necessary component of obedience!

Mckenzie: The most common reasons in my experience for missionary attrition would be little or no preparation of the wife for service overseas and an unwillingness or inability of the parents to take reasonable risks with their children.

Maigari: In my experience, there are a number of reasons which produce discouragement. These include no schooling for children or no proper health care, which may result in the death of children. Or missionaries may be discouraged with the missions office or home church and may feel it is better to leave than to continue in a pathetic situation. Some have felt the pressures from home: their district calling them to a pastorate or the needs of aging parents. Some have wanted to pursue higher education. Others were not really suitable for ministry in the first place due to their emotional and spiritual immaturity.

Schmidt: The major discussion regarding leaving the field or the ministry seems to revolve around educating children. What is proposed is for families to come home long enough to get the kids through high school and then return to the field. Unfortunately, some readjust to life in the USA and then never get it together again to return overseas.

I also suspect that many of the issues have to do with attitude and might fall into areas of candidacy, where they are chalked up to immaturity and allowable flaws. We seem to be allowing some people with personal idiosyncrasies to go to the field, assuming they will mature. They may endure and even survive on the field, but along the way they may create such a wake of stress and furor that the whole cause of Christ would be better served if they did return home. I am learning in my mature years to listen more to my intuitive inner senses and to make an issue of questionable areas as we screen candidates. I am no longer afraid to demand contingencies on candidates' acceptance.

WHAT THE CHURCH CAN DO

Q**Taylor:** What can the local church do to prevent attrition?

A**Cintrón:** The local church should prepare missionaries spiritually and emotionally to be able to deal with difficulties on the field. The church should also be very careful in its screening process. Missionary candidates should be proven by the church for both character and spiritual maturity.

Maigari: The church must have an open discussion of the cost of missionary service with whoever wants to serve. Once missionaries are on the field, the church should do what it can to main-

tain contact through writing letters, sending financial help, and even visiting when it is feasible. Church leadership should tell their candidates that they are part of a team, even though that team is not always in close physical proximity.

The local church should also be honest with the mission agency. If the church leaders do not feel that the applicant for mission service is suitable, they should say so, even though that kind of honesty may be painful. The local church should seek to give its members a variety of ministry experiences so that when one of the members applies for mission service, he or she is already proven in some kind of ministry in the church.

Schmidt: The church should be discerning and discriminating with potential candidates. A problem at home will most assuredly be a disaster on the field. A person not involved in the church at home will not be a fruitful missionary. A non-evangelist in the home church will never make disciples in the bush!

The church should also preach and practice the absolute, uncompromised, authoritative, and sovereign Lordship of Jesus Christ. I believe churches should support their own people to at least 35%, then pray, pray, and pray some more. They should leave the primary oversight and evaluation of the missionary and the field strategizing to an experienced mission agency with vision, seasoning, and resources.

Local churches need to realize that if they do their job and keen people are screened and sent to the field, it is highly likely they will in time rise to levels of administrative leadership.

When missionaries return home for the education of children and are given administrative positions, they ought not be cut off from their support, because these positions are necessary and the couple will often return to the field when their children's education is not an issue.

Nasser: The church leaders should be involved in serious counseling with each candidate. It should provide informal training in teamwork and ministry. The church should monitor personal growth, including candidates' response to authority, their interactions with believers from other congregations, their handling of money, their relationship to their spouse or those of the opposite sex, their skill at child rearing, etc.

Supporting each candidate's development is essential. The church should know the sending agency and should insist on regular reports. Church leadership should encourage short-term service. The church should know the gifts of each candidate. To try to work outside these guidelines is crazy!

Prado: The local church has often been left out in missions work. Here in Brazil, many agencies have sent missionaries who have no link with a local church. The local church should not give up the responsibility it has for its missionaries, and this preference should be made clear both to the agency and to the missionaries. Such a policy would prevent many premature returns.

The church should help candidates get adequate training. Such assistance would help counter the Latin American custom of sending missionaries to the field too quickly. As pastors, we should also help our people within the church to understand their commitment as the financial and spiritual rear guard for our missionaries. It would also help greatly to initiate a process of effective cooperation between the local church, the agency, and the candidate, with the goal of having a healthy integration of each one's function.

Mckenzie: We are working at a number of things in order to better prepare people for service overseas and, we hope, to minimize the risks of attrition.

First, we attempt to give opportunities for practical experiences for wives as well as husbands. In other words, where possible, we have a similar program of preparation at the home church level for both wife and husband. Next, trainees are urged to build something during their home church component of preparation, instead of simply being part of a maintenance program. They are encouraged to look for a need within the church's life, address that need, and then pass the leadership on by training another person prior to service overseas.

Where possible, we look for opportunities for service outside the church for a period of time—somewhere where trainees are on their own, having to make their own decisions and live with the consequences. Instead of just recommending that trainees find opportunities where their gifts can be used, we also urge them to attempt tasks where they will be stretched—with the possibility of failure. If they do fail, the experience provides an occasion to teach them how to handle failure.

We establish ways in which trainee families can be observed during the time of preparation, so that we can see how the husband and wife relate to each other and how the parents interact with the children. We attempt to be a lot more intentional in terms of evaluating the behavior of couples or families during the home church training component, not so much to use the results as a lever to determine whether a couple will serve overseas, but rather to determine any weaknesses and to work on those areas. We appoint a "buddy" (mature family) to be involved with each trainee/family during the home church training component.

We also use a recognized Christian counseling facility, again, not so much to weed out those who are unfit, but to strengthen the psychological and emotional well-being of trainees. The counseling figures as part of the preparation process. We encourage couples to attend marriage enrichment seminars.

We also promote the development of a special relationship with someone in the home church with whom the missionary can communicate freely. This person should be a good listener, who has the wisdom to know when to do nothing and when to take action. In my ministry as overseas missions pastor, I have this role, through correspondence, with a number of our people, and I have had to work hard at developing and maintaining that element of trust. Such correspondence is equivalent to a pastoral visit, not unlike that which takes place most days in a pastor's life.

Last but not least, it is important that missionaries be adequately financed. We endeavor to provide 80% to 90% of our missionaries' support needs. This means they do not have to spend months prior to departure drumming up funds. In addition, a larger portion

of their home leave can be spent in the home church.

HELPING "ATTRITS"

Q Taylor: What specific things should or can the local church do for those who "give up" or return early or who never go back to cross-cultural ministry?

A Nasser: Receive the missionaries as real people! They need attention, a human touch, acceptance, a hug. Wounds are healed by treating individuals with love, consideration, and mercy. Judgmental criticism has never helped to restore a wounded missionary. The church should attend to missionaries' basic needs, both physical and mental. Giving returned workers a good holiday can raise their spirits greatly. Counsel them lovingly. Reverse the steps that led them to leave the field, showing them how to return to the victory road. Respect them as workers. Don't demean them because they didn't meet expectations. With loving help, they can return to the ministry. The local church should also figure in the key role of mediator between the missionary and the agency to promote dialogue, if this has been broken.

Schmidt: The attitude a local church exhibits and communicates to a couple or individual is significant. If failure is the message, then it is unlikely the missionaries will return to the field. If a spirit of love and supportive understanding is conveyed, it is possible their missionary lives might be restored. In any event, no one can be judgmental if he has never been there. One missionary recently said to me, "My country of service is surely not my first choice of where to live and have my family. I can't say I even like the people. But I love Jesus a whole lot, and as long as that's where Jesus will have me, that's the place to be."

Maigari: The local church must keep in touch with, visit, and encourage returned missionaries to become involved in church planting in their home area. They should be encouraged not to lose sight of their mission ministries.

The church must exercise wisdom in each case. They may be called to discipline those who need it. They may need to encourage those who feel they have failed—to let them know that life is not over, so to speak. Returned missionaries are still the Lord's people, and He can use them no matter where they are or in what condition they find themselves.

Cintrón: The church's basic role in this case is to help returned missionaries enter into a process of inner healing and encourage them to greater preparation for the task.

Mckenzie: Among the most important things to do for those who return prematurely is to provide consistent pastoral care from someone with whom the returnees feel confident—someone who will allow the scum and pus to come out without a negative reaction. We also offer proven, recognized, professional Christian counseling when necessary. We provide assistance with all those things that would be provided for missionaries returning under normal circumstances—medical and tax matters, government benefits, job seeking, etc. Maximum resources are utilized to assist with the anticipated struggles that premature returnees face.

MISSION AGENCIES VS. CHURCHES

Q Taylor: How does the role of mission agencies differ from that of local churches in helping to keep missionaries serving effectively and happily in cross-cultural service?

A Maigari: I can answer this only in a general way. The mission agency is familiar with the specific cross-cultural circumstances of its missionaries and can provide specific help with equipping for the ministry, cross-cultural communication, dealing with culture shock and reverse culture shock, providing empathy (since it is likely they share the same experiences), and so on. The mission agency also handles field supervision, provides on-the-job training, helps in counseling and children's education, and gives prayer support. The local church prays and provides financial support for the missionary.

Cintrón: I believe that the mission agency looks after and supervises the work of the missionary, while the church is attentive to the physical, emotional, and spiritual well-being of the missionary.

Mckenzie: It seems to me the agency and home church ought to have a complementary working relationship. For example, the church is responsible for equipping and training; the agency ensures it has been done and is adequate. The church progressively evaluates; the agency makes the final evaluation. The church exercises all the pastoral care it can offer from the home end; the agency offers the on-site pastoral care that it alone can offer. The church debriefs and sets in place a program that ensures refreshment and restoration; the agency debriefs and relates with the church to ensure there is a balance between input from the agency and restoration and refreshment. The agency and church ought to be working together prior to the missionary's return so that a program is put in place that ensures adequate deputation for the agency and refreshment and restoration in the home church for the missionary.

Prado: There is still great confusion about the function of the local church and missionary agencies. Many functions have been duplicated. There is an urgent need to establish a forum of discussion with pastors and leaders of agencies so that these functions could be clarified. The local church is still, and always will be, the proving ground of the future missionary. The agency can never occupy the place of the local church. On the other hand, some of the agency's functions should be understood as supplementary to the local church.

Schmidt: The difference between the two might be likened to the military and civilian sectors of our society. Both may be at war with a common enemy. We never say, "The army is at war," but rather, "We are at war!" We are one country, one entity. The civilian sector provides the manpower, the resources, and even some watch care for the war. The civilian sector sends love, prayers, and concerned care packages. But Congress doesn't set up the strategy of the battles being fought. The war is fought by the army. Aunt Millie may make wonderful cookies and be a powerful prayer warrior, but she doesn't know warfare! Similarly in my view, the local church is joined in identity and partnership with mission agencies in a huge spiritual battle of unthinkable propor-

tions. The church best sends, prays for, and supports the warring missionary, but the mission is best equipped to wage the war. Two sectors of one entity. Neither can win it alone nor get along without the other. We are not in competition, but in partnership.

Nasser: I think mission agencies have a basic problem—they don't see missionaries from the same viewpoint as the sending church. I say this because missionaries are sent to the field with a few interviews and a lot of written materials. The relationships as Christians, human beings, and members of the congregation don't exist. The agency is the boss that covers their field work, but their father and mother are the local church. The problem gets much worse when missionaries abandon their relationship with their local church in order to affiliate themselves with an agency. In the end, they may be left without either support system.

EQUIPPING IN THE CHURCH

Q **Taylor:** In what areas and ways can the local church equip/train missionaries that a formal missionary training school/program cannot do?

A **Nasser:** Life! To walk with a person is a privilege. Formal study doesn't always promote these relationships. Financial help. Spiritual growth—not all schools hold this as a priority. Opportunities given for ministry—to preach, teach, and lead prayer groups. The local church is the best place for these things. Formal training might provide these opportunities, but unlike the school, the church is not a community of people who are there to judge performance. The church is looking for solutions—wanting to hear from God, to learn how to live, etc. The local church provides pastoral care and companionship, as it (often) includes the worker's family, past relationships, the spouse or fiancee's family, friends, etc. This context reveals the true person much more than a few interviews by professionals.

Cintrón: The main strength of the church, in my view, is that it can help develop good, biblical character and can provide a platform for ministry experience.

Maigari: Hopefully, a person's involvement in a local church has been much more long-term and has provided many more opportunities for ministry over the course of time than that provided by a school, which may last only a few months or not much more than a couple of years. This is on-the-job type training. The local church gives people a chance to discover their gifts and calling. The church can teach them about servanthood-type leadership, while a school may not do as much. However, I think that formal missionary training programs are equally necessary, since churches may not have the personnel to effectively teach what is needed. As I see it, the local church and the mission agency have different roles to play, but each complements the other. One is not a substitute for the other.

Prado: As I have already said, the local church is an excellent lab (yes) for knowing and training a missionary. Academic development is always important, but it will be in the church that the missionary candidate will effectively give signs of spiritual and emotional maturity, be it in planting another church, leading a small family group, etc.

Schmidt: Years ago at our local church, we established a "missions support group" which met periodically to help us remain accountable to our sense of call and missions burden. We read books and discussed them, heard one another's testimonies of progress or discouragements, held international dinners, interviewed visiting missionaries, and generally hung together for mutual support. I have a better vision for the possibilities for such a group now than I did then.

I do not think the local assembly, however large and sophisticated, can manage the strategy of a field missionary in today's complex world. What we find in our mission is that missionaries who go out to the field directly without agency backing discover that they need the things an agency can provide. They then come to our offices for the language, government, civic, financial, computer technical, and network support they lack. They think they can eschew these things and thus avoid overhead costs, but in the trenches, they decide they need them after all and run to the agency that is in place.

Mckenzie: There are several ways in which a local church can equip and train for overseas ministry that a formal missionary training programme cannot do. First, the church can provide practical opportunities for trainees to use their giftings and gain practical experience. Such opportunities take prospective missionaries out of their comfort zone and force them to put into practice the theory learnt at theological college. Trainees are stretched in new ways and must learn how to handle failure.

Second, within practical ministry in the local church, life opportunities are present for evaluation so that weaknesses and strengths can be determined. As a consequence, trainees can work on the weak areas so that they become strong.

Third, there is also the process of building a support network following time away at formal college training. Relationship building that leads to effective communication and prayer support can go a long way to minimise attrition. This network of relationships is something that time in college training cannot facilitate, and it is very obviously absent in those who are sent by their home church straight from college into service overseas.

Fourth, I think there is a lot the home church can do to assist trainees in self-preparation *prior* to any college training programme. Talking to trainees about self-preparation, in addition to providing them with a brochure on the subject, can get them going and can set them on the path to self-motivation and acceptance of their responsibilities.

FINAL THOUGHT

Insight from pastors into attrition issues is tremendously valuable, and the diversity of responses offered in this composite interview reflects a wealth of wisdom and experience. These resources are coupled with a deep pastoral commitment to members of the flock who serve as distant cross-cultural servants of Jesus Christ. If all pastors shared these concerns with equal passion, many of our attrition problems would be reduced.

25

An International Guide For Member Care Resources

Kelly O'Donnell

Member care services are not just for those who are struggling. *Everyone needs them!*

The purpose of this resource guide is to provide you with a reference tool in case you or your group need member care services.[1] The listings are not exhaustive. Rather, they include a good sampling that includes some 125 service organizations (primarily Christian groups) around the globe, most of which are actively involved in the care and development of mission personnel.

In general, the main services emphasized are pastoral care, psychological consultation, training, counseling, and medical advice. These member care services are meant to complement the various ones that mission agencies are already providing their own people. They are an important part of the overall member care strategy needed to help stimulate personal growth and ministry effectiveness.

To use this guide, look up the geographic area in which you are interested and then read the brief description of the services that are offered under each listing. Contact one or more of the listings for more specific information about services (types, fee structure, languages spoken, background and experience, or referrals). Several agencies also provide services outside of the country where they are located via field visits, fax communication, and electronic mail. It could also be helpful to contact the national or regional association of Evangelical missions for possible referrals. Remember to talk openly with and interview the potential counselor or consultant in order to insure a good fit between your needs and the types of services that he/she offers.

Finding member care resources for missionaries in creative access countries is usually done discreetly and by word of mouth, rather than via a "public" listing like this one. Be sensitive of security issues as you communicate with people in these countries.

---

1. This guide updates the "Member Care Resource Guide" published in *Evangelical Missions Quarterly*, January 1996. Used by permission.

Note that there are several other excellent service agencies that were not included here, due to space limitations or lack of information. Further, certain geographic areas are deliberately not listed or are deemphasized for security reasons, as well as because few service agencies are actually located within these regions. Please contact the author if there are other organizations and people that you think should be included in future updates of this guide.

AFRICA

GHANA

Africa Christian Mission
Seth Anyomi, Director
Box 2632
Accra, Ghana
Tel: 233 21 775268; Fax: 233 21 775268
E-mail: skanyomi@ncs.com.gh

Reentry help, debriefing for crisis/trauma, medical evaluation/care, referrals.

KENYA

Tumaini Counseling Centre
Roger Brown and Richard Bagge, Directors
P.O. Box 21141
Nairobi, Kenya
Tel/Fax: 254 2 724725
E-mail: roger_brown@aimint.org

A joint ministry of AIM/Wycliffe, providing individual, marital, and family counseling, debriefing, psychiatric consultation, team building, seminars, and a reference library.

GEM Counselling Centre
Emy Gichinga, Director
P.O. Box 44128
Nairobi, Kenya
Tel: 254 2 729922

General counseling.

Oasis Counseling Centre
Gladys Mwiti, Director
P.O. Box 76117
Nairobi, Kenya
Tel: 254 2 715023; Fax: 254 2 721157

General counseling.

REPUBLIC OF SOUTH AFRICA
(see also referrals from IACC in USA)

Beullah
P.O. Box 290
Wellington 7655, RSA
Tel: 27 21 864 1083

Retreat center for adults; rest and renewal.

Rosebank Union Church Counseling Center
David and Lorain Wilkinson, Coordinators
33 Cradock Ave.
Rosebank, Johannesburg, RSA
Tel: 27 11 788 5133; Fax: 27 11 880 5517

General counseling, crisis intervention, referrals.

ASIA

HONG KONG

Dr. Agatha Chan
c/o 1104 East Point Centre
555 Hennessy Road
Causeway Bay, Hong Kong
Tel: 852 2834 9536; Fax: 852 2577 9751

Counseling, training, assessment services, PTSD work, referrals. Speaks English and Cantonese.

Hong Kong Assoc. of Christian Missions
Terina Khoo, Contact/Psychologist
340 Portland Street, Unit 2, 6F
Mongkok, Kowloon, Hong Kong
Tel: 852 2392 8223; Fax: 852 2787 4299

Assessment, counseling, field visits.

Rebecca Dnistran
2B Shrewsbury #54, Stanley Fort
160 Wong Ma Kok Road
Stanley, Hong Kong
Tel: 852 533 9545; Fax: 852 2899 0773

Psychologist and counselor; works in English with families, individuals, couples.

INDIA

India Missions Association
M. C. Mathew, Health Advisor
48 First Main Road
East Shenoynagar
Madras 600 030, India

Tel: 91 44 617596; Fax: 91 44 611859

Currently involved with a proposal to set up an interagency health care team for missionaries in India. Referrals.

Christian Medical Association of India
2, A-3 Local Shopping Centre
Janakpuri, New Delhi 110058, India

INDONESIA

Counseling Department
Reformed Seminary of Indonesia
Dr. Paul Gunadi, Chairman
Jakarta, Indonesia

Possible referral source.

JAPAN

Member Care Task Force
Japan Evangelical Mission Association
OCC Building, 2-1 Kanda
Surugadai Chiyoda Ku, 101, Japan
Tel: 81 03 3295 1949

An interagency group to further coordinate member care; referrals.

MALAYSIA

Calvary Life Ministries
Pam Guneratnam, Director
Kuala Lumpur, Malaysia

General counseling and referrals.

PHILIPPINES

Alliance Biblical Seminary
George Blake, Contact
Metro Manila, Philippines

Offers an M.A. in counseling psychology and counseling for the Christian community.

Eirene Psychological Services
Naomi Basilio, Contact
3 C.M. Recto Street
8000 Davao City, Philippines
Tel: 63 82 221 4702

Counseling, assessment, and seminars in English and Tagalog.

SIL, Ortigas Center
Leslie Christian, Contact
P.O. Box 12962
1600 Pasig, Metro Manila, Philippines

Tel: 63 2 631 3839; Fax: 63 2 632 1216
E-mail: leslie.christian@sil.org

Counselor serving the Asia area for SIL; referrals.

Youth With A Mission
Brenda Bosch, Contact
P.O. Box 196
Q-Plaza P.O.
1900 Cainta, Rizal
Metro Manila, Philippines
Tel: 63 26 46759; Fax: 63 26 467368
E-mail: 103626.316@compuserve.com

Consultation in personnel development, debriefing, staff orientation, and reentry; referrals.

SINGAPORE

Member Care Associates, Asia
Ron and Barbara Rohnert-Noll,
    Coordinators
c/o 1 Dorset Road
Singapore
Tel: 65 291 9744; Fax: 65 299 5040
E-mail: 73422.3170@compuserve.com

Counselor training for Asians, crisis intervention, field visits, psychological consultation, seminars, team building, counseling, referrals.

Singapore Centre for Evangelism and Missions
Andre De Winne, Director
P.O. Box 1052
Raffles City, Singapore 9117
Tel: 65 299 4377; Fax: 65 291 8919
E-mail: scem@swiftech.com.sg

A group that has set up member care training events for agencies and churches; referrals.

TOUCH Community Services
Dr. Eliza Lian-Ding (psychologist)
Esther Wong (marriage/family counselor)
66 East Coast Road
#07-00 GRTH Building
Singapore 1542
Tel: 65 440 3141; Fax: 65 346 7986

Counseling, couple and family therapy, treatment for abuse survivors, referrals.

SOUTH KOREA

In Korea, most sending agencies and training centres see missionary care as an important part of their ministry. However, when it comes to missionary care by professionals on a full-time basis, Korea, like many countries, is in the initial stages. To my knowledge at this time, only the Global Missionary Fellowship provides professional care through its MK department. It is hoped that more systematic and professional efforts for missionary care will be made in the near future as Korean agencies and those from other countries accumulate expertise in this area.

General Assembly, Presbyterian Church

Sung Sam Kang, Mission Board Director
1007-3 Dachi 3-Dong
Kangnam-Ku, Seoul, Korea
Tel: 82 2 564 5253; Fax: 82 2 563 7716
E-mail: p564@chollian.dacom.com.co.kr

Referrals for training, counseling.

Global Missionary Training Center (GMTC)

Dr. David Tai-Woong Lee, Director
231-188, Mok 2-Dong
Yang Chun-Ku
Seoul 158-052, Korea
Tel: 82 2 649 3197
E-mail: gmtc@chollian.dacom.co.kr

M.K. Ministries Department

Global Missionary Fellowship
Ms. Ruth Baek or
Ms. Soon-Nam Park, Contacts
Kang-Nam
P.O. Box 1667
Seoul 135-616, Korea
Tel: 82 2 569 0716; Fax: 82 2 557 2088

TAIWAN

Counseling Services Center

Steve Spinella, Director
Ta Yi Street, Lane 29 #18, 2f-1
Taichung 404, Taiwan
Tel: 88 64 236 6145
E-mail: Spinella@ms5.hinet.net

Counseling and consultation for Christian expatriates.

THAILAND

Juniper Tree

P.O. Box 1
Petchasem Rd.
Hua Hin 77110, Thailand
Tel: 66 32 511 139; Fax: 66 32 511 140

Facility for rest and restoration in a quiet seaside setting, three-hour bus ride south of Bangkok.

Raintree Community Services

Esther Wakeman, Contact
P.O. Box 251
Chiangmai 5000, Thailand
Tel: 66 53 306 317; Fax: 66 53 306 419

Therapy and counseling in English and Thai for the Thai and expatriate community.

AUSTRALASIA

AUSTRALIA

Christian Psychological Services

Cliff Powell, Director
P.O. Box 640
Mona Vale, NSW 2103, Australia
Tel: 61 2 9997 1565; Fax: 61 2 9979 6943

Individual, marital, and family therapy; psychological assessment; ministry and mission applications; workshops.

Christian Synergy Centre

Kath Donovan and Ruth Myors, Directors
204 Wommara Avenue
Belmont North, NSW 2280, Australia
Tel/Fax: 61 49 458484

Retreats and seminars for candidates, missionaries on furlough, and retirees; missionary and pastoral assessment and selection; psychological testing; counseling.

Christian Wholeness Counselling Centre

John Warlow, Director
28 Palmer Street
Greenslopes, QLD 4120, Australia
Tel: 61 7 3847 3622; Fax: 61 7 3394 4876

Counseling by professional counselors for individuals and families; seminars and workshops.

El Kanah Counselling
Loris Gillin, Director
39 Sackville Street
Kew, VIC 3101, Australia
Tel: 61 3 9817 5654

Therapy and consultation services for individual, child, marital, and family issues; psychological assessment.

Lesmurdie Baptist Church
Counselling and Support Services
Colin Taylor, Coordinator
Brady Road
Lesmurdie, Western Australia
Tel: 61 9 291 9866; Fax: 61 9 291 5018

Counseling, counseling training, seminars, support services; has links with rural retreat centers.

NEW ZEALAND

Dr. Lorna Jenkins
P.O. Box 89126
Porbay, Auckland, New Zealand
Tel/Fax: 64 9 473 0349
E-mail: becejay@deepthnk.kiwi.gen.nz

Referral for children's material and ministries.

The Work Trust
Don Smith, Contact
Box 144
Wellington, New Zealand
Tel: 64 4 496 2312; Fax: 64 4 496 2341
E-mail: don.smith@mohwn.synet.net.nz

Psychologist, consults with several mission boards, referral source, currently helping to develop a list of NZ member care providers.

EUROPE

AUSTRIA

Barnabas Zentrum
Steve and Rita Williams, Directors
Stall 35
A-9832 Stall/Moelltal, Austria
Tel/Fax: 43 4823 315
E-mail: 100611.1632@compuserve.com

Retreat counseling program for vocational Christian workers, located in the Southern Alps. Runs 10-day programs of intensive counseling for singles and couples in small groups. All sessions in English, with future plans to have them in German also.

Schloss Mittersill
Judith Davids, Contact
5730 Mittersill, Austria
Tel: 43 6562 4523; Fax: 43 6562 4523 50
E-mail: 72376.3715@compuserve.com

Spiritual direction, individual/couple counseling in a retreat setting. Single-session counseling for those who are part of a course or conference, crisis counseling and short-term residential counseling.

BELGIUM

Center for Pastoral Counseling
Jef De Vriese, Contact
Heverlee/Leuven (by Brussels), Belgium

Graduate training in pastoral counseling, counseling services, possible source for referrals.

CYPRUS

Member Care Team
Box 7177
Lykavitos, 1642 Nicosia, Cyprus
Tel: 357 2 368392; Fax: 357 2 368596
E-mail: 75402.3041@compuserve.com

An interagency group that helps coordinate member care and referrals for the Middle East region. Has an extensive compilation of written resources related to cross-cultural life and work in the Middle East.

Oasis
David and Joyce Huggett, Directors
P.O. Box 80
Polis Chrysoc, Cyprus
Tel: 357 6 322241
E-mail: 100610.427@compuserve.com

Small retreat center offering guided retreats for individuals, couples, and small groups.

DENMARK

Danish Missionary Council
Birger Nygaard, General Secretary
Skt. Lukas Vej 13
2900 Hellerup, Denmark
Tel: 45 3961 2777; Fax: 45 3940 1954
E-mail: dmr@inform-bbs.dk

Has an organized network of groups and individuals that provide member care services to Danish missionaries in Denmark, including pre-field training, psychiatric consultation, counseling, debriefing, and graduate level training. The following listings for Denmark are part of this network.

DUO
Anne Karin Lauritzen, Coordinator
Torholmsvej 59 9800
Hjorring, Denmark
Tel: 45 9892 5097

A group which provides seminars and consultation on third-culture children.

Institut for Diakoni og Sjaelesorg
Benny Birk Mortensen, Coordinator
Kolonien Filadelfia
4293 Dinalund, Denmark
Tel: 45 5826 4200; Fax: 45 5826 4239

Debriefing for missionaries, individual counseling, retreats.

Missionary Fellowship
Ove Bro Henriksen, Coordinator
Gyvelvej 22
761 Ejstrupholm, Denmark
Tel: 45 7577 2904

Organizes gatherings, seminars, and camps for former missionaries.

FRANCE

Communaute des Diaconnesses de Reuilly
10, rue Porte de Buc
78000 Versailles, France

An evangelical community which offers self-guided retreats and worship services.

Famille et Jeunesse en Action
Claude and Ginette Gaasch, Coordinators
4, rue des Pins
68610 Lautenbach, France
Tel: 33 03 89 740656; Fax: 33 03 89 740657

Provides help in the area of family life and family problems, marriage preparation, family camps, and marriage enrichment.

International Family/Church Growth Institute
Walt and Patricia Stuart, Directors
13b, rue Principale
68610 Lautenbach, France
Tel/Fax: 33 03 89 763159
E-mail: 102234.2563@compuserve.com

Short-term residential and outpatient counseling, counselor training with an emphasis on marriage and family, family camps, re-entry and other seminars. Services provided in French, English, and German. This is the European headquarters, with affiliated groups in:

Austria (see Barnabas Zentrum)

France (see Famille et Jeunesse en Action)

Germany
Jay Adams and Libby Stephens
Black Forest Academy
Postfach 1109
79396 Kandern, Germany
Tel: 49 7626 91610
E-mail: 100273.1530@compuserve.com

Hungary
Ursula Spooner
International Christian School
Hata ut. 68, 2049 Diosd
Budapest, Hungary
Tel/Fax: 36 23 381986
E-mail: 102452.2132@compuserve.com

Le Rucher, Youth With A Mission
Erik Spruyt, Director
2067 Route de Tutegny
01170 Cessy, France
Tel: 33 04 50 283379; Fax: 33 04 50 283385
E-mail: 100412.2520@compuserve.com

Debriefing, counselor training, member care seminars, some lodging for rest/renewal (near Geneva).

Philippe Thomas
156 rue de la Zorn
57820 Lutzelbourg (by Strasbourg), France
Tel: 33 03 87 253634; Fax: 33 03 87 253861

General counseling in French and English, with specialties in trauma and crises. Also offers short-term residential counseling May–September, for up to two people.

GERMANY

Deutsche Gesellschaft fuer Biblisch Therapeutische Seelsorge
Michael Dietrich, Chairman
Hackstr. 60
70190 Stuttgart, Germany
Tel: 49 711 285230; Fax: 49 711 285 2399

Modular training course in Biblical Counseling. Has network of trained counselors in Germany, along with some regional offices.

Also has a residential counseling and psychotherapy clinic:

Bethel-Christliche Fachklinik
Charlottenstr. 33
75323 Bad Wildbad, Germany
Tel: 49 7081 1520; Fax: 49 7081 152174

Hohe Mark Klinik
Arne Hoffman, Contact
Friedlanderstrasse 2
61440 Oberusel, Germany
Tel: 49 6171 2040; Fax: 49 6171 204440
E-mail: 100420.2124@compuserve.com

Christian psychiatric facility with residential and outpatient services. Services in German with counseling also available in Polish, Russian, French, Swedish, and Dutch. Treatment for trauma and mental disorders.

IGNIS
Werner May, Director
Kanzler-Sturtzel-Str. 2
97318 Kitzingen, Germany
Tel: 49 9321 13300; Fax: 49 9321 133041

Counseling center, Christian graduate program in psychology, referral source for counselors in the German-speaking world. Also runs an inpatient psychiatric facility.

Member Care Network
Friedhilde Stricker, Contact
Kirchberg 2
74243 Largenbrettach, Germany
Tel: 49 7946 915131; Fax: 49 7946 915130
E-mail: hartmut.stricker@t-online.de

A developing network and referral source of member care providers who offer services in the German-speaking world—Austria, Germany, and Switzerland.

Renew International Counseling Service
Rhonda Pruitt, Contact
Kurfursten Str. 133
10785 Berlin, Germany
Fax: 49 30 265 1426
E-mail: 104521.1106@compuserve.com

Professional counseling for the missions community; seminars in Christian counseling and cross-cultural adjustment.

HUNGARY
(see also IFCI listing in France)

SHARE
David Brooks, Director
2049 Diosd
Ifjusag u. 11, Hungary
Tel: 36 23 381 951; Fax: 36 23 381 553
E-mail: 100263.723@compuserve.com

Educational support, consultation, and resources for missionary families in Europe and the CIS. Sponsors conferences and workshops dealing with educational issues. Publishes an annual review of educational options in Europe and the CIS. Budapest regional manager is Nancy Elwood. Also has a regional office in Romania:

Jack Thompson
Str. Th. Sperantia 96, Sector 3
Bucharest, Romania
Tel/Fax: 40 1 684 6010
E-mail: 74073.460@compuserve.com

NETHERLANDS

CVPPP
D. H. van Noort, Contact
Dr. van Dalellan 42
3851 JB Ermelo, Netherlands
Tel: 31 417 50090

An association for Christian mental health professionals throughout The Netherlands. Publishes a journal and organizes gatherings on psychological/spiritual topics.

Instituut voor Transculturele en Missionaire Psychologie (ITMP)
Margrete Bac-Fahner and
Marjan van Nus, Coordinators
Postbus 542
6710 BM Ede, Netherlands
Tel: 31 30 243 7673 or 31 318 639750
Fax: 31 318 591015
E-mail: cfahner@chsede.nl

Professional psychological services for missionaries, including counseling, therapy, assessment, testing, and training.

NORWAY

Diakonhjemmets International Senter
Mirjam Bergh, Contact
Capralhaugen 81
1342 Jar, Norway
Tel: 47 22 451808; Fax: 47 22 451810
E-mail: bergh@dis.no

Counseling, psychological consultation, referrals.

Instituut for Sjelesorg
Jorgen Korsvik, Contact
Postboks 60
3371 Vikersund, Norway
Tel: 47 32 788155

Christian counseling center; referrals.

Drs. Bjorn and Solveig Lande
c/o Norwegian Santal Mission
Hoenskollen 7
1370 Asker, Norway
Tel: 47 66 782897; Fax: 47 66 784217

Psychiatric consultation.

ROMANIA
(see SHARE in Hungary)

RUSSIAN FEDERATION

Moscow Christian School of Psychology
Alexander Valentinovich, Director
13 Yaroslavskaya Street
Moscow 129366, Russia
Tel/Fax: 7 95 283 5150
E-mail: wmah@ipras.msk.su

Graduate training in psychology; referrals.
USA office:
    c/o Dr. Janice Strength
    Tel: 714 491 7837
    E-mail: jmstreng@ix.netcom.com

SPAIN

Grupo de Asesoramiento Interprofesional
Robert Biddulf, Contact
Enrique Larreta 9, Bajo
28036 Madrid, Spain
E-mail: 100422.3357@compuserve.com

Christian mental health group including a counselor (speaks English and Spanish), psychologist, and two psychiatrists; referrals.

Member Care Group
Apdo. 109
29620 Torremolinos
Malaga, Spain
Tel/Fax: 34 52 382233
E-mail: 73633.662@compuserve.com

An interagency task force that helps coordinate member care services and referrals for North Africa. Offers seminars, brief counseling, retreats, field visits.

SWITZERLAND

Centre Chretien de Psychologie
Daniel and Denise Bouvier, Directors
13 rue de la Colombiere
1260 Nyon, Switzerland
Tel: 41 22 361 6505; Fax: 41 22 361 6507

Counseling in French and English; referrals.

Development Associates International
Scott Morey, Contact
Chemin des Croisettes 28
1066 Epalinges, Switzerland
Tel: 41 21 651 7761; Fax: 41 21 651 7762
E-mail: 100070.1445@compuserve.com

Leadership development and management consultation.

Evangelical Institute of Missiology
Stefan and Kathi Schmid, Coordinators
Route de Fenil 40
1806 St.-Legier, Switzerland
Tel: 41 21 943 1891; Fax: 41 21 943 4365

Courses in French for missionaries; annual summer retreat sponsored by the FMEF for French-speaking missionaries.

Klinik Sonnenhalde
Samuel Pfeifer, Medical Director
4125 Riehen (by Basel), Switzerland
Tel: 41 61 641 1313
E-mail: 100430.442@compuserve.com

Christian psychiatric hospital and outpatient counseling; referrals.

UNITED KINGDOM

All Nations Christian College
Easneye, Ware
Herts. SG12 8LX, England
Tel: 44 1920 461243; Fax: 44 1920 462997

A leading Bible college, primarily for missionaries. Has a retreat each year for Christian workers and a two-week preparation course for overseas workers.

Association of Christian Counselors
173 A Wokingham Rd.
Reading, Berkshire. RG6 1LT, England
Tel: 44 1734 662207; Fax: 44 1734 269635

Accreditation at two levels of counseling; recognition for training courses in Christian counseling; has a list of over 100 UK organizations and churches providing Christian counseling.

Care for Mission
Michael and Elizabeth Jones, Directors
Ellem Lodge, Duns TD11 3SG
Berwickshire, Scotland
Tel: 44 1361 890677; Fax: 44 1361 890329
E-mail: 100633.2065@compuserve.com

Residential and outpatient services for returning missionaries, including medical and functional assessment, debriefing, health advisory, and immunization service; psychological and medical assessment for candidates; agency consultation, educational seminars, and counseling for missionaries.

Children of Missionaries Education and Training (COMET)
Marion Knell, Chairperson
c/o P.O. Box 51
Loughborough, Leics. LE11 0ZQ, England
Tel: 44 1509 890268

Monitors MK matters and has developed a network of people involved with MK issues within EMA member societies.

Cornerstone
London, England
Tel: 44 181 424 8230

A network of professionally trained Christians offering psychotherapy/counseling services in the greater London area.

CWR, Waverley Abbey House
Waverley Lane
Farnham, Surrey GU9 8BR, England
Tel: 44 1252 783695; Fax: 44 1252 783657

Training courses in counseling and a variety of topics related to counseling, such as helping those with eating disorders, depression, sexual abuse, and marriage. Also has books, tapes, and specialist materials on counseling and Christian living.

EQUIP
Tony Horsfall, Director
Bawtry Hall
Bawtry, Doncaster DN10 6JH, England
Tel: 44 1302 710020; Fax: 44 1302 710027
E-mail: 101325.516@compuserve.com

Seminars and weekend workshops to prepare Christians for ministry, covering reentry for missionaries, marriage enrichment, parenting in missions, serving as senders, orientation for cross-cultural ministry, etc.

InterChange
Joy Lankester, Coordinator
c/o InterHealth (see address below)

Specialist in adult career guidance, vocational consultation for overseas workers, pre-assignment guidance for families.

InterHealth
Ted Lankester, Director
Partnership House
157 Waterloo Road
London SE1 8US, England
Tel: 44 171 902 9000; Fax: 44 171 928 0927
E-mail: 100636.1271@compuserve.com

Pre-travel health screening, travel health advice/written materials, immunizations, health supplies, medical exams upon return from overseas, psychological assessment, reentry debriefing, short- or long-term counseling, advisory and consultation service, workshops, psychiatric care/support.

Member Care Associates
Kelly and Michele O'Donnell, Coordinators
P.O. Box 4
High Wycombe, Bucks. HP14 3YX, England
Tel: 44 1494 484391; Fax: 44 1494 485917
E-mail: 102172.170@compuserve.com

Counseling including debriefing, team building, psychological assessment, seminars, case consultation, member care program consultation, and written resources.

Mission Encouragement
Janice Rowland, Director
P.O. Box 4034
Worthing, West Sussex BN14 7FS, England
Tel/Fax: 44 1903 211 50
E-mail: 106342.424@compuserve.com

Supportive field visits to missionaries in Europe.

MK Oasis
Anthony and Joan Sinclair
28 Salisbury Rd.
Mosley, Birmingham B13 8JT, England
Tel: 44 121 449 7496; Fax: 44 121 472 0425
E-mail: Anthony@mkoasis.demon.co.uk

Support for MKs and families via retreats, phone and individual counseling, family seminars, and some screening.

Network of Christians in Psychology
Michael Wang, Chairman
c/o University of Hull
Department of Psychology
Hull HU6 7RX, England
Tel: 44 482 465 933; Fax: 44 482 465 599

Referral source for Christian psychologists within the UK.

Readjustment Network
David Williams, Coordinator
Bawtry Hall
Bawtry, Doncaster DN10 6JH, England
Tel: 44 1302 710020; Fax: 44 1302 710027

Links missionaries who are returning to the UK with veteran missionaries who have already negotiated the reentry process.

Wellsprings
Marjorie Salmon, Coordinator
Bawtry Hall
Bawtry, Doncaster DN10 6JH, England
Tel: 44 1302 710020; Fax: 44 1302 710027

A residential service for overseas personnel and others needing time for refreshment and renewal. There would be opportunity to link with ongoing courses arranged by EQUIP. A resident nurse provides on-site coordination and service.

UK Notes
1. "Reorientation course for returning missionaries" (details from The Warden, Leasow House, Crowther Hall, Selly Oak, Birmingham B29 6QT, England).

2. "Residential Refresher Course" for Christian physicians, nurses, and midwives returning overseas (held at Oak Hill College in London; details from Overseas Support Secretary, Christian Medical Fellowship, 157 Waterloo Road, London SE1 8XN, England).

3. The Evangelical Missionary Alliance sponsors two gatherings each year for Personnel Secretaries.

4. *Vision Magazine*. A good source for places to go in the UK for rest and renewal, usually in rural, scenic surroundings.

NORTH AMERICA

CANADA

Amicus Ministries International
Claude Loney, Director
P.O. Box 1503
Peterborough, Ontario K9J 7H7, Canada
Tel: 705 742 5195; Fax: 705 742 1208
E-mail: 75672.173@compuserve.com

Retreats and counseling services for caregivers, including missionaries, pastors, and leaders.

Missionary Health Institute
Ken Gamble, Director
4000 Leslie Street
North York, Ontario M2K 2R9, Canada
Tel: 416 494 7512; Fax: 416 492 3740

Outpatient counseling, medical and tropical disease consultation/treatment, medical and psychological screening for pre-field and post-field; overseas seminars on health, conflict, stress; reentry seminars; crisis intervention on the field.

Missionary Internship
Claude Loney, Director
P.O. Box 1503
Peterborough, Ontario K9J 7H7, Canada
Tel: 705 742 1047; Fax: 705 742 1208
E-mail: 75672.1733@compuserve.com

Training for cross-cultural service, including pre-field orientation, language acquisition program, missionary family orientation; debriefing and reentry program.

UNITED STATES

Association of Christian Schools International (ACSI), Missions Office
Philip Renicks, Director
P.O. Box 35097
Colorado Springs, Colorado 80935, USA
Tel: 719 594 4612; Fax: 719 531 0631
E-mail: 102256.2544@compuserve.com

Resources for caregivers at MK schools and international Christian schools, including pre-field training, seminars and regional conferences, recruiting, and consultation services; also internships for student teachers.

ACMC

P.O. Box ACMC
Wheaton, Illinois 60189, USA
Tel: 312 260 1660

Written materials and other resources to help churches as they work in missions.

Barnabas International

Lareau Lindquist, Director
P.O. Box 11211
Rockford, Illinois 61126, USA
Tel: 815 395 1335; Fax: 815 395 1385
E-mail: 75453.2463@compuserve.com

Field visitation for teaching, preaching, pastoral care, clinical consultation, and counseling. Free monthly letter, "Encouragement." Marriage enrichment seminars. Also sponsors the annual "Pastors to Missionaries" seminar in Waxhaw, North Carolina.

Christian Association of Psych. Studies

Randolf Sanders, Director
P.O. Box 310400
New Braunfels, Texas 78131, USA
Tel: 210 629 CAPS; Fax: 210 629 2342

Referral source for Christian counselors and psychologists, primarily in the USA and in several other countries.

Christian Recovery International

Dale Ryan, Director
P.O. Box 11095
Whittier, California 90603, USA
Tel: 310 697 6201; Fax: 310 694 6930

Newsletters and resources for people recovering from addiction, abuse, and trauma.

Crisis Consulting International

Bob Klamser, Director
9452 Telephone Road, Suite 223
Ventura, California 93004, USA
Tel: 805 647 4329; Fax: 805 647 1630
E-mail: crisis.consulting.cci@iccs.sil.org

Trains and assists mission agencies to respond to terrorist threats and similar crises that affect their personnel.

Global Nomads

Norma McCraig, Director
P.O. Box 9584
Washington, DC, USA
Tel: 703 993 2975
E-mail: info@gni.org

An international, secular organization based in Washington, DC, focusing on the needs and adjustment issues of third-culture kids. Gives seminars and organizes campus groups at universities on the East Coast of the USA.

Heartstream Resources

Larry and Lois Dodds, Directors
101 Herman Lee Circle
Liverpool, Pennsylvania 17045, USA
Tel: 717 444 2374; Fax: 717 444 2574
E-mail: 72261.2634@compuserve.com

Psychological and medical consultation, training seminars, and counseling. Currently setting up a residential facility for intensive care and burnout treatment.

Interaction Ministries

David Pollock, Director
P.O. Box 158
Houghton, New York 14744, USA
Tel/Fax: 716 567 4598
E-mail: 75662.2070@compuserve.com

Seminars, consultation, and reentry programs dealing with missionary kids and families. Excellent referral source on TCKs.

Affiliated staff include:
David and Mary Ann Brooks—Hungary
Polly Chan—Hong Kong, Taiwan, Singapore
Judith Gjoen—Nordic countries
Anthony and Joan Sinclair—England
Gyoung Ae Ryoo—South Korea
Libby Stephens, Stephanie Hock—Germany

International Affiliates of the APA

International Affairs Office
American Psychological Association
Joan Buchanan, Director
750 First Street, NE
Washington, DC 20002, USA

Publishes a directory of about 3,000 psychologists from around the world who are affiliated with the APA. Possible referral source, although most may not be Christians.

International Assoc. of Christian Counselors

P.O. Box 739
Forest, Virginia 24551, USA
Tel: 800 526 8673

A new organization with which the American Association of Christian Counselors is affiliated. Its purpose is to bring together and encourage the development of national associations of Christian counselors.

Link Care Center
Brent Lindquist, Director
1734 West Shaw Avenue
Fresno, California 93711, USA
Tel: 209 439 5920; Fax: 209 439 2214
E-mail: 75027.2265@compuserve.com

Training, counseling, pre-field preparation, restoration, psychological evaluation, and reentry programs. Residential programs.

Makahiki Ministries
P.O. Box 415
Mariposa, California 95388, USA
Tel: 209 966 2988

A hospitality network in the USA providing housing for furloughs, rest, and renewal.

Marble Retreat
Louis and Melissa McBurney, Directors
139 Bannockburn
Marble, Colorado 81623, USA
Tel: 970 963 2499 or 888 21MARBLE
Fax: 970 963 0217
E-mail: 72040.1367@compuserve.com

Two-week sessions for crisis counseling for clergy (pastors, missionaries, anyone in Christian ministry).

Mental Health and Missions Conference
John Powell, Coordinator
Counseling Center
Michigan State University
East Lansing, Michigan 48823, USA

An informal gathering of over 100 people that meets each November at an inn in Indiana. Participants network, fellowship, and present papers on member care topics.

Missionary Care International
Len Cerny, Director
6291 Hilltop Place
Yorba Linda, California 92686, USA
Tel: 714 324 2212; Fax: 714 970 0819
E-mail: 74361.354@compuserve.com

Counseling, psychological assessment, seminars, field and e-mail consultation. Mobilization and training of mental health professionals for missions.

Missionary Care Services
Doug Feil and Lanell Schilling, Directors
141 West Davies

Littleton, Colorado 80120, USA
Tel: 303 730 1717; Fax: 303 717 1531
E-mail: jfeil@ares.csd.net

Counseling, assessment, and consultation services for missionaries and their families.

Mission Training International
Paul Nelson, Director
P.O. Box 50110
Colorado Springs, Colorado 80949, USA
Tel: 800 896 3710; Fax: 719 594 4682
E-mail: mintern@aol.com

Pre-field preparation for individuals and families, debriefing and reentry, language acquisition training, workshops on missionary care and development. Holds an annual consultation for member care workers.

MKs in Recovery
Sharon Koon, Director
P.O. Box 51
Reynoldsburg, Ohio 43068, USA
Tel/Fax: 614 861 8512

Newsletters, retreats, and networking for MKs abused in their childhood.

Mu Kappa
Jim and Ruth Lauer, Directors
1032 Twin Falls
De Soto, Texas 75115, USA
Tel: 214 230 1710

University fraternity to help missionary kids adjust to college and life in the USA. Provides and consults with reentry programs.

Narramore Christian Foundation
250 West Colorado Blvd., Suite 200
Arcadia, California 91007, USA
Tel: 818 821 8400; Fax: 818 821 8409
E-mail: 102132.3067@compuserve.com

Runs two MK reentry seminars each year; involved in several member care projects.

Operation Impact
Azusa Pacific University
Grace Barnes, Director
P.O. Box 7000
Azusa, California 91702, USA
Tel: 818 815 3848; Fax: 818 815 3868
E-mail: gbarnes@apu.edu

Courses and a master's degree program offered at different locations around the world on leadership training. Designed for missionaries and others.

Overseas Ministries Study Center

Gerald Anderson, Director
490 Prospect Street
Newhaven, Connecticut 06511, USA
Tel: 203 624 6672; Fax: 203 865 2857

Seminars for continuing education in cross-cultural ministries, research, publications, reference library. Has residential facilities for those studying.

Overseas Security Advisory Council (OSAC)

State Annex 10, 8th Floor
Washington, DC 20522, USA
Tel: 202 663 0533; Fax: 202 663 0868

Brochures and material on security precautions when living overseas, including preventing abduction, surviving hostage situations, and safeguarding one's family and business abroad.

Psychotherapy and Consultation Services

Fran White, Director
1272 Reading Court
Wheaton, Illinois 60187, USA
Tel: 708 668 6561

A staff of six therapists with significant mission experience. Provides counseling, consultation, and seminars on the field and within the USA.

Reconciliation Ministries

Esly Carvalho, Director
P.O. Box 26202
Colorado Springs, Colorado 80936, USA
Tel: 719 573 4670; Fax: 719 637 3481
E-mail: eslyregina@aol.com

Debriefing, field care, and team building services in Spanish, English, and Portuguese.

"Renewal" Houses

Here are a few of the many places available for rest and restoration for missionaries and ministers:

Break-A-Way (a division of Medical Ministry International), c/o Loe and Mary Jo Ferrante
Downing House in Denver, Colorado
Terre Haute in Indiana, coordinated by Dave and Kim Butts
Wears Valley Retreat, Knoxville, Tennessee
Cleft Rock in Kentucky, c/o Bob and Eddie Fields

Servants' Missionary Service

Ron and Sue Faircloth, Directors
P.O. Box 3488
Columbia, South Carolina 29230, USA
Tel: 803 754 2929; Fax: 803 786 8903
E-mail: 70413.2445@compuserve.com

Publishes/mails newsletters for missionaries.

Third Culture Family Services

Elsie Purnell, Director
1605 Elizabeth Street
Pasadena, California 91104, USA
Tel: 818 794 9406

Runs support groups for adult MKs in Southern California area. Also provides advice for MK-related concerns such as education, reentry, and pre-field preparation.

Training and Resource Center

Phil Elkins, Director
3800 Canon Blvd.
Altadena, California 91001, USA
Tel: 818 791 2000; Fax: 818 787 7906

Consultation, pre-field training, research.

Tuscarora Resource Center

Mount Bethel Christian Ministries
Lewis Judy, Director
870 Sunrise Blvd.
Mount Bethel, Pennsylvania 18343, USA
Tel: 717 897 5115; Fax: 717 897 0144

Counseling and assessment services for missionaries and ministers; housing for residential care.

North America Notes

Additional referral sources include the major evangelical mission associations:

1. IFMA
   John Orme, Director
   P.O. Box 3398
   Wheaton, Illinois 60189, USA
   Tel: 708 682 9270; Fax: 708 682 9278
   E-mail: ifma@aol.com

2. EFMA
   Paul McKaughan, Director
   1023 15th Street, NW, Suite 500
   Washington, DC 20005, USA
   Tel: 202 789 1500; Fax: 202 842 0392
   E-mail: 72143.1167@compuserve.com

3. World Evangelical Fellowship
   Missions Commission
   Bill Taylor, Director

4807 Palisade Drive
Austin, Texas 78731, USA
Tel: 512 467 8431; Fax: 512 467 2849
E-mail: 74742.133@compuserve.com

Christian organizations specializing in counseling and family life:
1. Focus on the Family
2. Minirth Meier Centers
3. Rosemead School of Psychology
4. Fuller School of Psychology
5. See also CAPS and IACC listings

E-mail forums for sharing member care-related information and needs:
1. Network of Associates for the Health of Expatriates (NOAHE)
   c/o Dr. Rick Johnson
   E-mail: drrickjohn@xc.org
2. Pastors to Missionaries Newsletter
   c/o Barnabas
   E-mail: 75453.2463@compuserve.com

LATIN AMERICA

ARGENTINA

Centro de Capacitacion Misionera Transcultural
Marcelo Abel, Director
Lima 933
Bo. General Paz
5000 Córdoba, Argentina

A regional missionary training center for cross-cultural missions.

ECUADOR

EIRENE
Carlos Pinto, Coordinator
c/o HCJB
Casilla 17-17-691
Quito, Ecuador
Tel: 59 32 43 512
E-mail: cpinto@hcjb.org.ec

The Latin American Association for Pastoral and Family Counseling. A referral source for Christian counselors in Latin America, speaking Spanish, Portuguese, and English.

GUATEMALA

COMIBAM International
Rudy Girón, Director
Apartado Postal 27-1, CP01907
Guatemala City, Guatemala
Tel: 502 2 500769; Fax: 502 2 300941

A missionary alliance for Latin America and a possible source of referrals.

SUGGESTED READINGS

Gardner, R., & Gardner, L. (1992). Training and using member care workers. In K. O'Donnell (Ed.), *Missionary care: Counting the cost for world evangelization* (pp. 315-331). Pasadena, CA: William Carey Library.

Johnston, L. (1988). Building relationships between mental health specialists and mission agencies. In K. O'Donnell (Ed.), *Helping missionaries grow: Readings in mental health and missions* (pp. 449-457). Pasadena, CA: William Carey Library.

Kelly O'Donnell *is a psychologist working as part of Youth With A Mission and Member Care Associates, an interagency member care group based in England. Together with his wife, Michele, he edited* **Helping Missionaries Grow** *(1988) and* **Missionary Care** *(1992). O'Donnell ministers in the areas of team building, counseling, family life, member care training, and program consultation, and he actively promotes member care in frontier missions. Address: P.O. Box 4, High Wycombe, Bucks. HP14 3YX, England.*

Part 5

Final Observations
And Outcomes

26

Challenging the Missions Stakeholders: Conclusions and Implications; Further Research

William D. Taylor

L ife stories of recent weeks:
These last three years on the field have been crushing ones. Our outward circumstances were tough to begin with, actually a matter of survival with the combination of stifling heat with suffocating humidity, little water, no electricity. We simply could not get away from it! When suffering comes from unbelievers or Muslims, it's understandable, but the worst crushing came from other missionaries within the body of Christ, even from leadership. We simply wanted to get out! But during the third year, we saw God opening our own eyes to let us know why He was orchestrating these things in our lives. We saw the worst of ourselves; we saw evil in our own lives. We had failed the spirituality test miserably. But then we began to discern God's purposes, even as our lives fell into the ground as the seed, to die, and then come back to life. God was crushing us to knock our shell off, in order that Christ would be revealed in us, and thus our people group would see Him and not us. Three years in the grinder. Then the power of Christ speaking to us. We are

on a lifetime plan with God. God brought brokenness to our own lives during this last term, but it was to teach us and to equip us for the long-term task. And we will return to our assignment early next year.

These blunt, self-revealing words came from Nigel and Tina, a young missionary couple who spent an evening with us last week. They had met in South Africa on a short-term mission project, married back home, and returned to that country to serve long term. Little did they know they would last less than two years in that first city-based ministry and that God would lead them to a remote region of a Portuguese-speaking African nation, where the Spirit was breaking through into a previously resistant people group. The original couple who recruited them to the team had left the field due to serious marital problems. But Nigel and Tina survived, learned profound lessons, saw the hand of God at work, are now taking their home leave—and they plan to return!

Theirs is but one of 11 family units with whom I have had close contact in the weeks of working on this last chapter. It has been my privilege to talk seriously with four couples en route to long-term missions; with three experienced couples in diverse contexts; with a family with 20 years of ministry facing another major transition; and with a gifted missiologist in her late 50s, realizing that her 32 years of cross-cultural Asian assignments had come to conclusion, and now she wondered what the future might hold for her at her age. I have replayed my conversations and correspondence with these people, pondering what keeps people in long-term missions and what causes people to leave early or unexpectedly. I have also reread and pondered our attrition questionnaire and its categories, the report by Peter Brierley (chapter 6), and the analysis by Detlef Blöcher and Jonathan Lewis (chapter 7), attempting to discern the implications.

AS WE APPROACH CLOSURE TO THIS BOOK

We finally conclude this book, with its wealth of information, statistics, and perspectives, with application to all those involved in or committed to the global cross-cultural enterprise. We have numbers, statistics, and specific causes for understandable and undesirable attrition from the perspective of 553 mission agency leaders in 14 nations, as well as countless personal case studies.

Our research demonstrates disturbing numbers, percentages, patterns, and conclusions. A few argue that things are not as bad as they might seem, but this dodges the issues that

need to be faced and obviously minimizes the loss of human potential and financial resources. I am fully convinced that there is much we can do right now, within our sphere of influence, to address these issues.

So what can we now say? What shall we do?

We are engaged in spiritual warfare, and understandably there are casualties. Some are the result of non-existent or inadequate pre-field screening (the fault of both the church and the mission agency); some wounds are self-inflicted; and in some cases our Evangelical structures have been destructive and wounding. Too many agencies are unable to face the task of bringing home those missionaries who either should never have gone out or who should leave the field—based on the testimony of both colleagues and the national church. In many cases, we do not know how to bring about or encourage needed healing. Serious self-evaluation must be done by church leadership, the academia and training leaders, and those who lead mission societies.

Cultural values play a significant role in the process of identifying the causes of attrition and reducing the problem. Western societies, such as those of the United States, place high value on bluntness, identification and resolution of problems, and the willingness (most of the time) to make changes. Asian societies, in contrast, tend to place higher value on "saving face," and they do not respond favorably to direct questions and problem solving, where the issues and answers may prove embarrassing. European, African, and Latin American societies have their own particular cultural norms that must be understood.

Another example of cultural differences comes in relation to generational realities. We were criticized early on for promulgating an Australian analysis of three current generations, as if we were imposing these categories on the rest of the world. Obviously, we are not doing that. But the fact is that every mission sending nation has a generational factor to grapple with from its own culture, and in every case these differences are proving critical to the movement. This is true not only in Australia and North America, but also in Asia and Africa.

Therefore, the reader of this chapter should know that I write primarily from my own cultural formation and experience. You will have to contextualize some of my observations and recommendations.

SPEAKING TO THE PRIME STAKEHOLDERS

We define a stakeholder as someone with a primary interest or investment (a "stake") in a program or project. Thus, for us, the missionary movement stakeholders will include the following seven individuals or entities, to whom we address these challenges. Who are these key players?

+ **Missionaries**—past, current, and future, including the tentmakers.
+ **Church leaders**—pastors, missions pastors, and missions committees.
+ **Missions mobilizers.**
+ **Missionary trainers, schools, and training programs.**
+ **Mission agencies or sending bodies.**
+ **National receiving churches**— where these exist.

+ **Member care providers**—pastors and professional counselors.

Let me suggest that all stakeholders use four markers as you read this final chapter.

Marker 1: The major Brierley tables (pages 92–94), which give the prime reasons for unpreventable and preventable attrition.

Marker 2: The major Blöcher and Lewis tables (pages 123–125), which give specific national attrition rates, as well as the other significant graphs.

Marker 3: The survey instrument (pages 363–370), with both the categories and detailed list of attrition factors.

Marker 4: The Donovan and Myors generational diagram (page 48).

Periodically refer to these four significant perspectives on attrition as you read this chapter, along with the section with particular application to yourself or your ministry. Ask God to help you grow your understanding of attrition and then identify your role in the solutions. Find yourself, your church, your mobilizing role, your training task, your mission leadership assignment, your receiving church challenge in light of these categories. What insight do you gain from this assessment?

1. The Missionaries Themselves

Previous Missionaries

When I think of previous missionaries, my mind flows back to my 17 years in Latin America, as I mull over the many colleagues who left our agency and other groups in that country to return home. Why did they leave? Were they pushouts, burnouts, dropouts, or never-should-have-gone-outs? How close did field reality match early expectations? What quality of pastoral care was provided for them? What kind of follow-up was provided after they left the field under less-than-ideal circumstances?

I suspect and hope that some of you as former missionaries will obtain a copy of this book. Or perhaps your mission colleagues might read it and be reminded of you or of others like you. Why did you leave active field ministry? Why did I leave Latin America for another ministry in my "passport country" after 17 years of cross-cultural service? What are the complex reasons given for leaving? Who really knows or understands the reasons for earlier-than-expected departure? Or do we simply give reasons that we and others could live with in the public domain?

Some of those who left and returned home were deeply hurt, and not a few were angry (at national and mission leaders, at colleagues, at a spouse, at themselves, at the sending church, at God). Other missionaries left and are glad they did. One former colleague stunned me with his blunt words, "The happiest day of my life was when I got on that plane, flew home, and knew I would never return to that country!" Should I be glad he left also?

To all who have served cross-culturally, we trust this book will help some of you put pieces of your life, perhaps some of them broken, into right perspective. I am totally convinced that the most important thing for you is not whether you are still officially a missionary. The question rather is, are you still walking passionately with the Triune God, still useful to the Kingdom, committed to God's global redemptive plan and future? Utilize your experience to further the Kingdom as a global mobilizer in your own sphere of influence.

Some final thoughts: Do not hide painful field experience and emotions under a carpet! Rather, face them directly. You may find valuable help coming from a gifted counselor or spiritual director. For some of you "former" ones, it might be necessary to seek healing of the broken relationships of the past. Is there any way you can let your former agency know what truly happened, for their good and yours?

Current Missionaries

I hope current missionaries will read this book, evaluate the causes of unpreventable and undesirable attrition, and then ask the question, Where do I fit here? Am I a missionary who is vulnerable to attrition? Why so? What would keep me in long-term ministry, whether in this location or another one? Be honest with yourself, and if married, work through these issues together with your spouse. What insights do you gain? You may discern a gifted colleague in pain, needing a word of encouragement. Your tangible support may help this man or woman get through the pain, darkness, and desert into fruitful ministry. We truly need each other.

Here's a more sobering question: Should you or others who simply are not where they should be stay in cross-cultural service? Would it not be best for you, your family, colleagues, agency, ministry, and the national church simply to consider seriously whether God truly wants you in this cross-cultural context? Some people get to field service from confused motives or easy screening, and since they can raise funds and apparently want to be missionaries, off they go—and stay for too long. Some become missionaries because they don't fit back home. Others run away from difficult home situations. Others simply do not possess the character traits, gift mix, or basic competencies for mission work. Still others have terrible family dynamics, but their dysfunctionality is covered up by being missionaries. Rare is the case where the agency or sending church closes the curtain on these missionaries and guides them back into their home context.

The Next Generation Of Missionaries

During the days I was composing this chapter, I spoke with four young couples who are committed to Christ and His global cause, tremendously gifted, and eager to serve long term in cross-cultural mission. One of them asked me a piercing question: "Bill, in light of what you have learned from this attrition study, what should we do to be sure we don't become some of your future attrition statistics?" This provoked a very fruitful exchange, and again I returned to two components of our study: the generational diagram and the categories of attrition. I also quizzed the couple on the nature of their practical and evaluated ministry experience prior to departure. Couples or individuals with minimal testing of life and spiritual gifting run the danger of failure in missions or any kind of vocational ministry. It is a wise church and agency that requires substantial evaluated ministry of future missionaries—and this means much more than simply being able to teach a children's Sunday school class!

Again I return to the generational issues before us and their application and implication in the lives of future missionaries. Here are some strong, reality-therapy words for the younger generation emerging into missions, a phenomenon in every missionary sending nation. Is there a place for you in the global enterprise? Absolutely! Will it be easy to make decisions, to prepare for this service, to find the right "team" and colleagues with which to work? Absolutely not—for all of you! Be wary of the emotional hype used by some to get you out into missions. You simply must develop substantial spiritual and personal "toughness" for missions, growing in your capacity to stick it out and be both flexible and creative at the same time. Most of you will have to work within existing structures, even as you plan your long-term strategy to change those very structures.

Some of you are turned off by the church and have difficulty finding a faith community that meets your needs. This is a difficult issue to resolve, for you are pro Jesus but not very pro local church. I don't really care what kind of local group of believers you get involved in, but you simply cannot afford to avoid the biblical imperatives of what Scripture calls the "church." Ask God to lead you to a church that does not pander to lower standards, but rather one that challenges your heart and mind, that prods you to holiness and to life commitment to Jesus, one that has a passion for the entire globe—from the local community to the far corners of the earth. You have to have a faith community you call your spiritual home/family, where your prayer support is rooted.

Many of you are frankly turned off by missions language. Good for you. So am I! So come up with new language that represents biblical, historical, and cultural realities. Uneasy with terms like "career missions" or "signing up for life"? Don't worry about it! Think of a series of five-year links in the chain of your life. Are you willing to give the King at least two links of your life, or perhaps more, in order for a people group or urban population to come to saving knowledge of Christ, and see them grow into a family of faith?

Seth and Rita, headed to Russia after seminary, asked me the other day, "How can we avoid 'attriting'?" My answer encouraged them to make the following commitments now:

1. Significant involvement in a local church, with true testing and use of your gifts, with genuine accountability for both of you.

2. Acquiring the right kind of training that focuses on character issues, spirituality, skills for ministry, and knowledge for life and ministry.

3. Reflection even now of the kind of life investment you want to make in Russia.

4. Dedication to strengthen your marriage and family, building together for the future.

5. Commitment to develop your church sending base, followed by a search for a field-based organization/agency that will partner with your church and that offers tangible field-team strategizing, supervision, and shepherding.

6. Decision to commit to long-term language learning and cultural adaptation.

Tentmaking Missionaries

Issues of attrition of tentmakers are real but at times elusive. But if we focus on the longer-term, intentional tentmaker—the one who goes out with clear vision of serving as a bivocational worker for the cause of Christ, the task is a bit easier. One veteran tentmaker told me that a high rate of attrition in the first four years was due to the following five causes:

+ Inadequate training.
+ Unmet or unrealistic expectations.
+ The stress of two jobs and cultural adjustment.
+ Lack of bonding to local Christians, and related security issues.
+ Lack of accountability.

Together, these factors generate great loneliness, loss of self-worth and value in ministry, and limited time for prayer and spiritual nourishment, ultimately leading to departure from the field.

Listen to a letter from a tentmaking couple who left Asia in pain:

Due to my continued weight loss and low energy, we decided to leave as soon as possible. I did go to a clinic for expatriates, but apparently nothing is really wrong medically. I do feel it's related to the stress of this teaching job, and Bob is having great difficulty mentally and emotionally in coping with the city noises and congestion. He's a country boy at heart, and the city is overwhelming. We did well at first, but other issues have surfaced regarding our character, personality, and giftedness; and all seems to indicate that this was the wrong job to take. It will be difficult to say good-bye. We have a mixed bag of emotions.

We have to be tentmaker realists. Too much fuzzy thinking has surrounded the movement. Significantly, the most recent world congress of the Tentmakers International Exchange, meeting in Australia in early 1997, expressed the urgent need for more pertinent training. As we tie tentmakers into attrition issues, we come up with some key questions to ask which can then be turned into discussion items and action plans to reduce attrition.

1. Who sends, supports financially, and prays for the tentmaking missionaries?

2. What kind of pre-field equipping have they had in order to integrate both vocations in the context of cross-cultural work?

3. What is the role of their sending church in their vocational plans?

4. Who is providing on-field shepherding, supervising, and strategizing?

A dear friend, now working in the Middle East as a tentmaker and in agency leadership, shared some reflections not too long ago as we talked about missionary attrition in his zone of the world.

I get overwhelmed almost on a daily basis. The tensions of tentmaking vis-à-vis ministry are tough. Combine them with the difficulty of being a field leader and not knowing how to do it.... Don't send us people without significant ministry experience. They don't have to possess a master's degree in theology, but they must be able to build a case using biblical motifs of revelation history, starting from Genesis on through the life of Christ. They must know the Bible and apologetics for Muslims—done on the field to understand the Muslim worldview.

2. The Local Church: Pastoral Team, Missions Committee, And/or Missions Pastor

When we began our attrition study in 1994, to be honest, most of the churches we talked with said they really did not have much of an attrition problem. But as time went on, as they understood the issues and tracked their own church missionary attrition, a transformation took place. Churches do have a problem, but they simply have not been fully aware of its dimensions. And now the attitude has changed radically. What's more, we had over 80 church missions leaders (including 64 in the USA and 12 in Ghana) complete our attrition questionnaire.

Here are some key questions for missions-minded churches:

1. Do you have records of your own attrition over the last decade, beyond just numbers and names?

2. Can you identify how many of "your" missionaries have left field ministry, regardless of reason?

3. Can you identify the causes of attrition of your former missionaries for the last, let's say, 10 years?

4. Are you able to put a financial cost figure to your attrition over the last 10 years?

5. What kind of responsibility does the church have for this attrition?

6. What can you do as a church to help those vulnerable to attrition?

7. In what ways are you partnering in pastoral care with the mission society of your missionaries?

8. When missionaries have returned under difficult circumstances, in what ways have you met wholistic/pastoral needs? Did the missionaries return to your church, or did they settle in an-

other church out of guilt, fear, shame, and disappointment?

9. What are you doing to stay in touch with your previous missionaries? Are they still walking with the Lord?

10. How are you utilizing the experience and expertise of those who return to your church—for your own local, cross-cultural ministries, as well as your global outreach?

A major transformation is taking place globally in terms of churches and missions. For years, many churches have offered a "pay and pray" kind of missions program. That is, missionaries seeking support have approached churches with money and have challenged them to financial (and of course prayer!) involvement. The churches, in turn, have checked out candidates (particularly in terms of their training and mission agency), and when they pass these tests, they become part of the church's supported missionary roster. The church pays and prays!

But radical changes are sweeping through churches in just about every country. Churches rightly are seeking a greater involvement, role, and responsibility in the total missions movement. These are encouraging changes, but they are also challenges for those—whether in churches, schools, or agencies—who have operated under the old system. The danger for local churches comes when they assume they can do everything needed: screening, equipping, sending, supporting, strategizing, and shepherding, on or off the field. Very few churches can pull all these things off successfully. And it is wrong to send gifted and committed missionaries into tough regions without provid-

ing the right kind of field-based support system.

The wiser churches develop two major strategic partnerships in their missions program. First, they provide the foundational equipping in terms of spirituality and character training, relational and ministry skill development, evaluated and accountable service. But they realize that some of their missionaries need specific pre-field, non-formal and/or formal training in biblical and theological areas, cross-cultural and Islamic studies, or other specific equipping for the task. Thus, they partner and "franchise" out some of the training to centers and schools which have a strong track record in specific fields. But the church guides the process.

Secondly, wise churches partner with field-based agencies with a strong track record of experience to provide the strategic services needed for the missionary, family, or team not only to survive but to thrive long term. And when the time comes for the missionary unit to return home, the church is there as the spiritual community to receive, encourage, and strengthen them. For those who return deeply wounded, the local church must become the gentle safety net that will receive them, seek healing for them from all sources, and seek the best future for them. This arrangement provides a double support system—one based on the field, the other in the local church.

So, to all churches committed to reducing attrition, some final words:

1. Don't attempt to provide/create the total missions infrastructure by yourself. Remember that small agencies (this includes churches also) have a higher attrition rate.

2. Develop careful (but not impossible) standards in the selection, screening, equipping, training, sending, and shepherding process. Be proactive in these areas.

3. Provide your own special kind of shepherding for missionaries, and also hold agencies accountable for the promised field-based shepherding. After all, if you provide a significant percentage of financial support, you are paying for these services!

4. Don't assume that Bible schools and seminaries are doing the job in terms of effective missionary training. Question the current process that focuses primarily on formal study plans and degrees. Ensure equipping that focuses on character and relationality, on ministry skills and substantial knowledge for missions.

Here is a case study of a good example of partnership between a mission agency and a local church. This particular agency's vision is a tough one: to plant churches, primarily through teams, among resistant peoples. Both the need and the strategy are clear, and this vision has attracted a significant number of gifted and committed young adults. But too many of them were very independent entrepreneurs with limited pre-field involvement in the life of a local church, much less in planting churches in their own culture. Consequently, issues of character and relationships fragmented families and church-planting teams. Limited ministry skills foundered quickly on the rocks of tough, cross-cultural reality. In recent years, the field-tested, new leader of this agency has identified the historic limitations and is taking steps to institute change.

The local church in mind has a vision of church planting in its own metropolitan area and has developed a strong movement of home groups (house churches), where leaders are equipped to serve as shepherds of these groups. Pastoral needs of the larger church are cascaded into the small groups, and those leaders have to grapple with the tough aspects of ministry as well as the more glorious ones. Home group shepherds (either singles or married couples), upon the multiplication of their house groups, see the ministry expand, and some become coaches of other shepherds. The requirement for future missionaries from this church is that they have served as home group shepherds and coaches. This becomes the arena for evaluating and shaping character and gift mixes for ministry. And the experience and skills acquired in this context become crucial foundations for cross-cultural ministry.

The new leader of the agency said to the church pastor, "If our missionaries in our restricted access nation had come with this testing of character and gifts, our attrition would have been dramatically reduced." And now the agency and the church have entered into a strategic partnership that essentially causes church planting to flow from the monocultural home field to the tougher cross-cultural field.

3. The Missions Mobilizers

These are very special people, and they are found around the world in every mission sending base. They are passionate and positive brothers and sisters, and we need them in the missions enterprise. They promote prayer in the churches; they offer special courses on world missions; they encourage the adoption of unreached people groups. Many of them are found in vibrant churches, or they serve in centers for world missions, or a few are loners. They provide all kinds of resources for missions—speakers, print, and video. They offer conferences, conventions, retreats, and all kinds of missions events. They are invaluable players!

Mobilizers have a strategic role in reducing missionary attrition, particularly at the front end of the movement to the nations and peoples without Christ. Here are some specific recommendations for missions mobilizers:

1. Be realistic about the true cost of world missions. Don't just promote without imparting knowledge of the price. Go beyond mobilization and motivation.

2. Be wary of emotionally charged decisions for missions that are not tempered by the maturity of those who have lived and served in long-term missions.

3. Promote a balance of short-term and longer-term missionary service. Remember that a prime reason unreached peoples are unreached is that they are hard to reach. They will probably be reached best by those who commit to long-term missions.

4. Do not shortcut the path to long-term, effective ministry. That is, stress the need for complete language learning as well as the study of history and culture. There is no substitute for language facility for someone planning to serve more than two years.

5. Finally, be wary of reductionisms that seriously affect the global enterprise. In other words, don't reduce the Great Commission to evangelization only; don't reduce the missionary geog-

raphy to one sector of the world; don't reduce the task by focusing too much on specific dates; don't reduce the job of planting churches to adopting people groups; don't reduce the challenge of relational and incarnational ministry to technological advances that make the task easy.

4. The Missionary Training Industry: Schools, Equipping Programs, Formal and Non-Formal Education

One of the major surprises of our study came when we attempted to trace the relationship between training and attrition. Perhaps we could have structured the question better or explained the issues in a different way. But the fact is that the response to this item from the older sending countries (OSC) placed inappropriate training in 20th place as a cause of attrition, though in the new sending countries (NSC) it came in ninth place. When we examine the specific NSC rating of training further, differences emerge. For Brazil, inappropriate training came in first place, and for Ghana, fifth. But review Detlef Blöcher and Jonathan Lewis's analysis (chapter 7) to see the key role that solid training provides.

The result generated mixed emotions for missionary trainers. How was it that inappropriate training was rated so low? Did it mean that trainers were doing a good job or a bad job? Others concluded dangerously, "Well, we knew all along that training was not very important anyway."

I too struggled with these findings, until I had one of those "Aha!" experiences when a new insight shone light on these issues. The fact is that missionaries seldom return home from lack of theoretical knowledge, particularly when they have had opportunity for formal and non-formal biblical and missionary training. But when little to no training is available or taken advantage of, then the results are clear and provide a warning.

The prime causes of preventable early return of missionaries cluster in areas of character and spirituality, relationships and interpersonal conflict. This is generally true for all nations in our survey. Now, what does this tell us about pre-field equipping and training? Who is responsible to focus on these prime weaknesses? It's simply an escape if those in the training industry say, "Well, that's just not our task. Let the church do that, or perhaps the mission agency should take a look at that aspect. We are called to focus on the formal, knowledge dimensions of training." Says who? My profound conviction is that formal and non-formal schools and programs that say they help train missionaries must ask some major questions about what they do and how they do it. Too many of the so-called missionary training schools are knowledge factories with nominal attention given to character development and community relationality. They may provide some skill equipping, but this is uneven also.

I detect around the world a broad-based questioning of formal theological education and missionary training values that base so much on schooling systems. The rejection comes from a diverse set of people: missionaries themselves, local sending churches, mission agencies, and the national churches. And this questioning is lead-ing to a crisis that will bring about real change. One of the major changes is that churches will downgrade the amount of resources they are willing to put into formal training. This alone should shake the educational industry!

The other change is coming from mission societies that are dissatisfied with the product of the schools. Their concerns have not been listened to, and the answer is not simply a matter of adding a new course to the already loaded curriculum. Agencies are already forming strategic alliances to develop a unique brand of shorter-term, non-formal equipping for missionaries. I know where this is already taking place in Australia and North America.

As we think of what can be done to reduce attrition, here are 10 recommendations for those involved in schools or programs that equip missionaries.

1. Be sure you partner with the sending church as you provide equipping. This requires personal dialogue with church leadership. Discern the kind of equipping the church is providing, what they ask of you, and then how you can meet their needs.

2. Take the bold steps to articulate a profile (in terms of character, skills, and knowledge) of an effective cross-cultural servant. Then study the kinds of curriculum (everything that contributes to teaching and learning) needed to develop that kind of servant.

3. Don't just add courses to cover more topics. Return to examine the totality of your curriculum (everything that contributes to teaching and learning) to determine how it matches the profile of the missionary needed today.

4. Remember that the younger generation of missionaries enter with

broken backgrounds, inadequate parenting, and character building experiences. Thus you will have to provide more careful in-house pastoral and counseling resources.

5. Evaluate how well you do in balancing these educational triads:

+ Training that meets the needs of character, skills, and knowledge.

+ Training that balances formal, nonformal, and informal education.

+ Training that takes into account the needs and desires of the church, mission agency, and national church.

6. Be sure your equipping is available to both husband and wife. Too many programs are directed only to the husband.

7. Consider developing a strategic equipping partnership between formal missionary training schools and some of the excellent non-formal programs now available in many nations. Your students can learn in different contexts and get credit if this is important.

8. Determine what kinds of formal training can be provided on the field itself, which means a partnership with both the agency and national church.

9. Develop a diagnostic tool that surveys your graduates from the last decade to get their evaluation of their studies and the changes they would suggest for the program or school.

10. Keep your own attrition records. How many of your graduates are still in the ministry for which they trained? For which reasons did they leave cross-cultural work? Is there any relation between their departure and their training?

5. Mission Agencies Or Sending Bodies

Our WEF attrition research primarily polled the opinion of mission agency leaders. They were accessible and generally (though not always!) willing to participate in the study. We also knew that the simple exercise of completing the survey would stimulate—or jolt—them into more careful examination of attrition issues within their own agency. A majority of those participating in our attrition workshop in April 1996 represented mission agencies. The value of the workshop was clear to them. One British personnel coordinator wrote shortly after that event, "Since the Consultation, I have made a study of our resignations for the years 1991–1995, basing it on the statistical records which I keep. It has emphasized the issue of first-term resignations, and from this I have made some specific recommendations about pastoral care in the first term and about the ways in which our leaders can assist our members better. Thus, I think the Consultation has proved its value for us."

Another mission leader wrote from India, "Already in the few weeks since our workshop, we have been able to implement changes in our agency to reduce our attrition. Thank you."

For an African leader at the workshop, the investigation stimulated him to examine his nation's major attrition causes: problems with the education of missionary children (lack of appropriate schooling in rural, Muslim areas); lack of cross-cultural pre-field training; cultural problems resulting from tribal values that emphasize a man's building his own home on his own piece of land (and how can missionaries do this far from home?); lack of financial resources to provide even a minimum salary for African missionaries; an administrative ruling of the parent denomination that allows their church planters to stay on as permanent pastors, thus leaving missionary rosters; and persecution (riots, harassment, even fear of martyrdom). It was encouraging to see this leader detail how his people were attempting to address each of these six issues.

Throughout this book, numerous references have been made to the role the sending body (church or agency) has in relation to attrition. What more can be said in this last chapter? Let me outline a series of 12 basic recommendations for mission agencies. Some of these may be relatively easy to implement; others require great courage, time investment, and the commitment to invest in new resources to identify and reduce attrition.

1. Reexamine your agency history, heritage, values, administrative structure, management style, and the age of your home and field leaders to discern whether these have a role in your attrition realities. Review the Brierley and McKaughan chapters in this light.

2. If you have not done so, carry out a serious attrition study at least for the previous decade or perhaps for the previous agency administration.

3. Institute a functional attrition tracking system for your agency.

4. Evaluate and strengthen your screening systems and pre-field orientation/training in order to reduce attrition. Learn the liberation of graciously saying "no" to some candidates, or something like, "It is our best observation and assessment at this point in your journey that joining our team is *not* what you should do."

5. Study the generational diagram in light of your own agency. What insights emerge? What space are you giving to proactive cultivation of younger leaders? What space are you giving in your agency for the creative, committed, and restless new generation of missionaries?

6. Evaluate your track record of providing a job description and assignment to missionaries and following through on the promises.

7. Develop and utilize an ongoing system to assess your missionary force, with reviews, self-evaluations, realistic goal setting, and course corrections. Be sure you have a way to discern those who might be vulnerable to attrition.

8. Ensure an acceptable system that enables field missionaries to evaluate the leadership immediately above them. Too many agencies impose leaders who do not represent field personnel.

9. Develop a survey that invites the candid evaluation of previous missionaries, assuring confidentiality and the serious nature of the study. A number of agencies have bravely done this with high-value results.

10. If you are an internationalized agency (multination personnel), be sure to institute sensitive ways to determine whether your leadership and systems are creating higher attrition.

11. Release pastoral care providers, ensuring they have the right gifts for that ministry and are respected by those needing the right kind of assistance.

12. Be sure you have a healthy exit interview system for your departing missionaries.

Some Final Words to Agencies

First, we all agree that it is impossible to eliminate undesirable attrition totally. I have often said, "Stuff happens!" Many times this "stuff" that happens is painful. But we can be proactive for change and thus significantly reduce attrition. One couple who were almost lost to missions said, "In our agency, those who needed the most pastoral care were those farthest from the mission centers and cities where the pastors hung out." I was stunned by a mission executive who told me, "Our missionaries don't need pastoral care." As I reflected on that remark, it said much about that leader, as well as about the lack of pastoral care the 150 missionaries in that particular agency were facing.

On occasion, there may be a valiant personnel director who attempts to track attrition, but higher leadership cuts off the study. I know of one agency where this actually happened. Fortunately, the new leader of that very agency is willing to search for that "hidden" study, update it, and then determine what can be learned from it. Too many times, attrition is caused by substantial differences between home office and field leadership. In some cases, the home team is creative and attracts creative new missionaries. Then the newcomers go to the field and face older leaders, who contribute to the early departure of those missionaries. In other cases, it's just the opposite, and newcomers endure the home office team, jumping through the hoops, in order to make it to the creative field team.

Finally, some thoughts on desirable or purposeful attrition: We need to help some missionaries leave without guilt and redirect them into their future back home, whether into other ministries or into some aspect of the secular marketplace. Mission leaders must face the reality that some have slipped through the system who should not be missionaries. In a few cases, unethical people are on the field. Others have developed their own kingdom far from the home country, and unfortunately, many of these people tend to be good at public relations. But they should not be missionaries! Praise to the fearless leader who speaks and acts truth with mercy here.

It is worth studying the observations coming from Blöcher and Lewis's study of the data regarding attrition in relation to the size of the mission agency. In all cases, whether preventable or unpreventable attrition, larger agencies had less attrition. The reasons are both simple and complex. Larger societies have greater room for "lateral movement," that is, if a missionary does not work out in one field, there is room to change assignments. Smaller agencies do not have this luxury. Larger agencies tend to provide more pastoral resources for missionaries than small ones. What does this say to smaller agencies? One recommendation is that they seek a pastoral partnership with other small societies or with a larger one that will provide the field-based services to keep missionaries surviving and thriving.

6. The National Receiving Church

Obviously there will not be a national church among unreached peoples during the early phases of ministry to them. But God's supernatural power will break through in time, and the national church, with its own institutions and systems, cultural dynamics and leadership, ecclesiology and training programs, will emerge. But the fact is that most of the current missions force serves where a national church exists. And this church has a vital role in the life of the expatriate missionary.

I shall never forget a visit to a Central American country early in my missionary service. I visited the pastor of a large city church and found a celebration going on. I asked my pastor friend what was happening, and he said to me, "We are giving a party to a North American missionary couple who are returning to their country soon after coming here. We don't know why they came, what they did, or why they are returning, but we can give them a happy send-off." What an insight into the national perspective on missionary attrition!

The other face of the national church and expatriate missionary attrition is that in many cases attrition is both a natural and a calculated departure of the foreigners. The job they came to do was completed. It was time to transfer leadership, responsibility, and authority to the national church. Therefore, such carefully planned closure is to be celebrated, appropriate words of appreciation should be stated to all, and then the new stage of national-led ministry begins. We have categorized this attrition as unpreventable or expected. But actually, these gifted veterans are prime candidates to serve in new contexts of cross-cultural ministry. There is a kind of myth in the saying, "Work yourself out of a job—and go home."

What is the national church's role in relation to the expatriate force? My initial observation is that this depends on the agency or denomination that has moved into that nation and culture. But there are some foundational recommendations to be made, always in the context of an existing church.

First, the national church must provide a national spiritual home for the missionary. Not all missionaries are mobile evangelists or church planters. Many have tasks that allow them to become vital members of the church. This means the pastor of that church is also the pastor of the missionary. It may also mean that the pastor will have to get involved in cases where the missionary has to be disciplined, perhaps prior to being sent home.

Second, the national church has a critical role in the early orientation and training of the newer mission force in terms of culture, language learning, history of the people, and history of the church. Such equipping must not be left only to the foreign mission agency or the even more distant sending church.

Third, the church becomes the spiritual family of the global family of Christ, and both national and missionary children become children of the churches around the world. Too many missionary kids grow up in half-way cultural bubbles of boarding schools and never seriously engage the national culture or the national church.

Fourth, the national church provides a kind of added accountability for the ministry of the expatriate family. The missionary has an assignment to fulfill and works under leadership. But how beautiful it is to see that same foreigner submitting voluntarily to the wisdom and experience of the national leaders.

Finally, when missionaries leave the field, for whatever reason, national leaders should be consulted for their reflections and opinions on these cases.

7. Member Care Providers

There is little more to say to these special players, both men and women, in the missions movement. Some of them are medical personnel watching out for missionaries' physical health. Others are shepherds of the flock, with special pastoral gifts for their task, as well as confidential access to missionaries. Still others are professional counselors and psychiatrists. Thanks go to Kelly O'Donnell and other pastors for their significant contributions to this book, including the international directory of member care providers (chapter 25).

What is the role of these unique people—men and women of equal but diverse gifts and personalities? First, they must serve carefully but with authority in the first stages of selection and screening, in both the church and the mission society. We need to develop the right kinds of personality tests that are appropriate for different languages and cultures. Thankfully, these are more and more available these days.

Secondly, member care services must be provided with total confidentiality. It is "death" when a counselor is seen as a secret channel of painful information to church and agency leaders. Whether it is special time spent on the field or a more prolonged ministry of redemption and restoration back home, the work of member care providers must be kept private. On occasion, we may have to face obvious, major exceptions where laws have been broken or where major biblical norms have been violated,

which affect the missionary's tenure on the field and in the mission.

Thirdly, member care networks must be fostered and built in our global missionary community. This is beginning to happen, and it is good news. Counseling and shepherding are delicate ministries and cannot easily be done cross-culturally. Therefore, internationalized mission societies must provide men and women from the diverse cultures to provide the proper member care.

SPEAKING ABOUT FUTURE RESEARCH

Other chapters have addressed the topic of further research into attrition issues. Peter Brierley (chapter 6) concludes his chapter with seven avenues of study. Detlef Blöcher and Jonathan Lewis (chapter 7) have added their own reflections. I want to single out some ideas that have particularly valuable potential.

Here is also a word to graduate-level theological institutions where students must do major theses and dissertations. The following catalog of research options offers ample opportunity for gifted men and women to fulfill their academic requirements, while at the same time accomplishing something that tangibly contributes to the missions cause. There are both quantitative and qualitative options.

First, on the broader dimension side of things, ReMAP can be replicated—with the improvements on the research that we can now implement—in other countries which would invite the study.

Second, ReMAP can be replicated in the 14 nations within 5–10 years, ideally with the same agencies and nations. Such a project would give opportunity to revisit the initial issues, evaluate reduction of attrition, and also revamp some of our research questions. Also, by this time a new generation of missionaries—with different backgrounds and personal needs—will be on the field.

Third, every mission sending church and mission agency serious about tracking and reducing their attrition can do their own internal study. This would probably be one of the most gratifying outcomes of the entire ReMAP venture.

Fourth, we need a serious study that listens to the up-to-now unheard voices that speak to attrition issues. Among these are the voices of former missionaries, particularly those who left under difficult circumstances. Such a study would require a carefully crafted research instrument, confidentiality, and a "neutral" body to receive and analyze the survey returns and write up the report. Will agencies provide information about their former members for this study? I believe the key ones will, for they want truth as well as healing of the wounded.

Fifth, we can develop case study profiles of agencies that have lower attrition rates, identifying the key administrative and leadership factors that keep missionaries in effective service.

Sixth, we need to study the factors which encourage effective, longer-term service. Our desire is not merely longevity—there are too many people in ministry who have done a poor job for too long! What we seek is to understand is the interaction between human and spiritual gift competency factors.

Seventh, we can develop more qualitative, personal studies. For example, we could study 10 families (family units) who have survived and thrived long term in cross-cultural ministry, and compare and contrast them with 10 families (family units) who returned earlier than expected. This research would require great sensitivity, and the results must be couched in language that preserves confidentiality. But it offers tremendous potential.

I conclude this section with these general thoughts on research sent to me by Jonathan Lewis.

Research has to flow out of research. We have uncovered some interesting relationships which could provide researchers, particularly graduate students, with some original hypotheses to test. We've even suggested some of these in this chapter. Yet I feel that the greatest contribution of this study has been the reexamination of mission as a wholistic process. "Failure" on the field may reflect poor decisions or choices which go back to pre-field days. We have found, for example, that high levels of expenditure on pastoral care (over 30%) apparently don't help reduce attrition, since this fact was associated with missions that actually had higher attrition rates. Is this because poor screening or pre-field training practices make it more necessary for pastoral attention when problems arise, which may not help keep people on the field because they really didn't belong there in the first place? This kind of hypothesis is hard to test, although it could be tried. But this information becomes most valuable when a mission that is spending high sums on pastoral care and still sees high attrition examines its screening and other pre-field procedures and modifies what they do, as they understand that more of the right kind of screening and more invested in the right kind of training will probably reduce their "pastoral care" bill and reduce their attrition. That kind of in-house "research" is what is going to produce results that help lower attrition.

FINALLY, BRINGING CLOSURE TO THIS BOOK

Just today I listened to a brave missionary couple speak of their recent, incredibly difficult term in South Asia. Their frank language was refreshing, and I honestly wept as I followed their story. It would not have surprised me, had they chosen to leave missions. But they are going back, and I admire them for this tough decision. In the process, the husband learned some major lessons about himself. From being a driven performer, he has discovered high priorities in life and has also realized how he can be a more sensitive husband to his wife in a Muslim culture, where the expatriate woman is exposed to many dehumanizing pressures.

This book has explored the causes and cures of missionary attrition among those whom we consider too valuable to lose. This attrition topic is a massive and dangerous iceberg that has to be dealt with in the right way and with the right tools. We have talked much about the cure side of attrition, but I want to conclude by addressing a final major question.

What keeps cross-cultural servants not only surviving (we all did that, and the difficult times came in waves), **but also thriving** (it can happen!) **in long-term missions?** Again, I do not assume that all missionaries should stay on the field, and I will focus on those who follow Jesus as King to the ends of the earth for the right reasons.

Here are eight principles that seem to undergird effective longevity of service.

1. Spirituality. We must focus time and time again on issues of deep spirituality and radical commitment to Jesus, tempered with a realistic vision of the cost of cross-cultural ministry. Never "sugar coat" this factor. Note again that lack of call and inadequate commitment were ranked high as attrition causes by our colleagues in the new sending nations. But lack of spirituality is not a problem only there. We must also unmask the pseudo-spirituality that infests so many leaders in our movement, where performance-driven behavior, "quota expectations," and guilt manipulate our choice brothers and sisters in missions.

2. Relational skills. We must emphasize (in pre-field practical ministry, as well as in whatever orientation and equipping are offered) the need for adequate relational skills for mission work. Monocultural people who have operated in their home cultures in a top-down hierarchical structure will have difficulty in missions. So will proud people. How many mission teams have collapsed for theological reasons? Some, of course. But many more have fallen apart because of interpersonal conflict. We will need to develop men and women with abilities of leadership and followership. We must be truthful enough to recommend to some that they not go into missions.

3. Ministry skills. We must stress the right skills for ministry. Where better should these foundational skills be revealed and honed but in the context of the local church? Do not assume that these skills will be developed in formal educational schools. We can also anticipate the future by encouraging in our mission force ongoing personal growth, where over the years different gifts and service opportunities will emerge. There is absolutely no substitute for genuine, extensive, intensive, evaluated, pre-field ministry as an antidote to attrition.

4. Training. We must encourage the right kind of knowledge mix for our missionaries. Not all will benefit from formal biblical, theological, or missiological study, but some will. And particularly if we are sending people to work in teams, some of those team members should have serious formal study. All team members will benefit from shorter-term courses that offer specific training for missions.

5. Church involvement. I underline again the strategic and growing role of the church in the entire missions enterprise. The church must know its mission force well, must have recognized prospective missionaries in the reality of that believing community, must have evaluated them in genuine ministry, and now must see that they are released for service in another country and culture. The church knows the missionaries, intercedes with power, sends, and financially supports their extension people. And the church stays in personal contact with their missionaries. It surprised me in our attrition study that sustained correspondence (more and more now, it is via e-mail) with the missionaries was seen as more valuable than even personal visits from people in the home country. And the best results come when the church significantly partners with the mission agency with their mutual careful screening of mission candidates.

6. On-field care. There is no substitute for adequate field-based member care. I was shocked at a case study of well-established mission agencies that will appoint a family to serve in an isolated region of Asia, but they base the closest team leader in London! This is simply and categorically wrong! Both churches and agencies must come to terms with adequate shepherding, strategizing, and supervising in the context of ministry.

7. Evaluation. We underline the need for periodic self-assessment and leader-guided evaluation of missionary personnel over the course of the years of service. This becomes a healthy tool for self-evaluation and also engenders the sense that the leaders care about the opinions of their staff. For many, this assessment becomes the platform for ongoing training for ministry, whether non-formal or formal in nature.

8. Closure. When the time comes for missionary service closure, be sure the missionary family is treated in the right way by both the mission agency and the sending church. You have an ongoing responsibility to these former servants long after they have departed the active role with you. Provide healthy exit interviews that allow opinions to flow in diverse ways. Release with blessing those who sense the Spirit guiding them from cross-cultural ministry into other ministries or vocations.

Yes, "stuff happens," and we cannot eliminate attrition. But we can significantly reduce not only attrition, but also the personal pain that accompanies it.

I return to March 1996, when my wife and I stood on the windswept island of Iona. Both Celtic and mission history washed over us as we relived the powerful testimony of those unique men and women of faith who evangelized Scotland and who would eventually send their missionaries as far away as the Ukraine and Byzantium. I remember again the Celtic missionary vision of *peregrinatio* (pilgrimage, or wanderlust to explore the unknown) under their symbol for the Holy Spirit, the wild goose. I gaze at their tricolored martyrdom: *red* martyrdom symbolized persecution, bloodshed, or giving one's life for Christ; *green* martyrdom spoke of self-denial and penitential acts that lead to personal holiness; and *white* martyrdom referred to leaving behind family, clan, and tribe to spread the cause of Christ, perhaps never returning home again.

Periodically I glimpse a piece of the glory of Revelation 7:9-10, painting the marvel of countless numbers from every nation, tribe, people, and language, standing before the throne and in front of the Lamb, wearing white robes and holding palm branches in their hands, and crying out loudly, "Salvation belongs to our God, who sits on the throne, and to the Lamb." We are not there yet. But we are closer to that day than ever before. And meanwhile, we will continue to select, equip, send, and support our global cross-cultural missions force, trusting that they will remain faithful until the Spirit sovereignly guides them into the next step of service.

William D. Taylor, Director of the WEF Missions Commission since 1986, was born in Costa Rica of missionary parents. He lived in Latin America for 30 years, 17 as a career missionary on the faculty of Seminario Teológico Centroamericano in Guatemala. Married to Yvonne, a native Texan, he has three children (all Generation Xers) who were all born in Guatemala. Taylor has edited **Internationalizing Missionary Training** *(1991) and* **Kingdom Partnerships for Synergy in Missions** *(1994) and has co-authored* **Crisis and Hope in Latin America** *with Emilio Antonio Núñez (1996). His passion is to finish well and to pack heaven with worshipers!*

Part 6

Additional Resources

Survey Instrument

LEAVING MISSIONARY SERVICE SURVEY

Introduction

Earlier this year, mission leaders from 10 nations met to craft a survey instrument to address the causes of early missionary withdrawal. In the United States the WEF Missions Commission, Missionary Internship, and the Mission Training and Resource Center have joined in partnership to attempt this study. We have surveyed most of the published literature on this subject. We are hereby soliciting from you unpublished or in-house studies known by you which were completed by senders or mission researchers.

This current survey aims at gaining insight primarily into the causes of avoidable missionary loss. We view this instrument and process as phase one in a multiple-phased effort. We will gather those interested for a workshop next year to share the results of this survey and to develop common tools which senders can use to complete annual in-depth analysis of the causes and solutions for unnecessary attrition.

We are committed to maintaining the anonymity of results of this survey as they relate to any particular agency or church. We are concerned that the results of the survey are not used to negatively impact either a sending entity or the mission enterprise as a whole.

William D. Taylor, WEF
512/467-8431

Phillip Elkins, MTRC
818/797-7903

1. Most Important Causes

Instructions

Here is a list of 26 reasons why missionaries leave missionary service, both preventable and unpreventable. Please indicate the <u>seven</u> most important reasons, out of these 26, which you believe are the reasons why missionaries have left your organization in the last five years. Rank your choices 1 to 7 with 1 being the most important reason.

Unpreventable Reasons

___ (a) **Normal retirement.** Retirement following normal completion of missionary service.

___ (b) **Political crisis.** Forced to leave missionary service due to war, government persecution, civil unrest, famine, etc.

___ (c) **Death in service.** Death or unexplained disappearance of serving missionary, spouse, or child.

___ (d) **Outside marriage.** Marriage to someone outside of the mission.

___ (e) **Change of job.** Change of job due to completion of assignment or move to a new post.

Marriage/Family Reasons

___ (f) **Child(ren).** Children unable to adapt to new culture, needs of education, health, or behavior.

___ (g) **Elderly parents.** Need of caring for aging parents.

___ (h) **Marriage/family conflicts.** Marriage or family conflicts, death of close family member.

Agency Reasons

___ (i) **Home support.** Inadequate financial, prayer, and/or other support from home country; high rate of inflation.

___ (j) **Disagreement with sending agency.** Disagreement with missionary sending body over policy, authority, etc.

___ (k) **Theological reasons.** Disagreement with the sending body over charismatic, ecclesiology, or other doctrines.

Personal Reasons

___ (l) **Immature spiritual life.** Problems related to spiritual life such as unmet spiritual needs, spiritual immaturity, etc.

___ (m) **Health problems.** Problems related to mental and/or physical health.

___ (n) **Inadequate commitment.** Lack of understanding of the cost and commitment involved in long-term missionary service.

___ (o) **Personal concerns.** Problems related to low self-esteem, dealing with stress, anger, unrealistic expectations, singleness, loneliness, etc.

___ (p) **Lack of call.** Lack of genuine spiritual call to missionary service, or loss of it.

___ (q) **Immoral lifestyle.** Immoral behavior, alcohol and/or drug abuse.

Team Reasons

___ (r) **Problems with peer missionaries.** Relationship problems with mission field leaders or fellow missionaries.

___ (s) **Problems with local leaders.** Relationship problems with local church leaders or other local colleagues.

Cultural Reasons

___ (t) **Poor cultural adaptation.** Unable to adapt to culture, customs, traditions, and living conditions of the country.

___ (u) **Language difficulties.** Unable to adequately learn the country's language.

Work-Related Reasons

___ (v) **Dismissal.** Dismissal due to inability to carry out duties and responsibilities satisfactorily.

___ (w) **Lack of job satisfaction.** Lack of job satisfaction due to heavy workload, lack of relevant skills, unsuitability to type of work, perceived failure in gaining converts, etc.

___ (x) **Inadequate supervision.** Inadequate, inappropriate, or authoritarian supervision of work by sending body, including lack of pastoral care, team building, and other support.

___ (y) **Inappropriate training.** Inadequate or inappropriate training and preparation for missionary work.

Other Reasons

___ (z) **Other reasons.** Other important reasons not mentioned above (specify).

_____

_____

2. Missionary Losses (part one)

Instructions

Please indicate the total number of your missionaries who left (for whatever reason) in 1992, 1993, and 1994, counting each couple as one unit.

(a) Total number of missionaries who left in year.
(b) How many were single women?
(c) How many were single men?
(d) How many were couples (as one unit)?

	(a)	(b)	(c)	(d)
1992	___	___	___	___
1993	___	___	___	___
1994	___	___	___	___
Total 1992–94	___	___	___	___

3. Missionary Losses (part two)

Instructions

Of the total number of missionaries who left between 1992 and 1994 (total in Q2(a) above), indicate the numbers due to the following reasons, as applicable:

(a) Unpreventable reasons   _____
(b) Marriage/family reasons   _____
(c) Missionary society/
     agency reasons   _____
(d) Personal reasons   _____
(e) Team reasons   _____
(f) Cultural reasons   _____
(g) Work-related reasons   _____
(h) Other reasons   _____
Total (as in Q2(a) above)   _____

Background Information

The following questions are aimed to give us more background information about your missionary agency/church. This information is essential to the study but will be treated in strictest confidence. The results will not be published in any way that identifies individual missionary sending bodies.

4. Personnel Numbers

Instructions

For the purpose of this study, career missionaries are defined as professionally trained for and fully engaged in long-term career missionary service. How many career missionaries (counting each couple as one unit) does your sending body serve? Please check the appropriate category.

___ (a) 1 to 10
___ (b) 11 to 25
___ (c) 26 to 50
___ (d) 51 to 100

___ (e) 101 to 200
___ (f) 201 to 500
___ (g) Over 500
___ (h) None

5. Organizational History

Instructions

For how many years has your organization been sending missionaries (both career and all others)? Please check the appropriate category.

___ (a) Under a year
___ (b) 1 to 2 years
___ (c) 3 to 10 years
___ (d) 11 to 25 years
___ (e) 26 to 50 years
___ (f) 51 to 100 years
___ (g) Over 100 years

6. Organizational Focus

Instructions

To which of the following categories does your organization send missionaries? If you have missionaries in more than one category, please rank in order from 1 to 4, where 1 represents the area in which you have the most missionaries.

___ (a) People within your own national boundaries who speak the national language and are culturally similar.
___ (b) People in foreign countries who are culturally similar and speak your national language.
___ (c) Ethnic groups within your own national boundaries of a different culture.
___ (d) People in foreign countries of a different culture and language.

7. Ministry Types

Instructions

In which of the following types of ministry are your missionaries involved? If your missionaries are involved in more than one type, please rank them in order from 1 to 6, where 1 represents the type of ministry in which you have the most missionaries and 6 the least.

___ (a) Helping the local church through administrative, pastoral, teaching, theological training, and other supportive work.
___ (b) Helping the national church through administrative, pastoral, teaching, theological training, and other supportive work.
___ (c) Involved in evangelism and church planting in areas where the evangelical church has an established presence.
___ (d) Involved in pioneer mission work among unreached, unchurched people groups where there is little or no evangelical presence.
___ (e) Providing a support service for evangelism and church planting such as Bible translation, aviation, literature, radio, etc.
___ (f) Involved in relief and development or institutional work such as famine relief, hospital (medical) work, etc.

8. Personnel Support

Instructions

Which of the following does your sending body provide for your missionaries? Please check all appropriate categories.

___ (a) Supervision by your appointed field leader.

___ (b) Pastoral oversight by someone other than your appointed supervisor.

___ (c) A detailed job description.

___ (d) Planned on-the-job training.

___ (e) Provision of annual leave (holidays).

___ (f) At least a yearly visit from someone in your sending body.

___ (g) Provision of schools, finances, or tutors for missionary children.

___ (h) A supportive team structure.

___ (i) At least a quarterly telephone call or letter from your office.

___ (j) Local/area conferences for mission personnel.

___ (k) Other types of support (specify).

_____

_____

_____

9. Resource Allocation To Personnel Support

Instructions

Please estimate what percentages of your sending body's resources are spent in the pastoral care and supervision of your missionaries on active service in terms of (a) time and (b) finance. Please check one item only in each column, i.e., of time and finance.

		Time	Finance
(a)	Under 1%	___	___
(b)	1%–5%	___	___
(c)	6%–19%	___	___
(d)	11%–20%	___	___
(e)	21%–30%	___	___
(f)	Over 30%	___	___

10. Training

Instructions

Please indicate which of the following types of training your career missionary candidates are required to complete before active service. Please check all appropriate categories.

___ (a) Degree course in missiological studies.

___ (b) Formal qualifications in missiological studies other than a degree.

___ (c) Completion of your organization's own course in missiological studies.

___ (d) Completion of a theological course or other professional training.

___ (e) Completion of a non-formal missionary training program.

___ (f) A short-term experience of living in a different culture.

___ (g) Cross-cultural orientation.

___ (h) None required.

___ (i) Other skills (specify).

_____

_____

11. Evaluation

Instructions

Please indicate, by checking all the appropriate categories, which of the following your organization undertakes in evaluating a career missionary's suitability for missionary service.

___ (a) Acceptance of your sending body's doctrinal statement.

___ (b) A clear statement of God's calling for mission service.

___ (c) Personal character references such as from the candidate's church.

___ (d) Previous experience of missionary type work.

___ (e) Previous experience of church work.

___ (f) Evaluation of health.

___ (g) Evaluation of communication and relationship skills.

___ (h) Evaluation of leadership and pastoral skills.

___ (i) Evaluation of candidate's marriage or singleness.

___ (j) Limits on the age or number of children, or other family restrictions.

___ (k) Psychological and/or personality testing.

___ (l) Firm promises of financial support.

___ (m) Ordination or its equivalent.

___ (n) Other conditions (specify).

_____

_____

12. Other Factors

Instructions

The following is a list of possible factors that may or may not be important in reducing to a minimum the number of missionaries who are lost through preventable reasons. Please indicate, in the first column, those which you believe are the three most important factors in preventing missionary loss, and then in the second column check those you consider to be the three least important factors.

M = Most Important
L = Least Important

	M	L
(a) A very supportive family and/or spouse.	___	___
(b) Regular contact with friends, church, and prayer partners from home.	___	___
(c) A clear calling to mission work from God.	___	___
(d) Good relationships with other missionaries and colleagues.	___	___
(e) Regular supervision, pastoral care, and other support.	___	___
(f) Ability to adapt to a different culture and learn languages.	___	___
(g) Ability to cope with stress and heavy workloads.	___	___
(h) Good relationships with supervisors and the sending body.	___	___
(i) Regular financial support from home country.	___	___
(j) Provision of appropriate and regular training.	___	___
(k) Ability to maintain a healthy spirituality without external support.	___	___
(l) Other factors (specify).	___	___

_____

_____

13. Respondent's Role

Instructions

As the respondent for this survey, what is your main role within your organization, mission agency, society, or church?

___ Mission director
___ Mission supervisor

___ Pastoral staff of sending
     church
___ Mission personnel officer
___ Former missionary
___ Other _____

Anonymity

We guarantee the anonymity of the information you have provided. Nevertheless, we need the name of your organization in order to identify those who have not responded to the survey and thus to request their cooperation again. Thank you again for your cooperation and trust.

Name of your agency/church:

_____

Mailing address:

_____

_____

Please mail to:
Phillip Elkins
Mission Training & Resource Center
P.O. Box 41155
Pasadena, CA 91114

LEAVING MISSIONARY SERVICE SURVEY: ADDENDUM FOR UNITED STATES AND CANADIAN MISSIONS

Introduction

In addition to the preceding worldwide survey, many countries are incorporating their own Addendum which seeks further information that is considered unique or specific to the country/region.

As those responsible for the survey in the US and Canada, we believe that the answers to the following questions will be very beneficial in understanding missionary losses in our countries. Thank you for your further participation.

Rationale

In the past 10 years, there have been significant changes in "mission," both in our understanding and in our practice. The following questions seek to understand the impact of these changes on our ability to recruit and maintain past levels of missionary numbers within our organizations.

1. Service

(Please check appropriate category)
      M = More
      S = Same
      L = Less

In relation to 10 years ago, you have changed in regard to:

	M	S	L
(a) Countries being served.	__	__	__
(b) People groups being served.	__	__	__
(c) National churches being worked with.	__	__	__

(d) If you are working with less national churches, would the reason be one of the following:
___ Handed over work to national church.
___ Reduced missionary force.
___ Unable to maintain presence in area.
___ Other _____
_____

2. Organizational

(Please check appropriate category)
Within the last 10 years, your organization has:

	Yes	No
(a) Formed partnership(s) with US/Canadian organization(s).	___	___
(b) Formed partnership(s) with non-US/Canadian organization(s).	___	___
(c) Developed a tentmaking or service department/ division.	___	___
(d) If yes to part (c), does new department have the same name?	___	___

3. Personnel

(Please check appropriate category)
V = Very significant
S = Significant
N = No change
In the past 10 years, the following may or may not be significant factors for your mission:

	V	S	N
(a) Increase in short-term workers (0–2 yrs).	___	___	___
(b) Increase in early retirees (45+ yrs) applying.	___	___	___
(c) Decrease in career missionaries.	___	___	___
(d) Change in roles, i.e., more specialists, rather than the "general missionary."	___	___	___

4. Financial

(Please check appropriate category)
V = Very significant
S = Significant
N = No change
In the past 10 years, the following may have affected your ability to send missionaries:

	V	S	N
(a) Increased cost in sending missionaries.	___	___	___
(b) Change in giving patterns within the Christian community, i.e., less general giving.	___	___	___

Attrition Tracking Guidelines For Mission Agencies

Phillip Elkins and Jonathan Lewis

The following Tracking Guide can help your organization collect, in-house, the information needed to analyze attrition. This is a *suggested* format and may be modified to suit your own needs. The Tracking Guide has two parts—one to use with missionaries departing for the field; the second, to use when a missionary leaves the field and has no plans to return.

USES FOR THE TRACKING GUIDE

Perhaps the most important function of the Tracking Guide is that it will help missionaries and mission administrators keep in mind the factors they depend on to select, prepare, and support missionaries on the field. The Tracking Guide will promote a constant review of these factors in the overall process of sending and maintaining the missionary task force. This could contribute significantly to alerting missions and missionaries of problem areas and allow time to compensate for them. When used as a part of a regular review process, the Tracking Guide can be a powerful tool in preventing unnecessary attrition.

Secondly, the information gathered should be used for planning purposes. Administrative decisions are only as good as the information upon which the decisions are based. Accurate records are an important source of that critical information. By simply tallying the weighted reasons for missionary departure from the field, church and missions administrators will be able to identify the areas of greatest weakness. If statistical analysis can be done on the data, relationships can be pinpointed between the causes of attrition and what the church or mission is or isn't doing in the areas of selection, training, and field support. The analysis will suggest specific courses of action aimed at preventing unnecessary attrition. With the limitations on time and resources which beset us all, sharpening our aim in dealing with the root causes of attrition will not only help reduce the number of those coming back, but also increase our overall effectiveness and stewardship.

This Tracking Guide takes the form of a survey instrument. It may be self-administered, but it will be more accurate if managed by a single interviewer.

The most practical way to gather the information initially may be through forms that are filled out. Whenever possible, the data should be transferred to a computer database or spreadsheet, where it can be tallied easily and used to obtain statistical information. If this is not possible, a manual filing system should be developed to allow easy access to the information as it is needed.

PART A:
LEAVING FOR THE FIELD

This questionnaire should be filled out initially as the missionary is sent out and then should be updated with each subsequent home leave. To start your tracking system, you may need to have a questionnaire filled out for each missionary presently on the field. It would be best to have an interviewer from the mission agency gather this information in order to assure consistency, but this may not always be possible.

1. Demographic Information

In the case of couples, a separate set of answers should be filled out for each person:

Name _____

Birth date _____ Age _____

How long has this person been a committed Christian? _____

Marital status:

___ Single woman
___ Single man
___ Married woman
___ Married man

If married, for how long to present partner? _____

Does this person come from a broken home (divorce or separation)?

Yes ___   No ___

Children's names	Birth date	Sex

2. Health

(a) Describe physical or emotional health issues affecting the missionary:

_____

_____

_____

(b) Has this individual submitted to psychological testing? If so, what is the evaluation?

___ Excellent   ___ Marginal

___ Good   ___ Not good

3. Calling

Is the individual strongly convinced of his/her call from God to go to the mission field?

Yes ___   No ___

Additional primary factors relating to decision to go (number in order of primary factors, 1–4):

___ (a) Responded to biblical mandate to go.

___ (b) Responded to knowledge of need of the unreached.

___ (c) Call was not clear, but he/she just felt it right to go.

___ (d) Calling was primarily from contact with missionaries.

___ (e) Teacher/pastor influence.

___ (f) Conferences/camps.

___ (g) Family influence.

4. Education and Training

(a) Last school year completed or degree earned _____

_____

(b) Formal Bible school or seminary training?

Yes ___   No ___

Number of years _____

Degree earned _____

(c) Missionary training program exclusively for missionaries?

Yes ___   No ___

Number of months _____

Did your agency run the training program?

Yes ___   No ___

Other (name or describe) _____

_____

_____

(d) Attended mission agency's orientation program?

Yes ___   No ___

Number of days _____

(e) Currently enrolled in some educational program?

Yes ___   No ___

Describe _____

_____

_____

5. Field Assignment

(a) Country of service _____

People group (if applicable)

_____

(b) Field assignment is:

___ In home country

___ Foreign country

___ Same or near culture

___ Definitely cross-cultural

(c) On loan to another organization?

Yes ___   No ___

Which? _____

(d) Specified length of current term:

_____

(e) Total number of years of previous missionary service _____

Primary Field Work

Check the missionary's primary responsibilities from the list below. Where there is more than one, write in the **percent** of total time budgeted to each activity. (The total of all percentages should add up to 100%.)

___ Church planting

___ National church

___ Evangelist

___ Pastoral work

___ Theological education

___ Administration

___ Field or area director

___ General education

___ Vocational education

___ Institutional administration

___ MK teacher

___ MK caregiver/dorm parent

___ Youth work

___ Children's work

___ Linguistics work

___ Literature

___ Radio/TV

___ Maintenance work

___ Secretary/bookkeeper/clerk

___ Development work

___ Refugee work

___ Social work among poor

___ Medical work

___ Tentmaking occupation

___ Other (specify)

_____

6. Selection

Check the selection criteria used with this missionary (check all that apply):

___ (a) Acceptance of a doctrinal statement.

___ (b) Psychological and/or personality testing.

___ (c) Clear statement of God's calling for mission service.

___ (d) Several positive personal character references.

___ (e) Proven ministry experience.

___ (f) Short-term missions experience.

___ (g) Required ordination (or equivalency).

___ (h) Limits on the number of children or other family restrictions upon entry.

___ (i) Evaluation of the marriage dynamic or singleness.

___ (j) Evaluation of relational skills.

___ (k) Predetermined amount of promised financial support.

___ (l) Evaluation of health.

___ (m) Other (specify):

_____

_____

7. Support

While the missionary is on the field, the following are elements that the sending church or agency provides. The missionary should rate each of the support items **that are provided** from 1–4 according to the value he or she places on each.

___ (a) Assignment of someone outside the mission to meet pastoral needs.

___ (b) Specific, detailed job description.

___ (c) Planned, on-field training for the specific job assignment.

___ (d) Time allotted annually for vacations (holidays).

___ (e) A visit from the home office at least every year.

___ (f) A call from the home office at least every month.

___ (g) A personalized letter, fax, or e-mail from the home office at least every month.

___ (h) Additional support for children's schooling (schools, finances, tutors, etc.).

___ (i) A team structure which provides spiritual and moral support.

___ (j) Direct supervision by a mission field leader.

___ (k) Other elements of field support your mission provides which you consider important:

_____

_____

_____

PART B: LEAVING THE FIELD

When a missionary leaves the field for whatever reason with no definite plans to return, the individual, as well as agency leaders, should use the following form to help determine the cause of attrition. This will be useful for your own records and will assist the WEF Missions Commission in replicating this attrition study with more accurate information in the future.

First, identify the reasons for departure that apply to this particular case. Then rank them in order of importance, **assigning each item a percentage value**. This is the only way to know how each of the reasons given is weighted in the overall decision to leave the field. In some cases, such as retirement or death, the factor will obviously be 100% of the reason. But in other more complex cases, the field departure will be due to a composite of reasons. This information can provide the mission with a better understanding of the situation. It also can be useful as the basis for in-depth interviews with the departing missionary.

Anticipated Reasons

___ (a) **Normal retirement.** Retirement following normal completion of missionary service or contract.

___ (b) **Completion of contract.** Completion of contract for a specified task or time period.

Political or Catastrophic Reasons

___ (c) **Political removal.** Forced removal from country due to war, government persecution, epidemics, famine, civil unrest, withdrawal of visa, or denial of visa extension.

___ (d) **Death in service.** Death or unexplained disappearance of serving missionary.

Marriage/Family Reasons

___ (e) **Children.** Children unable to adjust to new culture, schooling needs, health or behavioral problems.

___ (f) **Elderly parents.** Need to care for aging parents.

___ (g) **Marriage/family conflicts.** Marriage or family conflict, or death of spouse or child.

___ (h) **Outside marriage.** Marriage to someone outside mission.

Society or Agency Reasons

___ (i) **Home support.** Inadequate financial, prayer, and other support from home country.

___ (j) **Disagreement with sending agency.** Disagreement with mission agency over policy, authority, etc.

___ (k) **Theological reasons.** Disagreement with the mission agency over charismatic issues, church practice, or doctrinal issues.

Personal Reasons

___ (l) **Immature spiritual life.** Problems related to spiritual life such as unmet spiritual needs, lack of spiritual maturity, etc.

___ (m) **Health problems.** Problems related to mental or physical health.

___ (n) **Inadequate commitment.** Lack of understanding of the cost and commitment involved in long-term missionary service.

___ (o) **Personal concerns.** Problems related to low self-esteem, dealing with stress, anger, unrealistic expectations, the need to marry, loneliness, etc.

___ (p) **Lack of call.** Lack of conviction regarding a genuine call to missionary work, or loss of it.

___ (q) **Immoral lifestyle.** Immoral behavior, alcohol and drug abuse.

Team Reasons

___ (r) **Problems with peer missionaries.** Relationship problems with mission field leaders or fellow missionaries.

___ (s) **Problems with local leaders.** Relationship problems with local church leaders or other local colleagues.

Cultural Reasons

___ (t) **Poor cultural adaptation.** Unable to adapt to culture, customs, traditions, and living conditions of the country.

___ (u) **Language difficulties.** Unable to learn the country's language adequately.

Work-Related Reasons

___ (v) **Dismissal by agency.** Dismissal due to inability to carry out duties and responsibilities satisfactorily.

___ (w) **Lack of job satisfaction.** Lack of job satisfaction due to heavy workload, lack of relevant skills, unsuitability to type of work, perceived failure in gaining converts, etc.

___ (x) **Inadequate supervision.** Inadequate, inappropriate, or authoritarian supervision of work by mission agency, including lack of pastoral care, team building, and other support.

___ (y) **Inadequate training.** Inadequate or inappropriate training and preparation for missionary work.

Other Reasons

___ (z) **Other reasons.** Other important reasons not mentioned (specify):

_____

_____

INTERVIEWS

Part B of the above questionnaire should be accompanied, when possible, by in-depth interviews with those leaving the field, particularly when the primary reasons for leaving seem to fall in the category of preventable attrition. Such interviews can provide valuable insight into the whole attrition problem, which the more objective Tracking Guide may miss. A skilled interviewer will get to the bottom of the issues. There are always at least two sides to why missionaries leave the field early. Interviews will help get a more balanced picture and provide valuable insights.

Missions administrators must provide an opportunity for their returning missionaries to release what is in their hearts. Missionaries often need to talk about their reasons for leaving with those who in some way may be partly responsible. This should be done in an atmosphere of confidentiality, sympathy, and support, as opposed to exhibiting a defensive attitude. Just the act of listening is the most cathartic element of this activity and has real therapeutic value to the missionary. Praying with and for each returnee is an important element of this debriefing process. Such prayer can be the key to release and healing, which will promote further useful service. Many missionaries have retreated from active Christian fellowship over their disappointments with a mission organization. When administrators are humbly concerned for the welfare of their missionaries and are willing to listen to them, acknowledge their part in the matter, and learn from constructive criticism, healing can be achieved for the missionaries and positive growth and change for the mission.

Index